Wings, Women, and War

❖ ❖ ❖ ❖ ❖ ❖ ❖ ❖ ❖ ❖ ❖ ❖ ❖ ❖ ❖ ❖

Wings, Women, and War

SOVIET AIRWOMEN IN WORLD WAR II COMBAT

Reina Pennington

Foreword by John Erickson

UNIVERSITY PRESS OF KANSAS

Published by the University Press of Kansas (Lawrence, Kansas 66045), which was organized by the Kansas Board of Regents and is operated and funded by Emporia State University, Fort Hays State University, Kansas State University, Pittsburg State University, the University of Kansas, and Wichita State University.

Library of Congress Cataloging-in-Publication Data

Pennington, Reina, 1956–

Wings, women, and war : Soviet airwomen in World War II combat / Reina Pennington ; foreword by John Erickson.

p. cm. — (Modern war studies)

Includes bibliographical references and index.

ISBN 978-0-7006-1145-4 (cloth : alk. paper)

ISBN 978-0-7006-1554-4 (pbk. : alk. paper)

1. World War, 1939–1945—Participation, Female.   2. Soviet Union. Voenno-Vozdushnye Sily.   3. World War, 1939–1945—Aerial operations, Soviet.   4. World War, 1939–1945—Regimental histories—Soviet Union. I. Title: Soviet airwomen in World War II combat.   II. Erickson, John. III. Title.   IV. Series.

D810.W7 P45 2001

940.54'4947'082—dc21   2001003126

British Library Cataloguing in Publication Data is available.

Printed in the United States of America

10 9 8 7 6 5 4 3

Contents

Photo galleries follow pages 80 and 144.

Maps

❖   ❖   ❖   ❖   ❖   ❖   ❖

Foreword

For the historian and for the general reader, the Eastern Front 1941–1945 is still in many respects "undiscovered country," recent access to former Soviet archives and wartime records notwithstanding. We are generally familiar with the great dramas, the epic battles, the monstrous cruelties, and the inhuman costs of warfare in the east. They made up the pulp of wartime propaganda and they stimulate present-day literary sensationalism, but the innate mysteries of morale and motivation remain largely undiscovered.

Russian historians have avidly pursued the so-called blank spots and have opened up fresh avenues of research, one informative instance being Elena Senyavskaya's sociopsychological profile of the Soviet wartime generation and her larger work on the psychology of twentieth-century war, *Psikhologiya voiny v XX veke. Istoricheskii opyt Rossii* (1999), covering Russia's experience from the Russo-Japanese War to Afghanistan. Within the ambit of that experience, Russian women at large and Soviet women in particular have occupied a singularly important place. Save for ritualistic recognition of women, piousness, and hyperbole, this historical contribution had long been undiscovered or, worse, deliberately ignored. This is the dimension Dr. Reina Pennington identifies, investigates, and illuminates in *Wings, Women, and War*. In conveying wholly fresh, vivid, often unique, and revealing insights into the role of Soviet women aircrews in war, Dr. Pennington also contributes directly to the debate and controversy outside Russia surrounding the commitment of women to front-line operational roles that put them in harm's way.

Commanded by Marina Raskova, the all-female Aviation Group 122 was formed in October 1941. It trained pilots, navigators, mechanics, and ground crews for three regiments—the 586th Fighter, 587th Day Bomber, and 588th Night Bomber Regiments—none formally designated "women's regiments" nor otherwise distinguished by special flying gear, nor indeed uniforms, until 1943. The regiments flew more than 30,000 combat missions and included at least two fighter aces within their ranks. This must be considered a unique phenomenon in its own right, not easily dismissed as a mere propaganda ploy, though some have tried. A shortage of pilots does not account for this step. The aerial massacre carried out by the Luftwaffe in June 1941 destroyed aircraft wholesale but left pilots largely unscathed. Put at its most mundane, women's regiments proved to be useful and effective, all to the satisfaction of the Soviet command, particularly Air Marshals Vershinin and Novikov, but that mundanity conceals a plethora of intricate and compelling questions.

Although this is primarily a study of Soviet women in combat aviation, Dr. Pennington throws a great deal of light on the attitude of Soviet men toward women fliers and what effect their presence had on performance. The initial masculine reaction varied between skepticism and outright hostility, but once the women's regiments showed acceptable performance in combat, their assimilation into operational units was not difficult. Masculine acceptance and adaptability evidently developed fastest where men were assigned to women's regiments or flew with other women. Soviet pilots who refused to fly with women claimed that this was to protect the women. This was not so. Most probably it was to protect themselves, since they were doubtful of the women's abilities. The effect was to prevent women from flying with experienced pilots. Whatever the motive, evidently this attitude soon wore off once the women pilots began to fight and to do so successfully.

Dr. Pennington has drawn on a formidable and fascinating array of evidence: archives, interviews with veterans of the women's regiments and the men who flew with them, letters, photographs, regimental histories, regimental albums, and unpublished memoirs. Clearly, she established a great rapport with the former women combat aviators. She repays this with a cool, objective, and intensely intimate analysis of the women fighter pilots and of others who made up the complement of the women's regiments—navigators, armorers, and flight mechanics. There is no piousness, no hyperbole, yet much of this book is deeply moving: the loss, hardship, stress, heroism, and failure.

What distinguishes the book is not only the collection of data, much of it new, but also the level of analysis. There have been other studies of

Soviet women at war, which Dr. Pennington acknowledges, but on the whole, the coverage has been meager or largely confined to biographical material. What sets *Wings, Women, and War* apart is the level of analysis. One of the most fascinating aspects of the book is the investigation of the attitudes of the women combat pilots toward the question of women and war, their postwar fortunes, and the nature of gender roles in Soviet society—indeed, the whole question of gender roles. What emerges quite unequivocally in this context is that official Soviet cognizance of women in combat roles, coupled with the wartime integration of women into the military system, was not intended to bring about any fundamental change in gender roles in Soviet society. There are issues here that will interest military sociologists, military historians, economists, psychologists, and specialists in gender studies. The great value of this study is that there are so few examples of women in combat roles on the scale furnished by the wartime Soviet Union—when men and women showed equal willingness to fight, when there was equal participation in the business of war (killing not excluded), and when risks regardless of gender were equal. What female persistence achieved during the "Great Patriotic War," albeit as a wartime concession and in the face of entrenched opposition, was a suspension of the argument against the presence of women in the front lines on the traditional grounds of suitability, physiology, or psychology. It was, as Dr. Pennington puts it, "a temporary expansion of gender roles."

If that expansion is interesting, then the contraction is doubly so. Here the reader will find a pertinent analysis of some of the causes, as well as opinions and reactions of the women themselves. For understandable reasons, after the prolonged stress of front-line service, many women simply wanted a return to normality, meaning home and family. There was also a horribly ruined world waiting to be rebuilt. What is surprising, however, is not merely the contraction of that temporary expansion of gender roles but the abrupt and brutal rejection of it. The ejection of women from the military (for that is what it amounted to) bore all the signs of a deliberate and preordained decision. It was made abundantly plain that women could not expect permanent military careers. The same specious wartime argument about "protecting" women was also trotted out. The fact of the physical displacement of women from the military had its fictional counterpart in postwar writing, where front-line women steadily disappeared from view. The "celebration of women" did not include the wartime aces.

Dr. Pennington has presented a unique record of a unique situation, rich in important insights and lessons that have immediate relevance for present-day circumstances. Many thousands of women served with the Soviet armed forces during the "Great Patriotic War." Those committed to a combat role operated largely at subunit, battery, or weapons crew level. Where they exercised command it was principally at platoon level. Officer rank ranged from senior lieutenant to lieutenant colonel. The three women's air regiments were exceptions, operational entities that provide a substantial base to examine in depth and over time the combat role of women under conditions of maximum stress, great risk, and acute personal danger.

What adds further validity to this study is that here like is compared with like. No special exceptions were made for the women's aviation regiments. They operated exactly as did other regiments in terms of type and number of missions. Dr. Pennington presents convincing evidence that the women's regiments performed on a par with the male regiments, that exemplary combat performance on the part of women aircrews was not specifically related to either gender integration or gender segregation. This is an absolutely key point, making *Wings, Women, and War* mandatory reading for those having anything to do with the manning of armed forces in the twenty-first century.

The overriding issue is the degree to which the admission of women to combat roles will or will not debilitate overall combat performance. Its import was graphically illustrated by General Sir Charles Guthrie, the outgoing chief of the British Defence Staff. General Guthrie observed that an "incremental approach" had been taken to "widening the roles for women" in the armed forces, and a study is presently under way to investigate the suitability of women for "close combat roles." The general is unsure whether "the nation is ready for such a step." His main concern, however, from what he defines as his perspective, is that "nothing, I repeat nothing," should damage "the combat effectiveness of the British Armed Forces."

I strongly urge the general to advise his study group to take up Dr. Pennington's book, for nowhere else will he, his successor, and their colleagues find such a volume of unique and invaluable data—behavioral, institutional, and operational. The argument is not, as General Guthrie seems to suspect, about gender balance, or "equality as an end in itself." It is essentially about combat effectiveness, and Soviet women aircrews demonstrated in terms of tactical front-line performance that they possessed, in the words of a leading male Soviet fighter pilot, "an iron character, a steady hand and an accurate eye." That is not about equality or balance; it is simply about being good at the job, which is exactly what the battlefield demands.

John Erickson
University of Edinburgh

Acknowledgments

First and foremost, I am grateful to my mother, Gloria Knight Pennington, who made many sacrifices while providing both moral and financial support. She took me flying when I was a child, never dreaming that aviation would affect my life in so many ways. My uncle, John W. Knight II, gave me the airline ticket that enabled me to go to Russia in 1993, and my dear friends Ruth Donnellan and the late Rick Bennett gave me money for travel expenses. Anne Noggle graciously shared with me the store of materials she brought from Russia; she also provided continuing friendship and financial assistance for a research trip. Fellow writers Angelia Dorman and Lew Reed encouraged me at times when the task seemed impossible.

In the academic world I had both mentors and tormentors. The latter need not be named; the former deserve special thanks. At the University of South Carolina, my research adviser S. P. MacKenzie was unfailingly encouraging, and former department chair Peter Becker helped me obtain financial support. My friend Christine White of Pennsylvania State brought me important papers from Russia. Richard Stites of Georgetown and Peter Paret of Princeton made substantive and editorial suggestions on earlier work that was incorporated into this book. Von Hardesty of the Smithsonian, John Erickson of the University of Edinburgh, and David Glantz were all profoundly supportive and provided the best possible examples of scholarly mentoring.

I am deeply indebted to the many friends in Russia who assisted me with this project, especially Margarita Ponomareva, Vladimir Ravkin, Aleksandr Gridnev, Ekaterina Polunina, Vladimir Pasportnikov, and Inna Pasportnikova. These veterans and friends of veterans were generous with their time, photos, and letters. I will never forget the weeks I spent in their company; the excursions we made together; the interviews given with tears, smiles, and outrage over old injustices; or the dinners, stories, and songs we shared.

Abbreviations and Translations

❖   ❖   ❖   ❖   ❖   ❖   ❖

BAD	bomber aviation division	*bombardirovochnaia aviatsionnaia diviziia*
BAK	bomber aviation corps	*bombardirovochnyi aviatsionnyi korpus*
BAO	airfield service battalion	*batal'on aerodromnogo obsluzhivaniia*
BAP	bomber aviation regiment	*bombardirovochnyi aviatsionnyi polk*
Gv	Guards	*gvardeiskii*
HSU	Hero of the Soviet Union	*geroi sovetskogo soiuza*
IA	Fighter Aviation	*istrebitel'naia aviatsiia*
IA/PVO	Fighter Aviation of the Air Defense Force	*istrebitel'naia aviatsiia protivovozdushnoi oborony*
IAD	fighter aviation division	*istrebitel'naia aviatsionnaia diviziia*
IAE	fighter aviation squadron	*istrebitel'naia aviatsionnaia eskadril'ia*
IAK	fighter aviation corps	*istrebitel'nyi aviatsionnyi korpus*
IAP	fighter aviation regiment	*istrebitel'nyi aviatsionnyi polk*
Komsomol	Young Communist League	*Kommunisticheskii Soiuz Molodezhi*
NBAD	night bomber aviation division	*nochnaia bombardirovochnaia aviatsionnaia diviziia*
NBAP	night bomber aviation regiment	*nochnoi bombardirovochnyi aviatsionnyi polk*
NKO	People's Commissariat of Defense	*Narodnyi komissariat oborony*

OAP	Separate Air Regiment	*otdel'nyi aviatsionnyi polk*
PVO	Air Defense Force	*protivovozdushnaia oborona*
ShAP	ground attack aviation regiment	*shturmovoi aviatsionnyi polk*
TsAMO	Central Archive of the United Armed Forces of the Commonwealth of Independent States in Podolsk	*Tsentral'nyi arkhiv Ob'edinennykh Vooruzhennykh Sil Soiuza Nezavisimykh Gosudarstv*
VA	air army	*vozdushnaia armiia*
VVS	(military) Air Force	*Voenno-vozdushnyie sily*

Introduction

"Warfare is . . . the one human activity from which women, with the most insignificant exceptions, have always and everywhere stood apart. . . . Women . . . do not fight . . . and they never, in any military sense, fight men."[1] So writes the eminent military historian John Keegan. It has often been said that one of the first casualties of war is truth, and that seems to be the case here. If historians have failed to note the presence of military women in their study of history, it is simply a case of selective blindness. Keegan notes the "military historians' habitual reluctance to call a spade a spade,"[2] but Keegan himself suffers an all-too-common form of that reluctance regarding the military history of women. Women were the "invisible combatants" of the Second World War, according to historian D'Ann Campbell.[3] This book discusses the history of one important group of those invisible combatants.

The Soviet Union was unique in world history in its use of large numbers of women in combat. During both world wars and its civil war, women fought on the front lines.[4] Soviet women engaged in combat in all branches of service, as well as in partisan units, in addition to their massive employment in combat support services.[5] They were an important part of the Soviet military in the Second World War; by the end of 1943, more than 800,000 women were in military service—about 8 percent of the total personnel. Altogether, as many as a million Soviet women (including partisans) served in the military; half of them were at the front.[6] Soviet women were also the only female combatants who fought outside the borders of their own country during the Second World War.

The Soviet Union was the first state to allow women pilots to fly combat missions, in a rare historical example of state sponsorship of women in combat roles. Women pilots in other countries flew military aircraft, including the Women's Airforce Service Pilots in the United States, but those women were relegated to support roles. They performed ferry, test, and training functions and took the risks associated with those duties, and some were fired on by enemies. But only the Soviet women pilots could fire back; only Soviet women dropped bombs and fought in air combat. Women's aviation units were formed early in the war: in October 1941, the all-female Aviation Group 122 was formed under the command of the famous pilot Marina Raskova (sometimes characterized as a Russian Amelia Earhart). The 122nd trained the entire personnel—pilots, navigators, mechanics, and ground crews—for three new regiments: the 586th Fighter Aviation Regiment, the 587th Day Bomber Aviation Regiment, and the 588th Night Bomber Aviation Regiment.[7] The women's regiments carried no special designation; their unit numbers and titles were standard military designations. They were not formally called "women's" regiments, in the manner that American and British women's support units were so designated. The women used standard Soviet flying clothing and equipment; they did not receive uniforms designed for women until 1943. In general, the 586th, 587th, and 588th were officially regarded as typical military regiments in all respects except their initial recruitment. These combat regiments were activated beginning in early 1942 and served until the end of the war in 1945.[8] They flew a combined total of more than 30,000 combat sorties, produced at least thirty Heroes of the Soviet Union (of the thirty-three female aviators who received that medal for wartime service), and included in their ranks at least two fighter aces.[9] Two of the regiments received the elite "Guards" appellation, with the 587th becoming the 125th Guards Dive Bomber Aviation Regiment and the 588th redesignated the 46th Guards Night Bomber Aviation Regiment. (Following Soviet custom, and to avoid confusion, the regiments that were redesignated during the war are hereafter referred to by their Guards numbers.)

Some Westerners have maintained that these units were created primarily as a public relations exercise.[10] If such were the case, one would expect to find evidence that these units were carefully planned, an official policy on the recruitment and promotion of women, and a strong propaganda emphasis on women's roles in the military; however, none of these things existed. Another common assumption is that women's wartime units were born of desperation. Rarely, however, is an effort made to define "desperation." Conventional wisdom equates desperation with personnel shortages and suggests that women were accepted into military service to replace soldiers killed in action or to free up men to go to the front. Although this appears to have been an important motivation in other situations, it was not a factor in the formation of the women's aviation regiments. At the time they were created, in October 1941, there was no shortage of pilots in the Soviet Air Force—there was, however, a severe shortage of aircraft.

Were Soviet women's aviation regiments created by the government primarily as an exercise in public relations? Were they merely a desperate measure, created to free up male pilots for front-line duty? Was it instead Marina Raskova's personal influence with Stalin that instigated the creation of the 122nd Air Group? How well did the women pilots measure up in combat? Was their mere presence disruptive to unit cohesion? How successful was the gender integration of two of the regiments? The opening of the Soviet military archives on the Second World War created a new opportunity to examine these questions. And recent developments in the former Soviet Union have made it much easier to locate and interview veterans; such interviews can validate and expand on the accounts given in the memoir literature.

There has been little written in English about the Soviet women aviators, and the quality of those materials is uneven. This book provides the first scholarly survey of how and why three women's aviation regiments were formed in the Soviet Union during the Second World War, how they were integrated into the Soviet armed forces, and their recruitment, training, and combat service.

1

Before the War

The historical experience of Russian and Soviet women as aviators and combatants set the context for the Soviet wartime experience. Although there were isolated instances of women who fought throughout Russian and Soviet history, they were rarely encouraged to do so. However, there were historical and legal precedents in the Soviet Union that made it easier for women to fight than in other countries. This, combined with a general belief that Russian women were physically strong, set the stage for the mass entry of women into combat in the Second World War.

❖ ❖ ❖

THE HISTORICAL CONTEXT OF WOMEN IN COMBAT: FACT AND LEGEND

There is a legendary tradition in Russia of strong, combative women—perhaps more so than in any other country. For example, one legendary homeland of the Amazons was the south Russian steppes, where archaeologists have discovered ancient burial sites of women with weapons in Georgia, Ukraine, and Russia—areas of traditional Sarmatian culture. Dating primarily from the fourth and third centuries B.C., these women's graves contained swords, armor, lance heads, and archery gear.[1] Russian folk literature includes tales of the *polianitsy*, or warrior heroines, who were credited with powerful physiques and who conquered men in single combat.[2] These legends were not unknown to the average Russian. One commander of an engineering battalion said, "If we recall history, we'll see that at all times Russian women not only saw their husbands, brothers and sons off to the battlefields and grieved and waited for them, but in perilous times also stood beside their men."[3]

Legend and perception are one thing; actual experience is often quite different. In practice, Russian women (like most women throughout history) were expected to be subservient to men and were hardly regarded as suitable for fighting. Despite that fact, there are a number of documented cases of women who participated in combat. Perhaps the most famous was Nadezhda Durova, who fought as an Uhlan officer in the Russian cavalry during the early nineteenth century. In male disguise, Durova saw combat in 1807 and 1812–1814 in the wars against Napoleon. Her disguise was eventually discovered, but Tsar Alexander I permitted Durova to continue to serve because of her several decorations for heroism; she was the only woman to win the St. George Cross until the end of the First World War.[4] A century later, a number of young women joined the Russian army during the First World War. According to Alfred G. Meyer, "a surprisingly high number eventually succeeded in joining a fighting unit," and many were decorated.[5]

The most dramatic precedent for Soviet women in combat was set by the "Women's Battalion of Death" commanded by Maria Bochkareva in 1917.[6] Bochkareva was a peasant woman who received permission from the tsar to enlist in the infantry as a line soldier early in World War I.[7] She served with some distinction, was wounded on at least three occasions, and received several medals. After the February Revolution, Bochkareva was taken to Petrograd to meet the War Minister of the new Provisional Government, Aleksandr Kerensky.[8] When asked for her suggestions on a way to alleviate the deteriorating morale at the front, Bochkareva suggested forming a "Women's Battalion of Death": a unit of 300 women that would "serve as an example to the army and lead the men into battle."[9] Bochkareva's stated purpose was "to shame the men in the trenches by having the women go over the top first."[10] Bochkareva initially recruited 2,000 women, but her insistence on rigid discipline, severe punishments for minor infractions, and absolute authoritarianism soon thinned the ranks to around 300 recruits.[11] The battalion went to the front in July 1917.[12] It participated in one inconclusive action, when the women's battalion and a group of officers attempted to inspire the IX Corps to conduct an offensive. Bochkareva claimed that their attack was successful, resulting in the capture of many prisoners, but they were then left stranded with no rein-forcements or supplies. They were eventually forced to retreat and sus-tained heavy casualties.[13]

As the situation in revolutionary Russia deteriorated, Bochkareva found herself on the losing side. Although she violently opposed the Bolsheviks, Bochkareva also engaged in heated arguments with Kerensky, who in-sisted that she cease her stern punishments and permit representative committees in the battalion.[14] She went to America and England in late 1917, then returned to Russia to join the anti-Bolshevik White forces dur-ing the Russian Civil War; her subsequent fate is unknown. The Women's Battalion of Death attempted to protect Kerensky from the Bolsheviks dur-ing the October Revolution in Petrograd. There are conflicting reports as to their fate.[15]

Women who supported the Provisional Government, like the Women's Battalion of Death, fought on the losing side. Other women were militant supporters of socialism and of the Bolshevik Party. Even before coming to power, the Bolsheviks, like good Marxists, supported full legal equality for women. Many women were active in the Bolshevik cause, but their participation was "always at secondary or lower levels of leadership," and as historian Richard Stites notes: "This pattern would be repeated with the Bolsheviks in the Civil War, when the female commissar stood beside, but slightly behind, the male commander; and it would be repeated in Soviet society at large after the war, when the trained Communist woman acted out the role of deputy, assistant, or vice-director in almost every walk of life."[16] After the Bolsheviks secured power and formed the new Soviet state, women's legal status changed dramatically. It was believed that when socialism was achieved and the bourgeoisie eliminated, men and women naturally would become equals; there could be no gender discrim-ination in a socialist state.[17] The Bolsheviks proclaimed the full emancipa-tion and enfranchisement of women; they even appointed one woman, Alexandra Kollontai, as a government minister. The Soviet Union became the first major country in the world to give women full citizenship and legal equality.[18]

The Bolsheviks' 1918 decree establishing universal military service obli-gated only men, but it did permit women to volunteer for service.[19] About 66,000 women, or 2 percent of military personnel, served in the Red Army during the Russian Civil War; most served in traditional support roles such as nursing. Some women did take positions that involved leadership or combat roles, such as those who served as commissars and soldiers. No special attention was given to the potential problems of integrating women into the military. By definition, gender discrimination was inherent in the class struggle of capitalism and could not exist in a socialist state.[20] There was a certain utopianism about the whole issue, as noted by Griesse and Stites:

> Men were expected, officially, to accept women in combat as a matter of course, without sexist resistance or pious welcome speeches. The reality, of course, did not always match the slogans and aspirations of the regime. . . . A prominent Bolshevik woman herself recalls how she had to assert her right to operate as a purely military person and not as a woman (a commander contemptuously explained that he had no sidesaddle for her). Yet this same woman was notorious for her violence and even cruelty in action.[21]

The situation began to change under Stalin. Griesse and Stites believe that only the idea of female equality remained: "When Stalin consolidated his power in the early 1930s, much of the early Bolshevik feminism was muted. . . . But both the facts and the myths of women's emancipation in Soviet Russia still remained very much alive in the popular mind."[22] The universal military service laws of 1925 and 1939 were similar to the 1918 decree; only men were subject to regular conscription. Women with certain skills, such as medical training, could be mobilized in emergencies.[23] Women were allowed to volunteer for service, although they were strongly discouraged from doing so: "Pronatalist, sexist, and suspicious of spontaneity, Stalinism assured that the Soviet high command would have a deeply ambivalent attitude to the participation of women in the next war."[24]

WOMEN IN AVIATION IN THE PREWAR PERIOD

Aviation developed more slowly in Russia than in the West. Even so, there were a few women who flew even in the imperial period. At least two women, Lidiia Zverevskaia and Liubov Galanshchikova, reportedly received pilot's licenses in 1911.[25] The Western magazine *Flying* reported in June 1913 that "two Russian women . . . have studied aviation, and passed their tests at the German flying grounds at Johannisthal." One of those women, Galanshchikova, set an international women's altitude record.[26] The other, Princess Evgeniia Mikhailovna Shakhovskaia, was interested in military flying. In 1912, when Italy and Turkey were at war, she proposed to the Italian government that she be allowed to fly as an aerial reconnaissance pilot. Although the Italians refused her offer, Shakhovskaia was later hailed as "the first military airwoman" in the world when she became an air scout for the Russian Army in the First World War.[27] Princess Shakhovskaia obtained the tsar's permission to serve as a reconnaissance pilot, although she did not hold military rank and did not participate in combat.[28] Another woman, Nadezhda Degtereva, reportedly disguised herself as a boy and entered military air service in 1914. Like Shakhovskaia, she flew reconnaissance missions. Her disguise was discovered when she was forced to seek medical attention after being wounded while flying over enemy lines.[29] Sofiia Alexandrovna Dolgorunaia is also reported to have flown for the Air Service in 1917, after Kerensky opened military service to women.[30]

After the Bolshevik Revolution and the end of the civil war, women pilots flew as air-club instructors or with the civil air fleet, though a small number of women served in the Red Army as pilots from at least 1923. Women did not find it easy to obtain military training; there was a great deal of social opposition to women entering military service. However, since the Soviet Union was the first country in the world to proclaim legal equality for women, the military flying schools and Osoaviakhim (the two organizations that offered flight training) could not legally refuse entry to qualified women. Women who stayed the bureaucratic course and refused to bow to sometimes severe peer pressure did become pilots and even military pilots.

It was through the paramilitary organization Osoaviakhim (the Society for Cooperation in Defense and Aviation-Chemical Development) that most Soviet women received flight training. Osoaviakhim was founded in 1927 to train teenagers and young adults in quasi-military skills such as defense and chemical warfare, marksmanship, and parachuting.[31] By the early 1930s, Osoaviakhim also began developing a network of air clubs to provide flight training in light aircraft. The Soviet government put a great deal of emphasis on the importance of aviation. Vast expanses of Soviet territory were still not linked by roads or railways; air travel was seen as the most promising means of transportation to these distant areas. The second Five-Year Plan dictated a tripling of civil aviation routes through-out the country.[32] Many pilots would be needed if this vision of a huge network of air transportation were to become a reality.

Young women were encouraged to participate in all facets of Osoavia-khim training. However, despite this official and legal support, most women had to struggle to get into flight training. Marina Chechneva (subsequently a night bomber pilot and a Hero of the Soviet Union) described the manner in which her male flying club instructor discouraged her from seeking a career as a pilot as being typical of the time:

> Quite a few women were studying at the air club; however, the atti-tude of many of the instructors towards them was, to put it mildly, less than enthusiastic. The instructors took women in their groups unwillingly. That was clear. Women were only beginning to enter avi-ation. Not everyone believed that we would be able to work in this field on an equal basis with men. The example of famous women pi-lots did not convince the skeptics. "Aviation is not a woman's affair," they declared repeatedly, and tried in every way possible to dissuade young women from joining the air club.[33]

Chechneva went on to say that her flight commander once told her that even though he knew many women pilots whose skills were quite as good as men's, women were simply not meant to be in aviation. Nina Ras-popova related a similar story. In 1932, she was sent by the regional Kom-somol to a pilots' school, but when she and another girl arrived, she said "the commander of the school said he wouldn't admit us because we were girls, but the government said they must admit us, so I was enrolled."[34]

Even when the air club instructors were supportive, many young women faced opposition from their parents. Antonina Bondareva, later a Guards lieutenant in the 46th, related the following story:

> When I was in the seventh grade, an airplane came to our town. In 1936 it seemed something extraordinary. A campaign was launched spontaneously: "Young Boys and Girls, Take Up Aviation!" Being a Komsomol member, I was, of course, in the front ranks and immedi-ately joined an air club. Father was dead against it, though. Until then all the members of my family had been steelworkers, with several generations of blast-furnace operators. My father believed that a woman could be a steelworker but never a pilot.[35]

Nevertheless, many young women persevered and learned to fly. By 1941, 100 to 150 air clubs had been established; one out of every three or four pilots trained in these air clubs was a woman.[36] The purpose of this training, at least for young men, was to help prepare them for either active or reserve military duty. The men who received flight training at air clubs were registered in the military reserve forces, but women were not; no provision was made for women pilots to play a military role.

❖ ❖ ❖

WOMEN IN MILITARY AVIATION

Osoaviakhim provided an introduction to combat-related skills such as shooting and flying to thousands of young people in schools and factories. At the same time, regular military forces were being expanded, especially during the late 1930s, as the probability of imminent war was widely recognized. However, women were still not encouraged to pursue careers in the military. Even so, a few women were admitted to military aviation in the prewar years. There were two means of becoming an officer in the Soviet military: promotion from the enlisted ranks, and entry into a service academy. The most common way for a woman to become a military pilot was through a military flying school. The military schools combined both flight training and officer training; graduates became pilots and officers at the same time.

The first woman to become a military pilot under Soviet rule was Zinaida Kokorina. After her test-pilot husband died in a crash, she entered the Egorevsk Military Aviation School. The school administration apparently opposed Kokorina's acceptance but could not find a reason to deny her application.[37] She completed training as a pilot, finished advanced firing and bombing courses, and was accepted as a military flier, first class.[38] Kokorina's example would prove to be typical: women who applied to enter a military aviation school were invariably denied their first request. Raisa Aronova recalled:

> I heard that the surest path to aviation was through the military flying school . . . I sent a letter. "I cannot conceive of a life for myself without aviation," it said frankly. I awaited a reply impatiently. And one arrived: "Women, at the present time, are not being accepted at the military flying schools."[39]

The women who succeeded did so through persistent applications. When the administration could find no legal reason to deny them, and the women refused to be discouraged, they were usually admitted. Some women who achieved admittance did so by finding a civilian job at the school, which gave them, in time, more of an insider's status. For example, in the early 1930s, Polina Osipenko (who later set many international aviation records) was a young poultry keeper on a state farm near the Sea of Azov. She applied to the Kacha Aviation School near Sevastopol; rather than being offered a student's slot, she was given the job of waitress in the school cafeteria. She took the position—and then reportedly hounded the head of the school until he agreed to accept her as a student. Osipenko graduated with a military commission and flew in fighter squadrons before the war, achieving the position of flight commander.[40]

One of the most significant cases is that of Marina Raskova, who was a famous navigator and pilot in Soviet aviation in the 1930s and subsequently became commander of the first women's military aviation group. In 1933, Raskova became the first woman to qualify as an air force navigator.[41] In 1934, she began teaching air navigation at the Zhukovskii Air Academy; Raskova was apparently the first female instructor at the academy. She was twenty-two years old.[42] Raskova also began pilot training in 1934 with the Moscow Center Airclub. She qualified as a pilot, then as a flying instructor. In August 1935, she competed in the first women's cross-country flight in sports planes, flying from Leningrad to Moscow.[43] During 1937 and 1938, while continuing to teach at the Zhukovskii Air Academy, Raskova began to participate in a series of world-record flights (such as the 1938 flight described later). In 1939 or 1940, Raskova entered the M. V. Frunze Academy, the first institution of higher military education established by the Soviets after the revolution and a prestigious center of military study and research. It trained command-level military officers; its graduates included many marshals of the Soviet Union, such as Zhukov, Novikov, Konev, Rokossovskii, and Chuikov. A Soviet history of the Frunze Academy makes special note of Raskova's presence.[44]

INTERNATIONAL COMPETITION AND WORLD AVIATION RECORDS

Soviet aviation was a realm of excitement in the late 1930s. The achievements of Soviet aviators were an important means of public justification for the Stalin regime.[45] There was immense propaganda value in setting world aviation records or completing challenging flights. Airplanes were a tangible product of Soviet industrialization, and the records set by Soviet pilots demonstrated the superiority of Soviet training. Such flights "proved" the ability of the Soviet Union to compete with Western nations industrially and commercially. Moreover, such achievements carried implications of military capability, as a Soviet author noted in 1938: "should . . . Comrade Stalin issue the order to fly . . . to any point on the globe, there will be the aeroplanes and thousands upon thousands of Soviet pilots—*men and women*—courageous, resolute and devoted to the Land of Soviets, to carry out such an order for the good and glory of their country."[46] Historian Robert Tucker has identified a "hierarchy of hero cults" as a major feature of Stalinist culture. In this hierarchy, aviators (inspired by Stalin) were very near the top:

> Below the apex were cults of deceased leaders . . . and then small cults of living comrades of Stalin, notably Voroshilov. Below these were the much publicized heroes from the common folk: labor heroes and heroines like Stakhanov . . . heroic Polar explorers . . . Stalinist falcons like Chkalov who set new world records for long-distance flights . . . Stalin was in the hearts and minds of airmen heroes as they flew their dangerous missions.[47]

According to Kenneth Whiting, the aviation achievements of the 1930s "did much to bolster Soviet confidences in both flying personnel and Soviet aircraft, with the enthusiastic assistance of the Soviet media—the whole business resembled the later arduous Soviet approach to the Olympic games."[48] General A. S. Yakovlev, a member of the presidium of the 1935 Central Council, was closely associated with the Central Aeroclub of the Osoaviakhim. Yakovlev recalled that up to 1939, aviation achievements had kept pace with the propaganda campaign, but afterward, the public image of aviation had dangerously surpassed reality.[49] This would lead to unrealistic expectations, and disappointment, during the early days of the war.

The idolization of Soviet fliers (and other heroes) was thus encouraged by the Soviet government. Because of the inspirational role Stalin allegedly played, publicity about aviation served to strengthen Stalin's position. The cadre of aviation heroes included a small but influential number of Soviet women pilots, including women who held military rank such as Polina

Osipenko and Marina Raskova.[50] The ability to complete long-range flights had important implications. It aided the development of a fast transport system that could deliver mail, passengers, and freight from Moscow to the far reaches of the country in hours, rather than days or weeks.

THE FLIGHT OF THE *RODINA*

The Soviets had a particular interest in long-distance flights. Soviet writers of the 1930s were well aware of the military ramifications of long-range flights, as shown in the following passage:

> In war, long-range aircraft determine to a great extent the success of an attack. This applies particularly to bombers. Long-range bombing planes may penetrate far into the hinterland of the adversary, deal a blow where it is least expected, paralyse the activity of large industrial centres, important railway junctions, and powerful defence enterprises, which are, as a rule, located far from the borders. Long-range bombing planes can cross the territories of several so-called neutral states, reach their destination, drop their load and return to their bases.[51]

It was not just men who were interested in flying for distance; aviators such as Marina Raskova, Polina Osipenko, and Valentina Grizodubova established a number of women's distance records during the 1930s.[52] Setting distance records was regarded as "the most honoured" of aviation feats.[53] But women's participation in long-distance flights had connotations beyond mere sports flying. When Soviet women performed such flights, there was a multifaceted propaganda benefit. In addition to demonstrating the industrial and military capability of the Soviet Union, these flights allowed the Soviets to portray not only their aircraft but also their women as superior products of socialism. Coverage in newspapers, magazines, and books ensured that the Soviet public was well informed of the feats of the female pilots—perhaps as an inspiration to women who toiled in factories or on collective farms, an example of what the "new Soviet woman" could achieve. By 1939, Soviet women fliers had captured more aviation records than women of any other country.[54]

The record-setting *Rodina* flight in late 1938 is the best known of the Soviet women's aviation achievements in this period.[55] An examination of this most famous prewar flight by Soviet women, and of the decision-making process and propaganda surrounding it, serves to illuminate the impact and importance of these flights. The three women of the crew of the *Rodina* were Marina Raskova, Polina Osipenko, and Valentina Grizodubova. The goal of the flight was to set a new international women's record for straight-line distance.[56] The idea for the flight was Grizodubova's; it was she who applied for official permission to conduct the flight. While Raskova and Osipenko were preparing for and carrying out another distance flight from Sevastopol to Arkhangelsk, Grizodubova was planning what would be known as "the flight of the *Rodina*." The flight attracted high-level interest; Lazar Brontman claimed that Grizodubova was summoned to the Kremlin to discuss the flight. The route and type of aircraft that should be used were discussed at length in a two-hour meeting between Grizodubova and Stalin that also included important leaders such as Molotov, Voroshilov, Ezhov, Loktionov, and Gromov. The prototype twin-engine ANT-37 (a converted DB-2 long-range bomber) to be named *Rodina* (motherland) was selected for the flight. The route would be from Moscow to Komsomolsk in the Far East, covering more than 6,500 kilometers. Brontman and Khvat's 1938 book, *The Heroic Flight of the Rodina*, includes the claim (typical of Soviet writing of that time) that "Comrade Stalin made a number of valuable practical suggestions for the guidance of the crew," using the example that "when [Stalin] heard that there was no radio station on the north coast of Lake Baikal, he suggested that one be built there forthwith."[57]

Stalin's personal interest and involvement in this flight and his personal acquaintance with the women pilots may have been a factor in his approval of the formation of the women's combat regiments during the war. Brontman related an interesting story, which he claims was told to him by Polina Osipenko. On 18 July there was a reception for the *Rodina* crew at Molotov's dacha; the guests included Stalin and many famous test pilots and aircraft designers. Osipenko is quoted by Brontman as making the following short speech during the dinner:

> I raised a toast and said that more attention should be devoted to women striving to work in the Army. I cited examples of women working on collective farms, drew a parallel between the latter and the Red

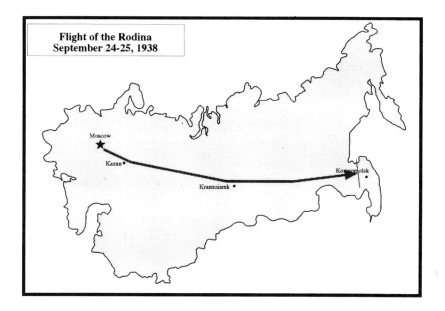

Flight of the Rodina
September 24-25, 1938

Army, and pointed out that women could be of great use in the Army as well. Comrade Stalin supported me. He began to talk about this to Comrade Voroshilov. He asked me a number of questions about the work of women fliers.[58]

In August, about a month before the scheduled date of the flight, the crew settled in at Shchelkovo Airfield to complete their preparations. They were often interrupted for newspaper interviews and photographs. At dawn on 24 September 1938, Raskova, Osipenko, and Grizodubova were ready to make their flight. They had written a letter to Stalin extolling the virtues of Soviet aviation, which was given to a *Pravda* correspondent. Dressed in heavy flying gear—fur trousers, jackets, and boots—they buckled on revolvers and examined their parachutes. A press conference was held that was attended by M. M. Kaganovich (People's Commissar of the Defense Industry) and various bureaucrats. In accordance with International Aeronautic Federation regulations, three sealed barographs were placed in the fuselage, which would provide proof that the flight was made with no stops; the fuel tanks were sealed to prove that they were not refilled during the flight.[59] Finally the *Rodina* was able to take off. The flight was expected to last twenty-five to thirty hours.

Unexpectedly bad weather and icing conditions caused communications to deteriorate, and no reports were received from the *Rodina* after the first ten hours.[60] The aircraft completed most of its planned route, but poor visibility near the destination prevented the crew from locating one of the few possible airfields in the area. They were running low on fuel, apparently because the ground crews had failed to top off the tanks after preflight engine warm-ups, and the women realized they would have to make a forced landing.[61] The aircraft's emergency procedures called for the navigator to bail out of the airplane before a forced landing. The navigator's cockpit in the nose of the plane was vulnerable if the aircraft nosed over in a bad landing, and there was no access from that cockpit to the rest of the plane. Raskova jumped out but accidentally left behind her emergency kit. She expected to touch ground very close to the landing spot. Instead, she spent ten days wandering in the taiga with little food and no water. Grizodubova and Osipenko remained with the *Rodina* (which was stuck in mire in the middle of a swamp), trying to signal for help with pistols and the emergency radio.

In the meantime, a massive air search was conducted by Soviet air clubs and military aviation in the Far East. A vast area—nearly 2 million square kilometers—had to be covered. According to Brontman and Khvat, "scores of aeroplanes and hundreds of people organized into search parties set out in all directions, exploring taiga, plain and gorge." During the search, a midair collision of two rescue planes killed sixteen people, including a high-ranking air force official—a fact that was kept secret for decades.[62] The *Rodina* was finally located eight days after the landing, and a rescue team was dropped in by parachute; Raskova finally found the *Rodina* the next day. On the tenth day, the entire group began the journey back to civilization, first on foot, then by collapsible canoe (Raskova, whose legs were injured, had to be carried out by stretcher).

A great deal of publicity attended the rescue, with daily newspaper updates—but only after the aircraft had been located.[63] The start of the mission received prominent coverage in *Pravda*; but when the aircraft went missing, the newspaper was strangely silent, printing only tiny notices about the search. After the *Rodina* was found, coverage once more exploded, with articles virtually every day detailing the progress of the crew's return to Moscow. Brontman reports that a crowd of "tens of thousands of people" gathered to meet them at the first stop on their journey back to Moscow. Raskova was the focus of much of the media attention; her dramatic story of ten days alone in the taiga made the front page of

Pravda on 13 October. Raskova, Grizodubova, and Osipenko arrived back in Moscow on 27 October as heroes. The *Rodina* had covered 5,947 kilometers of straight-line distance and 6,450 kilometers actual distance in twenty-six hours and twenty-nine minutes. It broke the women's international straight-line distance record by more than 1,500 kilometers and at the same time established a new women's international nonstop broken-line distance record. The women were met at the Belorussia Railway Station by Nikita Khrushchev (then secretary of the Central Committee of the Ukraine) and Kaganovich. A parade procession carried them to the Kremlin, where Stalin reportedly greeted them with kisses. Raskova sat next to Stalin during a long dinner, at which he made a speech about the ancient times of matriarchy in Russia. He concluded by saying, "today these three women have avenged the heavy centuries of the oppression of women."[64] Raskova, Grizodubova, and Osipenko became the first women to receive the Hero of the Soviet Union award, and the only women to receive it before the war.[65]

SIGNIFICANCE OF THE WOMEN'S PREWAR FLIGHTS

As the threat of war increased, the feats of Soviet aviation became more and more significant. Soviet fliers were the objects of adulation comparable to that of American film stars of the period, but with the added aura of the warrior. The names of the women pilots figured prominently in media coverage. In the five years before the Second World War, women fliers such as Raskova received significant attention from the press—both Soviet and Western. Stalin took a personal interest in the women's flights and invited the women fliers to the Kremlin—as he did the famous male aviators. Stalin's personal interest and involvement in these flights, which are documented in contemporary sources, are pertinent to the questions raised in this study.[66] Kenneth Bailes noted that "during the 1930s, Stalin and his associates used world records in aviation as a means of winning support for his regime at home and abroad, and of counterbalancing the effect of the purges." He remarked that "Stalin's own name and reputation were more closely associated with the practice of technological legitimation than any other major leader during this period, and aviation was one of the most spectacular forms this practice took."[67] Stalin's involvement in the 1930s with famous women pilots—the Kremlin receptions, the public recognition, the medals—has already been discussed. Stalin even acted as a pallbearer at the 1939 funeral of Polina Osipenko, who had been killed in a crash.[68] Stalin's longtime interest in aviation and his personal acquaintance with the women pilots were almost certainly factors in his approval of the formation of the women's combat regiments during the war.

Alexander Werth, a Russian-born American journalist, was in the Soviet Union during the late 1930s and through the war. He noted that in 1938–1939, "more or less everybody was aware of the Nazi danger," and clashes with the Japanese and the war in Spain had increased the Soviet sense of standing alone against the world. The Soviet people anticipated and feared war. In important ways, the names of women aviators such as Raskova were closely linked with Stalin. Werth also linked them with the country's preparations for war:

> No wonder that in those days people looked to the Army for protection and that for example some women ace-fliers like Valentina Grizodubova, Polina Osipenko and Marina Raskova became popular idols. When in May 1939 one of them, Polina Osipenko, and the ace-flier Serov were killed in an air-crash, it was like a day of national mourning; they were given a public funeral in Red Square, and the pallbearers included Stalin, Molotov, Beria and other leaders.[69]

According to Werth, the propaganda surrounding these flights was purposely increased just before the signing of the Soviet-German Non-Aggression Pact in August 1939:

> Aviation Day had been celebrated on August 18, and half the front page of *Pravda* that day was occupied by a drawing showing Stalin and Voroshilov surveying a boundless airfield with thousands of planes on it . . . and recalled some of the outstanding feats of Soviet aviation in recent years and their heroes—Chkalov, Gromov, Grizodubova, Raskova and Osipenko.[70]

One female pilot wrote of Moscow in the late 1930s, "In those years, the names of Grizodubova and Raskova . . . were on everyone's lips."[71] Raskova was the best known of the women aviators of her day for several reasons. The most spectacular women's flight was that of the *Rodina*. Of the three women involved, Osipenko died in 1939, but Grizodubova was still an active aviator. However, it was Raskova who wrote a book about the flight, *Zapiski Shturmana* (Notes of a Navigator).[72] The account of her ordeal during her ten days in the taiga was the stuff of adventure novels. Many women pilots stated in their memoirs or in interviews that Raskova's example inspired them to learn to fly. Raisa Aronova's comment is typical: "Indeed it was precisely [Raskova], with her vivid biography, who kindled in me the love of aviation. I admired her record-breaking flights, and after reading her *Notes of a Navigator*, firmly decided to connect my own life with aviation."[73] It was not only Raskova's fame and flying skill but also her endurance during her trial of survival that won her the love of other women. In a 1993 interview, Valentina Kravchenko emphasized Raskova's achievement: "I am a Siberian. I know what it is to be in the taiga in September. It was *very* cold."[74]

Raskova said that after the flight, she and her colleagues received many letters asking them to tell the story of how they became pilots: "tens of hundreds of girls asked for advice and help on how to enter flying school." In the introduction to her book, Raskova cautioned that her entry into aviation was not the typical path of the majority of Soviet women pilots.[75] However, both Raskova and Osipenko published articles in the late 1930s encouraging women to become pilots (and to enter other nontraditional occupations).[76] Pilot Evgeniia Zhigulenko recalled her opinion of Raskova in prewar days: "Marina Raskova was an exceptional person. A famous pilot and Hero of the Soviet Union, she was still a simple, kind woman. She helped many young women who wanted to fly."[77] Some women veterans have also voiced the opinion that Grizodubova was not as personable as Raskova, and was less interested in "women's issues" than in simply flying. According to Inna Pasportnikova, "Raskova and Grizodubova both received many, many letters from women pilots who wanted to fly. But Grizodubova didn't want to work with women."[78]

A Soviet journalist writing in 1975 similarly commented on Raskova's influence on women before the war: "Marina Raskova, the famous aviator, was the idol of many young women who joined air clubs before the war."[79] Natalia Kravtsova, a pilot with the 46th who flew 982 combat sorties, remembered that in 1938 she had saved pictures of Raskova from newspapers and magazines.[80] Liliia Litviak (who left the 586th to fly with the 73rd Guards Fighter Regiment and became a double ace before her death in 1943) also kept pictures of Raskova and the other women pilots in her notebook.[81] The publicity that surrounded the achievements of Raskova and the others was another important factor in setting the stage for the formation of women's combat aviation regiments. The public was accustomed, to some degree, to the idea of women flying under arduous, even heroic, conditions. The names of women pilots were linked in the public mind with feats of aviation that clearly had military overtones.

2

Recruitment and Training of

Aviation Group 122

❖ ❖ ❖ ❖ ❖ ❖ ❖ ❖ ❖ ❖ ❖ ❖ ❖ ❖ ❖

When the Germans invaded the Soviet Union on 22 June 1941, only a few
Soviet women were actively serving in military aviation units. There were,
however, many hundreds, possibly thousands, of trained women pilots in
the civilian sector who were graduates of the Osoaviakhim air clubs. Like
many other Soviet women, many of these pilots immediately volunteered
for active duty. Unlike most other women, the pilots had a highly technical
skill to offer: the ability to fly aircraft. Nevertheless, the women pilots were
all turned down during the first weeks of the war. Those who were already
employed as air-club instructors were told that it was vital for them to
remain behind to train new pilots while the male instructors went to the
front. Nadia Popova, a veteran pilot of the night bomber regiment who
flew 852 combat missions, related a typical experience. When the war
broke out, Popova was a nineteen-year-old aviation instructor in the Do-
netsk region of Ukraine. She said, "the day after the war broke I joined
everyone else trying to enlist. I was flatly refused; they weren't taking
women pilots."[1] Evgeniia Zhigulenko, another Po-2 pilot with nearly 1,000
wartime missions, told a similar story: "It's true that in the first months of
the war women were not enlisted in aviation units. Women could only
serve as nurses, communications operators, or antiaircraft gunners, even
though many of them had been members of aviation clubs before the
war."[2]

When the war began, there was no recruitment or mobilization plan in place to utilize the large number of trained women pilots in the Soviet Union. In fact, there seems to have been no plan for the large-scale military mobilization of women. Only women with selected technical skills (medical, veterinary, and communications) were liable to conscription. According to Cottam, "no separate army women's organizations or policies on conscription and promotion appear to have existed."[3] It appears that women who served in *combat* units in the ground forces, as well as the air force, were volunteers.[4] As the war progressed, there were some mobilizations of women, particularly for the air defense forces, rear services, and support specialties such as communications. These mobilizations occurred long after the formation of the women's aviation regiments. In any event, the recruitment and formation of the women's aviation regiments were handled quite differently from those of later mobilizations. Aviation Group 122 was formed in early October 1941. The unit, which was recruited entirely from women volunteers, was not created through the usual military channels. Instead, primary selection of volunteers was handled by the Central Committee of the Komsomol (the Young Communist League, a Party organization for youth). The women who were selected for the aviation regiments did not receive military status until the completion of their training.[5]

THE ROLE OF MARINA RASKOVA AND POPULAR DEMAND

Precisely how the decision was made to form an all-women's aviation group, and which agencies and personnel were involved, is not clear. What is known is that Marina Raskova, who was the unit's commander, was closely connected with the unit's formation. In fact, it seems to have been Raskova's idea to form the regiments—an idea that she pushed through a reluctant military establishment by the force of her persistence and with the backing of Joseph Stalin. According to Soviet author Aleksandr Magid (who wrote a unit history of the 46th Night Bomber Regiment), "in the October days of 1941, when the Motherland was enduring difficult times, *upon the initiative of Hero of the Soviet Union Marina Raskova*, there began a voluntary recruitment of women-patriots into aviation."[6] Mitroshenkov also claimed that it was Raskova who "proposed the formation" of the women's aviation units.[7] In various accounts, Raskova went to the Defense Ministry, "the authorities," or directly to Stalin and convinced them that women's combat aviation regiments should be created.

It has been suggested that it is unlikely that an individual like Raskova could have been responsible for the creation of a military unit.[8] It might seem more likely that the idea actually originated at Air Forces Headquarters, at the Defense Ministry, or even with Stalin himself and that Raskova was selected as the best and most popular woman to command the group. There is no evidence to disprove this theory; there is also little evidence to support it. Personnel shortages had not reached a critical point; the military had shown no inclination to recruit women or to publicize their participation in the service. The creation of women's regiments on this relatively limited scale served no military purpose beyond that of any typical aviation regiment. There was no government policy or propaganda campaign to support such a move from the military. And it seems unlikely that the idea originated with Stalin. Given the nature of the personality cult, if it had been Stalin who first decided to form women's aviation regiments, he would have been publicly credited with the idea. After all, many other ideas and innovations were attributed to him that were probably not his own. Yet this was not the case with the women's aviation regiments.

Raskova was an extremely well-known figure in Soviet popular culture, as well as a highly skilled aviator. She was a member of the Supreme Soviet and had a certain degree of access to high levels of government. She held an air force commission and knew the chain of military command. Moreover, she knew Stalin personally. It would not have been difficult for her to gain a hearing for her idea at Air Force Headquarters or even directly from Stalin.[9] One Western writer even claims that "prewar gossip, mostly foreign, linked [Stalin's] name to two prominent Russian women, [including] Marina Raskova, the long-distance flier."[10] Although it seems unlikely that there was a romantic connection between Raskova and Stalin, it is clear from her own autobiography that she knew him personally.[11] This connection may have given her additional influence, even if she went to the Defense Ministry rather than directly to Stalin.

According to General-Lieutenant of Aviation Aleksandr Beliakov, "Marina went to the government with a petition to organize women's combat aviation regiments." Beliakov was Raskova's department chief at the Zhukovskii Academy before the war and a Hero of the Soviet Union for his participation in the 1936 nonstop Moscow-to-America flight with Valerii

Chkalov.[12] An article by General A. V. Nikitin, chief of the Main Directorate for Instruction, Formation, and Combat Training of the air force, said that "in the very first days of the Great Patriotic War, HSU Marina Raskova appeared at VVS [air force] headquarters. . . . Characteristically, she didn't talk only about herself, but about the many other women pilots who passionately wanted to defend their homeland. Stubbornly, so characteristic of Raskova, she soon was able to get her way."[13] Pilot Nadia Popova related a similar tale, reflecting the way most of the women veterans remember Raskova's role:

> Marina Raskova, a pilot famous for her world record nonstop flight to Asia, proposed the formation of a separate women's air regiment, tapping the unconsidered resource of thousands of women who had learned to fly in the sports schools before the war. The Defence Ministry agreed and asked her to form three regiments—fighter, short-range bomber and night bomber units—composed solely of women.[14]

Evgeniia Zhigulenko recalled a similar story. Her story is particularly revealing in suggesting that Soviet Air Force Headquarters considered the formation of the women's regiments to be strictly Raskova's concern:

> A friend of mine and I wanted to be pilots. We camped out on many a doorstep, but we were always turned down. Then we got hold of the telephone number of the Air Force headquarters. We called there several times, trying to get somebody to talk to us. . . . Finally, we got passes. A colonel met us, saying, "What is it, girls?" "We're going to sit here until you assign us to an aviation unit," we responded. The colonel first frowned, then smiled: "You should have said so in the first place. You're in luck—Marina Raskova is forming a group of women pilots. Go see her."[15]

Despite her influence, Raskova apparently did not have an easy time getting approval for the women's regiments. According to A. Skopintseva:

> Upon the initiative of Hero of the Soviet Union Marina Raskova . . . three women's aviation regiments were formed. . . . It was not easy for Raskova to convince those who came out against her idea for the creation of women's aviation regiments, who tried to prove that war was not a woman's affair. Coming forward on behalf of one thousand women and girls, who appealed to her at the beginning of the war

with patriotic letters, Raskova stubbornly demonstrated that if the war had become a nationwide matter, then it was impossible not to reckon with the patriotic feelings of women. . . . Persistence won out.[16]

Raskova had a strong hand to play with the Soviet authorities. In addition to her strong qualifications as a pilot and leader, the women she sought to recruit were highly skilled. The women pilots in these regiments were not just Osoaviakhim trained; most of them were air-club instructors and well regarded for this skill. In his study of Osoaviakhim, William Odom suggested that the quality of training was very high, as evidenced by comments from a number of foreign observers.[17] So Raskova was, for the most part, enlisting not raw recruits but skilled pilots who could almost immediately contribute to the war effort.

The Soviet women who joined Raskova's unit clearly believed that she played the key role in the formation of the women's units. Women veterans have repeatedly emphasized the strength of Raskova's character. Navigator Valentina Kravchenko said in 1993, "She was very respected. She was very nice, irresistible . . . I wish you could have seen her when she was alive."[18] Galina Brok-Beltsova remarked on the confidence and skill she observed among the women pilots and navigators and said, "It was all because of Marina Raskova; she was their ideal, their hero. We all need an ideal, an example to follow."[19]

Nina Ivakina, who was Komsomol organizer of the 586th Fighter Aviation Regiment during the war, told a Soviet journalist in a 1975 interview, "I showed you this picture [of Raskova] to remind you that it was Raskova who initiated our three regiments." The journalist was also told:

The day after Nazi Germany's sneak attack on the Soviet Union, Raskova began receiving letters from women air club trainees with the request: "Help me get to the front, into an air force unit." With a briefcase full of these letters, Raskova, a deputy to the USSR Supreme Soviet, went to the Defense Ministry. After hours of discussion, she was authorized to form the three regiments.[20]

Some of the women veterans stress the role of public pressure in the formation of the regiments. "They didn't recruit us. We besieged them with requests, demanded. It was only because of the greatest pressure from us that we were taken."[21] Many of the women who served in the aviation regiments believe that petitions by women and a letter-writing campaign also played a role.[22] Evgeniia Zhigulenko recalled:

When the war started, many of my female peers started writing letters to the government. We demanded to be taken into the army. Of course, they didn't take us. And then Marina Raskova, a famous pilot whom we fondly called the grandmother of Soviet aviation even though she was only twenty-three or twenty-four years old, went to Stalin about this. And, strange as it may seem, this monster told her, "You understand, future generations will not forgive us for sacrificing young girls." It was she herself who told us this, this fascinating woman.

   She said to Stalin, "You know, they are running away to the front all the same, they are taking things into their own hands, and it will be worse, you understand, if they steal airplanes to go." . . . And we had just such an incident. There were several girls who had asked to go to the front, and they were turned down. So they stole a fighter plane and flew off to fight. They just couldn't wait. . . . And because of this, they formed first a group, then three aviation regiments.[23]

Little information has come to light on Stalin's role in the decision to create the women's aviation regiments. Even if the idea was originally Raskova's, it had to be approved at the highest levels—probably by Stalin himself. Unfortunately, information about decision making at the highest levels of the Soviet government and military during Stalin's rule is still scanty. However, Walter Laqueur provides some insight into the way things probably worked:

It is crucial for the understanding of totalitarian regimes to recognize that while not all decisions are actually made in and by the center, *no truly important decision is made without the knowledge, let alone against the wish, of the leader.* It is equally important to realize that while not all decisions are made by the supreme leader, all *could* in principle have been made by him.[24]

Laqueur's analysis of Soviet decision making likely applies to the case in point. For example, Stalin was reported to be directly concerned with the subsequent mobilization of women for the air defense forces. In the spring of 1942 (six months after the formation of the women's aviation unit), 100,000 women were conscripted specifically for the newly created national Air Defense Force (PVO). D. A. Zhuravlev, former commander of the Moscow front of air defense and later the Western Front of air defense,

wrote that Stalin took a personal interest in the women's training and billeting. Zhuravlev noted the many letters from women received by the
Party, the Komsomol, and Stalin and stated that answering the women's
demands to serve was one of the reasons the Central Committee justified
the recruitment.[25] Stalin undoubtedly played an important role in the decision to form women's aviation regiments, as he did in the later mobilization of women for air defense duty. Although the idea probably originated
with Raskova, Stalin almost certainly had to approve such a concept before
the Defense Ministry could agree to implement it.

Raskova apparently retained Stalin's support throughout the training of
the regiments. Aleksandr Gridnev related the comments of one male major,
made to him in the spring of 1942: "[Marina Raskova] enjoys a good reputation at the top. She can get anything, if she wants to." The major recalled
that once Raskova was in the office of the chief of the Engels school, being
reprimanded for some problem (real or perceived) in the behavior of her
students. She happened to receive a personal call from Stalin just at that
time. The person who answered the phone yelled out that Raskova was
being called to speak to Stalin. The chief (and probably everyone else
within earshot) sprang to attention. Stalin asked Raskova how training
was progressing and whether she was receiving the support of the local
organizations. She assured him that everything was fine. After that call,
the chief apparently ceased his complaints.[26]

A further indication of Raskova's key role is the fact that when she died
in January 1943, some of the women pilots feared that the regiments would
be dissolved.[27] They believed that without her presence and influence, the
military would simply disband the women's units. Raskova's death also
illuminated her connection to Stalin, as shown in the media. A memorial
article in the military newspaper *Krasnaia zvezda* was signed by all sorts of
luminaries (Novikov, Shakhurin, Grizodubova, Yakovlev, Nikitin, Levin),
including Stalin. The text stated that "Comrade Stalin, friend and teacher
to Soviet pilots, with love and care followed the creative growth of Marina
Raskova."[28]

Fifty years after the war, the women pilots still stressed the key role
played by Raskova. When Soviet researcher Svetlana Alexiyevich sent out
requests for remembrances of women and war, most of the women who
responded identified their units in the usual way—by number or by name
("the Zhelezniak Brigade," "the Minsk underground organization"). The
women pilots, however, usually associated themselves specifically with

Raskova. One group letter began, "Greetings from women pilots of Marina Raskova's air regiment."[29] The regiments continue to be known commonly as "Raskova's regiments."

At least one woman veteran presented a somewhat different view of Raskova's role. M. A. Kazarinova, the chief of staff of the 122nd and later the 125th, described the day in October 1941 when she was summoned to the 122nd assembly point. She claimed that Raskova recognized that Kazarinova would have preferred to remain in her old regiment and said that Raskova told her that "Valia [Grizodubova] and I also intended to fly in the same crew and asked to be sent to the front, but the command decided otherwise"; she said that "headquarters has assigned us a very great task."[30] This seems to imply that Raskova did not initiate the request to form women's regiments. There are several possible explanations for this apparent discrepancy. First, one must examine Kazarinova's motivation and credibility. There is evidence that Kazarinova censored and edited materials on several occasions to glorify her sister (and possibly herself) at the expense of other veterans. Some veterans accuse her of vengeful and vindictive actions after the war. Kazarinova, to a great extent, worked in Raskova's shadow; perhaps she wished to minimize Raskova's role. Kazarinova herself was replaced as chief of staff of the 125th by a man in October 1943.[31] Second, Kazarinova simply may have been in error; there are other errors (apparently intentional) in her article. For example, Kazarinova implied that her sister, who later became commander of the 586th, was present during the forming of the 122nd; other sources state that Tamara Kazarinova did not arrive until several weeks later, when the group was already at Engels.[32] Third, it is possible that Raskova did indeed ask to go to the front and was refused. The Soviet government might have been reluctant during the first days of the war to permit someone of Raskova's fame to risk herself in combat. It was some time before Grizodubova was assigned to the front, as commander of a long-range transport unit. Grizodubova's case also provides a fourth reason to question Kazarinova's story: if it was the higher command that decided to form women's regiments, why was Raskova assigned to the group but not Grizodubova?

The sources strongly indicate that forming the women's regiments was Raskova's idea.[33] Raskova exerted a strong personal influence on the organization and character of the women's aviation units, to such an extent that many of the women in those units identified themselves as much with her as by their regimental numbers. Raskova inspired many young women to learn to fly before the war. The memoirs of the women aviators who flew under her and the published sources overwhelmingly suggest that Raskova's petition, supported by the requests of hundreds of young women, was the primary reason that the Soviet government formed the women's aviation regiments.

ORGANIZATION AND RECRUITMENT

It is probable that when Raskova made her famous 8 September 1941 speech at a "women's antifascist meeting" in Moscow, she had not yet received approval to form the women's regiments—but had reason to believe that her petition would be approved. The speech was broadcast by radio and reprinted in major newspapers. In it, Raskova said, "the Soviet woman—she is the hundreds of thousands of drivers, tractor operators, *and pilots,* who are *ready at any moment to sit down in a combat machine and plunge into battle. . . .* Dear sisters! The hour has come for harsh retribution! *Stand in the ranks of the warriors for freedom . . . !*"[34] Many veterans remember that speech to this day. If Raskova had not already received hundreds of letters from young women who wanted to become combat pilots, she certainly did in the days and weeks following that speech.

Ekaterina Migunova, Raskova's old friend from the Zhukovskii Academy and later her deputy chief of staff in the 125th, wrote that she was working on the staff of the Operational Directorate of the VVS during the early days of the war. One day in September 1941, Raskova came to see her:

"Now listen, it's most important!" Marina looked around and, making sure that there was no one in the corridor, lowered her voice and said: "This conversation is strictly between us. The decision has been made about the formation of women's combat aviation regiments. The formation will be accomplished on a strictly volunteer basis, with a call-up of women pilots from the Civil Air Fleet, airclubs, and the Osoaviakhim schools, and of women among regular VVS personnel. Here in the VVS this matter has been dragged out for an incredibly long time. I had to appeal to Commissar Aleksei Ivanovich Shakhurin, to ask him to speed up the decision on this question. He promised to support the proposal, and he fulfilled his promise. Now it can only turn out successfully![35]

Raskova then told Migunova that things were still progressing slowly, but they would have to move quickly once orders were received. A "tremendous flood of letters" proved that they had plenty of volunteers, but they would have to train the entire personnel themselves: technicians, armorers, instrument mechanics, radio operators, and staff workers. "There will be many worries and difficulties," Raskova stressed, and she asked Migunova to join her staff. "There's only a small cadre of women-commanders in the VVS, but they all absolutely must be won over to this work."[36]

Migunova recalled thinking to herself, "with her fame, her authority, and the opportunity to socialize with the greatest leaders of the state, Raskova could, without exerting any sort of effort, choose for herself a government post" where she could serve her country without any risk to her life.[37] But she knew that Raskova, who was working at the People's Commissariat of Defense (NKO), had been unable to ignore the pleas of the women pilots. Migunova provided an explanation for Raskova's decision to form separate women's units rather than simply assisting the women in being accepted for duty through regular military channels:

Of course, it would have been possible to decide the question more simply, without special measures, as it was decided during the civil war. Women together with men could undergo special training in training units and schools, and as part of men's units, could take part in combat activities at the front. However, in view of the mass desire of women to go to the front, such a decision now seemed incorrect. There arose the question of forming special women's aviation units, in order that in more favorable conditions for them, then women could develop in full measure their flying and command abilities.[38]

According to Migunova, Raskova's idea met resistance from the VVS. Many senior officers thought that "in such difficult times for the country, there was no time to waste on such 'experiments.' " But Raskova apparently persuaded them by agreeing to take complete responsibility for the formation and training of the new units. Her persuasive abilities were no doubt greatly augmented by the support of A. I. Shakhurin, People's Commissar of Aviation Industry, "known for his tough-minded efficiency."[39] It seems likely that Stalin's influence was also a factor; even if he did not intervene directly, the mere association of his name with Raskova's was undoubtedly important. Given the apparent resistance within the VVS, Raskova probably could not have pushed her idea through without taking advantage of her personal connections in high places.

Order No. 0099 of the People's Commissariat of Defense, dated 8 October 1941, directed that by 1 December, three regiments would be formed and trained for combat work. Those regiments would be the 586th Fighter Aviation Regiment (to be equipped with Yak-1 fighters), the 587th Short-Range Bomber Aviation Regiment (to receive Su-2 bombers from the reserves), and the 46th Night Bomber Regiment (which would receive U-2 biplanes). The high command of the VVS was directed to staff the regiments with women from the military and civil air fleets and from Osoavi-akhim.[40] Aviation Group 122 (as it was later designated) was to be staffed entirely by women. Not only pilots but also women who would be trained as navigators, mechanics, armorers, and all other support personnel had to be recruited. Navigators were recruited from among students at universities and technical schools; mechanics and technicians were recruited primarily among factory and technical workers. The recruitment for the 122nd was handled primarily through Komsomol channels and by word of mouth; there is no evidence that the call for volunteers received wide publicity. The majority of the volunteers were from Moscow, or were studying or working in Moscow, when the call went out.

Most volunteers heard about the recruitment on 10 October 1941—the date on which Soviet troops pulled back to the Mozhaisk Line only fifty miles west of Moscow.[41] For example, Polina Gelman recalled how she found out about the call for volunteers. "[On 10 October 1941] all the [university] students were digging antitank ditches along the Belorussian road near Moscow. Among the students the rumor was going around that girls were being taken into aviation. My girlfriend was studying at the Moscow Aviation Institute. She said that she had already received orders. The next morning, I submitted all the paperwork to the Komsomol Central Committee."[42]

The Central Committee of the Komsomol sent instructions to its district committees and Komsomol units in factories and educational institutions. It was easy to locate volunteers for pilot and navigator positions through the Komsomols of air clubs and universities. But women suited to be mechanics and staff were also needed. The Komsomols were directed to select female volunteers who were strong and had some sort of technical background. These nonflying volunteers did not know that they were being recruited for aviation; they simply wanted to get to the front.[43] The volunteers filled out questionnaires; they were interviewed, warned about the hardships of military service, and asked to think carefully before agreeing to volunteer for duty. Aronova described the Komsomol selection process as "stringent and thorough."[44] Those selected by the local Komsomols were then sent to Raskova.

At no point were the women volunteers required to undergo extended medical testing or tests of physical fitness. Inna Pasportnikova, who had the physically demanding job of mechanic, told me, "There was no medical commission. Before Engels we were based at Zhukov, and there was a doctor there, but I never saw him. No one ever asked me about my strength."[45] It might seem odd that there were no tests of strength, endurance, or physical fitness or even thorough medical examinations. These girls, especially those selected as armorers and mechanics, would have to lift heavy weights and needed strength to endure their duties. It seems that the Soviets simply assumed that the women would be able to do the job; after all, Soviet women had borne the brunt of physical labor in Russia for centuries. Ellen Jones indicates that the Soviets traditionally took the physical strength of their women as a given. "Soviet reliance on females for harsh, physically demanding labor was not at all new," she notes. "The same social values that allowed the use of Soviet women in hard, menial labor probably facilitated their participation in combat in World War II."[46] Western observers commented on the incredible endurance of Russian women during the war. One British pilot who flew with a Royal Air Force unit near Murmansk wrote about a group of a dozen Russian girls he had watched sawing up and loading timber. Stiff and bored after days on a transport ship, he decided to help the girls out:

> The party was under the command of a girl of about twenty, a qualified engineer. They worked away for three hours like absolute fury, the engineer-girl working the hardest of the lot. . . . Once a lorry was loaded up with sawn timber, the girls would sit down for a breather and start smoking and singing. And then, when another lorry would come up, they'd start in all over again. About halfway through the loading and sawing I felt that I had strained every muscle of my body . . . but every time I sat down for a rest, there would appear another

girl at the end of a log weighing half a ton . . . and back one would have to go to the treadmill of labour out of pure shame—explaining that one had been three weeks aboard ship, and one was not quite in one's natural athletic condition.[47]

The elite among the volunteers were the women who were already flying as military or civil pilots when the war began. Raskova and Grizodubova were not the only famous women pilots; everyone knew the names of the *piaterka*, five women pilots whose aerobatic team, based at Tushino Airfield in Moscow, performed at many air shows and parades. Three of those women, Evgeniia Prokhorova, Raisa Beliaeva, and Valeriia Khomiakova, joined Raskova's group; all were assigned to the fighter regiment.[48] However, many women who already had positions in aviation did not want to be transferred to "women's" regiments; they preferred to remain where they were. Some were opposed to the idea of separate women's regiments; Valentina Grizodubova was vehemently against the idea.[49] Klavdiia Iliushina, a military engineer, asked to be sent from the factory where she was working to the front, but she was sent to Raskova's unit instead. She was not happy about being in an all-female regiment. She recalled, "When I first came to the regiment, I was not pleased. I wasn't used to working with girls, for I had always worked with men. The girls seemed noisy, and . . . [the ground personnel] were from a very common strata of society."[50]

It is difficult to generalize about why many women on active military duty resisted being reassigned to Raskova's unit. Some, like Grizodubova, seemed to oppose the segregation of women into separate units. Most of them simply may have wanted to stay where they were; those who had managed to find positions at the front had no desire to return to Moscow and waste time training when they could be fighting. Women in operational units had already formed bonds with their comrades in arms. In general, the women who had managed to get positions in some sort of front-line unit resisted a transfer, while women working in the rear as instructors or transport pilots eagerly sought to join Raskova's group; it was their chance to get to the front.

Some women pilots were transferred during the formation of the 122nd. One example is Nadezhda Fedutenko (later a bomber pilot with the 125th). As a civil aviation pilot for six years before the war, she had accumulated thousands of flying hours. When the war began, Fedutenko was flying the

R-5 with the Kiev Special Group of Civil Aviation, dropping supplies to encircled troops, evacuating the wounded, and transporting senior officers; she completed about 200 combat flights before arriving at the 122nd.[51] Other women arrived later, often because they had difficulty getting released from their duties, despite the transfer orders. Marina Chechneva, an air-club instructor, had been evacuated with her club to Stalingrad to train pilots for the front. She was able to achieve a transfer only after the 122nd had arrived at Engels.[52] Engineer Irina Emel'ianova recalled that she was unable to transfer to the 122nd until mid-November, despite her repeated requests to be sent to the front since the first day of the war.[53] Olga Yamshchikova was working as an air-club instructor in Siberia; after repeated requests, and with Raskova's assistance, she was finally transferred to the 586th in the fall of 1942.[54]

Some women pilots were not transferred until much later in the war. Liuba Gubina, a pilot with the Special Purpose Western Group of Civil Aviation, was not transferred to the 125th until April 1943.[55] Valentina Petrochenkova, later a pilot with the 586th, also arrived late, although she desperately wanted to join Raskova's group. As an air-club instructor, she had been evacuated to Stalingrad to train pilots for the VVS. Then she was reassigned to train *desantniki*, airborne troops. She was sent to a tiny airfield where there was a single Po-2 and told that after she trained sixty soldiers in parachute jumping, she would finally be released to the women's regiments. A group of thirty could be trained at once, and it took a month for each group. The main restrictions were the weather (prevailing wind conditions on the steppe limited jump time to the dawn hours) and the fact that Petrochenkova had to pack all the parachutes herself: "In one day, I could take fifteen people. Then I had to pack all the parachutes, and I could only pack fifteen in one day."[56] By the time Petrochenkova was released, it was the fall of 1943. She was sent to Penza for fighter upgrade training. It was not a pleasant experience. She said, "At first the commander refused to take me. He said he recently had three girls there (including Akimova and Batrakova) and he was sick and tired of them. . . . He thought I would go away, but I didn't." Petrochenkova vowed to sit outside his door until he changed his mind. She sat all through the night, not daring to leave even to go to the bathroom. "I was afraid that if I left, the watchman would never let me back. In the morning [the commander] changed his mind and decided to see how I flew. I had 300 hours in the UT-2 and T-1. I already had experience with small planes. They were designed for aerial aerobatics. And when he flew with me, he was pleased with my technique." Petrochenkova finally joined the 586th in November 1943 at Kiev. She was then required to take another twenty days of training before she was considered ready for combat missions.[57]

Although most of the women recruited for the aviation regiments were young and single, some were married and some had children. Many of the married women had lost husbands or children in the war. Dusia Nosal', who became the first woman aviator to be awarded the Hero of the Soviet Union (HSU) during the war, lost her baby in the bombing at the beginning of the war (and was later killed in action herself).[58] Other mothers left their children with relatives. Marina Raskova had an eight-year-old daughter whom she left in the care of her mother. Pasportnikova recalled that "the main complication was with women with children. There had to be someone to take care of the children."[59]

But not all women who were already in military aviation were transferred to Raskova's group. Some remained where they were and served out the war in male regiments. Those volunteers who were in Moscow by early October were sent to the Zhukovskii Air Force Engineering Academy, where they would be interviewed before final selections were made.[60]

❖ ❖ ❖

SELECTION OF PERSONNEL

While the call for volunteers was proceeding, Raskova gathered the core staff for the new aviation group. She pulled together a small group of women who already held military rank, including Captain Militsa Kazarinova, Major Tamara Kazarinova (according to some sources), battalion commissar Lina Eliseeva, political worker Evdokiia Rachkevich, Captains E. A. Semenova and Vera Lomako, armaments engineer Galina Volova, and engineer third class Olga Kulikova. Initially they worked in some spare rooms at the special services school of the VVS, in Petrovsky Park.[61]

Among the most interesting characters on Raskova's staff were the Kazarinova sisters, Militsa and Tamara. Militsa was named as Raskova's chief of staff, first in the 122nd and later in the 125th; Tamara became the first commander of the 586th. Both sisters were held in some awe by the recruits because they were career military officers—but also because of their strict and even harsh demeanor. Galina Markova noted that although the sisters did not look very much alike, "both their characters were notable for their hardness and determination."[62] She described Militsa as a woman who was always brisk, organized, and efficient, who "set an example of unfailing military discipline" but was also "hypercritical and distrustful."[63] Migunova said that, unlike Raskova, Militsa Kazarinova thought that there was only one way to treat subordinates: "one doesn't joke with them, one demands their obedience." Migunova also noted that Militsa "considered even the tiniest deviation from regulations to be impermissible."[64] Even in physical appearance, the Kazarinovas were stern. Migunova said that Militsa was graceful and good-looking, but "it was as if she protested against her own femininity: she wore leather pants, cut her pretty curly hair very short, and chain-smoked cigarettes."[65] Their hard, cold nature was often explained by the fact that the Kazarinovas had served among so many men. Aleksandra Makunina, who later worked as chief of staff under Tamara Kazarinova, recalled, "The two sisters were graduates of military school. They were regular officers and they always showed their masculine character."[66] Migunova, who was Militsa Kazarinova's deputy, said that "she was emphatically cold in the way she treated people. Evidently this was the result of the fact that she served a long time in men's units where she was the only woman."[67]

But other members of the women's group had similar backgrounds and remained "unmasculinized." Raskova and Migunova had often served as the only women on military staffs. Oddly, despite the Kazarinova sisters' military backgrounds and supposedly "glowing" records, neither remained in her operational post for more than a few months, and there is little discussion and no hard proof of why they left (or were removed). But they had an influence all out of proportion to their actual service. Militsa, as editor of both editions of *V nebe frontovom*, the major collection of memoirs by veterans of all three regiments, was able to control much of the published history of the regiments.

It must have been incredibly difficult to accomplish the task of forming the 122nd at this particular time. These were terrible days in Moscow, and the Germans were practically on the doorstep. On 12 October, the Germans occupied Kalinin; on the fourteenth, the Soviets were forced to retreat from Mozhaisk. Mass evacuations were already in process; women and children were sent away first, followed by important government offices and many elements of industry. Radio reports, though heavily censored, were still alarming; everyone knew that Moscow was in imminent danger of occupation.[68] Many of the women volunteers went directly from digging trenches to the 122nd assembly point; they knew that the situation was grave. Inhabitants of the city were increasingly agitated, yet it was precisely at this moment that Raskova persisted with her work. One wonders whether the VVS tried to persuade her to delay the process. Unfortunately, sources do not reveal much about this.

The volunteers selected by the Komsomol, civil aviation, and the military were sent to an assembly point in Moscow. Captains Lomako and Rachkevich saw that the volunteers were fed and assigned rooms. On 13 October 1941, interviews and final selections began at the Zhukovskii Air Force Engineering Academy. "The huge corridors of the special services school were filled with girls in blue overcoats and leather flying coats, and among them like stains of color stood out the most varied civilian attire—from sports skiing costumes to dresses sewn in the latest fashion. The whole crowd seethed like an upset anthill," Migunova recalled. Some of the volunteers had already discovered that three regiments would eventually be formed, and there were some strong preferences about assignments.[69] A day or two earlier, most of the volunteers would have been happy to get to the front as a medic, if that was the only way they could serve. Now that they were certain of a position in aviation, they began to hope for jobs in line with their skills. All the pilots wanted to remain pilots, and nearly all of them wanted to fly fighters.

A Mandate Commission, or credentials committee, interviewed each volunteer individually.[70] So many women pilots applied that only those with the strongest flying backgrounds made the cut for the pilots' group. The field in which experience was most lacking was Raskova's own— navigation. Virtually no women navigators had been trained before the war, and training a navigator was no easy task. Raskova looked for women with a technical education—nearly all the upper-level university students, especially those from scientific fields, ended up as navigators—or women who were pilots and therefore knew a little navigation already. Many volunteers who had trained as pilots in air clubs but were neither air-club instructors nor pilots by profession were selected as navigators. According to Migunova, the Kherson Osoaviakhim produced instructor pilots with strong backgrounds in navigation. "Raskova entered the women pilots who had completed this school into the navigators' group. They protested, pointing out that they wanted to be pilots, that their place was at the controls of a combat aircraft, but it was all in vain. Here Marina was adamant and made no concessions."[71]

Raskova personally interviewed every volunteer. Migunova said, "Marina talked with every girl for a long time, trying to determine where and how best to utilize her, in accordance with her profession, training and preferences. As far as possible, she took into consideration personal desires, but sometimes . . . she had to exercise her authority."[72] Aronova wrote that during her personal interview, Raskova asked her what position she hoped for. "I only want to be a pilot!" she replied. Raskova answered, "But you see, you don't have enough flights—only 50 hours altogether." Aronova had to accept a slot as a navigator (though eventually she was retrained as a pilot).[73] Valentina Kravchenko was another pilot who had to accept a navigator's slot. Before the war, she had been an instructor pilot at Saratov and logged 724 flying hours. But she had also attended specialized navigation training; her fate was sealed in the 122nd.[74] Migunova recalled:

> The women pilots from civil aviation stuck together solidly and independently. They didn't express their wishes aloud. Many of them, such as Evgenia Timofeeva, Evdokia Bershanskaia, and Nadezhda Fedutenko, knew one another, and had many flights on the air routes or as instructors. But they were worried, when entering the room where the committee was meeting. Each one leaving the room was at once surrounded and bombarded with questions: "Where did you end up?" Some left beaming—their dream had come true; others were not lucky, and they were distressed.[75]

Even among the volunteers without flying experience, there was a marked preference for particular jobs. Many wanted to be mechanics; the armorers' jobs were less desirable. But here too the Mandate Commission had its criteria for selection: "those who were stronger physically or who were acquainted with any sort of technical work were assigned to the group of armorers, engine mechanics, and other kinds of aviation specialists." The girls who were selected to be clerks or staff workers were bitterly disappointed; many cried. Migunova said, "It seemed to them that all their hopes had collapsed. . . . 'My girlfriends will be fighting, but I will sit and pore over papers!' "[76]

On 14 October, uniforms were issued. There were no women's uniforms at this time. "They gave us men's clothing, right down to the underwear," which was often too large for the women.[77] Pants could be hitched up with belts and the cuffs could be rolled up, but footwear was a real problem. The boots were far too large for the women—most were sizes 40 to 43, an average size for men, but women normally wore sizes 34 to 36.[78] If the oversized uniforms made them look ludicrous, the boots made them clumsy. Uniforms could eventually be altered, but the only thing to do with too-big boots was to stuff the toes and shuffle. The women used foot-cloths to wind around their feet and ankles, but even so, their feet swam inside the boots.[79]

The next day, 15 October, Raskova received orders to evacuate the aviation group immediately to Engels and to complete the formation and training there.[80] According to Markova, Raskova had been urging VVS headquarters to come to a decision about this matter, as it was obvious that the aviation group could not be formed in Moscow. Markova said that Raskova sent Migunova to VVS headquarters to expedite the orders.[81] After the evacuation orders were received, Raskova had to go to the railroad station in person to try to arrange transportation, but the commandant could not guarantee that any railcars would be available for several days. He told her that he could approve transportation only if a *Narkom*, a People's Commissar of Defense, called him. Raskova promptly telephoned Shakhurin; on the sixteenth, he told her that a train had been arranged for the next day.[82]

❖ ❖ ❖

JOURNEY TO ENGELS

On 17 October, as the German Army offensive against Moscow was reaching its peak, the entire contingent of Aviation Group 122 boarded a train headed east. There was a virtual panic in the city among the civilian population that had started on the previous day; there were rumors that the Germans would occupy the city at any moment. During the night of 16–17 October, 100 trains carrying 150,000 people reportedly left Moscow.[83]

The girls were formed up in the dark and marched in their shuffling columns to be loaded onto railcars waiting near Belorussia Railway Station.[84] The group was arranged, according to one veteran, by the source of the recruits. The women who were civil aviation and air-club instructor pilots were in the first rows; most of these women already possessed

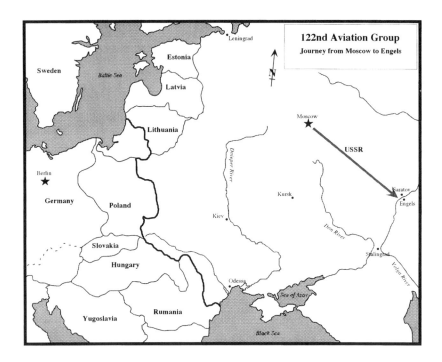

decent uniforms and knew how to march. In the middle were the students; behind them, the factory workers and technicians. Bringing up the rear, tripping over the hem of her oversized overcoat, marched a "tiny soldier with a huge rucksack on her back, upon which was written in large letters in indelible pencil, 'Khoroshilova.'" The girl was determined not to be parted from her pack; the result was that everyone knew her name, and she became the object of many jokes.[85]

It was exceptionally cold (four degrees below zero Fahrenheit)—a harbinger of the difficult winter in store.[86] Most of the recruits did not know that their destination was Engels, a city on the Volga River some 500 miles to the southeast, where a large aviation school was located. The girls found out their destination only after the train was under way.[87] Just how many women were in that group is difficult to determine. One memoir stated that it was about 200; a Western writer who interviewed veterans said it was 1,000.[88] One of the three regiments formed from the 122nd would arrive at its first combat post with 112 personnel.[89] A figure of between 300 and 400 initial recruits seems most likely.[90]

The women spent nine days on the train. The journey east was slow; the train was often forced to stand on sidings and at stations for long periods to allow the passage of other, more urgent trains. Rail traffic was heavy. Trains moved west with troops and supplies; trains moved east with evacuated citizens, bureaucratic staffs, and factory equipment, machines, and workers.[91] The 122nd occupied several railroad cars—not passenger cars, but heated freight cars used to transport troops.[92] At least the cars were capable of being heated, but Migunova wrote that they were cold and dark inside.[93] Personnel were divided into groups; pilots, navigators, mechanics, and staff personnel each had their own cars.[94] At one point, the 122nd's cars were uncoupled from the eastward train, and Raskova and Militsa Kazarinova were forced to make their way to the station commandant from their distant siding, crawling beneath twelve rows of trains, to arrange for further transport.[95]

During the journey, they were sometimes thirsty, and food was difficult to obtain. Migunova said they lived on bread and herring; sugar for tea was almost impossible to obtain.[96] Kravchenko remembered one incident when the girls were so hungry they stole food: "When we went to Engels we were in cars that weren't ever meant for people—and we had no food. At one station we saw a lot of fresh cabbage. We jumped off and took it to the train and ate it fresh, just like rabbits. Then Kazarinova discovered us and made us take it all back. But to the end of the war, we called each other 'brother rabbit' because of this."[97] There was, of course, no possibility of bathing or washing one's hair. Militsa Kazarinova later commented on how these conditions reduced the girls' permed or lengthy hair to a terrible state and implied that her comments inspired Raskova to issue orders that the girls' hair be cut immediately after arrival.[98]

Raskova spent time in each of the cars during the course of the journey. Aronova recalled that Raskova "was always fresh, neat, energetic. Her authority and simply her personal charm in large part contributed to the strengthening of discipline and order in our still motley military unit."[99] The girls passed the time on the long journey studying military regulations, singing, and tailoring their uniforms. They slept a lot; Raskova told them to "rest, because ahead lie very demanding studies."[100]

TRAINING AND EQUIPPING THE REGIMENTS AT ENGELS

On 25 October 1941, the 122nd arrived at the Engels station in the dark, in fog and rain.[101] No one met them; the town was in blackout. Raskova and

Kazarinova found the officer on duty at the Engels garrison, who showed them to the gymnasium of the Red Army House, which had been turned into a dormitory for the 122nd.[102] Kazarinova wrote that a small room with a carpet, a wide double bed, and fresh flowers had been designated for Raskova. Raskova was angry and demanded that the bed and carpet be removed, since the girls did not have such things, and that two cots be brought in so that she and Kazarinova could share the room.[103] According to Migunova, the three of them shared a room in a former barbershop, which was narrow, cold, and drafty. At times the room became so unbearably cold that winter that they took refuge with women whose quarters were warmer.[104]

Raskova reported to the garrison commander at Engels, a Colonel Bagaev, who informed her that he had received notification that her aviation group's provisional designation would be "Number 122" until the three combat regiments could be formed. He asked, "Are you certain you'll succeed in this thing you've started?" She assured him that she was.[105]

The first order given was for all girls to report to the garrison barbershop and get a "boy-style" haircut.[106] Then studies began in earnest. During the next few months, the members of the 122nd underwent an extremely condensed, intensive course of training. First there were ten courses a day plus two hours of drill; navigators studied Morse code for an additional hour and rose earlier than the other students, sleeping only five or six hours a night.[107] To prepare the girls for the difficult conditions at the front, Raskova from time to time sounded an alarm in the middle of the night, requiring everyone to dress and form up outdoors in less than five minutes. When she discovered some girls had cheated by donning their overcoats over their nightshirts, she made them march around the airfield with the cold wind blowing on their bare legs.[108]

On 7 November 1941, the anniversary of the revolution, the members of the 122nd took the military oath. Migunova wrote that Raskova made a speech after all the personnel had taken the oath; she reminded them that "history remembers those women who participated in battles." She reminded them of Joan of Arc; Nadezhda Durova, who fought in the war of 1812; and the partisan Vasilisa Kozhina, who also fought against Napoleon. She mentioned the many women who had fought during the Russian Civil War. Raskova continued:

> But all of these women were individuals, and they fought in men's units. Such were conditions then. We are Soviet women, women of a

free socialist nation. In our constitution it is written that women have equal rights in all fields of activity. Today you took the military oath, you vowed to faithfully defend the homeland. So let's vow once more, together, to stand to our last breath in defense of our beloved homeland.[109]

Aronova also remembered Raskova's speech that day: "She always spoke well, her words came from the heart and therefore easily penetrated our hearts too. I especially remember one sentence: 'Study persistently, with perseverance,' she said, 'the examination will be given on the field of battle.' "[110]

The flight training program that normally took three years was condensed into less than six months. Pilots training for fighter and dive bomber assignments accrued a minimum of 500 flying hours. Training included classroom and flying lessons and sometimes lasted fourteen hours a day.[111] The mechanic trainees, most of whom had little previous experience, worked as much as fifteen hours a day in Russian winter weather. The training was stringent and demanding—more so than that of many male pilots, who were being rushed to the front from accelerated programs with only sixty-five flying hours.[112] Still, some observers questioned whether it would be sufficient to prepare the women for war.

The women were not readily accepted by the staff and instructors at Engels. Migunova noted that their arrival there was "a curiosity and a surprise" and that many of the men made fun of them.[113] The majority of the women had little or no military training; they found it difficult at first to remember military courtesies and often forgot to use proper forms of address with one another or even with superiors. Their uniforms were ill fitted and their boots were too big; their marching was a disgrace. Because of all this, many men seem to have considered them disrespectful, frivolous, or worse. As might be expected, the women's behavior fell under close scrutiny, and some men were only too ready to find fault. There is also evidence that some of the wives of the Engels staff were not thrilled with the presence of the women students. Aleksandr Gridnev recalled the comments of one male major from Engels who told him that Raskova had once been called into the office of Colonel Bagaev, who complained to her: "I'm getting complaints from the wives of the instructors who are teaching your women pilots. Just what do you think they're doing with the instructors in the evenings? They're fooling around, destroying families."

Raskova calmly replied that the women students were not doing any such thing, but were studying hard, working overtime to complete their program. Then she commented, "And you're the garrison chief; you're the last person I'd expect to interest himself in women's gossip."[114]

The male instructors were not accustomed to working with women, and some found it difficult to adjust. One instructor, G. N. Meniailenko, recalled that the men had real trouble controlling their language. Normally when male students made mistakes, "we swore at them on the ground and sometimes in the air as well. But it was forbidden to do anything like that while instructing the pilots of Marina Raskova's regiment. When it happened, they were offended and even cried. . . . We had to rein ourselves in."[115]

Raskova directly supervised all training.[116] According to Marina Chechneva (veteran pilot of the 46th and author of several books), "Raskova was the organizer of combat training. . . . She devoted a great deal of time to checking that we were at our studies, she took exams and tests in many disciplines, not only teaching, but also constantly studying herself."[117] By all accounts, Raskova probably drove herself too hard. She was involved in the training of all three regiments, and since one regiment was training for night work, it was a twenty-four-hour-a-day job. Markova noted that Raskova was sometimes so tired she did not have the strength to undress at night and slept on top of the bed in her uniform.[118] When Eliseeva tried to convince Raskova that it was essential to rest, Raskova replied, "We'll rest when the war is over."[119] The following passage from one of Chechneva's books, which describes Raskova during the training of the 122nd at Engels, is informative:

> At any time of the day [Raskova] could be found beside her girls: she conducted critiques, she flew, she talked with people, she gave orders, she attentively supervised her subordinates, she taught them. It seemed that she never rested; in any event, she was continually seeing to affairs. We did not notice in Marina Mikhailovna any outward signs of fatigue. She knew how to stay in control of herself. To all of us it seemed that this woman possessed unprecedented energy.[120]

Ekaterina Fedotova, later a flight commander in the 125th, noted that Raskova "studied the new Pe-2 aircraft together with us, at night was at the takeoff line with the night bombers, and in the morning—on the flightline with the fighter pilots." Once she went to Raskova's office and found her sleeping on top of a table. When she tried to leave without disturbing her, Raskova opened her eyes and, without moving, said, "Give your report. I'm listening."[121] Migunova reported that Raskova was able to fall asleep instantly and wake up just as quickly.[122] But the ability to catnap was only a small help. Markova wrote that Raskova's appearance grew increasingly older and sterner.[123] Migunova also observed that although Raskova was young, only thirty years old, her face grew paler and paler from strain: "Sometimes Marina even smoked a cigarette, trying to dispel the fatigue," although she noted that Raskova had not smoked before the war.[124] Migunova was always surprised and a bit shocked to see Raskova smoking. Raskova once told her, "It's nothing; when the war is over, I give you my word—I'll stop smoking! You're right, it's not the sort of thing for a woman to do, but after all we're all now occupied with something that is not 'women's business.'"[125] Kravchenko recalled, "Once Grizodubova came to Engels. Migunova and I overheard her talking to Raskova. 'What will you do with those *women*?' she said to Raskova, and she invited her to join her own regiment. I was afraid. I was so afraid Raskova would go."[126]

On occasion, Raskova would sneak away from her work late at night to play piano; she was a talented musician. Migunova wrote that Raskova would make up some excuse for Kazarinova, whom she apparently felt compelled to deceive, rather than admit that she wanted to take a break. Migunova sometimes accompanied Raskova; they played the piano in turn, or played duets. They loved Brahms's "Hungarian Dances," the dances from Glinka's opera "Ivan Susanin," and Schubert's "Unfinished Symphony." Migunova noted that she felt no pangs of conscience about deceiving Kazarinova.[127]

The women appear to have genuinely loved Raskova. Many commented that the impression she made on them in person was even more profound than when they had idolized her from afar. Aronova wrote about discussions among the new recruits after their first meetings with Raskova. "I was happy when I learned I could volunteer to go to the front," Aronova told Katia Dospanova the night after their selection interviews in Moscow. "I was doubly happy when it turned out to be with Raskova. What an exceptionally charming woman! Did you think so, too?" Dospanova replied, "Positively! It seems to me that Raskova is one of those people about whom there cannot be two opinions."[128]

Raskova was not without a sense of humor. Inna Pasportnikova remembered an incident involving the first time Raskova noticed future fighter pilot Liliia Litviak. The women had recently been issued winter uniforms. At the morning roll call, Pasportnikova recalled, Raskova suddenly commanded Litviak to step forward:

> Liliia took a step forward and the whole formation burst out laughing. Instead of a brown fur uniform collar, she was showing off a white, fluffy one with ringlets.
>
> "Litviak, what do you have on your shoulders?" asked Raskova.
>
> "A goatskin collar," Litviak replied. "Why, doesn't it suit me?" The goatskin looked suspiciously like the stuff used to line our new winter boots.
>
> "It suits you," said Raskova. "When did you do this?"
>
> "Last night," Litviak answered.
>
> Of course, we all laughed, but Raskova said sternly: "You'll have to spend one more night without sleeping, Litviak, and sew back on the collar that is supposed to be on that uniform!"
>
> I looked at Litviak then: small, delicate, and beautiful; still completely a little girl. How could she be a strong, courageous, tough-willed fighter pilot? Here she was making herself collars from fur boot linings. And what was she going to wear on her feet inside her boots? Blood was flowing and people were dying, and she was thinking about what suited her and didn't suit her? What sort of frivolity! I never imagined then that I would become the aircraft mechanic in the crew of Lidia Vladimirovna Litviak (Liliia, as she preferred to be called), or that she would become the only woman in the world to have 15 enemy aircraft to her credit—killed by her in difficult air battles.[129]

But it would be many months before future pilots like Litviak would see combat. In the meantime, all the women students had to survive their first winter in the military. The airfield at Engels was located in a bare, treeless, windswept plain, the better to feel the full effects of the winter of 1941–1942, which started early and was severe.[130] As German troops defended themselves against the first Russian counteroffensive outside Moscow, half frozen in their summer uniforms, the women pilots of the 122nd began their combat training in open-cockpit aircraft—the same type of aircraft that would be flown by many of them for the duration of the war.

Flight training for the navigators began on 25 January 1942. The entire

group could be taken together on a TB-3 aircraft; they flew lengthy missions that at first left some of the student-navigators, who were unused to
flying, white-faced and glassy-eyed from airsickness. Navigators also flew
with male instructor-pilots in the R-5 trainer and other aircraft.[131] As soon
as flying training began, Raskova and her staff began to evaluate which
women should go to which regiments. Up to that time, the volunteers had
been divided only into specialty groups: pilot, navigator, mechanic, and
so forth. Now it was time for more difficult decisions: Who would get to
fly in fighters? Who would go to bombers? And who would be stuck for
the rest of the war in the open-cockpit biplanes? It was obvious that the
women chosen to fly fighters had to have outstanding skills, not only as
pilots but also as navigators. But good pilots were needed in all three regiments.

Raskova and her staff spent many nights discussing how the personnel
should be distributed. One of the most critical decisions was who would
be chosen to command each regiment.[132] Raskova had already decided that
she would command the day bomber group herself. Commissar Eliseeva
suggested that Bershanskaia would be a good choice to command the
night bombers; she was an experienced instructor and had flown in civil
aviation. Kazarinova protested: "She has no combat experience." "None
of us has that sort of experience," Eliseeva reminded her. Raskova agreed
that Bershanskaia should be appointed to the night bombers. Bershanskaia
did not want the position, however; she wanted to become a fighter pilot.
She tried to protest on the grounds that she had no command experience.
There were several days of repeated discussions during which Bershanskaia "stubbornly refused" to accept the job. She was at last persuaded to
accept the position of commander of the 588th Night Bomber Aviation
Regiment.[133]

The selection of a commander for the fighter regiment was more difficult. According to Markova, Raskova "could not even identify a single
person to whom she could entrust the fighter regiment." Even when the
fighter pilots had been selected and begun training in the Yak-1 fighter
aircraft, Raskova still had not named a commander.[134] Tamara Kazarinova
then arrived at Engels as the designated commander. Her appearance was
somewhat abrupt, and there is little information about how she was chosen.[135] Another odd thing is that although one or two sources state that
Tamara Kazarinova was part of the initial staff of the 122nd, her name is
not mentioned again until her sudden arrival at Engels. There is no expla-

nation of her whereabouts between early October and early December. Since Raskova was clearly acquainted with Kazarinova, yet Markova emphasized Raskova's indecision in choosing a commander for the fighter regiment, it is apparent that Kazarinova was not Raskova's first choice. Kazarinova had a supposedly glowing record as an air force officer and had been awarded the Order of Lenin in 1937 for an unspecified accomplishment. The fact that Raskova apparently did not consider her earlier seems odd—unless Raskova had reason to dislike or distrust Kazarinova. It is possible that the Kazarinova sisters used their influence to have Tamara appointed commander of the 586th over Raskova's head. Given the reported conflicts between Raskova and Militsa Kazarinova, it is also possible that both sisters were forced on Raskova, not chosen by her.

On 9 December 1941, the 586th was officially created by order of Stalin, and Kazarinova was designated its commander.[136] On 8 February 1942, Raskova announced the staff of the night bomber regiment: Evdokia Davydovna Bershanskaia, commander; Evdokiia Yakovlevna Rachkevich, commissar. Squadron and flight members of all three regiments were read out. There were three aircraft and crews in each flight *(zveno)* and three flights in each squadron *(eskadril'ia)*.

Throughout this period, Raskova continued to receive letters from young women who wanted to join the regiments; some brave souls even set out on foot and made their way to Engels, begging to be allowed to join. Some arrived with no money and no food. Some were accepted, like Sasha Votintseva, who became a navigator; others were sent home. Some pilots continued to arrive as late as the spring of 1942 (including Katia Musatova, Tonia Skoblikova, Masha Kirillova, and Sasha Egorova, all four from Ufa). Other women arrived completely against their will; Kseniia Sanchuk had been flying partisan resupply and medical evacuation missions on the Western Front and unhappily begged Raskova to allow her to return.[137]

In February, the 588th's Po-2 aircraft (called the U-2 until 1943) were delivered, and the regiment received its official designation.[138] One terrible accident during training is remembered by all the veterans. On 10 March 1942, four students from the night bomber regiment were killed: Liliia Tormosina and her navigator Nadia Komogortseva, and Ania Malakhova and navigator Marina Vinogradova. By a miracle, Ira Sebrova and Rufa Gasheva survived; their airplane grazed the ground and was damaged, but they managed to land safely.[139] Polunina remembered that day: "Komogortseva got lost. It was at night, there was a lot of snow, and she ran out of fuel. Sebrova managed to make a forced landing. But Malakhova, Komogortseva, Tormosina, and Vinogradova were killed." Few details are available about the reason for the accident. Polunina charged that "[Nadezhda] Popova was to blame."[140]

According to a Soviet historian writing in 1960, Popova had been the flight commander on what started as an ordinary training flight. She led two other Po-2s piloted by Tormosina and Sebrova on a practice bombing run on a dark but clear night. Somehow Popova lost her two wingmen and returned by herself to the airfield. The next day, searchers discovered the wreckage of two airplanes; the bodies of Tormosina and Komogortseva were in one plane, but Sebrova and Gasheva had walked away from their aircraft and made their way back to the town. The deaths of Malakhova and Vinogradova are not mentioned.[141]

Aronova wrote that this accident delayed the regiment's scheduled departure for the front, originally planned for 1 April, for more than a month.[142] The 46th would have been the first regiment to achieve operational status, but instead, the 586th became the first to complete training and fly out to its duty airfield. On 16 April 1942, the 586th was assigned to active duty as part of Fighter Aviation of the Air Defense Force (IA/PVO), rather than to the VVS.[143] Its first posting was only a few miles from Engels, for its mission was to protect fixed targets near Saratov (factories, rail junctions, and so forth) against enemy bombers. Although this was an important mission, it was not exactly on the front lines of the war, so there was not much excitement or ceremony surrounding the 586th's departure from Engels.

It was late May when the 588th at last received orders to go to the front. Aronova recalled that after being at Engels for seven months, the crews of the 588th prepared to leave with great enthusiasm, throwing around jokes and retorts. On the morning of their departure, 23 May 1942, garrison commander Colonel Bagaev made a short speech:

> Today, for the first time, a women's regiment leaves our airfield for the front. You do not fly on awesome machines, but on training aircraft. And it's true that you yourselves are not excessively awesome in appearance. But I am certain that in these light-winged airplanes, you will be able to inflict heavy blows on the enemy. Let fly with you my fatherly wish: success to you and combat glory![144]

What is interesting about this speech is that Bagaev clearly did not regard the 586th's post in IA/PVO as being "at the front"; after all, the 586th had officially entered active service more than a month earlier than the 588th.

Raskova worked hard to ensure that the regiments received the aircraft they had been promised. She used her personal contacts in high places, often going outside the usual chain of command, and aircraft acquisition was particularly controversial. Ekaterina Polunina (a mechanic with the 586th during the war and now the unit historian) believes that the only reason Raskova got new Yak fighters for the regiment was that she was a friend of I. S. Levin, director from 1940 to 1950 of the Saratov Aviation Factory, which produced Yak-1 and Yak-3 fighters.[145] Levin, who later attained the rank of general-major, moved in high circles: he knew Stalin and worked intimately with famed aircraft designer A. S. Yakovlev.[146] He first met Raskova in Moscow in 1938, during the preparations for the flight of the *Rodina*. He was later involved in the search for that aircraft, as he was then working as director of the Irkutsk Aviation Factory. Levin recalled that in October 1941, he received a call from General A. V. Nikitin, chief of the Main Directorate for Instruction, Formation, and Combat Training of the VVS. Nikitin notified Levin that according to an order of the Stavka of the Supreme High Command, three aviation regiments were being formed from volunteer women pilots; one regiment would be equipped with Yak-1 aircraft. Nikitin asked Levin to assist the women in mastering the new technical equipment: "Raskova, whose mission it is to form the regiments, will be coming to see you. Help her."[147] In January 1942, Levin received orders to deliver twenty-four Yak-1s to the 586th. At that time, there was no shortage of pilots in the Soviet air forces; however, there was a severe shortage of aircraft.[148] Levin says that there were bitter jokes among his staff when the order came through. There were front-line pilots—male pilots—waiting at the factory airfield for airplanes, they pointed out. Were the available aircraft now to go instead to a bunch of girls?[149] Even some male engineers based with the 586th at Anisovka echoed the same views: "[The women] demand to be equipped with new planes, without waiting for their turn, mind you, and here are the planes. At the front there is one plane for every five pilots, all of old design, and here each girl has got a personal fighter. And not just any fighter, but the best design—Yakovlev."[150]

The 586th took delivery of its aircraft on 20–21 February 1942.[151] Levin described how a large group of pilots and other personnel from the 586th came to visit the factory. Although some of Levin's staff still resisted the idea of giving precious fighters to the women, he noted that there was a very positive effect on the workers once they actually met the women pilots: "Our aerodrome kids were transformed. Exhausted, fatigued from sleepless nights, from stressful work in the freezing cold, they somehow at once pulled themselves up, and began to drop by the barbershop more often."[152]

Irina Emel'ianova, a technician who later became deputy engineer of the regiment for special equipment, remembered that when the pilots brought the new Yaks back to the base, the bort numbers painted on the fuselages all ended in zeroes—10, 20, 30, 40, and so on. Some aircraft were painted white, others khaki; all were on skis for winter operations. All the Yaks had radios, but most could only receive, not transmit. There were ten aircraft for each squadron, but only one, for the squadron commander, had a transmitting radio. Emel'ianova recalled that "our girls refused to fly without transmitters, and they won." It was part of Emel'ianova's job to equip the remaining aircraft with transmitters.[153] It must have taken some real effort on Raskova's part to acquire radios for the fighters. It was not until late 1942, at Stalingrad, that transmitting radios were commonly used in fighter aircraft; the success of this measure inspired the decision to equip all fighters with radio sets.[154] Raskova had reached the same conclusion nearly a year before the VVS decision. (This coup, however, did not extend to the other regiments; the Po-2s never had radios, and the Pe-2s eventually given to the bomber regiment were equipped only with radio transmitters late in the war.)[155]

The 587th Bomber Aviation Regiment was originally scheduled to fly the Su-2 light bomber. But when training flights on three Su-2s began in late December, everyone was unhappy. The outdated airplanes smoked, leaked oil, were slow, and burned a lot of fuel. Everyone knew that they had been scheduled to be taken out of production, which meant that getting spare parts would become increasingly difficult. Raskova decided to appeal to the *Narkomat* for a newer-model day bomber.[156] Raskova apparently had to go to Moscow to force a decision on aircraft for the 587th. According to Markova, she appealed once more to Shakhurin. Raskova seems to have already decided on the Pe-2; Markova reported that Shakhurin tried to discourage Raskova and suggested that if she waited a bit, maybe the American "Boston" bombers that were expected to arrive via Lend-Lease shipments would be a more suitable aircraft for the 587th.

Raskova said that the regiment could not wait that long, and if men could fly the Pe-2, so could the women.[157]

The official change in aircraft was directed in NKO Order No. 0497, dated 19 June 1942 and titled "On the conversion of the 587th Aviation Regiment to a new equipment table with the Pe-2 aircraft." The order was signed by the commander of the VVS, General-Lieutenant Novikov.[158] Raskova returned to Engels in late June 1942 and announced that they would be receiving the brand-new Pe-2 dive-bomber—the newest and most complicated bomber of its day. They were expected to be fully operational within four months.[159]

When the announcement was made to the regiment, some of the women immediately voiced doubts about whether they could learn to fly such a sophisticated aircraft in such a short time. Raskova told the women that she had been offered the American "Boston" aircraft for the regiment—a good airplane, but the supply of spare parts was uncertain. "Besides that, the Pe-2 is an excellent, Soviet-produced aircraft, and we should be proud that they have trusted us to master such a machine."[160] Several of the women veterans emphasized to me that Raskova would not even consider American aircraft; Valentina Kravchenko's comment was typical: "Raskova insisted that all the women's regiments fly only aircraft made in the Soviet Union."[161] Militsa Kazarinova wrote that "the fact that they gave these aircraft to the regiment was the great contribution of M. M. Raskova. She managed to prove and to persuade the command that women pilots could not only master the technique of flying the Pe-2, but could successfully fly combat missions in it."[162] Migunova wrote that "the news that the women's regiment was transitioning to the Pe-2 created a real sensation in our garrison. Male pilots took it as a personal insult."[163]

The acquisition of the Pe-2 meant that the 587th was short-staffed. The Su-2 carried a two-person crew (pilot and navigator), but the Pe-2 carried a third crew member: a radio operator–gunner. This latter position required a fair amount of physical strength. One of the few women to become a radio operator–gunner in the regiment, Antonina Khokhlova-Dubkova, pointed out that it took sixty kilograms of force to pull the lever that recharged the machine gun, using the left arm. "I could never do it on the ground because it was very hard," she said, "but in the air it was one, two, and it was recharged!"[164]

Moreover, the Pe-2 was far more sophisticated technologically; four additional people were required for each ground crew. Time was too short to permit a new cycle of recruitment and training to fill the additional positions with women.[165] Raskova realized that she would have to accept men into the regiment if she hoped to get to the front by the end of 1942. She was not happy with this decision but could see no other solution. The majority of the new personnel were men who were called up from the reserves.[166]

Twenty brand-new Pe-2 bombers arrived at the 587th in July 1942. A last, each pilot had her own aircraft—the one she would fly in combat.[167] Basic training for the Pe-2 (aircraft design, armament, and navigation) was provided by the staff at Engels. But when it came time to study combat tactics, more experienced instructors from the school at Lipetsk and pilots with combat experience were brought in.[168] One of the instructor pilots who trained the women to fly the Pe-2 described just how challenging that airplane was:

> The Pe-2 was quite strict in its demands on flying technique, especially when one engine was out, and it didn't brook slow pilot reactions. Even so, it was a good dive bomber, with a large safety margin and tolerance for high g-loads. Strong pilots liked this airplane—weak ones feared it. Of course, for a woman to fly the Pe-2 . . . was a real achievement.[169]

Some of the particular challenges in flying the Pe-2 included taking off with a full bomb load, adapting to the design of its cockpit, flying it on one engine, and landing the aircraft. The cockpit was structured to accommodate a pilot who was taller than most of the women; some of the shorter ones had to strain to reach the rudders and certain instruments. The control stick was very "heavy" and hard to manipulate during takeoff when the aircraft was heavily loaded. Since the pilot had to operate the throttles with the left hand, she had to pull the stick back and get the nose up with only one hand. Women Pe-2 veterans recall that navigators would sometimes assist the pilot in pulling back the stick or would brace the pilot's back during takeoff. Landing was difficult due to the high speed required—a problem on rough wartime airfields. But the veterans also remember the airplane with great affection. The speed was almost as great as that of a fighter, and it had the latest equipment and weapon systems.

Since there were no dual controls in the airplane, the first time a pilot flew the Pe-2 would be a solo. The first woman pilot to solo on the Pe-2 was the commander of the 2nd squadron, Evgeniia Timofeeva. Everyone knew that there would be intense pressure on the first woman to fly the aircraft; every man at the airfield would be watching. Timofeeva, an experienced civil aviation pilot, volunteered to be the first. She soloed without incident and made a good landing.[170]

An instructor with special skills, a Major Kalachikov, was sent from the 9th Reserve Aviation Regiment to train the 587th pilots in dive-bombing. Migunova said that when he arrived, he regarded the assignment as "a whim of HSU Raskova's." He made no secret of his opinion that the whole idea was a "ridiculous game" and that women could not possibly learn dive-bombing. Migunova said that Raskova heard him out, smiling, and asked him simply to test the women's flying skills and then decide whether to continue with training. The squadron commanders were tested first, and Kalachikov conceded that they did not fly badly: "But after all, those are the commanders; the rest are children!" But the remaining pilots also passed his test, and Kalachikov apologized to Raskova and agreed to teach them how to dive-bomb.[171] Dive-bombing in the Pe-2 was a difficult skill for anyone. The twin-engine aircraft flew as fast as a fighter, and during a high-speed dive, the g-forces were almost as high as in a maneuvering fighter. The pilot had to be absolutely attentive and respond instantly in order to hit the target accurately, and then strong enough to pull out of the steep dive—and when possible evading the inevitable ground fire of the enemy.

Ekaterina Musatova-Fedotova, a Pe-2 pilot, never took her job for granted. She regarded the airplane as "probably the best in either the German or the Soviet Air Force," but one that was "complex and difficult for women to fly, especially small women who were slim and hungry." The controls were designed for taller individuals, and many women had to put two or three pillows behind their backs. The plane was so heavy on takeoff, and required so much force to pull back the control stick to get the tail up, that it was common for navigators to push against the pilot's back to brace her.[172]

Retraining on the Pe-2 was completed on 23 November 1942; twenty crews were declared to be combat ready. Twelve crews had received training in techniques of dive-bombing. Throughout the course of training, the crews as a whole accumulated 1,776 flying hours (554 in the Pe-2) and 5,835 flights (1,276 in the Pe-2). Pilots had an average of 88 hours in the Pe-2. As of 1 December 1942, the regiment was declared ready for duty and, in accordance with an order from VVS headquarters, was assigned to the 8th Air Army on the Western Front.[173]

Raskova apparently did not hesitate to use her name and influence to get the best equipment she could manage for "her" regiments. Some observers thought that this was unfair, preferential treatment. Perhaps Raskova thought that the women were laboring under a number of inequities already: they had little military training and no combat experience. Unlike newly trained male pilots who were assimilated into squadrons where there were experienced and battle-seasoned veterans, the women would be entering combat duty cold. From that point of view, which Raskova almost certainly shared, it was not unreasonable to give the new women's regiments the best equipment that could be obtained.

The 122nd was a temporary unit that existed from October 1941 until the spring of 1942. Its sole purpose was the training and equipping of three combat aviation regiments: the 586th Fighter Regiment, the 587th Bomber Regiment, and the 588th Night Bomber Regiment. These regiments became operational beginning early in 1942 and were transferred to combat commands. When the last regiment became operational, the work of the 122nd was completed.

WHY WOMEN?

The 586th, 587th (later 125th Guards), and 588th (later 46th Guards) were the first women's combat aviation units in the world. Why did the Soviet Union decide to create them? Several possible explanations can be examined: first, that the women's regiments were created primarily to alleviate a shortage of personnel (that is, out of desperation); second, that they were created for propaganda purposes; and third, that they were created primarily because of popular demand and the persistence of Marina Raskova. The most likely explanation is that all three factors were involved. Raskova's key role has already been discussed; the issues of desperation and propaganda are covered below.

Personnel Shortages

In virtually all countries where women were recruited into the military for combat duty, personnel shortages (that is, desperation or necessity) have been cited as the main factor. Western observers have often assumed that sheer desperation led countries such as the Soviet Union, Israel, and Yugoslavia to use women in combat. "Desperation" is usually conceived in terms of a combination of personnel shortages and imminent danger to the homeland; a desperate country, in this view, will recruit anyone—even children, old people, and women—to fight. There is a basis for speculating that the Soviets created the women's regiments primarily due to shortages of personnel. For example, necessity was clearly the reason women were first recruited into other nontraditional roles in the prewar Soviet Union. Acute shortages of workers in industry had developed by 1930, which drove a "new perspective" in official publications supporting the introduction of women workers into new fields; quotas for women were even established in some industries.[174] But the personnel shortages in industry were the result of the effects of collectivization, the purges, and the rapid industrialization of the Soviet economy. By the time the war began, the Soviets had largely recovered. After all, their air force was the largest in the world on the eve of the war. Furthermore, what occurred in Soviet industry in the 1930s was *not* seen in the Soviet military during the war. No quotas were established, except in air defense; no preexisting plan for recruiting women was evident; and women were not exhorted to join the army. Griesse and Stites noted the emphasis on support, rather than combat, roles for women early in the war: "only a handful of women . . . were estimated to have been in the service when the war broke out . . . there was military and civilian resistance to augmenting their numbers during the first year. There were a few volunteers in 1941, but they were usually channeled into support, not combat, roles."[175]

In late 1941—at the time of the formation of the women's aviation regiments—personnel losses were not a major factor in convincing the Soviets to permit women to enter combat roles. By 1942, the situation was different; mobilizations of women were conducted, and by the latter part of the war, any woman who was childless and not involved in critical industrial or governmental work was subject to mobilization.[176] Personnel shortages *were* the main reason for the recruitment of women into the PVO in 1942. Colonel General of Artillery Zhuravlev wrote that when the Central Committee discussed the recruitment of women for the PVO, it was justified for two reasons: it would answer the women's demands to serve, and it would also release men for front-line duty.[177] In the 1942 recruitment of women, there were specific goals for the percentages of men to be replaced in the PVO; women were to replace eight of ten men in antiaircraft artillery, three of five in machine gun crews, and varying percentages in most other roles. In fact, "they were to release the entire male rear-services personnel serving in private and noncommissioned officer ranks."[178]

The recruitment of Soviet women later in the war, particularly into the PVO, seems to have been justified primarily in terms of freeing men for combat. Therefore, many analysts assume that the creation of the women's aviation regiments was also driven by sheer necessity.[179] But although personnel shortages may have instigated other mobilizations of women, it is unlikely that they were the driving factor for the creation of the Soviet women's aviation units in 1941. The fact is, at the time the regiments were formed, there was no shortage of pilots in the Soviet Air Force. Although the Soviets had lost more than 7,500 aircraft by September 1941, most of the aircraft had been destroyed on the ground; relatively few pilots had been killed. As historian Von Hardesty emphasizes, "concealed in the confusion of Soviet reversals, was the survival of a significant number of VVS pilots, other air personnel, and technicians. For the prolonged struggle ahead, the Soviet Air Force did not face, as one might have expected, an acute shortage of flight crews."[180] Furthermore, for every woman pilot who had been trained before the war there were two or three male pilots, many of whom were still on reserve status and available for duty.

What is perhaps most amazing is not that the Soviet Union was willing to accept women pilots for combat service but that it was willing to give them airplanes. At the time the 122nd was formed, there was a severe shortage of aircraft. The devastating aircraft losses suffered by the VVS during the invasion had been bad enough; in addition, hundreds of factories were being relocated to the Ural Mountains, delaying production and delivery of aircraft and parts for months. The Soviets were so short of aircraft at this time, especially bombers, that they adapted all sorts of trainers (the obsolete Po-2 biplane) and transports (the Li-2/DC-3) for military use. Many Soviets thought that precious aircraft, especially the newer designs, should go to regiments already at the front, not to a bunch of "girls." I. S. Levin, director of the Yak fighter factory in Saratov, wrote that some members of his staff were bitter about the decision to give new fighters to the 586th.[181] And 586th commander Aleksandr Gridnev recalled similar complaints from some male engineers.[182]

Moreover, although women were recruited for air defense specifically to replace men—to free them for front-line duty—such was not the case with the aviation regiments. The women's regiments did not free men for combat, since they themselves were combat units. It could be argued that if there was no real shortage of pilots, perhaps a *perceived* shortage was a factor in creating women's units. This seems unlikely in view of the other factors mentioned earlier that weighed against forming women's regiments (scarcity of aircraft, augmenting rather than replacing men). Furthermore, if perceived shortages drove the VVS to create women's regiments, there should have been recruitment on a larger scale, and there should have been provision for a longer-term, if not continuous, infusion of women, since overall pilot casualties could only be expected to increase. A onetime recruitment of women pilots might be reasonable if there had been an initially heavy loss of pilots, but it has already been demonstrated that this was not the case.

Desperation alone, whether presumed or real, is not a sufficient reason for a state to allow women into combat. Other countries that faced far greater shortages of personnel, such as Germany at the end of World War II, never allowed women to fight.[183] It seems obvious that other factors were at least as important as desperation.

Propaganda and Morale Factors

Western observers have speculated that when women were mobilized for combat, it was primarily for propaganda, rather than military, purposes.[184] Cold-war analyst George Quester stated this point of view in a 1977 article:

> The use of females in combat service in the past has been defensive strategy. . . . When one's country is invaded, women wind up in guerrilla battalions as in Yugoslavia, or *are portrayed* as regular infantry as in Russia. . . . Whether or not this characterization is valid, it always has been effective propaganda. A nation forced to send its women into combat must be the underdog, the nation that has been threatened, the nation that cares the very most about the justice of its cause.[185]

If Quester was right, then one would expect to see women used primarily in "showcase" positions or units, with a great deal of press coverage. In particular, the Soviet Union would have encouraged reports about the women pilots and other women combatants in the foreign press if its primary goal was, as Quester suggested, to portray itself as the underdog and to encourage international sympathy and support. Was there, in the Second World War, a propaganda campaign devoted to the issue of women in combat, in general, and to the women who flew in the combat aviation regiments, in particular? If so, what forms did the propaganda take, and what were its purposes? At what audience was it aimed—Soviet women, the broader Soviet public, or foreigners?

There is little evidence that the Soviets glorified their women in combat to the foreign press corps, even to female reporters. Correspondents and writers such as Margaret Bourke-White, Erskine Caldwell, and Alexander Werth make no mention of women in combat in their books about the war. Caldwell and Bourke-White wrote books about the early days of the war.[186] Werth, who was in the Soviet Union for the entire war except the period November 1941 through May 1942, wrote several books. In his thousand-page *Russia at War*, he never mentioned Soviet women fliers or any other women in combat—despite two references to Raskova's flying achievements before the war.[187] Werth recounted many wartime press conferences in detail, and he specifically assessed Soviet wartime propaganda in several chapters of his book. The only propaganda efforts directed toward women that he noted are those urging women to join the labor force. He reported that a typical appeal to women was a poster saying, "Women, go and work on the collective farms, replace the men now in the Army!"[188] Historian Gregory Smith noted a similar emphasis in his study of wartime Moscow.[189] And on 8 October 1941 (in the middle of the recruitment and assembly of the 122nd Air Group volunteers in Moscow), Werth noted only a "routine article" in *Pravda* on "The Work of Women in War-Time" —in factories and on farms.[190] There is no indication that the Soviets specifically arranged for Western correspondents to meet the women aviators. Any exposure to the Western press seems to have occurred by chance. For example, on one occasion, an American journalist happened to see a female night bomber pilot during a 1944 women's conference in Moscow and commented to his colleagues that the Soviets were obviously trying to fool them by hanging a few medals on the girl. She responded by showing him her logbook with its 800 combat sorties; his reaction is not noted.[191]

The women fliers and other women combatants were also virtually ignored in the writings of the most famous Soviet war correspondents, such as Konstantin Simonov, Vasili Grossman, and Ilya Ehrenburg.[192] These writers were as famous to the Soviets as Edward R. Murrow and Ernie Pyle were to Americans. For example, Werth said that Ehrenburg "was a very important factor in the great battle for Russian morale in the summer of 1942; every soldier in the Army read Ehrenburg; and partisans in the enemy rear are known to have readily swopped [*sic*] any spare tommy gun for a bundle of Ehrenburg clippings.''[193] Ehrenburg wrote about the Soviet pilots who flew during the Spanish Civil War and about the French pilots who flew in the famous Normandie-Nieman squadron as part of the Soviet Air Force during the Second World War, but he did not mention the women pilots.[194] Simonov was the most famous wartime poet, as well as one of the most popular journalists. His poem "Wait for Me" was the best known of the entire war. It urged the Soviet woman to fulfill the role expected of her in war: to wait for her man to return from the front.

These writers published primarily in military publications such as the military newspaper *Krasnaia Zvezda*. They wrote numerous articles glorifying nurses and civilian women who had suffered under German occupation. If propaganda was the primary reason for allowing women in combat, the Soviets would have assigned these top correspondents to the story.

Not only did the Soviets fail to propagandize their military women to the press; these women were also neglected in one of the most critical forms of internal propaganda: Stalin's speeches. The Soviet people anticipated these speeches, especially in the early days of the war, eagerly and anxiously. According to Werth, "in wartime Russia . . . every official utterance, and especially any word from Stalin was awaited with a desperate kind of hope.''[195] Stalin's most important speeches were probably those given in Red Square on the anniversary of the revolution in November. In these speeches, he noted the achievements of "workers and employees, *men and women*," and *"men and women* collective farmers," even *"men and women* guerrilla fighters"—but only "Red Army and Red Navy *comrades*.''[196] Although the term *comrade* can include both sexes, it lacks the special emphasis present in the other categories. If Stalin had wished to stress women's role in combat, he would have used a different word, such as the popular *girl-soldier* commonly used in works about the women.[197] In Stalin's 6 November 1944 speech, made when hundreds of thousands of women had served at the front, he noted the contribution of Soviet women to the war effort but did not mention the fact that women had actually participated in combat. On the contrary, he stressed the role of women as supporting the men who did the fighting:

The matchless labor exploits of the Soviet women . . . will go down forever in history; for it is they that have borne the brunt of the work in the factories and mills and on the collective and state farms. . . . They have shown themselves worthy of their fathers and sons, husbands and brothers, who are defending their homeland against the German fascist fiends.[198]

There was, of course, *some* media coverage of women in combat. Although the women pilots did not rate coverage from the top correspondents, there were occasional articles about them in *Ogonek,* a political-literary weekly publication intended for young adults, and scattered items in popular newspapers. Much of the Soviet press coverage of the women pilots was published only in "women's" publications such as *Rabotnitsa* (Woman Worker) and *Krestianka* (Woman Peasant). Other coverage of the women pilots was in the form of the popular "letters from the front" format, in which soldiers wrote about their experiences for the newspapers. For example, two pilots of the night bomber regiment published a short piece in *Izvestiia* in 1945; this article was published on 8 March, International Women's Day, and therefore falls into the category of token publicity for that holiday, rather than true recognition of the pilots' achievements, since it is doubtful that many men read the Women's Day editions.[199]

Members of the 586th Fighter Aviation Regiment received the first important propaganda coverage during the war. A pilot of that regiment, Valeriia Khomiakova, was hailed as the first woman in the world to shoot down an enemy aircraft. On 24 September 1942, she destroyed a Junkers-88 bomber over Saratov—in a nighttime engagement on her first combat patrol.[200] The magazine *Ogonek* printed a full-page article about the event.[201] Fighter aces Litviak and Budanova were natural "heroes" for the press. One of the first wartime articles about them occurred as a sidebar to an article about Raskova's death. A photo of Litviak, Budanova, and Maria Kuznetsova was captioned, "youthful replacements trained by Marina Raskova," and the article noted that the women pilots had destroyed a German bomber near Stalingrad.[202] Litviak and Budanova received more prominent coverage with a cover photo on the 20 April 1943 issue of *Ogonek;* a short inside blurb detailed their accomplishments. In true Soviet fashion, their collective, rather than individual, achievements were honored; the magazine gave a combined number of combat missions and kills to date for the two pilots.[203] Overall, however, it was the "night witches" of the 46th who garnered the most attention from the Soviet media. This may be partly due to the fact that some of the earlier "stars," such as Raskova, Litviak, and Budanova, were killed in action before the end of the war.[204] The greater publicity might also be because the 46th was the only one of the three women's regiments to remain all female throughout the war, and so was the only "true" women's aviation unit in the latter part of the war.[205]

There is one other reason that the 46th received the most propaganda coverage: these women pilots were seen as more vulnerable than the others. The 46th flew the outmoded wooden biplane, the Po-2, while the other units flew modern fighters and bombers. The image of women flying this frail little plane into the jaws of death undoubtedly appealed to the press.[206] An American reporter would probably have described them as "feisty"—an adjective that denotes someone who is full of spirit but essentially powerless. That the Soviets held this sort of image of the 46th pilots is evident in the title of an *Ogonek* feature article about them: "Eaglets."[207] Male pilots also flew the Po-2 in combat and were often described with the popular bird-of-prey monikers ("falcons," "eagles")—but never with the diminutive form, which can only be regarded as patronizing. The frequent use of the term *girl-pilots (devushki-letchiki)* further supports the thesis that the women pilots were not regarded on equal terms with the men. Most Soviet pilots during the war were quite young, but the men were never described as *boy-pilots*.

Social anthropologist Sharon Macdonald believes that society makes the experience of women warriors acceptable by "recasting" their stories in one of two ways: either the women are portrayed as unnatural, "manly" creatures, or else their femininity is stressed and their traditional female virtues are played up while their role in combat is explained as due strictly to exceptional circumstances.[208] The Soviets took the second approach. There was a strong emphasis on how "women remained women" even at the front. A number of wartime photographs, for example, were obviously staged to fit society's conceptions of how women at war would behave. One woman pilot is shown standing beside her plane in full flight gear, primping before a huge mirror; other photos show the women in dugouts decorated with flowers, reading to one another and sewing.[209] Although the women did sew in their off-duty time, there is no mention in the memoirs that pilots had mirrors brought planeside as part of their preflight routine.

In recent interviews, the women veterans recall receiving little public attention during the war. The former chief of staff of the 46th, Irina Rako-bolskaia, recalled that most of the coverage was in localized "front-line newspapers" published by the Red Army:

> They wrote a lot about us during the war in the front-line newspa-pers—at first, it is true, under male last names. It was like the regi-ment was classified secret. Maybe they were afraid that we wouldn't be equal to the situation. Later on, when we became Guards and the first Hero appeared, they began to write in newspapers and maga-zines, and writers came to the regiment.[210]

When asked whether the famous correspondents wrote about them, navigator Polina Gelman replied:

> Ehrenburg was never with us. Simonov, it seems, wrote something. It seems in some sort of introduction to an article, no more than a single page. But I can't say exactly, now. The Poles wrote about us, and the French from the "Normandie-Nieman" squadron. I don't remember the name of the French count (there were two counts, who became Heroes of the Soviet Union), but he wrote that "the Germans called [them] 'night witches,' but we admired these wonderful sorcer-esses."[211]

If the women of the 46th and a few of the fighter pilots received some media coverage, there was virtually none about the 125th Guards Bomber Regiment. Navigator Valentina Kravchenko has said that neither she nor Valentin Markov, the regimental commander, could remember publicity of any sort during the war.[212] Kravchenko claimed that "the Germans knew about our regiment, but there were no newsmen or cameramen at our regiment . . . nobody wrote about our regiment during the war. For the Soviet people it was like a secret regiment, carrying out secret assign-ments. Only at the victory parade in Moscow [in 1945] did the country learn about our existence."[213] On the whole, there was no large-scale pro-paganda campaign about the women pilots. Griesse and Stites, in a broad survey of the literature, found little publicity emphasizing the role of women in combat, especially early in the war:

> When the Germans invaded in June 1941, the initial response of the government in regard to women was to stress the already growing

theme of separation of functions: men to the front and women to re-place them at the bench and on the farm. This was the major public theme in the early months of the war.[214]

Most of the propaganda that did exist seems to have been aimed at rais-ing the morale of the women themselves, rather than attempting to publi-cize their role or to socialize male attitudes. For example, the women's units heard lectures about traditional Russian women who fought, as well as "biographies of leading contemporary female soldiers."[215] It seems doubtful that men's units heard the same lectures.

It is interesting to note that after the war began, the Soviets resurrected the history of Nadezhda Durova, "the cavalry maiden" who disguised her-self as a man and fought in the Napoleonic wars. Durova, it seems, would have been a good role model for their new Soviet woman who could do anything—a real Russian heroine. Yet Durova's works, which went out of print shortly after their publication in the mid-1800s, had not been re-printed by the Soviets; Durova's monarchist loyalties may have accounted for this.[216] It is even more likely that before the war, the Soviets simply did not wish to glorify a woman who was a decorated military officer. If the Soviets had wished to encourage women to seek military careers, Durova's works undoubtedly would have been reprinted much sooner.[217] After the Soviets decided to use women in combat, however (and after the creation of the women's aviation regiments), Durova's history became a useful pro-paganda tool, albeit in a "sovietized" version. The text of Durova's own memoirs was not reprinted until 1960, but two highly romanticized works loosely based on her memoirs (*Kama Foundling*, a novel, and *Nadezhda Du-rova*, a play) appeared in 1942. Durova became a posterized heroine, more a patriotic exhortation than a historically legitimate role model.[218]

A short biography of Durova, also published in 1942, was more accurate in its facts than the novel or the play, but historian Mary Zirin noted that the author "misuses [Durova's] frank passages on the fatigue and physical stress she underwent to make it quite clear to Soviet women that a military career was not for them."[219] It is possible that there was an intentional effort here to add some leaven to the bread—to show Soviet women heroic examples, but also to stress that these examples pertained only to extreme conditions and were not appropriate in everyday life. Durova's own words were not heard during the war.[220] Even so, many women saw Durova as a heroic figure to be emulated. The members of the 122nd attended a performance of the play on 23 February 1942 in Saratov. Raskova made a speech after the play, comparing Durova's situation with their own and stressing their own advantages:

> Well, girls, someday there will be plays written and performed about us. We have been called to continue the glorious traditions of the Russian woman-soldier. We don't face the sort of obstacles and conventionalities that prevented Nadezhda Durova from displaying in full measure the courage and heroism of the Russian woman. Everything has been given to us: the right to defend the Homeland, and aircraft, and weapons.[221]

It seems clear that the Soviet government's primary purpose in forming the aviation units was not to create a propaganda tool. However, there are other motivations for propagandization. Was it merely to improve morale and motivation, perhaps by shaming the men into action? After all, that was Bochkareva's stated motive in forming the Women's Battalions of Death under the Provisional Government in 1917. Decades later, historian Richard Abraham still echoed that view of the women's units in the First World War: "A symptom of the government's uncertainty over army morale was the formation of an exclusively female military unit."[222]

The morale factor was certainly important to the Soviets. For example, in a 1942 speech to political workers of the Moscow Air Defense Front, President M. I. Kalinin claimed that women soldiers had a very positive effect on morale. It was not the women's bravery, endurance, or skill that he praised, however; it was their "civilizing and ennobling effect," the fact that the men started cleaning their quarters and doing their laundry.[223] Much the same could be said, however, of women in noncombat roles, such as female entertainers who visited the front.[224] The Soviets hardly needed to put tens of thousands of women into combat roles to convince male soldiers to wash their socks. Kalinin may have been attempting to derive propaganda value from the situation, but it is ludicrous to assume that the Soviet government's main goal in allowing so many women to fight was to improve either the men's morale or their hygiene.

Propaganda can also be used as a tool to change social perceptions and values. Did the Soviets hope to socialize the population into accepting a new role for women—not just during the war, but in the future as well? The Soviet people had already come to accept the idea of the working woman. In Soviet Russia, unlike in France or the United States, women had been quickly and rather easily assimilated into the working classes. In the West, women were seen as competitors for jobs. In the Soviet Union, the rapid industrialization and collectivization of the 1930s changed the nature of work for all citizens; there were few Soviet women who could afford not to work. So any resistance to women in the military was not due to Soviet men being unused to seeing women in the workplace. In the Soviet Union, the resistance was specifically to the idea of women in combat.

Historian Kazimiera J. Cottam mentioned "an educational campaign aimed mainly at male commanders," but did not seem to regard it as particularly successful.[225] Nancy Loring Goldman, a specialist in the social psychology of military personnel, noted that although "political and ideological mobilization" was a factor in the Soviet use of women in combat, "the Soviets have nonetheless exhibited their own brand of conservatism; the presence of women at the front was resisted. . . . resentment and ridicule continued to stalk Soviet women soldiers in all services even at their most dedicated and heroic moments."[226] Grigorii Tokaev, a Soviet pilot who was on the faculty of the Zhukovskii Academy when the war began, expressed a typical male attitude. One of his assistants, a woman who was a senior lieutenant, had heard that Tokaev would be commanding an air force regiment, and she asked to join. Tokaev wrote, "I had difficulty in persuading her that there had not been any such assignment. I should, however, confess that even if there had been, with myself in charge, I should have refused her. I had then, and still have, rigid views on women in men's uniform: in war, women play a more important role by remaining the gentle sex."[227] Ironically, Tokaev himself later attempted to join Valentina Grizodubova's regiment, rather than be evacuated to the rear with the academy staff. Apparently, his "rigid views on women in men's uniform" were flexible enough to allow him to consider working for a woman commander, if that was the only way he could get to the front.[228]

If there was an officially created and supported propaganda effort to persuade Soviet men to accept women as combatants, it was not well conceived. Most of the women's stories do not reveal strong support for their efforts. Instead, they recall continually fighting a resistant system in order to achieve their goals. Despite their equal legal rights, they constantly encountered men in positions of authority who actively discouraged them from trying to fly before the war and from joining combat units after the war began. Many Soviet women have reported the stigma they faced as women at the front, both during and after the war. For example, one woman recalled the reception she met: "I went [home] as a heroine, never thinking that a girl from the front line could be received the way I was . . . I came to know insults, I heard offensive words." She then recounted the reaction of her new in-laws to their son's front-line marriage: "Who have you got married to? An army girl. Why, you have two younger sisters. Who will marry them now?"[229] The pervasive belief persisted that any woman who went to the front was looking for action in more ways than one. Women who fought were tainted by the camp-follower image.

To whatever extent women's aviation units were formed to support propaganda goals, those goals were for the short term only. The rapid demobilization of women from active duty after the war, and the exclusion of women from service academies since that time, indicates that the Soviets never intended to create an ongoing tradition of military women. Leila Rupp, in her study of U.S. and German mobilization of women, noted that both used the wartime media to achieve a rapid change in women's images. Rupp also stressed the temporary nature of that change. The idea of "Rosie the Riveter" was encouraged by the U.S. government, but ultimately, Rosie did not change the status of American women.[230] The vast majority of American women who gained work in factories during the war lost it when the boys came home. Anne Griesse noted that "women were never received as part of the military elite" and that two policies in 1943 highlighted the true attitudes of the Soviet regime toward women in the military: the first was a new policy of gender segregation in primary and secondary schools (with special sessions during which girls learned domestic skills while boys took military classes), and the second was the creation of the Suvorov cadet schools, to which female students were not admitted.[231]

There was a deliberate policy to downplay the role of women in combat that began even before the end of the war. Gregory Smith's analysis shows that the image of Soviet women as strong and independent peaked in late 1941; as early as 1942, women were given decreasing press coverage every year, and the family was given increasing attention.[232] Olga Mishakova, a member of the editorial board of *Krestianka* and author of several wartime pamphlets about women in the war, wrote in March 1945, "in the Red Army . . . women very energetically showed themselves as pilots, snipers, automatic gunners [etc.]. . . . But they don't forget about their *primary duty* to nation and state, that of *motherhood*."[233] This statement appeared in

Pravda and carried the implied official weight of that publication. Mishako-va's position was an omen of the pro-natalist policies promulgated after the war's end. The August–September 1944 issue of *Rabotnitsa*, the maga-zine for working women, was dedicated to motherhood.[234] Carol Berkin and Clara Lovett believe that this sort of "patriotic motherhood" originates "in the determination of political leadership to preserve patriarchy."[235]

In July 1945, President Kalinin spoke to a gathering of recently demobi-lized women soldiers. Although he acknowledged their strength and hero-ism, he made no mention of continued military careers; his main concern was that they quickly find civilian jobs. His final advice to them was:

> Apart from everything else, there is one more thing you have done. Equality for women has existed in our country since the very first day of the October Revolution. But you have won equality for women in yet another sphere: in the defence of your country arms in hand. You have won equal rights for women in a field in which they hitherto have not taken such a direct part. But allow me, as one grown wise with years, to say to you: do not give yourself airs in your future practical work. Do not talk about the services you rendered, let others do it for you. That will be better.[236]

Kalinin's speech is revealing. He claimed that the women had "won equal rights" as soldiers, which implied that the military had become a potential career for women. Yet Kalinin urged the women to forget their combat service as soon as possible. The same man who had pinned the gold star of the Hero of the Soviet Union on Marina Raskova in 1938 now urged women not to even talk about their combat achievements.[237] It seems unlikely that the same sort of speech was made to male war veterans.

It seems clear that the Soviets sought only to derive propaganda value from an existing situation and to justify the presence of those women who were already in combat. The goal of Soviet wartime propaganda was to show that it was acceptable—but not necessarily desirable—for a woman to fulfill the role of military pilot. Although propaganda and morale bene-fits were derived from the existence of the women's regiments, there is little evidence that publicity was the main factor behind their formation. Top Soviet leaders did not propagandize these regiments in any significant way, and little information was given to the foreign press or to important Soviet war correspondents on the women aviators. Furthermore, the avia-tion units were formed less than four months after the beginning of the war, at a time when the only propaganda concerning women targeted agricultural and industrial jobs. There was no publicity attending the formation of the women's regiments or their initial entry into combat duty.

Wartime propaganda about these units was used at least partially to mobilize women for temporary military service and to make that service acceptable to society—at least until the war was over. The publicity that attended the women's aviation units after they had proved themselves did not seek to recruit women into aviation but was geared primarily toward inspiring women to serve in other roles. The Soviets began playing down the accomplishments of the women pilots, and all women combatants, as soon as the end of the war was in sight. The Soviets did not publicize the women pilots in such a way as to foster long-range changes in gender roles in society. Instead, the propaganda surrounding the women pilots had a more short-lived purpose: "to build morale, instill outrage, incite to vengeance, encourage through praise and inspire through example."[238] Any image of the new Soviet woman as military officer and pilot that resulted from wartime propaganda was far outweighed by the overwhelming emphasis on the Soviet woman as mother, wife, and builder of society. Where the Americans had Uncle Sam, the Soviets had Mother Russia. Soviet women were constantly reminded that their true place was on the home front, not the battlefront.

The women veterans themselves do not believe that they received undue attention from the press. "It didn't seem that [the press] devoted too much attention [to us]," wrote Polina Gelman. And they certainly do not believe that their regiments were merely a propaganda ploy. As Gelman pointed out, "After all, girls were killed; how could this have been propaganda?"[239]

OFF TO COMBAT

The three regiments formed from Aviation Group 122 had widely different missions and aircraft. The women aviators flew fighters, dive-bombers, and night bombers; they engaged in combat on different fronts under different commands. These three regiments were the only aviation regiments that were originally assigned all-female personnel. The exigencies of war were such that two of the three eventually included some men as well as women, primarily among the enlisted and technical ranks in ground support positions. These regiments are therefore an interesting case study in the relative merits of combat units both segregated and integrated by gender.

In addition to these regiments, some Soviet women pilots flew in mostly male units. For example, Valentina Grizodubova, Raskova's pilot on the *Rodina*, became the commander of the 101st Long-Range Air Regiment, a bomber-transport unit. Other women flew in dive-bomber, reconnaissance, and ground attack regiments. Most of these women had already attained military rank prior to the war. A separate chapter about these women follows the chapters on the three women's regiments. The fighter pilots from the 586th who were assigned to other regiments, either temporarily (during Stalingrad) or permanently (Liliia Litviak and Katia Budanova), are discussed in that chapter.

It is impossible to truly appreciate the relatively brief histories of the wartime experiences of the women aviators that are presented in this book without an understanding of the overall context of the war on the Eastern Front. The best general histories are John Erickson's two-volume set, *The Road to Stalingrad* and *The Road to Berlin*, and the more recent military history by David M. Glantz and Jonathan M. House, *When Titans Clashed: How the Red Army Stopped Hitler*.[240] Both these histories neglect the air war, a failing that is addressed in Von Hardesty's outstanding *Red Phoenix: The Rise of Soviet Air Power 1941–1945*.[241] Hardesty points out that Western historians have been so taken with the image of the apparent destruction of the Soviet Air Force during the first weeks of the war that they often fail to recognize the incredible recovery of the VVS—a situation that would be analogous to eternally characterizing the U.S. Navy by its defeat at Pearl Harbor. But the fact is that the Soviet Air Force (as Hardesty notes) recovered the strategic initiative in the air by 1943 and thereafter applied "overwhelming air power against the enemy in a series of decisive campaigns."[242]

Hardesty describes some of the unique characteristics of the war on the Eastern Front: "The arena for air operations in the east was vast and demanding, with no exact parallel anywhere in World War II. . . . The enormity of the landscape can be fully appreciated if we realize that from the fall of 1941 to the fall of 1943, the width of the Eastern Front was never less than 2,400 miles. In late 1942 the front extended for 3,000 miles."[243] Other important aspects of the air war include severe attrition on both sides and extremes of weather that made maintenance, logistics, and combat operations extraordinarily difficult at times. Much has been made of the hardships endured by the German Army on the Eastern Front; however, the Soviets—including the members of the women's aviation regiments—suffered those same hardships. "The Soviet Air Force, targeted as the first victim of Operation Barbarossa . . . emerged at the conclusion of World War II as the most powerful tactical air arm in the world," noted Hardesty; "no air force had suffered greater losses, endured more hardships, or experienced such a dramatic rebirth from the ashes of defeat as had the VVS between 1941 and 1945."[244] The experience of the Soviet women's regiments is one component of that phoenix-like rebirth.

3

The 46th Guards Night Bomber

Aviation Regiment

❖   ❖   ❖   ❖   ❖   ❖   ❖   ❖   ❖   ❖   ❖   ❖   ❖   ❖   ❖

Unit designations:	588th Night Bomber Aviation Regiment (February 1942–February 1943) 46th Guards Night Bomber Aviation Regiment (February 1943–1945)
Honorary designations:	Guards; Tamansky; Orders of the Red Banner and Suvorov III class[1]
Dates of service:	27 May 1942–9 May 1945 (disbanded 15 October 1945)
Divisional subordination:	218 NBAD; 132 NBAD; 325 NBAD[2]
Primary areas of operation:	Stalingrad, Krasnodar, Novorossiysk, Kerch', Sevastopol', Minsk, Warsaw, Berlin
Commander:	Evdokiia Bershanskaia
Aircraft flown:	Po-2
Combat missions:	24,000 +
Heroes of the Soviet Union:	24

The best known of the three women's regiments is the 588th Night Bomber Aviation Regiment, which was redesignated the 46th Guards Night Bomber Aviation Regiment (GvNBAP) in 1943. The 46th was commonly known as the "night witches," a phrase attributed to the Germans, whose troops were harassed and bombed by the regiment during hours of darkness. The idea of using an open-cockpit biplane as a combat aircraft might seem inconceivable to us today, but dozens of Soviet women (and hundreds of men) flew the Po-2 as a night bomber in the Second World War.

Pilot Nina Raspopova gives a dramatic account of just how fragile the Po-2 could be. In late 1942, Raspopova and her navigator Larisa Radchikova were conducting a night bombing sortie against a German bridgehead on the Terek River.[3] Raspopova's plane was caught in an enemy searchlight and hit by antiaircraft fire; she remembered, "my left foot slipped down into an empty space below me; the bottom of the cockpit had been shot away. I felt something hot streaming down my left arm and leg—I was wounded."[4] Blinded by the lights, with gas streaming from a damaged fuel tank and carrying no parachutes, Raspopova had to try to land the aircraft. She managed to get across the river and down to the ground, but the wood-framed plane had been so badly shot up that Raspopova noticed "large splinters were sticking out my body." Together with her wounded navigator, armed only with a pistol, Raspopova managed to find her way back to friendly territory, and within two months she was flying again.[5] This resilience in the face of terrible odds was typical of the aircrews of this regiment—and noteworthy enough to be mentioned when the unit was redesignated as a Guards regiment.[6]

The 46th first saw combat in June 1942 on the Southern Front, where it bombed river crossings of the Mius and Don Rivers and participated in the battle for Stavropol. In August through December 1942, the 46th flew in defense of the Transcaucasus. In January 1943, it flew in the regions of Stavropol and the Kuban, and in March through September, near the Taman peninsula and for the liberation of Novorossiysk. For its service during this period, the regiment was redesignated Guards and received the honorary name of "Taman." In November 1943 through May 1944, the 46th flew at Kerch, the Crimea, and Sevastopol. June and July 1944 saw the 46th at Mogilev, Minsk, and other locations in Belorussia. In August 1944, the regiment was in Poland; in January 1945, in western Prussia; and in March, it participated in the liberation of Gdansk. The regiment ended its combat service in April and May 1945 near the Oder River. It had operated continuously on the front lines for three years.[7]

The 46th GvNBAP was the only one of the three original regiments that remained all female throughout the war—a fact that every veteran stresses, sometimes in capital letters and underlined, as in a 1993 letter from Polina Gelman to the author: "OF THE THREE WOMEN'S REGIMENTS FORMED FROM

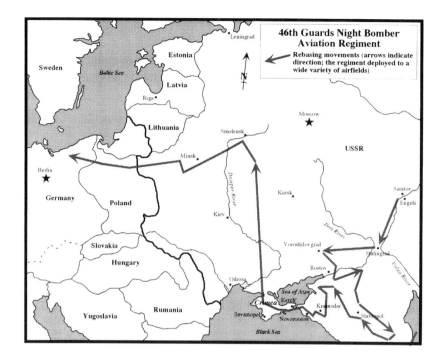

46th Guards Night Bomber Aviation Regiment

Rebasing movements (arrows indicate direction; the regiment deployed to a wide variety of airfields)

THE 122ND AVIATION GROUP, ONLY THE *46TH GUARDS TAMAN (588 BAP) REMAINED PURELY FEMALE UNTIL THE END OF THE WAR.*"[8] Former chief of staff Irina Rakobolskaia emphasized the same point: "Not a single man served in our regiment during the entire war."[9] The members of the 46th were proud of their all-female status and refused offers to integrate the regiment. For example, on 8 March 1944, in honor of International Women's Day, the 46th was visited by Marshal K. K. Rokossovskii, commander of the 2nd Belorussian Front, and K. A. Vershinin, commander of the 4th Air Army. Before the assembled regiment, Rokossovskii turned to Vershinin and said, "It's probably hard for the girls to do everything themselves. Maybe we should send them ten or twenty men to help hang bombs and do other heavy work?" But the women protested loudly, "We don't need any helpers, we're managing just fine on our own!"[10] In fact, a male radio mechanic was once assigned to the 46th in mid-1943 for a special equipment installation. Rakobolskaia said, "He was a shy, modest little fellow. He went to the dining hall alone, after us. . . . After about a week, the uniform branch sent him some women's underwear. Whether this was done accidentally or on purpose, you had to laugh a little. He couldn't take it, and requested to be sent back to his home unit. And so we re-mained without any men."[11]

The 46th had a single commander throughout the war—Evdokiia Bershanskaia, who reluctantly accepted the position (see chapter 2). Bershanskaia was a comparatively experienced pilot. She entered the Bataisk Aviation School in 1931 and became an instructor pilot. She was serving in civil aviation when she received orders to go to Moscow and join the 122nd.[12] The veterans seem to be unanimous in their admiration for Bershanskaia. Polina Gelman, a navigator and Hero of the Soviet Union, wrote, "We relied on one another as if we were family. Our commander, Lt. Col. Evdokiia Davydovna Bershanskaia, played a tremendous role in this. I'm very old, I served a long time in the army, and worked in many places. I had many commanders. But I never met such a wonderful person as our commander."[13] Bershanskaia was unaccustomed to giving orders and unfamiliar with military discipline. Yet she was unafraid to innovate, and under her leadership, the 46th became one of the top-performing Po-2 night bomber regiments in the Soviet military. Bershanskaia insti-tuted a system of in-house training to provide continual replacements for flying personnel, which meant that the 46th was never taken out of action for regeneration. The sheer endurance of the 46th's crews in three years of unbroken combat service is evidence that Bershanskaia's style was effec-tive, if somewhat unorthodox. Bershanskaia would later be singled out for mention as one of twelve "remarkable air regiment commanders" in the VVS.[14]

Of the three women's regiments, the 46th was the most ill equipped. It flew night bombing missions in the Po-2 biplane—a wood and canvas, open-cockpit relic from the 1930s. The Po-2 was no one's idea of a good combat aircraft. It was certainly not the first choice of the women who were assigned to the 46th; nearly all the pilots (including Bershanskaia) would have preferred fighters, and the navigators longed for the Pe-2. It was not only women pilots who regarded the Po-2 as a less-than-desirable combat aircraft. One of the women navigators of the 46th pointed out that "before the war [the Po-2] had been used by flying clubs for instruction and no one would have dreamed of using it for military purposes."[15] Nei-ther parachutes nor self-defense machine guns were carried until the end of the war; before that, the Po-2s had no weapons except the four small bomb racks. It also lacked a radio and any sophisticated instrumentation.

Mark Gallai, a famous test pilot and HSU, described what it was like to fly the Po-2 in combat:

> It means coming under fire from anti-aircraft weapons of every cali-bre, up to and including submachine guns (the Po-2 flew extremely low, sometimes at zero altitude), it means enemy night-fighters, blind-ing searchlights and often bad weather, too: low cloud, fog, snow, ice, and gales that throw a light aircraft from one wingtip to the other and wrench the controls from your hands. . . . And all this in a Po-2, which is small, slow and as easily set alight as a match.[16]

But it was precisely in these aircraft that the 46th left the training base at Engels for combat duty on 23 May 1942, having been assigned to the 4th Air Army on the Southern Front in the Donets Basin region. The training group commander, Marina Raskova, accompanied them to their new base, leading the regiment on its two-day journey. The contingent of twenty Po-2s stopped overnight at an intermediary airfield, then continued on early the following morning. They stopped once for refueling, then pro-ceeded to their destination of Morozovskaia.[17] Ten minutes away from landing, an incident occurred that was to have unfortunate repercussions. Fighter aircraft appeared in the air. "Katia, look, it's our escort," navigator Raisa Aronova told her pilot, who replied that they should be certain the fighters were friendly. The fighter pilots did not take up standard escort formation but began acting strangely, flying all around the Po-2s, first on the right, then on the left, sometimes passing very close to them. Aronova saw the red stars on the aircraft and realized it was Soviet pilots who were playing with them. Unfortunately, some of the other women remembered warnings they had received about enemy aircraft in the area. Without much experience in aircraft recognition, they thought the fighters were attacking them and scattered out of their formation. "The fighter pilots, pleased with the effect they had produced, but perhaps surprised by such a turn of events, withdrew to a respectful distance, and then just disap-peared from sight," recalled Aronova. The Po-2s managed to re-form in time to make a proper landing, but the damage was done to whatever hope they might have had of being regarded as savvy military pilots. After the women landed, some male pilots on the field taunted them, calling out, "Hey, spineless, can't you tell a star from a swastika?"[18]

The 46th was based at the village of Trud Gorniaka, not far from Moro-zovskaia. If the flight to their first front-line base was traumatic, at least they felt at home after they arrived: according to Aronova, the airfield service battalion (BAO) had arranged billeting in the huts of local residents, and a dining area was set up under some trees. It was a pleasant surprise compared to the earthen dugouts they had expected—and one of the few times during the war the women were so nicely accommodated.[19] Polina Gelman remembers this rather differently: "The first base was very small, at a small village. We called our place 'Hotel Flying Horses' because we lived in a stable."

The first visitor was the commander of the 4th Air Army, General Vershinin. He wrote that he met with the regiment and asked a number of questions about the sort of training they had received, then explained that they would be assigned to the 218th Night Bomber Aviation Division, which already had regiments of SB and R-5 aircraft.[20] The following day, the commander of the 218th, D. D. Popov, and his commissar arrived to inspect the 46th. Popov did not disguise his lack of enthusiasm at having a women's regiment placed under his command. Aronova noted that from the peculiar manner of the inspection, the women had the distinct impression that "the division commander was far from ecstatic about the situation he found himself in," and he walked around with a "stony, impenetrable face." Even Magid, who neglected to mention the fighter "attack" on the Po-2s in his history of the 46th, commented on Popov's gloomy manner: "He acted as though he was only interested in the equipment. His face was sullen. He asked nothing, said nothing, silently walking from aircraft to aircraft, not even glancing to the side."[21] Popov had already made up his mind about the usefulness of a women's regiment. The day before the 46th arrived, Popov had received a call from a General Ustinov of the army staff, demanding that a regiment of night bombers be assigned to his control. Popov told him, "I'll give you a brand new regiment . . . it's a women's Po-2 regiment. In fact, you can keep them permanently." The general reportedly replied, "Don't get so distressed, the regiment's a good one. Raskova led it." Popov was apparently not so sure; he told his commissar, "We've seen everything now. They're giving us some sort of little girls, and in Po-2s to boot."[22]

It was not only the women who remarked on the distrust of the 46th by its new division commander.[23] Vershinin wrote that Popov called him after the inspection and complained, "I've received 112 little princesses. Just what am I supposed to do with them?" Vershinin noted the annoyance in Popov's voice and replied, "They're not little princesses, Dmitrii Dmitrievich, but full-fledged pilots. And, like all the other pilots, they're going to fight against the enemy." Vershinin suggested that the women be gradually introduced into combat missions. "I'll do all that, comrade general," replied Popov, "but after all there's never been such a thing as women fighting in the air." Vershinin responded, "No, there hasn't, Dmitrii Dmitrievich. Therefore it falls to you to teach them combat work. And you're responsible for them, naturally."[24]

Popov decided that after demonstrating "lack of discipline" by scattering under the fighter "attack," the 46th should wait another two weeks before flying its first combat sortie in order to receive additional training. The women were "alarmed and chagrined"; after burning to get to the front for so many months, this was not the reception they had hoped for. Their own commissar felt it necessary to try to raise their spirits. "Don't lose heart, girls! We will have to prove in action that we can defend the homeland as well as the men."[25] First, however, they would have to prove themselves in training. The division navigator, a Major Nechepurenko, was sent from Morozovskaia to train the navigators on combat flying techniques, especially on how to maintain their orientation during very low altitude flights. Aronova reported that the women enjoyed practicing this sort of flying very much.[26] The regimental chief of staff, Irina Rakobolskaia, admitted that the unit had been hastily trained and sent to the front quickly due to military necessity, which resulted in "accidents caused by inexperience, and difficulties with military discipline." Rakobolskaia estimated that it took two to three months for the regiment to reach proficiency.[27]

After being inspected and double-checked on its flying proficiency, the regiment finally received its first combat mission in early June 1942.[28] Only three aircraft, flown by the regimental and squadron commanders, participated in that first sortie.[29] The 46th received another setback on this first mission: one of the aircraft failed to return. Its fate was not discovered until 1965, when the bodies of the crew were located. From local villagers it was learned that the women had been wounded by ground fire; they managed to land the aircraft, but both pilot and navigator died. The Germans, who occupied the area where the Po-2 landed, had searched the bodies for documents, then thrown them aside. They were later buried by the villagers.[30]

Despite this setback, the 46th was soon fully combat operational and flew many missions during the summer of 1942. General Vershinin noted the particularly dangerous nature of night bombing missions for the 218th Division (and thus the 46th Regiment) during this period.[31] This was, in many ways, the most difficult period of the war. The Germans had renewed their offensive and pushed deep into Russia, all the way to Stalingrad. Polina Gelman recalled the stress of that time, when it seemed that her country was in ruins:

> I remember a night when I flew with tears on my face. We were pushed back from the Ukraine to the Caucasus. We were bombing the advancing columns of German tanks. They were advancing so fast that we had not time to change bases. We didn't even have maps. It was August and September, we could not harvest grain, so they burned it. And so I was crying. Because it was my country and it was burning. This was the time they read Stalin's Order No. 227: not one more step back.[32]

The 46th went next to the North Caucasus Front, a particularly demanding area for flying. The mountainous terrain created dangerous up- and downdrafts; wind shear could crash an airplane. Mist and fog were constant hazards; three people were killed in one midair collision. Supplies were often difficult to obtain, and the food was monotonous. From September through December 1942, Annisovskaia was the main base of the 46th. Despite the challenges, the regiment performed well and was recognized on the anniversary of the Bolshevik Revolution. On 7 November, General Vershinin visited the regiment with the commander of the Transcaucasus Front, General Tiulenev, to present medals to ten women and commemorative watches to another thirty-two.[33]

Although the Po-2 carried only a light bomb load and could attack only light targets (troops, unarmored vehicles, and the like), most sources evaluate the night bombing raids as effective; in general, "harassment raids worked well" because they "forced the enemy on all fronts to take precautions, lose sleep, and on occasion suffer the loss of a storage area or fuel depot." The rugged reliability of the Po-2 and its basing right behind the front lines enabled it to maintain continuous harassment of German troops throughout the year, even in bad weather.[34] The Germans themselves admitted that it would be "wrong to underestimate the effects of the attacks, since they were so unpredictable and therefore were extremely disturbing . . . [they] reduced the already short rest of the troops and had an adverse effect on supply operations, although the actual physical damage done in the raids was small."[35]

One area of pride for the 46th veterans is the number of missions they performed. Because of the limited range of the aircraft, such regiments were based very near the front and could fly repeated missions, limited only by fatigue and the approach of daylight. On average, the Po-2 crews flew five to ten missions each night, with an occasional "maximum effort" of as many as fifteen missions a night.[36] For example, one archival report notes that even during the relatively short nights of August and September 1942, each aircrew averaged no fewer than five flights per night, with the majority of the crews making seven to eight flights per night; at times, the regiment completed eighty to ninety combat sorties in a night, or twelve to fifteen flights per crew.[37]

Rakobolskaia pointed out that it was seasonal darkness, more than the short duration of flights, that made it possible to achieve high sortie rates. "Each flight usually took 45–50 minutes. During the long winter nights we had 12–14 flights. The pilots were so tired they never even came out of the cockpit. In the winter they even brought hot tea to the aircraft." On an average night, the 46th might be ordered to perform 100 flights during the night. Rakobolskaia recalled that "325 was the maximum number of flights in one night."[38] When asked in a 1993 interview why the women went to such lengths to fly record numbers of missions, Rakobolskaia replied, "Out of enthusiasm. In order to prove that we could do anything."[39] Twenty years earlier, she had written that outperforming men was also a factor: "We were not content just standing on par with men's regiments. We had to constantly increase the daily number of sorties."[40]

When asked why the women drove themselves so hard, Polina Gelman replied, "The regiment was all-volunteer. Everyone was a patriot. Often they hadn't even completed a landing before they were already spoiling to carry out the next flight. The men even attempted to stop us, they said, 'the less you fly, the longer you'll live.' "[41] Veterans of the 46th felt that conditions were better in their all-female unit. Rakobolskaia commented, "I believe that women fight more effectively in a separate unit than together with men. The friendship is stronger, things are simpler, there is greater responsibility. I have talked a great deal with women who fought among men. It was more difficult for them than for us."[42] Gelman's statement about the number of combat flights she achieved (860 total) is also revealing about the combat motivation of the 46th personnel:

The Rodina *at Shchelkovsky Airfield before its 1938 flight. Left to right: Valentina Grizodubova, Polina Osipenko, Marina Raskova. (Courtesy Valentina Savitskaia-Kravchenko.)*

Marina Raskova, 1939. (Courtesy Valentina Savitskaia-Kravchenko.)

Marina Raskova (in white beret), 1939. (Courtesy Valentina Savitskaia-Kravchenko.)

Pilots of the prewar female aerobatics team (the piaterka). Left to right: Glukhovtseva, Beliaeva, Khomiakova, Popova, Prokhorova. (Courtesy Aleksandr Gridnev.)

Pilots Mariia Batrakova and Valentina Petrochenkova of the 586th IAP. (Courtesy Valentina Petrochenkova-Neminushchaia.)

Militsa Kazarinova (left) and Tamara Kazarinova (right). (Reprinted from Kazarinova, Kravtsova, and Poliantseva, V nebe frontovom, *2nd ed., 7, 279.)*

An example of the oversized men's clothing that was issued to the women aviators. (Courtesy Aleksandr Gridnev.)

Liliia Litviak. (Courtesy Inna Vladimirovna Pasportnikova.)

Po-2. *(Reprinted from Magid,* Gvardeiskii Tamanskii, *24.)*

Pilot Mariia Kuznetsova of the 586th IAP with mechanic Piotr Pshenichnikov (holding mirror) in 1944. (Courtesy Aleksandr Gridnev.)

Pilots of the 586th IAP in a dugout at Voronezh, 1943. (Courtesy Aleksandr Gridnev.)

Evdokiia Bershanskaia, commander of the 46th GvNBAP. (Reprinted from Magid, Gvardeiskii Tamanskii, *65.)*

Nina Raspopova (left) and Larisa Radchikova (right). (Reprinted from Magid, Gvardeiskii Tamanskii, 28, 33.)

Polina Gelman. (Courtesy Polina Gelman.)

Irina Rakobolskaia. (Reprinted from Magid, Gvardeiskii Tamanskii, *163.)*

Mechanics and armorers of the 46th GvNBAP. (Reprinted from Magid, Gvardeiskii Tamanskii, *103.)*

The 46th GvNBAP in September 1943, before the attack at Novorossiysk. (Reprinted from Kazarinova, Kravtsova, and Poliantseva, V nebe frontovom, *2nd ed., 197.)*

Opposite: Po-2 inscribed "To avenge our comrades: Tania Makarova and Vera Belik!" (Reprinted from Magid, Gvardeiskii Tamanskii, *225.) Above: Evdokiia Nikulina (left) and Evgeniia Rudneva by the prop of a Po-2. (Reprinted from Magid,* Gvardeiskii Tamanskii, *95.)*

Ground and air crews of a Pe-2, including Galina Brok-Beltsova (standing, last on right) and Antonina Bondareva-Spitsina (next to Brok-Beltsova). (Courtesy Valentina Savitskaia-Kravchenko.)

Valentin Markov, commander of the 125th GvBAP. (Reprinted from Kazarinova, Kravtsova, and Poliantseva, V nebe frontovom, *2nd ed., 90.)*

Valentin Markov (on right). (Courtesy Valentina Savitskaia Kravchenko.)

Valentina Kravchenko, regimental navigator for the 125th GvBAP. (Reprinted from Kazarinova and Poliantseva, V nebe frontovom, 1st ed., 61.)

Members of the 125th GvBAP. Valentina Kravchenko is fourth from the left. (Courtesy Valentina Savitskaia-Kravchenko.)

Pilot Mariia Lapunova (left) and navigator Nadezhda Vasil'eva in front of a Pe-2. (Reprinted from Kazarinova and Poliantseva, V nebe frontovom, 1st ed., 55.)

Without a break in the course of three years, without rest or leave, I flew on average 5–10 combat flights a night in the fire of ground batteries and in the blinding beams of searchlights. But that's the way it is in war. Whoever didn't want to be there could leave. There weren't any people like that in our regiment. Only the dying and the wounded left. And the wounded, after the hospital, even despite the protests of the doctor returned to the regiment and continued to fight and even to perish.[43]

Maintaining such a sortie rate inevitably took a toll on the aircrews. Even a single mission was stressful. Evgeniia Zhigulenko described the experience of attacking a German position at night: "There is a superhuman psychic overstrain when you are blinded by the searchlights and deafened by the explosions of antiaircraft shells and fire all around you."[44] This could lead to disorientation and even a crash if the pilot became unable to distinguish the ground from the sky. Larisa Litvinova-Rozanova also mentioned "overstrain" and disorientation, as well as physical discomfort: "we inhaled the gunpowder, choking and coughing, unable to breathe, from the anti-aircraft gunfire bursting around us." This could go on for fifteen minutes, for as long as the plane was caught by German searchlights.[45] And after the challenges of finding a target in enemy territory, navigating in the dark without the help of special instruments, and making an attack while avoiding the enemy response, aircrews still had to find their way home. Given the fact that the regiment moved frequently and utilized rough auxiliary fields to get close to the front, just returning after a mission was stressful. The regiment could not use bright landing lights to illuminate the field for fear of bringing in enemy attacks. Often the Po-2s had to land by the light of kerosene lanterns or headlights from vehicles. Rakobolskaia recalled that the pilots joked, "Soon we'll have to land by the light of the commander's cigarette."[46] Aronova recalled, "Even I find it difficult to believe sometimes that we, young girls, could endure such incredible stress in our combat work. Apparently, our moral strength was immeasurable."[47]

The stress manifested itself even when aircrews were supposedly resting. Mariia Smirnova recalled that aircrews often had trouble falling asleep after missions because of tension, as well as difficulty trying to sleep during the daylight hours while working at night. She remembered that "we slept two to four hours each day throughout the four years of the war."[48]

Larisa Litvinova-Rozanova also talked about the lack of sleep, which could cause pilots to fall asleep during missions. The need for sleep was so desperate, she said, that "we even had a kind of agreement between the pilot and the navigator that one of us would sleep going to the target and the other returning to the airfield." She believed that there were times when both members of an aircrew may have dozed off from sheer exhaustion. It was accepted practice in the Red Army, as in the United States, for military doctors to provide stimulants; Litvinova-Rozanova noted that "our doctor gave us pills nicknamed Coca-Cola to keep us awake," which could contribute to difficulties sleeping after a mission.[49]

Rakobolskaia explained a new method for maintaining and servicing aircraft that enabled the regiment to increase even further the number of flights it made. This was one of several innovations in the 46th:

> There is a regulation that says every mechanic and armorer had to service their own plane. So there would be a crowd at the airfield. It was dark. The mechanics tried to see if [each plane landing] was their own plane. Mechanics had to meet planes and help them to their hardstands. Mechanics had to hold the wing at the takeoff point.
>
> If each mechanic only worked on her own plane, we could only manage two flights per night. . . . And so we used groups of mechanics, each with a specialty. One met planes, another refueled. . . . Armorers worked in groups of three, and there were two such groups. The bombs weighed 50 kg. A truck from BAO unloaded bombs, an armorer had to unwind the lead and lift the bomb first on her knees, then under the wing. On the nights of maximum activity, each girl had to lift three tons of bombs. So we worked. It was not according to the regulations. But because of the better organizing of the work we managed to do more.[50]

Rakobolskaia described this new servicing system as a factory with a "well-functioning conveyor belt." It enabled the 46th to "turn" an aircraft (refuel and rearm it) in only five minutes—a major factor in achieving the high sortie rate of the regiment. Furthermore, according to Rakobolskaia, "in this way we began to win our secret competition with the men's regiments." Although the method produced excellent results, it was not adopted by other units. Rakobolskaia, as chief of staff, urged the regimental engineer to send a report on their method to the division, but the engineer was reprimanded for violating regulations on how to maintain

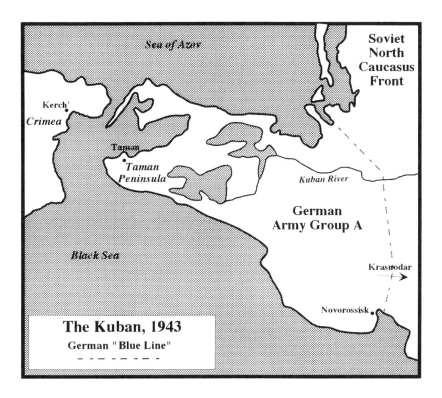

Map labels:
Sea of Azov
Soviet North Caucasus Front
Kerch'
Crimea
Taman
Taman Peninsula
Kuban River
German Army Group A
Black Sea
Krasnodar
Novorossisk

The Kuban, 1943
German "Blue Line"

aircraft. Nevertheless, the regiment continued to employ its unique servicing system throughout the war.[51]

The regiment was next transferred to the Kuban and based near Krasnodar through September 1943. The combat situation was intense, and the flights were demanding and hazardous. Extremes of weather and rough terrain continued to present challenges to the Po-2 pilots. In February 1943, in recognition of its success in combat, the regiment received its Guards appellation and was renamed as the 46th Guards Night Bomber Aviation Regiment.[52] Rakobolskaia said that "in our division at that time there was another regiment of Po-2 [which] did not receive Guards. Then we were transferred to another division where there were five regiments, four of them Po-2, and they also did not receive Guards throughout the war." When asked why the 46th was honored while the other units in these divisions were not, Rakobolskaia said, "We flew many more flights."[53]

There was no men's Po-2 regiment such as ours, in which there were so many Heroes of the Soviet Union—only in ours. Usually, there were 1–3 in a regiment, but we had 23, and the title of Hero by law was conferred if a pilot or navigator completed more than 500 combat flights—successful flights. Our Heroes, as a rule, had more than 700 flights. A. I. Sebrova was able to make 1,008 combat flights.[54]

Soon afterward, the unit began operations in the Crimea, where crews would take part in offensive operations in the breakthrough of the German "Blue Line" on the Taman peninsula and participate in the liberation of Novorossiysk. In April 1943, pilot Evdokiia Nosal' and navigator Irina Kashirina were performing a mission near Novorossiysk. Nosal' was considered an experienced pilot, with more than 353 combat flights. After dropping its bombs, the Po-2 was attacked by a German fighter, and Nosal' was shot in the head and killed. Kashirina, who had been retrained from mechanic to navigator not long before, managed to fly the aircraft back to the airfield. Nosal' was posthumously awarded the HSU medal—the first in the regiment.[55] Kashirina herself was killed in action not long after.[56]

Kashirina's performance reveals the way in which the 46th managed to maintain its exclusively female personnel during the war. Irina Rakobolskaia, the chief of staff, recalled, "We began ourselves to retrain our own personnel as replacements." The system arose almost by chance. "Because the Po-2 was a training aircraft, there were linked controls in both cockpits. Frequently on the return flight, the pilot allowed the navigator to practice flying. It was not difficult to retrain a navigator to be a pilot." The frequency of flights gave ample opportunity for retraining. When they realized that several navigators had become competent pilots, Rakobolskaia says that they devised a formal system: "First we retrained one or two people, then we organized a group. When we first went to the front, we had 112 people, two squadrons, each with ten aircraft. By the end, I don't know, about 300, no more. But then at the front when we became Guards, we had three squadrons, and we made a fourth squadron ourselves in order to do training."[57] Rakobolskaia explained, "We turned navigators into pilots, and trained new navigators from among the mechanics, and made armorers of the girl-volunteers who were just arriving at the front. Sometimes pilots arrived who had been trained in air clubs in the rear. The regiment flew combat missions at night, and the training groups worked during the day."[58] Zhigulenko, Meklin, and Rudneva were navigators who became pilots in this way.

The 46th was apparently able to acquire new recruits to fill the vacancies among the mechanics and armorers who were retrained. By this method, the 46th managed to create a third operational squadron within the regiment, which was required when it made Guards. Marina Chechneva was put in charge of the fourth training squadron, which provided replacements for crews lost in combat. This innovation in training was entirely self-generated. As Rakobolskaia recalled, "We never asked permission for this." They just did it because it seemed a sensible thing to do.[59] This "pipeline" of internal training helped the regiment cope with wartime casualties.

The worst single incident of casualties was on 31 July 1943, when the 46th lost four crews (eight people) to night fighters, which had not previously been encountered. Pilot Larisa Litvinova-Rozanova, who participated in that mission, recalled seeing the first Po-2 destroyed. "The strangest thing was that no antiaircraft shells were exploding in the air; the antiaircraft guns were silent, but still it was on fire."[60] Then a second Po-2 was caught in the searchlight, but still there was no fire from the ground. Litvinova-Rozanova remembered feeling "a bitter tickling in my throat" as she realized that, for the first time, the Germans were using night fighters. A third aircraft went down, and she was next in line. She continued to the target but dove to an extremely low altitude, lower than was a usual safe altitude for a bomb release. After dropping her bombs, Litvinova-Rozanova cut her engine and managed to evade detection by the enemy, starting up again only when she was dangerously close to the ground. The pilot who followed her in sequence to the target failed to grasp the situation and became the fourth victim. "That night we lost eight girls in ten minutes," said Litvinova-Rozanova. "For our whole wartime experience it was our worst, most horrible, tragic night."[61] Further missions were canceled that night, and by the next night, the regiment received support from Soviet night fighters.

Altogether, sixteen women died in the fighting over the Kuban and the Taman peninsula in the summer and fall of 1943.[62] Eight crews were detailed from late August to October 1943 to operate in conjunction with the Black Sea Fleet battalions, which were attempting to seize Novorossiysk. The women flew over and between sea and mountains in extremely rough air conditions. The rest of the regiment was flying in support of the fight to regain the Taman peninsula. In October 1943, the 46th was awarded the "Taman" appellation for its service in that area.[63]

Rakobolskaia described typical tactics used by the night bombers:

The Po-2 aircraft always flew alone on missions. They never flew in pairs. But they cooperated over the target. The time of flight from one crew to the next varied by 3–5 minutes. When each following crew approached the target, the crew flying before them was just circling the target for bombing. Usually the searchlights picked them up and the antiaircraft guns were firing. Then the second crew bombed the searchlights, and the first—the target. It was necessary to take into consideration that usually the aircraft went to the target at altitudes of 1,000–1,300 meters, cut the gas above the target and approached on a glide, so the noise of the engine was not audible, and the aircraft identification lights were not lit. They bombed from a lower altitude, but no lower than 400 meters, otherwise fragments from your own bombs might hit the aircraft—the speed was slow, the aircraft simply was not able to get away from them. Prior to bombing they threw out illuminating flares (SAB), which hung from parachutes and illuminated the target. After releasing the bombs, the pilot could descend [powerfully] and leave the target at very low altitude.[64]

Late in 1943, the 46th was transferred to the 2nd Belorussian Front under the command of Marshal Rokossovskii. Instead of flying in mountains and over the sea, the Po-2s now flew from such "runways" as streets and roads, open fields, and clearings in the woods. In the spring of 1944, the 46th supported the army offensive at Kerch.[65] Regimental engineer Klavdiia Iliushina described the confusing situation during this period: "First our troops were encircled, then they were not. The Germans and our troops were all mixed in close proximity." Iliushina recalled a particular morning when the aircrews were asleep in their tents as troops began to approach. Unable to identify the soldiers, the women pulled out their weapons and were prepared to fire on them, but the soldiers identified themselves as friendly just in time.[66]

In the early months of 1944, the regiment experienced some of its most trying missions, in support of amphibious operations in the Crimea. Evgeniia Zhigulenko recalled one terrifying flight when she attacked a German weapons storage area. Upon leaving the target, her aircraft was hit by antiaircraft fire, stalled, turned upside down, and recovered: "I called to my navigator to give me directions, but there was no reaction. I turned in my seat and to my horror found no navigator."[67] Zhigulenko was certain her navigator had fallen out of the aircraft during the stall and said, "I found myself whispering to my mama to help me." She managed to crash-land on the beach and, miraculously, found her navigator still alive. "While we were stalling, her seat had fallen to the bottom of the cabin, and her leg had stuck into the broken floor."[68]

By July 1944, the 46th was in northeast Poland. On 25 August 1944, pilot Tania Makarova and navigator Vera Belik were attacked by an enemy fighter as they tried to return to base; their aircraft caught fire and was consumed in flames before a forced landing could be made. One of their friends from the 46th, Larisa Litvinova, revealed some bitterness when she wrote, "If they had had parachutes, they could have been saved. But we flew the Po-2 without parachutes, preferring to take a few additional kilograms of bomb load. The only salvation in a situation like that was to get on the ground." The Po-2, made of wood and fabric, burned like a candle; once it caught fire, it was difficult to manage a landing before the airplane and crew were consumed.[69]

The crews of the 46th did not begin flying with parachutes until late 1944. It was believed that parachutes would rarely save anyone's life. Moreover, weight was always a major consideration in such a light aircraft; the Po-2 had to carry fewer bombs to accommodate the weight of parachutes. Rakobolskaia noted that "until 1944, we flew without parachutes. No one flew with parachutes in these aircraft before the war. The frame of mind was such that if you caught fire over enemy territory, it would be better to die than with the help of a parachute to be taken prisoner. And if you were damaged over our own territory, then you would be able to land the aircraft somehow."[70] Many veterans recalled that they would rather have died than be captured. Rakobolskaia also noted that even after they began carrying parachutes, only one person's life was saved. Navigator Rufina Gasheva and her pilot, Olga Sanfirova, both bailed out of a damaged Po-2. Unfortunately, their parachutes landed them in a minefield; Sanfirova was killed.[71]

September to December 1944 was a fairly slack time for the regiment, as there were no major army operations in their area to support. There were still occasional nights of "maximum" effort. On 26 December 1944, the regiment received notification that four more women had been awarded the HSU: Mariia Smirnova, Evdokiia Nikulina, Evdokiia Pas'ko, and (posthumously) Evgeniia Rudneva. According to a regimental album edited by Bershanskaia, the 46th lost a total of thirty-one people in the war, or approximately 27 percent of the total flying personnel assigned during the war.[72]

By January 1945, the 46th was in East Prussia. The final period of the war was one of heavy activity for the regiment, which supported the furious fighting in Poland. It was then rebased to Buchgoltz, northwest of Berlin, and supported the Soviet Army in its final push for the German capital. In August 1945, ten crews from the 46th were called to participate in the victory parade in Moscow, celebrating Air Force Day. The regiment was officially disbanded on 15 October 1945. The subsequent fate of its personnel is examined in chapter 7.

According to Polina Gelman, the 46th "was not only equal to the men's regiments according to effectiveness and other indices, but was among the first."[73] I asked her to explain what these indices were:

> The effectiveness was determined by the accuracy of the hits from bombing and shooting. After completing a mission everyone had to report his results and the results of others, as he saw them, what and where it happened. Crews from other regiments reported on our results, as did ground reconnaissance—in fact, we worked for them. It was easy to verify everything, everything was recorded: the number of combat flights, of bombs dropped, of rounds fired. . . . In the 4th Air Army our regiment was always first or among the first.[74]

Moreover, Gelman stated that "our regiment firmly held first place among all in the Air Forces for the number of flights."[75] She believes that "female thoroughness and sense of responsibility obviously played a role in this."[76] Other members of the 46th voice similar views. Senior Lieutenant Serafima Amosova-Taranenko related this comparison:

> On one airfield where we were stationed there were two regiments, one female and one male. We had the same missions, the same aircraft, and the same targets, so we worked together. The female regiment performed better and made more combat flights each night than the male regiment. The male pilots before a flight started smoking and talking, but the women even had supper in the cockpit of their aircraft.[77]

Eighteen pilots and six navigators of the 46th received the highest military honor, the Hero of the Soviet Union title—a far greater proportion than in the other women's regiments (the 125th received five HSU awards, the 586th none, and four women pilots in other units were awarded the HSU).[78] There are differing opinions as to why the 46th received such a disproportionate number of Hero awards. A number of veterans of other regiments believe that the commissar of the 46th, Rachkevich, had a great deal of influence and that many of the Hero medals were due to her efforts. At least one veteran of the 586th Fighter Aviation Regiment recognized that although there was a much better chance of receiving medals in the 46th, there was also a much greater risk of mortality. Irina Favorskaia recalled that Raskova offered her the chance to go to the Po-2s rather than to fighters, but she turned it down. "I didn't realize that if I had agreed to go I would either be dead, or I would be a Hero of the Soviet Union."[79] However, Gelman thought there were so many Heroes in the 46th because "this was the only regiment among the three . . . that was completely women, from the start to the finish. In the others, men also served." She also pointed out that "one of the fundamental criteria for the award was the quality and quantity of successful combat flights." She herself received the HSU, she said, for making 860 successful combat flights.[80]

Historian Von Hardesty assessed the performance of the 46th as comparable to that of other Po-2 regiments; in his view, they "made a significant impact on German troops by maintaining a sustained air presence over the battle zone."[81] General Boris Eremin agreed with this assessment. Chief of staff Irina Rakobolskaia noted that "nobody made any allowances for our youth or sex. They demanded from us nothing less than from a men's regiment."[82]

4

The 125th Guards Bomber

Aviation Regiment

❖ ❖ ❖ ❖ ❖ ❖ ❖ ❖ ❖ ❖ ❖ ❖ ❖ ❖ ❖ ❖

Unit designations:	587th Bomber Aviation Regiment (January 1943–23 September 1943)
	125th Guards Bomber Aviation Regiment (23 September 1943–1947)[1]
Honorary designations:	Guards; Borisovsky; Orders of Suvorov and Kutuzov III class; named for Hero of the Soviet Union Marina Raskova[2]
Dates of service:	January 1943–May 1945 (disbanded 29 February 1947)
Divisional subordination:	270 BAD/2 BAK, 223 BAD/1 GvBAK, 4 GvBAD/1 GvBAK, 5 GvBAK[3]
Primary areas of operation:	Stalingrad, Tambov, Vysedki, Borisoglebsk, Yezovnia, Orsha, Grislinen (Poland), Ponevezys
Commanders:	Marina Raskova, Valentin Markov
Aircraft flown:	Pe-2
Combat missions:	1,134 (980,000 tons of bombs dropped)
Heroes of the Soviet Union:	5

The 125th was the last of the three regiments to enter active service, primarily because the crews had trained on the Su-2 but were then equipped with the brand-new Pe-2 bomber at the last minute.[4] This formidable, top-of-the-line combat aircraft was the source of pride and a constant challenge to its crews. For example, navigator Galina Brok-Beltsova recalled a mission she flew late in the war, when the 125th and a "sister" regiment of male pilots were conducting sorties in East Prussia. It was decided to maximize the bomb load by reducing the amount of fuel on the aircraft, but the calculations were in error. Too much weight in an aircraft and too little fuel can make for a tricky takeoff, which Brok-Beltsova and her crew were about to experience firsthand. "A Pe-2 from a male regiment took off just before us, crashed into a hangar, and exploded, not being able to clear the hangar," Brok-Beltsova told an interviewer. "We were next in line to take off. You have to forbid yourself from thinking that your plane will end up the same way." The pilot, Antonina Bondareva-Spitsina, managed to get the plane off the ground, and the mission was completed successfully. Brok-Beltsova regarded this as "a victory—not over the German troops but over ourselves. You fight your own cowardliness."[5]

The Pe-2 was not only more difficult to fly than the Su-2 but also required a crew of three, rather than two. As was discussed in chapter 2, some men were assigned to the regiment as gunners, mechanics, and engineers.[6] Militsa Kazarinova was replaced as chief of staff of the 125th by a man in October 1943.[7] As in many similar bomber units, the regiment sustained heavy casualties, particularly during the winter of 1943–1944. Replacement crews brought the unit back to full strength in the summer of 1944, and the 125th participated in the great summer offensive that year. The regimental album does not list the names of casualties but mentions the deaths of twenty-two flying personnel, a rate of 22 percent, throughout the course of the war.[8] Archival materials indicate a higher casualty rate, listing a total of forty-six flying personnel lost during the war.[9] One veteran pilot told an interviewer in the early 1990s that forty-seven aircrew members in the 125th had died during the war.[10] One navigator regarded the casualty rate as somewhat lower than that in male regiments.[11]

The first commander of the 125th was Marina Raskova. Tragically, Raskova's command lasted only a few months; she never saw combat. This least known of Raskova's regiments started the war with a catastrophe, performed heroically for two and a half years, and ended in obscurity.

The 125th received orders in late November 1942 to join the 8th Air Army on the Western Front, but in attempting to reach its first operational base, it was repeatedly delayed by weather. The regiment left Engels on 1

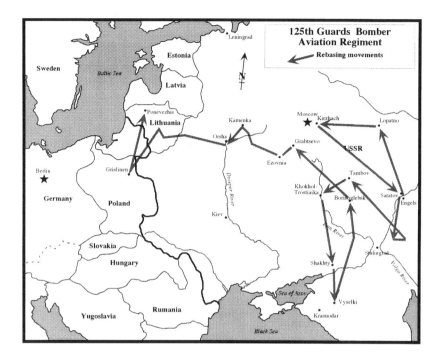

December 1942 and made what was supposed to be just an overnight stop but turned out to be a ten-day ordeal. The weather closed in and prevented all flying. The crews were housed in filthy dugouts; each morning, they rose before dawn, prepared the aircraft to fly, and hoped for a break in the weather. When no break appeared, the water was drained from the aircraft radiators to prevent freezing, and the crews were forced to sit out another day. Finally, on 10 December, the storm broke unexpectedly. When the regiment hurried to prepare its aircraft for flight, they discovered that the local airfield service battalion (BAO) support unit had failed to supply enough warm water to fill all the radiators. Only one squadron could take off; Nadezhda Fedutenko took the first squadron on ahead, while Raskova remained with Evgeniia Timofeeva's second squadron.[12] The winter storms settled in again the next day, grounding the second squadron for another ten days. Raskova, in the meantime, was called to Moscow for new orders. Raskova told Timofeeva to take off at the first opportunity and join Fedutenko's squadron. Upon arriving in Moscow, Raskova received orders reassigning her regiment to the Stalingrad Front. Both squadrons now in-dependently set out for the new base, but two aircraft with engine trouble were left behind at a transit airfield. Severe storms continued to ground the squadrons at various places en route to Stalingrad. In short, the situation was a real mess.[13]

Finally, on 28 December 1942, Timofeeva's second squadron landed at its front-line airfield; the staff and ground crews had already arrived by train. The 125th was assigned to the 270th Division of the 8th Air Army.[14] It was now the first squadron's turn to be stranded at an intermediate airfield. Ekaterina Migunova, the regimental chief of staff who was with the second squadron, wrote that they had no access to a radio or newspapers at their front-line base and had no news about either the first squadron or Raskova, who had gone to retrieve the aircraft with engine trouble.[15] Raskova had returned to the airfield where her own Pe-2 and the two aircraft with engine trouble were still waiting. The problem aircraft were repaired, and on the afternoon of 4 January, when there was finally a break in the weather, the three Pe-2s took off and set a course for Stalingrad. While they were en route, the storm closed in once more; visibility was quickly reduced to almost zero. Aleksandr Gridnev has suggested that Raskova should not have attempted the flight because the weather was worse than prescribed minimum conditions. However, a navigator who was with Raskova's group, Zina Stepanova, said that although there were reports of unpredictable weather, they had been informed by Moscow that their flight route was clear all the way to Stalingrad. They started out at an altitude of 1,900 meters, but after an hour and a half, conditions began to deteriorate, and they reduced their altitude to get below the clouds. By 4 P.M., the Pe-2s were down to 450 meters, and the clouds and fog had made visibility almost nil. The aircraft were separated from one another; unable to locate an airfield, and with darkness closing in, they had no choice but to try to land.[16] Two of the Pe-2s managed to make forced landings in a field, but Raskova's aircraft crashed, killing everyone aboard: Raskova, the regimental navigator (Kirill Il'ich Khil'), and Raskova's gunner (N. N. Erofeev), as well as a mechanic who was hitching a ride (V. I. Kruglov).[17]

It was two days before the wreckage was found.[18] The search plane that found Raskova's crash site was from the Yakovlev factory in Saratov; the factory's director, I. S. Levin, was Raskova's old friend, with whose family she had spent many happy hours. Levin himself called Moscow to convey the news, and he was directed to prepare Raskova's body, which would be sent by a special train to Moscow for interment in Red Square. The three other members of Raskova's crew (all male) were buried together in a common grave in Saratov.[19]

For ten days, the newspapers carried tributes, copies of speeches, and letters signed by people such as Stalin, Nikitin, and Grizodubova.[20] Nikitin and Shakhurin, who had given her so much support in creating the women's regiments, were among the pallbearers. Raskova's remains were interred by the Kremlin Wall; hers was reportedly the first state funeral of the war.[21] It was not until 9 January that the members of the 125th were informed of Raskova's death.[22] Valentina Kravchenko remembered, "Our commissar gathered us together in a big dugout and told us what had happened. We just cried. She truly affected our regiment. Maybe everything was different without her."[23] Her death was a severe blow to the regiment. If Raskova, one of the most famous and experienced women aviators in the country, could be killed in a crash, they had to question their own skills. Evgeniia Timofeeva, the deputy commander of the regiment, wondered whether "all the effort expended in mastering the complicated aircraft [was] in vain."[24]

The 125th was sitting at Karabidaevka, situated on the west side of the Volga River, south of Engels and east of Stalingrad.[25] Timofeeva awaited orders to proceed to a front-line airfield. A representative from the 8th Air Army arrived with orders for Timofeeva to take temporary command of the regiment and to prepare for a high-altitude mission.[26] She wrote that she was "literally stunned" at the thought of replacing Raskova and having to lead the regiment in its first combat mission. She wanted to refuse but thought to herself, "Such an answer could make headquarters think that with Raskova's death, the women's regiment had become pointless, and then they would disperse our collective to various units." And so she agreed. But many were concerned about "the fate of our orphaned regiment."[27] Timofeeva was in temporary command of the 125th from 15 January until 2 February 1943.[28] Kravchenko described Timofeeva's character: "She was very loved by everyone in the regiment. Timofeeva was a little older than the rest of us; she was already a mother. Her husband was at the front, and they left two children behind in Vinnitsa with a grandmother, but the town had been occupied by the Germans during the time Timofeeva went to Moscow [to join Raskova's group]."[29] Now Timofeeva had to add the stress of unexpectedly finding herself in regimental command to the ongoing fears about the safety of her family. Kravchenko said that Timofeeva appealed to Raskova's old flying partner from the 1930s, Valentina Grizodubova, and asked her to take over for Raskova, but Grizodubova never bothered to answer. "We didn't want a man as our commander," said Kravchenko. "We would even have accepted Grizodu-bova."[30]

The weather continued to be severe, with subfreezing temperatures. Timofeeva ordered the regiment to continue training. The 125th shared an airfield on the west bank of the Volga River, north of Stalingrad, with the 10th Leningrad Bomber Aviation Regiment (BAP).[31] According to Timofeeva, the 10th taught them to locate targets, maneuver against antiaircraft guns, and deflect attacks by enemy fighters.[32] Timofeeva stressed that there was excellent cooperation between the 10th and the 125th, but other members of the regiment recalled difficulties in gaining the acceptance of male pilots. Galina Ol'khovskaia, a squadron navigator, wrote that when they arrived at the front, they were met "with distrust in the division. The male pilots could not accept the idea that, just like them, some girls had mastered complicated equipment and would be able to complete any sort of combat mission." Even so, Ol'khovskaia claimed that the women were accepted after a few flights proved their abilities.[33]

On 20 January 1943, the VVS ordered the 125th transferred from the 8th Air Army to the control of the 16th Air Army.[34] The 125th's first mission was on 28 January 1943, during the Battle of Stalingrad. Two Pe-2s from the 125th were included in a nine-aircraft formation led by the 10th BAP.[35] Using the famous tractor factory as an orientation point, they successfully bombed their target. Someone jokingly referred to the male lead pilots as the "old men," a nickname that stuck. The 125th and the 10th continued to fly together until the end of the war. Three aircraft from the 125th were again included in another regiment's sortie on 29 January. On 30 January 1943, the 125th began flying combat missions independently, without "leaders" from the 10th.[36] During this period, the 125th's targets were enemy defensive positions, firing points, and troops in the northeastern region of Stalingrad, near the tractor factory.[37]

At this time, the 125th gained its second commander, Major Valentin Markov, an experienced pilot. Markov had already been commander of a bomber regiment and was recovering from battle injuries when he was reassigned to the 125th. He wrote that in January 1943, he was urgently called to Moscow by General A. V. Nikitin, the chief of the Main Directorate for Instruction, Formation, and Combat Training of the VVS.[38] Nikitin asked, "You know, of course, about the death of Marina Raskova; what if we assign you as commander of the women's dive bomber regiment?" When Markov hesitated, Nikitin said, "The order has already been signed." Markov did not, at the time, regard the reassignment as a good thing. Neither did his friends. As he left Nikitin's office, he met several old friends and told them about his new command; he said, "They looked at me with obvious pity."[39] He admitted that he was angry about the assignment and agreed with his friends, who predicted that he "would have to go through hell in that regiment."[40]

Markov arrived at the 125th on 2 February 1943. The regiment, which was now assigned to the Don Front, was on a mission when he arrived. As the aircraft returned, he noted that the women pilots landed correctly. He decided to inspect some of the airplanes. When he looked into one gunner's cockpit, he noticed that the machine guns were thickly covered in grease. "Who's the armorer?" he asked. "I am," said a girl, who ran up to the airplane smiling. "Quit smiling and explain why the machine guns are greased like this. They won't be able to fire." Tears filled the armorer's eyes. Markov, accustomed to military discipline, was nonplussed and hurried away. He decided to call a formation and gave the following speech:

> I am your new commander. I warn you that I will be holding you strictly accountable. There will be no sort of allowances made because you are women, so don't expect them. I ask you to make it a point to remember this. You, of course, have already fulfilled combat missions, but still too few to consider yourselves experienced fighters. We will begin with discipline.[41]

Many of the women remember that speech. Valentina Kravchenko, who later became Markov's navigator, told me that most of the women were angry and hostile to Markov. "He was tall and thin. We did not like him. He was so shy. . . . He was afraid to look at us."[42] They admitted that they had hoped the new commander would somehow be like Raskova, but "he was young, thin, and very stern in appearance," wrote Fedotova—so thin that, according to Kravchenko, "Behind his back we called him 'bayonet.' "[43] His warning, "We will begin with discipline," struck them like a blow; they thought their discipline was quite good. And when Markov implemented rules about things such as clean collars on uniforms and cleaning airplanes twice, Fedotova noted that "in our hearts we mutinied against the new commander."[44]

What is interesting about this reluctance to accept a male commander is the fact that the 125th was already integrated. As discussed in chapter 2, the unit received a number of male personnel when it was upgraded during training from the two-seat Su-2 to the three-seat Pe-2. Kravchenko commented on this situation, noting that "there were some men" in the regiment, mostly gunners on the aircrews, but "the pilots and navigators were all women," as well as the majority of ground personnel.[45] A total of seventy-five women flew in the 125th, but aside from the gunners, the only men who flew were Markov and a male navigator who arrived at the same time.

Markov then conducted intensive work with the staff and squadron commanders. His navigator, Nikolai Nikitin, was optimistic; he had talked with the navigators and thought that they were not badly trained. Markov, however, still had doubts about the ability of the women pilots to perform in combat. He began training them on formation flying; it was critical in Soviet bomber tactics to maintain a formation in which the defensive guns of the bombers gave optimal coverage for the group. Thus, for the twin-engined Pe-2, one of the most dangerous situations in combat was to lose an engine. Not only was the Pe-2 difficult to control on one engine, but its speed was reduced when only one engine was operating. This meant that the pilot would have trouble maintaining her place in formation, and without the protection of the formation, she would be vulnerable to enemy fighters. Markov also arranged for joint training with Soviet fighters in their spare time; the regiment was still flying missions over Stalingrad.[46] As time passed, Markov said that "sometimes, seeing how the girl armorers hung heavy bombs from the aircraft, how the mechanics prepared the airplanes at night, in snowstorms and frost, I thought: 'well okay, we men are supposed to do all this . . . but them?! They, who for the most part are still girls . . . how they must love our homeland!' "[47]

Interestingly, Kravchenko believes that Markov gained the trust of the regiment because he became more "like a woman." When asked to explain what she meant, she said that Markov had been advised by the regimental doctor, Ponomareva: "She was a good psychologist and knew how to talk to us. He never raised his voice to us but he did to the men. I think that she persuaded him not to yell at us, because we would resent it."[48] Eventually, the women changed his secret nickname of "the bayonet" to the public nickname of "Batia" (Daddy).[49] Gunner Antonina Khokhlova-Dubkova believed that "we survived the war because of our regimental commander" and his constant concern for the welfare of his crews. She says, "He chose routes so that we evaded the ground attacks of the anti-aircraft guns and also the German fighters; he knew the situation very well. He told us always to stick together."[50]

Markov, despite his initial misgivings, was later deeply proud of the performance of his regiment. He was especially pleased to hear how the commander of a men's bomber regiment at the same airfield chewed out pilots who had committed errors by saying, "What sort of landing was that you made today? Eh? Did you see how the girls landed? Just how does that make me look in front of them? It's a shame and nothing else!"[51] Kravchenko noted that Markov was aware that the women had to prove their abilities to their comrades, especially to the other regiments in their division: "Markov decided to arrange some training tests during a break in the battles, at Tambov. It was like a demonstration, so the men could see how we flew. Their attitude changed after that."[52] Markov himself pointed out that the senior commanders did not differentiate between the men's regiments and the women's. "The girls were proud of this," he wrote. "But, speaking frankly, sometimes I wished that the commanders had not forgotten that our regiment was women's, and that they would not throw us into the very thick of things."[53] Markov's assessment was that his regiment was treated the same as male regiments and given the same sort of combat assignments.[54] He noted, "During the war there was no difference between this regiment and any male regiments. We lived in dugouts, as did the other regiments, and flew on the same missions, not more or less dangerous."[55]

However, the women's attitudes toward men's regiments was not all one of competition. Pilot Mariia Dolina recalled that at one point, the 125th was stationed near a male air regiment; relations were so cordial that "about half our regiment made happy marriages with members of that regiment."[56] Dolina herself married a navigator from that unit; after his death in 1972, she reunited with the man who had been the armorer on her own crew and married him. "We had been through the hardships of war together so we knew each other well," she noted; "my friends told us that two broken hearts had been united."[57]

The 125th was transferred to the 223rd Bomber Aviation Division (2nd Bomber Aviation Corps) of the 4th Air Army on the North Caucasus Front and, from 27 April to 9 May 1943, also worked in conjunction with the 56th Army in the Crimea.[58] Markov regarded this period as the "main combat training" for the regiment due to heavy opposition from the Luftwaffe.[59] This required the regiment to use low-level bombing tactics, since dive-bombing would expose them to enemy aircraft. The regiment was typically based about fifty kilometers from the front lines; the Pe-2 carried enough fuel for missions of up to two and a half hours. The Pe-2 was one of the most sophisticated aircraft in the inventory, and the turn time between missions was one to two hours. This permitted each crew to fly two to three sorties per day. The pace was intense for both aircrews and ground personnel. Armorer Evgeniia Zapolnova-Ageeva recalled, "The flights could not be delayed even for one minute, because it was all coordinated with fighter regiments that escorted the bombers."[60] This meant that ground crews had to work at the same pace, regardless of the weather. Zapolnova-Ageeva noted that at times, such as during the Battle of Stalingrad, temperatures were far below freezing, and since some work had to be done with bare hands, there were cases of frostbite; at other times, such as in the Kuban, the heat was so severe that touching the metal parts of the aircraft caused burns.[61] Another armorer, Anna Kirilina, said that her job entailed mounting and arming ten bombs of 100 kilograms each to the aircraft for each mission. She too recalled getting frostbite and hiding it to avoid being sent to the rear.[62]

On 4 May 1943, the 125th received its honorary designation, "named for HSU Marina Raskova."[63] From 24 May to 2 July, it supported the 37th Army in the North Caucasus. During this period (April through July 1943), the 125th was based near Krasnodar. Four people were wounded and two were killed, including one air fitter (technician), who apparently was ambushed by "Vlasov's bandits."[64] In this period, a regimental album noted, the 125th engaged in six air battles, shot down five enemy fighters, and lost five Pe-2 aircraft.[65] The album reprinted an information bulletin from the 4th Air Army describing an air battle on 2 June 1943. Timofeeva was leading a nine-ship formation, one of three "niners," in a group attack. Cloud cover forced the bombers to descend to 1,000 meters, separating them from their fighter escort. During the target run, Timofeeva's group was attacked by eight Me-109s; they managed to shoot down four. They credited this achievement to their strict adherence to maintaining formation and following the plan of fire they had practiced. This engagement was considered significant enough to be highlighted in the official history of the 4th Air Army.[66]

From 19 July 1943 to 20 June 1944, the 125th was part of the 223rd Bomber Aviation Division and was based at airfields near Grabstevo, Ezovnia, and Ivanevo and participated in the battles of Kursk and Smolensk. Two crews (six people) were lost to antiaircraft fire, one on 28 August and one on 22 October 1943; four more personnel were listed as dead by December.[67] On 9 September, an aircraft was shot down and the crew bailed out; pilot A. S. Egorova landed safely and returned to the regiment, but navigator N. D. Karaseva and gunner A. P. Kudriantsev were captured by German troops.[68] Two technicians were killed during this period in the crash of a Douglass transport.[69] On 17 September, pilot K. Ia. Fomicheva and navigator G. P. Turabelidze were wounded and their gunner killed; Turabelidze's injuries were so severe that she was invalided out of service.[70] Casualties were severe enough to cause someone in VVS to send some replacements. Pilot Antonina Bondareva-Spitsina noted that she had been stuck as a flight instructor all this time and was finally allowed to join Raskova's units in 1943, when she was sent to the 125th.[71]

On 7 September 1943, while still assigned to the 1st Air Army on the Western Front, the unit was redesignated from the 587th to the 125th Guards Bomber Aviation Regiment; at the same time, the 223rd Bomber Aviation Division was redesignated the 4th Guards Bomber Aviation Division, and its parent unit, the 2nd Bomber Aviation Corps, became the 1st Guards Bomber Aviation Corps.[72] Kravchenko noted that the 125th was second regiment in its division to be named Guards; one male regiment in the division had become Guards earlier, and the third did so after the 125th was designated.[73] The 125th would remain assigned to the same division for the duration of the war, although the division would be reassigned to other air armies on various fronts.[74]

One compelling story of self-sacrifice in the 125th is that of Liuba Gubina. On 14 October 1943, the 125th was flying a mission near El'nia in the usual nine-ship formation when Gubina's aircraft lost an engine to antiaircraft fire. Unable to maintain airspeed and altitude, Gubina was forced to drop out of the main formation, but her two wingmen stayed with her. They were attacked by Messerschmitts; one Pe-2 caught fire, and the crew was forced to bail out. The pilot and navigator of a second Pe-2 were killed, although the gunner escaped. Gubina's aircraft was attacked and badly damaged. She ordered the navigator and gunner to bail out, but the navigator's parachute harness snagged a machine gun turret; she hung from the aircraft, trying to free herself. The Pe-2 was spiraling toward the ground, with little control left, but the pilot stayed at the controls, jerking the control stick until her navigator was able to slip free. By this time, Gubina was too low to bail out herself, and she crashed with her airplane.[75]

Like most regiments, the 125th had one or two light aircraft (usually Po-2s or similar types) in addition to its combat aircraft, used to transport the staff and to serve as communications and ambulance aircraft. In the 125th, it was Galina Chapligina's job to fly as "liaison pilot" in the Ut-2, an open biplane like the Po-2 but of somewhat newer design.[76] Kravchenko recalled, "Chapligina had a very special position in our regiment. When one of our planes had been shot down, she went there and looked. She brought back bodies or pieces of bodies. . . . She was a master of her plane, she could land anywhere. She could have been a combat pilot."[77] Chapligina had more work doing body retrieval than she thought she could bear at times.[78]

In April 1944, the regiment received personnel reinforcements to replace the casualties. Nine flight crews arrived, all women who had been trained in the 3rd Reserves at Ioshkar-Ola by a female instructor pilot, one Senior Lieutenant G. Bel'tsova.[79] In June, the 125th joined the 5th Guards Bomber Aviation Corps (GvBAK) of the 16th Air Army on the 3rd Belorussian Front; it was subsequently based at Shel'ganovo, Kamenka, and Balbasovo. During a 23 June 1944 mission, one Pe-2 was shot down; pilot Klavdiia Fomicheva and navigator Galina Dzhunkovskaia managed to bail out, although they sustained burns, but the gunner was killed.[80] On 10 July 1944, the regiment received the honorary name "Borisovsky" for its participation in the capture of the city of Borisov.[81] From 22 July to 29 December 1944, the 125th remained with the 5th GvBAK but was transferred to the 1st TransBaltic Front, where its main targets were enemy troops, tanks, and artillery. During missions on 24 July, pilot E. M. Maliutina and navigator E. V. Azarkina were severely wounded; navigator E. V. Guruleva received a light wound. All three returned to the regiment after treatment.[82] The official history of the 16th Air Army noted the contribution of the 125th during this period and made special mention of Fedutenko, Fomicheva, Zubkova, Dolina, and Maliutina. It also mentioned that members of the 125th, together with other regiments, assisted in the harvest in Lithuania in September 1944 in their off-duty time.[83]

Although the tide of the war had turned in 1944 and the Red Army was on the offensive, aircrews were far from complacent. Some of the heaviest fighting of the war occurred in this period as the Soviets began advancing into enemy territories. Navigator Evgeniia Guruleva-Smirnova recalled her fears:

What I feared most on flying missions was being captured by the fascists. We were also afraid of being punished for not fulfilling a combat mission. We couldn't turn around and go back without completing the mission. If we didn't complete our assignment, we could be imprisoned.[84]

Punishments were not uncommon. Armorer Ekaterina Chuikova stated that she had been arrested during the war and noted, "There was hardly a person who was not arrested at some time," usually for conducting black-market exchanges with local peasants. Chuikova said they used to trade some of the men's underwear they were issued for potatoes or milk, finding the latter items more useful. But she was caught once by the regimental commissar and spent three days in the guardhouse.[85]

Gunner Antonina Khokhlova-Dubkova recalled a particularly gruesome incident in this period. It was during a large attack involving aircraft from both the 125th and another Pe-2 regiment. Dubkova's aircraft was hit, but the pilot managed to land in a small clearing. Dubkova says:

The other plane that was on fire was flown by the men's crew. Probably they were conceited young boys not very well trained—they couldn't make it the last one hundred meters to that open space where we landed. They crashed in the forest and burned before our eyes. Because there was no one else around, we had to pick up their remains: one arm, one leg, all smoked and roasted. I thought I would never look at any meat after that. Well, life is life. So we collected the remains of that crew, all three of them, torn apart. No heads, all apart. We gathered them together. There was a parachute intact, so we ripped the parachute apart, covered the remains, and buried them.[86]

During the winter of 1944, the 125th conducted repeated raids on Libava in the Baltic. On 22 December 1944, a German fighter shot down a Pe-2; the gunner (Absaliamova) escaped by parachute, but the pilot and navigator (Matiukhina and Kezina) were killed. At first the crew's fate was not known; Absaliamova landed among artillerymen, and it took her several days to return to the regiment. She then reported that their Pe-2 had been on fire when the pilot ordered her to jump out. The bodies of the pilot and navigator were not discovered for another twenty years.[87]

The 125th (still part of the 5th GvBAK) fought on the 1st Pribaltic and 3rd Belorussian Fronts from January to May 1945, in western Prussia.[88]

During the latter part of the war, the 125th flew in conjunction with the famous French Normandie-Nieman fighter regiment, which applauded the women's courage and performance. On 19 February, the 125th was awarded the Order of Kutuzov.[89] On 18 April 1945, an armorer was killed in an accident. The 5th GvBAK was transferred once more, to the Leningrad Front, for operations with the 15th Air Army in the Baltic during the final week of the war.[90] Six members of the regiment were awarded medals in June 1945 for the capture of Konigsberg.[91] On 28 May, the regiment was awarded the Order of Suvorov.[92] All five women who received the Hero of the Soviet Union (three pilots and two navigators) were awarded that medal on 18 August 1945.[93] Markov later expressed regret that so few of his aviators received the HSU. When he learned how many members of the 46th had received the award, he said that if he could do it over again, he would recommend many more of his personnel for the HSU.[94]

After the war, crews from the 125th participated in some of the big victory parades. Ten crews were trained in early June 1945 at Monino airfield near Moscow for the air show that took place on 24 June.[95] Ten crews (probably the same ten) also flew in air shows in Kazan' and Belgrade, Yugoslavia. Markov was reassigned sometime in early 1945, and the command of the 125th changed hands at least twice in the next two years, first to Semen Titenko and then to F. I. Liakh.[96] The regiment was not formally disbanded until 28 February 1947. Some of the women continued on active duty with the regiment up to that point, although the regiment was reduced to about half strength in 1946.[97]

Markov remained in the VVS and attained the rank of lieutenant-general of aviation before his retirement.[98] Markov married one of the 125th navigators, Galina Dzhunkovskaia, after the war. Although they fell in love at the front, their relationship was not openly acknowledged. Of course, most people in the regiment realized that the two were in love. But when Kravchenko was asked about the effects of the relationship between Markov and Dzhunkovskaia, she mused, "Did it disrupt the work? No, of course not. I think they tried even harder to show each other how well they worked."[99]

Markov's ultimate assessment was that "the women in my regiment were self-disciplined, careful, and obedient to orders . . . they never whimpered and never complained and were very courageous. If I compare my experience of commanding the male and female regiments, to some extent at the end of the war it was easier for me to command this female regiment. They had the strong spirit of a collective unit."[100]

5

The 586th Fighter Aviation Regiment

❖ ❖ ❖ ❖ ❖ ❖ ❖ ❖ ❖ ❖ ❖ ❖ ❖ ❖ ❖

Unit designations: 586th Fighter Aviation Regiment
Honorary designations: none
Dates of service: 16 April 1942–May 1945
Divisional subordination: 144 IAD, 101 IAD, 9 IAK[1]
Primary areas of operation: Saratov, Voronezh, Kostornaia, Kursk, Kiev,
                             Zhitomir, Kotovsk, Bel'tsy, Debrecen,
                             Budapest (Hungary)
Commanders: Tamara Kazarinova, Aleksandr Gridnev
Aircraft flown: Yak-1/7b/9[2]
Combat missions: 4,419 (38 enemy aircraft destroyed in 125 air
                             battles)
Heroes of the Soviet Union: none

In April 1943, two Soviet fighter pilots, Raisa Surnachevskaia and Tamara Pamiatnykh, engaged a group of forty-two German bombers and shot down four. Pamiatnykh and Surnachevskaia were scrambled to intercept two enemy reconnaissance aircraft. When they reached the patrol area, they discovered instead two groups of German bombers—forty-two aircraft in all. Their regimental commander, who was in the command post when they radioed for instructions, said, "What was there to do? I got on the radio and commanded them, 'Attack!' "

Attack they did. Driving a wedge into the German formation, the pilots managed to scatter the bombers, forcing them to drop their bombs well short of target. Moreover, each woman shot down two enemy bombers.

The target of the German attack, a rail junction crowded with Soviet troops and fuel supplies, remained unscathed. "Some representatives from Great Britain saw all of this," wrote Aleksandr Gridnev, their commander. "They reported it to the King of England, and he sent the girls inscribed gold watches. But our own people never even found the time to give them the [gold star of the] Hero of the Soviet Union medal. I believe this is one of the most distinguished victories of the entire war. They should hang two gold stars on each of them for this."[3]

The pilots of the 586th Fighter Aviation Regiment received little recognition either in their own time or from history. In its ranks, the 586th included some of the best pilots the Soviets had to offer. Three members of a well-known prewar women's aerobatic team, which performed before crowds of thousands at Tushino Airfield in Moscow, flew with the regiment during the war: Raisa Beliaeva, Valeriia Khomiakova, and team leader Evgeniia Prokhorova.[4] Fighter aces Liliia Litviak and Katia Budanova were first assigned to the 586th before transferring to another regiment. However, the history of the 586th is the source of disagreements and disputes. Controversies focus on the capabilities and reasons for dismissal of its first commander, Tamara Kazarinova; the circumstances surrounding the deaths of all the women just mentioned; and the reasons for its failure to achieve Guards status or to receive a single Hero of the Soviet Union award.[5]

The 586th Fighter Aviation Regiment served from April 1942 through May 1945 as part of Fighter Aviation of the Air Defense Force of the Soviet Union (IA/PVO). Flying modern Yak-series fighter aircraft, the unit completed more than 9,000 flights, of which 4,419 were combat sorties; 38 enemy aircraft were destroyed and 42 damaged in 125 air engagements. The 586th Fighter Aviation Regiment was assigned to protect fixed targets such as airfields, cities, and transportation nodes from enemy attacks. The regiment supported the Battle of Stalingrad (sending some of its pilots to augment all-male fighter regiments) and performed air defense duties at Voronezh, Kursk, Kiev, Debrecen, Budapest, and Vienna.[6] The regiment was most active during the middle period of the war, especially while based near Voronezh and Kursk. During the first and last months of its existence, the 586th was based in areas where enemy activity was relatively light.[7] By 1944, the Luftwaffe had increasing difficulty mustering forces to attack the fixed targets defended by PVO regiments.[8] Although the 586th began the war with all female pilots, it later included male pilots as well: women and men flew and fought side by side in the 586th.

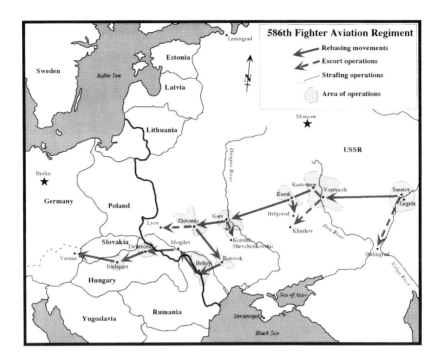

The first commander of the 586th was Major Tamara Aleksandrovna Kazarinova, one of two Kazarinova sisters who served in the aviation regiments. It was under her command that the 586th began its active service on 16 April 1942 as part of the 144th Fighter Aviation Division of IA/PVO.[9] Her command was brief—just over six months—a fact that is often not evident from the published sources. She did not evoke the sort of loyalty that Marina Raskova received, but many veterans of the 586th still credit Kazarinova with trying her best. By most accounts, Kazarinova was not a very likable person. Unlike the popular Raskova, she was stiff and severe. Kazarinova was strict, harsh, and cold—traditionally "masculine" in her style.

Aleksandra Makunina, the 586th chief of staff who worked closely with Kazarinova, recalled that "we kept a distance between us. [Once I received an] urgent order . . . about a combat mission . . . and went to her to report. I had to confirm with her which particular crews should go on this mission. She told me 'next time make your own decision.' " Kazarinova never permitted conversations about personal matters. "Though we spent a lot of time together at the command post, I was always afraid to ask her personal questions. I didn't even try to ask. She wouldn't permit it," Makunina said in a 1993 interview. "I knew nothing about her personal life. Yes, she was a lonely woman. Maybe because of this she was so strict. She never asked me anything about my life, or whether I received letters from home."[10]

Mechanic Elena Karakorskaia expressed a somewhat different opinion: "I knew Kazarinova well. She was very strict and severe in appearance, but nobody knew how sweet she was. She knew every girl in the regiment and she spoke so well about everyone. Raskova valued her very highly. She had some quarrels with Raskova because she thought that Raskova was letting girls into combat too early. Kazarinova thought there should be more training."[11] During the same interview, Chief of Chemical Services Nina Slovokhotova disagreed, saying, "She was too strict. Maybe because she wasn't a Party member . . . Kulikova [the commissar] hated her."[12]

All accounts agree that Kazarinova rarely, if ever, flew after she took command. Some pilots believed that it was because she was incapable of flying a high-performance aircraft like the Yak fighter. According to published accounts, the reason was that she had injured her leg during an air raid and the wound had never healed properly. For example, Makunina wrote in an official history that in the fall of 1942 "Kazarinova's health got worse. The unhealed wound made itself felt. Tamara Aleksandrovna began to limp a little more and stopped flying."[13] In a 1993 interview, Makunina confirmed that Kazarinova was indeed physically unable to fly:

> She could not fly in fighters because she was wounded in the leg while she was in the Caucasus. . . . Yes, I saw the blood on her leg. I once came to her in the morning and knocked because I had something urgent to report. I apologized because I saw her without one boot on, and there was blood on her foot. She always covered it up, but she walked with a limp. I remember that I asked her if I could help her with anything, should I call the doctor? She said, don't pay attention to this, it's a trifle.[14]

Whatever the reasons, the fact is that Kazarinova did not fly her own regiment's aircraft. Considering that the most experienced pilots had been sent to this regiment, it seems obvious that they would be uneasy about taking orders and receiving their training from someone who did not understand the airplane. Kazarinova's successor, Aleksandr Gridnev, has raised many questions concerning Kazarinova's character and abilities. For one thing, Gridnev claimed that Kazarinova was linked with the commander of the IA/PVO, General Osipenko (husband of the late Polina Osipenko), and Gridnev had a very unfavorable view of both of them:

Fighter Aviation of PVO was headed by General Osipenko, who was illiterate in all regards, especially in respect to tactical flying questions, as he did not fly fighter aircraft himself. He had, however, received the Order of Lenin in 1937. And when the 586th Fighter Aviation Regiment was formed, Osipenko placed Tamara Kazarinova in command of this regiment, who was completely ignorant regarding tactical flying and did not fly fighters, but who had also been awarded, in 1937, just like Osipenko, the Order of Lenin. For what were such high honors given? After all, there weren't any real accomplishments in aviation in 1937. They awarded it only for denunciations, for the exposure of "enemies of the people."[15]

For nine and a half months, from 24 April 1942 through 10 February 1943, the 586th was based at Anisovka near Saratov. During this period, the regiment conducted 509 combat sorties, 32 of them at night.[16] But all was not well with the 586th. Gridnev asserted that Kazarinova was at odds with her squadron commanders right from the start (information he claims to have received from the squadron commanders themselves—all of whom were killed in action during the war). Gridnev stated that it was the most experienced and skillful pilots in the regiment, including those who had flown on the prewar women's aerobatic team, who most strenuously opposed Kazarinova: "Prokhorova, Beliaeva, and Khomiakova . . . immediately became enemies with the commander, who didn't know how to fly a fighter. They clashed, and those three pilots demanded that the commander be changed."[17]

According to Gridnev, the dissatisfaction within the regiment became severe enough to involve the division commander, a Colonel Starostenko. There were some in the regiment who supported Kazarinova, though Gridnev said that Evgeniia Prokhorova called them "toadies" whose loyalty was based on self-protection. The division commander tried to appease both sides by calling an official conference of the party members and activists in the regiment, but according to Gridnev, he was unable to achieve a reconciliation. Gridnev said that the pilots of the first squadron (Raisa Beliaeva, Ekaterina Budanova, Liliia Litviak, and Klavdiia Nechaeva) were especially vocal in their opposition, along with the second squadron commander and her deputy (Prokhorova and Valeriia Khomiakova). Gridnev wrote that "all of them requested that Kazarinova be removed from the regiment as not being suitable for filling the position. But the division commander did not have the authority to remove a regimental commander from her post and he reported the 'incident' to the IA/PVO command."[18]

For the time being, Kazarinova remained in command. On 10 September 1942, she sent eight pilots from the first squadron of the 586th to Stalingrad as replacements for aviation regiments there that had endured heavy casualties. Four of those pilots returned to the 586th within a few months, but Nechaeva was killed at Stalingrad, and Litviak, Budanova, and Antonina Lebedeva continued to serve in various men's regiments (all three were killed in action during the summer of 1943).[19] There was something odd about the transfer of these pilots. Why would half the pilots of a brand-new women's regiment suddenly be sent away? Raskova was still alive, and she always fought to keep the women together. Moreover, the 586th was part of the PVO. Why were pilots pulled from this air defense unit to reinforce VVS front-line regiments? Even stranger was the fact that one group was sent to a regiment that did not even fly the same model fighter, which created difficulties in support and rearmament.[20]

Gridnev claimed that the idea was Osipenko's. He believes that after receiving Starostenko's report of the complaints about Kazarinova, "General Osipenko found a 'fitting' way out of the situation that had developed . . . under the pretext of rendering assistance to Stalingrad, he sent from the regiment the entire "rebelling" squadron of Beliaeva, in their brand new airplanes, with their maintenance personnel, to Stalingrad."[21] This not only removed the troublemakers from the 586th, but also split them from one another: "From the time they landed, the squadron was divided and sent to different regiments, and there was no squadron anymore."[22] Ironically, some of these women went on to become the best-known female fighter pilots of the war, even achieving ace status. Sending them away from the 586th gave them the chance to get into front-line fighting, but their accomplishments were credited to their new regiments and not to the 586th. During the Battle of Stalingrad, Litviak became the first woman in the world to shoot down an enemy aircraft. When the other women later returned to the 586th, Litviak and Budanova (and their ground crews) asked to remain with their new unit. Litviak went on to achieve twelve personal kills plus three shared kills before her death in air combat in August 1943; she was posthumously awarded the Hero of the Soviet Union.

In the meantime, Valeriia Khomiakova, who stayed with the 586th at Anisovka, became the first woman in the world to shoot down an enemy aircraft at night. On 24 September 1942, she destroyed a Ju-88 bomber over

Saratov—in a nighttime engagement on her first combat patrol.[23] This is the first official kill credited to the 586th.[24] Less than two weeks later, Khomiakova was dead—killed during a night flight on 5 October 1942. The circumstances of the untimely death of the first pilot in the 586th to score a kill were never explained in published materials. For example, Raisa Aronova noted in the 1980 edition of her memoirs that "the circumstances of [Khomiakova's] death to this time remain not entirely clear, as far as I know."[25] Only recently did some veterans of the 586th agree to discuss the incident.

Khomiakova had been sent to Moscow on 29 September to receive recognition for her achievement in shooting down the German night bomber. She was interviewed by magazines and newspapers and met with the Soviet president, M. I. Kalinin. When she arrived back at Anisovka at few days later, she was fatigued from the long journey, Polunina recalled, but she was immediately assigned to night alert duty anyway.[26] Karakorskaia recalled that Khomiakova "was very tired, and I could not believe she had been appointed to duty. We had a very bad doctor at the regiment; he was also to blame. I could not believe Kazarinova [put her on alert]."[27] Gridnev related the details of Khomiakova's death, which he said he had heard from Prokhorova:

> [Khomiakova] is sitting in the cockpit, strapped in. The engine is warm and ready for immediate start. The radio is checked and the ammunition is ready. So what did Kazarinova do? . . . Kazarinova put [the mechanic] Polunina into the plane and said, "let the pilot rest in the dugout." The pilot went into the dugout and went to sleep. Then there was the signal to take off. Polunina started the engine, someone ran to the dugout to wake up the pilot, who ran to the plane, jumped in, and then took off. But her vision wasn't adapted to the darkness. The night was dark and she could not see. She took off blindly and she could not see the direction. There were no guidance lights in the direction of takeoff. So she could not hold the direction and she crashed into an obstacle, crashed and died.[28]

Several veterans agreed with these basic facts of the story. At the very least, the veterans agreed that Kazarinova demonstrated extremely poor judgment in this matter. What Gridnev found astonishing was that there was no investigation of the accident. "Prokhorova raised her voice against Kazarinova about this and demanded that she be brought to account. The other pilots were silent." Gridnev said that "they wrote it up as if the death occurred in battle. They made the case as a combat loss, and such losses were not investigated. And so they could not be blamed legally."[29] Even so, according to Gridnev, "General Gromadin removed Kazarinova after that, and ordered Osipenko to bring her to investigation . . . Osipenko put Kazarinova on his staff, but she should have been imprisoned because of the accident, because she was responsible for the death of Khomiakova. But Osipenko took her, half-secretly, nobody knew about this, to the staff."[30] Makunina confirms that Kazarinova was recalled to Moscow to work on the staff of the PVO.[31] Some of the other veterans also believe that Kazarinova was considered to be at fault for the accident. For example, even Polunina said that "Kazarinova and Kulikova were both punished after the death of Khomiakova, but Kazarinova was removed and Kulikova was not."[32] This is in contradiction to the published sources—including one written by Makunina (but edited by Militsa Kazarinova, the sister of Tamara Kazarinova)—which state that Kazarinova was removed from command for health reasons.[33] It seems apparent that Kazarinova was lacking in military judgment and would not have made a good wartime commander.

After Kazarinova was removed, a Major Beliakov was appointed temporary commander of the regiment.[34] The regiment was initially composed of two squadrons; a third squadron of male pilots was added in the fall of 1942. Many aviation regiments were being expanded from two to three squadrons at this time as aircraft production began to increase; in addition, the 586th was still short a full squadron of pilots who had been sent to Stalingrad.[35] Little has been written about the men who served in the 586th. As Gridnev noted, "They fail to mention the men's squadron. It is as though it was never in the regiment at all."[36]

Major Aleksandr Gridnev, former commander of the 82nd Fighter Aviation Regiment, became the second commander of the 586th. Gridnev had a checkered past, as far as the NKVD (the predecessor to the KGB) was concerned: he had been arrested twice—once in 1937, and again in 1942. The 1937 arrest was in connection with the "Tukhachevsky affair." Gridnev's father had known Tukhachevsky (a hero of the Russian Civil War who was a victim of the 1937 purges), and Gridnev himself had kept a picture of the famous marshal. Gridnev was not convicted but was released back to active duty with a black mark on his record.

The second arrest was more serious. According to Gridnev's memoirs, he was never convicted of wrongdoing in his second arrest either, although he endured a lengthy investigation. On 13 August 1942, while he was with the 82nd Fighter Aviation Regiment in Baku, he was directed to prepare a ten-fighter escort for a special transport plane carrying an important passenger. Gridnev took nine pilots to Krasnovodsk the next evening and awaited orders. The following morning, he received orders from General Osipenko to accompany a transport to the island of Mayak. Gridnev and his pilots were put on cockpit readiness and waited for the arrival of the transport. As they waited, a dust storm blew up, of the sort locally called an "Afghanets." By the time the Li-2 carrying the VIP arrived, visibility had been dangerously reduced. Gridnev wrote that to carry out the escort flight "would have been suicide, because the aircraft were sure to collide." The fighters themselves could endanger the transport if they attempted to maintain formation under those conditions. Gridnev decided to fly a solo escort, to reduce the chance of a midair collision. But as he taxied to the takeoff point, the garrison commander ran out and forbade him to fly. The Li-2 pilot did not wait for the escort but continued on his route. Back at the command post, the garrison chief read Gridnev an order, signed by Stalin, forbidding flights in the Krasnovodsk area during Afghanets conditions due to previous accidents.

The storm cleared by evening, and Gridnev and his pilots returned to Baku, where Gridnev was immediately arrested (along with his corps commander, Colonel I. G. Puntus). He was accused of purposefully endangering the life of the chief of the NKVD, Lavrenty Beria—the VIP passenger who had been on board the Li-2 transport. They charged that Gridnev was attempting to gain revenge for Tukhachevsky and that he had tried to take off by himself in order to shoot down the transport without witnesses. Puntus was accused of being Gridnev's accomplice. Gridnev remained in jail from mid-August until mid-October; he said that the investigation consisted of repeated late-night interrogations and "involved the use of force." But Gridnev had supporters, who gathered proof that his refusal to fly had been justified and in accordance with Stalin's orders. General-Colonel Gromadin, the PVO commander and Osipenko's superior, supported Gridnev and Puntus. They were finally released "on probation," and Puntus was assigned to the 102nd Fighter Aviation Division while Gridnev received the command of the 586th. But Gridnev claimed that Osipenko was bent on harming him; after all, Osipenko was the one who had accused Gridnev in the first place. Gridnev wrote that throughout the remainder of the war, Osipenko took every opportunity to remind him that Beria had never "had his say" about Gridnev; it was a sword of Damocles that haunted Gridnev for years.[37]

Gridnev arrived at Anisovka on 14 October 1942, relieving Major Beliakov. He called a regimental formation of the 586th to introduce himself and formally announce the change of command; then he asked whether there were any questions. There were two main questions from the pilots. First, they wanted to know how long they were going to be stuck at Anisovka. Gridnev replied that the regiment was scheduled to be relocated to the front once it had proved its readiness to his satisfaction; this created a lot of excitement. The second question was, "Have you come to the regiment for long?" Gridnev thought for a moment and then replied, "Forever."[38]

The women accepted Gridnev and still speak of him as a good commander. Despite the stress he must have been under after his arrest, and the fact that commanding a women's regiment was not his first choice of duty, Gridnev did not become bitter. Even Makunina, Kazarinova's defender, said, " 'Batia,' he was the real commander of the regiment. He was only ordinary-looking, but he was very funny . . . he's an excellent storyteller, with a great sense of humor. It was very pleasant to be in his company. He tried to appear very serious but his eyes were smiling. I have only good memories of Gridnev."[39]

Gridnev recalled one tragedy that occurred just after his arrival. It had been raining for several days, delaying training. On 15 October, the sun shone and everyone rushed to begin their flights—the first Gridnev had observed as commander. About an hour after flying had started, a young pilot from the men's squadron was working on takeoff and landing techniques (what we might call "touch and go's"). As the Yak-1 came in on one gliding landing pass, a Po-2 suddenly appeared at extremely low altitude on a perpendicular course to the fighter. A collision appeared inevitable, but the biplane pilot managed to pull his aircraft up abruptly, missing the Yak. The Po-2 stalled and crashed from 100 feet altitude, killing the pilot. It turned out that the Po-2 pilot was from a local communications squadron. There was a mail sack in the rear cockpit, as well as a huge bunch of flowers that the pilot had apparently intended to scatter over the airfield from the air. He had been in the habit of making low-altitude passes and rocking his wings at the women on previous visits.[40]

At least some of the men assigned to the 586th, like Gridnev himself, seem to have been "on parole." Gridnev recalled one male pilot who arrived in late October 1942. At first, Gridnev was quite excited to see him; he had met him earlier at IA/PVO headquarters. The pilot, Chulochnikov, was an experienced squadron commander. But Chulochnikov seemed oddly uncomfortable when he greeted Gridnev. Then he handed Gridnev a document that stated that Chulochnikov had been sent to the 586th, to serve in whatever position Gridnev deemed fit, to work out an eight-year sentence for cowardice in combat. Gridnev was ready to judge him guilty until proven innocent, but Chulochnikov pleaded that he had been unjustly sentenced and begged to be allowed to prove himself in combat. Gridnev finally agreed to give him a chance. Chulochnikov became the commander of the men's squadron in the 586th.[41]

Before taking command in the fall of 1942, Gridnev had encountered the 586th once before. He had stopped with a group of pilots from the 82nd to refuel at Anisovka in May 1942 and had asked whether there was really a women's regiment there. He was told that there was, and one male engineer eagerly began informing him just how poorly prepared the women were: "Judge for yourself, is it really possible for anyone to master flying fighters in just a few months? . . . They've learned how to take off and land, and now they think of themselves as fighter pilots, they have all sorts of pretensions." A few minutes later, a Yak-1 took off and began performing aerobatic maneuvers over the field. It attracted everyone's attention, and Gridnev spotted the women pilots, who had come outside to watch the show. The women, as well as Gridnev's male pilots, began cheering and applauding; all were impressed with the pilot. "Who's that pilot?" asked one of Gridnev's pilots. A female mechanic answered, "It's one of the women from the second squadron." The male engineer who had been denigrating the women's training protested: "What's with you—that's a joke! What woman can fly like that? It's Major Beliakov flying." Someone pointed out that Beliakov, who had been instructing in ground training that day, was standing with the women pilots. The pilot performing the aerobatics display turned out to be Zhenia Prokhorova.[42]

Prokhorova was an incredibly talented pilot. She had two world records in gliders and had been the leader of the prewar women's aerobatic team. Prokhorova became a squadron commander and flew twelve to fourteen hours a day, training the less experienced pilots. When Gridnev took command at the 586th, he said that he quickly noticed that Prokhorova was "the idol of all the women pilots, the technicians, in fact, the entire personnel of the regiment." They talked about her even more than they did about

Raskova, according to Gridnev. Prokhorova was not externally impressive—of average height with an athletic build. She spoke in a cultured voice but could not pronounce the sound "r" properly.[43] "One would not call her a beauty," Gridnev noted. "She had big features, a chin that was rather heavy, and a short neck that didn't go well with her delicate figure. Nature was unfair to her with this odd disproportion." However, Gridnev noted that Prokhorova was a "perfect shot" against both towed and ground targets.

Gridnev conducted additional training for the regiment throughout October and November, following the plan of "Combat Training Course 42." This training consisted of daytime work in formation and group coordination in flights and squadrons, with target practice against towed targets. Navigation flights were also conducted, and solo flights for perfecting piloting techniques were assigned. Another part of the regimen was night intercept flights, which involved single fighters being vectored by radar against prearranged targets. At the same time, the regiment was still responsible for night alert duty, always keeping some fighters at Readiness One and Two.

Gridnev recalled being upset by an article in the "combat newspaper" of the second squadron that stated that when one flight finished its work earlier than the others, it was given time off. This was justified by the old Russian saying, "When work is done, have your fun." Gridnev instituted a new philosophy: "When work is done, help your chum." He tried to instill a greater sense of mutual assistance in which "the stronger helped the less strong always, in everything, on the ground and in the air."[44]

The flying weather at Anisovka was nearly perfect in the fall of 1942, but living conditions left a lot to be desired. Gridnev recalled one incident in November: The usually unflappable Prokhorova was on a night training flight when they noticed her aircraft jinking and maneuvering oddly. There seemed to be a mechanical problem with the aircraft. Prokhorova was yelling incomprehensibly on the radio; all they could make out was that she wanted to land. Gridnev called out the emergency vehicles. Prokhorova came straight in against the pattern, the aircraft still moving jerkily, but managed a smooth landing. The instant the plane stopped, Prokhorova switched off the engine, leaped from the cockpit, and ran from the plane. Everyone thought the Yak-1 was about to explode.

"They're in the plane," she tried to explain. Gridnev was mystified. "Who's in the plane?" he asked. "The mice." It turned out that after Prokhorova had begun her maneuvers, several mice fell out of some hiding place in the cockpit and began scrambling around on her neck and face.

Fearless in every other way, Prokhorova had a phobia about rodents. Gridnev admitted, "There really were thousands and thousands of rats and mice in the fall and winter of 1942." Hordes of the rodents infested the Volga steppes; they particularly loved the earthen dugouts and storehouses of the airfields. There were so many of them in the dining halls that they were routinely crushed under people's feet. Mass migrations sometimes caused trains to stop, the wheels jammed with crushed rodents.[45]

Mechanic Inna Pasportnikova also stressed the miserable conditions at Anisovka: "The mosquitoes were horrible there. We were just devoured. We had to button up everything and they still got us, even at night."[46] Deputy engineer of the regiment for special equipment Irina Emel'ianova agreed: "Life at Anisovka was very difficult indeed," she said. The pilots lived in wooden "summerhouses," which in the winter were cold and drafty. Each was equipped with a brick stove; "it was very warm near the stove, but three steps away it was cold. And so they made earthen dugouts and moved there." Baths were a rare luxury—too scarce a commodity for the women to receive special treatment. "Every ten days, we went to the bathhouse in Saratov," Emel'ianova recalled. "We hung a sheet between the rooms; there were men in the other room."[47]

Life was more difficult for the mechanics and armorers than for the pilots. Flying personnel received better food, better clothing, and better accommodations. Since some of the mechanics had also been pilots before the war, it was hard for them to accept this inferior position, especially in a "classless" society. But the women have stressed that their envy of the pilots was not personal. As mechanic Irina Favorskaia put it, "We did not have black envy toward our pilots, just white envy."[48]

One of the important duties of the 586th was to provide fighter escorts for various types of VIPs. Although these were a relatively small percentage of flights—about 7 percent of the regiment's total combat sorties—they were considered high-profile missions due to the rank and prominence of the persons being escorted. Typically, the 586th Yaks escorted an Li-2 transport that carried a high-ranking officer and his staff. This sort of escort mission was usually assigned to PVO fighters, rather than pulling aircraft from VVS units that were supporting the ground forces. On one of the first escort missions, during the summer of 1942, General-Major Gromadin's Li-2 had been escorted by four pilots of the 586th (Nechaeva, Surnachevskaia, Shakhova, and Kuznetsova); the women were thereafter promoted to officer rank.[49]

Gridnev received orders in December 1942 to take four planes to Sred-niaia Akhtuba near Stalingrad to meet a VIP transport. With pilots Mordo-sevich, Beliaeva, and Burdina, he flew to the designated point and landed to refuel. The local garrison commander refused to provide the fuel, claim-ing that he was part of the VVS and had not received any orders to refuel PVO aircraft. In the meantime, the Li-2 transport arrived; after circling several times, its pilot finally realized that there was some problem with the escort and landed. Unfortunately, the transport hit a bomb hole at the end of the runway and broke a wheel. When Nikita Khrushchev, political officer for the Stalingrad Front, emerged from the plane, the garrison com-mander hopped into action. The repairs to the Li-2 delayed the planned flight until the next morning. Khrushchev invited the fighter pilots to his quarters and explained that they would be visiting a camp for German prisoners of war; he asked whether the pilots would like to accompany him into the camp. They eagerly agreed, hoping to meet some German pilots, but most of the prisoners were from the 6th Army at Stalingrad. Gridnev recalled that many were dressed in just the way the Soviet news-papers portrayed them: short of winter clothing, they had stuffed their coats with rags and blankets and often wore huge peasant-woven "straw galoshes" to try to keep their feet warm.

Another escort mission in December 1942 ended in tragedy. Gridnev was ordered to send six aircraft to Kuibyshev for an escort mission; Belia-kov, Prokhorova, Pankratova, Pozhidaeva, Borisov, and Mordosevich were assigned the mission. Borisov's plane developed trouble en route, forcing him to return to base; the others reached Kuibyshev but were grounded for several days by weather. Finally, the fighters received orders to fly, although the weather was still so bad that Beliakov concocted "mechanical difficulties" for two aircraft. Only three Yaks (flown by Beliakov, Mordo-sevich, and Prokhorova) accompanied an Li-2 toward Uralsk. The weather deteriorated even further, making visibility almost zero, and the group was unable to reach the intended airfield. The transport aircraft had much better instruments for flying in weather than the fighters did, and it man-aged to land safely on the open steppe. The fighters were "left to their own devices," and each made a forced landing in the snow. Beliakov attempted a normal (gear-down) landing; his aircraft overturned, but he survived the crash. Mordosevich was able to make a belly landing; the plane was ru-ined, but he was uninjured. Prokhorova was not so lucky; while attempt-ing a landing in the whiteout, one wing struck "the only mound on that spacious flat steppe," flipping her aircraft as it landed. Gridnev wrote that a "cross-country vehicle" was sent to pick up the passengers and crew of the transport, but no one searched for Prokhorova until the next day. Beliakov found her trapped in her overturned plane, apparently frozen to death. She had no external injuries.

Gridnev believed that there were many irregularities about this incident. A PVO regiment was already located in Kuibyshev. Why hadn't it been assigned the escort mission? He questioned why an escort was required at all; the flight took place far from the front, where no enemy flights had been reported, and in weather in which no German would have attempted to fly. Gridnev was admittedly bitter about the episode. In his memoirs he wrote, "Prokhorova was thrown away by the stupid incompetence of a pseudo-commander. . . . Was anybody punished for the death of a pilot and the loss of three combat aircraft?" Gridnev said that if there was any sort of investigation, its results were never revealed. The casualty was written off as a "combat loss," just as Khomiakova's death had been.

This is where Gridnev is at odds with other veterans. They do not dispute the facts of the deaths of Khomiakova or Prokhorova, but they believe that it is acceptable to consider them combat losses. Gridnev's point is that calling these deaths combat losses precluded any investigations. Other veterans point out that the families were comforted by the belief that their daughters had died in the line of duty.[50] Biographical sketches of the women by unit historian Ekaterina Polunina provide no insight: "On 6 October 1942 during a night flight on a combat mission, V. D. Khomiakova was killed. . . . E. F. Prokhorova was killed on 3 December 1942, fulfilling an especially crucial combat mission."[51]

Gridnev provided information during our interviews that he did not include in his memoirs, which he had self-censored in the hope that they would be published. He told me that he believed that Khomiakova, Beliaeva, and Prokhorova were purposely sent into dangerous and unreasonable circumstances in order to hasten their deaths: "I understood then, and so I understand now, that Kazarinova and Osipenko had a plan to destroy [them]."[52]

The 586th was transferred to the 101st Fighter Aviation Division (9th Fighter Aviation Corps, IA/PVO) and was based at Voronezh from 13 February until 16 August 1943—the site of some of the most intense combat activity the regiment would experience. "During that time at Voronezh, every pilot had about three times the usual work," Gridnev noted. "The food was terrible. Then suddenly they overloaded us with American food. When they sent us the American food, it was a feast—canned meat, dried eggs, canned milk."[53] During this period, the 586th performed a total of 934 flights (total flying time of 901 hours 31 minutes) and is credited with shooting down seven Ju-88 bombers and three FW-190 fighters.[54] It was also during this period that pilots Surnachevskaia and Pamiatnykh engaged the forty-two German aircraft, as described in the beginning of this chapter.

On 26 June 1943, Lieutenant Colonel Gridnev and Senior Lieutenant Lisitsina were involved in an air engagement near Belgorod that garnered them coverage in *Pravda*. Gridnev and Lisitsina attacked a formation of Ju-88 bombers, escorted by three FW-190 fighters; Gridnev shot down a fighter, and Lisitsina a bomber. Gridnev, now out of ammunition, was pursued by the two remaining fighters. During a series of evasive maneuvers, he took the Germans into the clouds, where they collided with each other. Gridnev and Lisitsina safely returned to base.[55] The 586th continued to receive assignments for a variety of escort missions. On 19 April 1943, four Yaks led by Senior Lieutenant Pamiatnykh escorted General-Major Antontsev.[56] On 9, 12, and 13 June 1943, the 586th provided escorts for General-Lieutenant Korniets; Senior Lieutenant Beliaeva was in charge of these flights.[57] Six fighters from the 586th, led by Senior Lieutenant Yamshchikova, on 14 July 1943 escorted the Li-2 of a General-Colonel Khodiakov from Voronezh to Kursk.[58]

One of the pilots from the prewar aerobatic team was still with the 586th at this time. Raisa Beliaeva had been sent to Stalingrad, where Soviet pilots suffered a high casualty rate. But Beliaeva was among those who survived; in fact, at Stalingrad, she scored two kills. Together with Kuznetsova and Shakova, Beliaeva returned to the 586th in late December 1942.[59] Gridnev remembered her as one of the best pilots he ever knew. "Beliaeva was an exceptional person. It seemed that her body was not even like other bodies; she could withstand very high g's. During training flights she could beat any man. . . . I never met any man like her. She could withstand so many g's that when you were flying against her, you'd black out trying to keep up with her."[60] Others shared Gridnev's high assessment of Beliaeva's ability. Olga Yamshchikova, who knew Beliaeva from childhood, wrote that she was strong and dexterous, absolutely tireless, and "she could literally do anything." Yamshchikova wrote at length of Beliaeva's skill and passion for flying; "I never met a person who loved their profession more than she did."[61]

But Gridnev said that Kazarinova and Osipenko were still waiting for an opportunity to get rid of Beliaeva, which presented itself when the 586th was at Voronezh: "Kazarinova and Osipenko did not like her, and they always tried to hurt her."[62] Preparations were under way for the battle of Kursk. "We were under tremendous strain," Gridnev recalled, "and during this period of time, Beliaeva was the person who performed the best."[63] The Luftwaffe had adopted a new tactic for attacking Soviet tanks, troops, and trains by flying at extremely low altitudes. The Soviets were unable to use radar to detect the flights or to vector fighters against them. "Then Beliaeva came up to me and asked, 'Let me try to force them to fly a little higher. But I have one condition: you must agree to let me perform some aerobatics when I return.' " Gridnev said that he agreed on the condition that she perform only ascending maneuvers—even though aerobatics of any sort were technically against regulations.

Beliaeva was successful in forcing a group of German aircraft into the detection and interception range of Soviet fighters. When she returned to the airfield, she launched her Yak into a series of maneuvers. Unfortunately, General Osipenko had arrived at the airfield and observed Beliaeva's performance. "[Osipenko] was a very crude person," Gridnev said. "He swore at me with four-letter words. He said, 'She will be arrested for forty-five days for a violation of flight regulations.' " Beliaeva had landed and was walking toward them as her aircraft was being prepared for the next mission. Just at that moment, the regiment received a radio warning that German bombers were inbound against a nearby railway station where troops were being unloaded. Osipenko had already left, and Gridnev had not yet called guards to carry out the order to arrest Beliaeva. In the meantime, she heard the alert and ran back to her plane and took off. When she returned from another successful mission, having diverted the German bombers from the rail junction, Osipenko appeared once more and declared that Beliaeva was to be grounded permanently for evading arrest.

But Beliaeva was irrepressible. As she awaited the orders that would discharge her from aviation, the regiment's airfield came under repeated night bombardment, requiring that additional aircraft be put on night alert. Gridnev placed himself on first readiness, and a male pilot who had been specially detailed to the 586th from 9th Corps took second readiness. One night, Gridnev was launched against an inbound German bomber. Gridnev recalled that he thought that it was the other man who took off to assist him. "But then in the air I heard the voice of Beliaeva, and not Bankovsky. She transmitted that she saw the enemy. She attacked and set him on fire, and he exploded from his own bombs. We returned together. . . . They wanted to expel us both from aviation because we did not act according to regulations." However, General Gromadin (Osipenko's superior) appeared the next day. "He shook hands with Beliaeva and said that if the bomber had gotten through to Lisitsa station, many people could have died." Gromadin ensured that Beliaeva was reinstated to active flying status.[64]

Unfortunately, Beliaeva did not enjoy her reinstatement for long. On 19 July 1943, she was killed in a crash. Gridnev said that Beliaeva was test-flying a fighter that had been repaired with some defective parts, and during the test, the aircraft went out of control.[65] Polunina's biography states that Beliaeva was "returning from a combat mission" when she was killed.[66] Yamshchikova's memoir said the same thing, although she wrote at length about how Beliaeva often flew aerobatics and tested newly repaired aircraft.[67] All accounts agree that Beliaeva was unable to pull the aircraft out of a spin, though she managed at the last moment to divert it from the populated section of the airfield. She crashed into the ground. Yamshchikova's account is particularly heartrending. She wrote that she ran out to the crash site, a hole in which the wreckage of Beliaeva's aircraft was burning. People were hastily shoveling dirt onto the flames. Yamshchikova lost control of herself and began screaming at them to dig out the pilot; she even pulled her pistol and ordered them to try to save Beliaeva. The regimental commander (Gridnev, though she does not name him) quietly ordered that her pistol be taken away until she calmed down. Yamshchikova wrote that she hardly wanted to live; she had lost her husband at the beginning of the war, and now her best friend. She was roused from her depression when she was told that Beliaeva's husband, a night fighter pilot, had been summoned from a nearby airfield. He had been told only that his wife was wounded; it was left to Yamshchikova to inform him of Beliaeva's death.[68]

Beliaeva's death affected the whole regiment. "We lost a heroic pilot, and all the regiment was crying," Gridnev told me. "I also was crying. When we buried her I made a speech, and I cried during the speech."[69] Beliaeva's husband, who had refused to believe his wife was dead, fainted when he was shown her body. Yamshchikova said that she did not cry at the funeral; "my heart had once more turned to stone."[70]

All the pilots who had opposed Kazarinova in mid-1942 were dead by mid-1943. Gridnev suspected that Kazarinova was bent on vengeance not only against the women pilots who had opposed her but against him as well: "From my first steps I met her influence. She always tried to harm the regiment; she didn't want it to be better than when she was commander."[71] Gridnev believed that Kazarinova prevented the 586th from receiving the Guards designation:

> After Voronezh we were prepared to receive Guards. A special photo reporter came and took pictures for two months. Then a film crew. They even shot real air battles. And the photographer and cinema operators were of the highest class. In our regiment two commissions were at work, the internal regimental commission, and the corps commission, and they prepared the documents for Guard.[72]

Gridnev said that Kazarinova came personally to pick up the Guards materials, supposedly to hand-deliver them to Moscow: "Colonel Sergeich who was chairman of the commission signed the document and Kazarinova also signed it. They stamped it. Two guys were with her. They took all the materials, got on the aircraft, and went to Moscow." Within a week, the 586th received Guards clothing.[73]

But time passed, and the 586th never received official notification of its new Guards number. Because of the demands of war and frequent rebasing, it was not always easy to track down the source of administrative delays. Finally, Gridnev discovered that an old friend of his was working on the staff of the IA/PVO: "He said that the materials never reached the staff. But in the staff department, they knew that Kazarinova brought the materials to Moscow." Later, Gridnev said that he was told by another person that when Kazarinova was leaving the 586th for Moscow, she "told a staff worker at the 9th Fighter Aviation Corps, Colonel Khil'nevich, that she categorically objected to the fact that Gridnev, this 'upholder of honor' from the Tukhachevsky-Gomarnikovsky rabble, was going to receive the Guards designation."[74] Gridnev believed that Kazarinova simply destroyed the materials to prevent the regiment from receiving Guards under another commander.[75] Other veterans confirmed that Kazarinova did see the Guards materials, but they did not know whether she transported them or not.[76]

The 586th next spent a month at Kastornoe (18 August to 17 September 1943), followed by two and a half months at an airfield called Kursk-West (17 September to 5 December 1943). There were a total of 261 combat sorties in this period.[77] On 5 December 1943, the 586th was assigned missions covering targets in the area of Kiev, Ukraine. Enemy flights were rare; the only German aircraft encountered were single reconnaissance aircraft. In a period of two months, the regiment flew 199 sorties (190 hours 34 minutes) but engaged enemy aircraft only three times.[78] From 4 to 15 February 1944, the 586th was rebased to Zhuliany and was assigned the mission of performing strafing ground attack flights against the encircled German troops at Korsun'-Shevchenkovskiy. During this period, Gridnev and Burdina each shot down an Me-109 and shared a kill against a Ju-52.[79]

The 586th was next based for more than five months at Zhitomir-Skomorokhi (21 March to 2 September 1944), where it protected fixed targets and rail junctions.[80] In seven daytime air engagements, Gridnev and Surnachevskaia shared a kill against an He-177, and Korolev and Tsokaev shot down a Ju-88. There were also eight nighttime engagements; during one, Burdina destroyed a Ju-88. The 586th flew 611 combat sorties (725 hours 12 minutes), which included 274 flights covering fixed targets, 237 flights to intercept enemy reconnaissance aircraft, 35 night sorties against bombers, 49 flights to escort Li-2 transports, and 14 free-hunt sorties.[81] On 21 July 1944, four Yaks (Gridnev, Burdina, Shakhova, and Batrakova) escorted Marshal Voronov of the artillery forces.

The 586th spent two weeks at Kotovsk (2 to 14 September) and was transferred back to the 141st Fighter Aviation Division on 7 September 1944.[82] Next it was rebased to Beltsy for ten weeks (7 October to 20 December), where its mission was to cover the Dnestr River crossings.[83] There was little enemy activity in this area during this period.[84] The 586th was rebased to Debrecen, Hungary, on 23 February 1945.[85] Again, enemy activity was almost negligible; only twelve combat sorties were recorded for a two-month period.[86]

The 586th spent the last two weeks of the war, from 25 April 1945, at Tsinkot airfield near Budapest.[87] There was very little flying to be done. However, Gridnev made some interesting observations about the behavior of Soviet forces in the area. He observed that senior officers condoned corruption and theft: "Government planes landed [at our] airfield, Li-2's. They were loaded with safes full of gold and silver, cutlery, dishes."[88] Malinovsky, the commander of the Second Front, had issued orders that every aircraft was to be checked for unauthorized cargo. But Gridnev got into trouble when he tried to enforce the order:

They invited me to the division staff. They were so kind to me. They said, "Aleksandr Vasilevich, the war is over. We'll disband the women's regiment. Would you like to continue serving in the army after the war?" "Yes, I'm a professional, a fighter pilot." "So you can choose between two positions. One is deputy corps commander." I answered, "No, I don't want to be someone's assistant. I want to work alone." "Then please accept the 39th Guards Regiment." I said, "Thank you, with pleasure." So I was appointed commander of the 39th, which was in Kiev.[89]

Gridnev discovered that he had been duped when he arrived in Kiev; instead of taking command of the 39th, he received new orders—to go to a sanatorium to recover from "poor health." A few months after Gridnev's departure, the 586th was disbanded.[90]

The 586th never received its Guards designation, and no pilots received the Hero of the Soviet Union medal while assigned to the regiment.[91] This unit was not, however, in the front lines of battle; it was part of the air defense forces protecting rear areas from German attack. Altogether, the PVO is credited with only about 10 percent of the total German aircraft shot down during the war (VVS and the ground forces claim the rest).[92] As historian K. J. Cottam has noted, "the opportunity for displaying spectacular heroism in the [586th] was limited."[93] Several veterans of the 586th say that one reason none of their pilots received the HSU was that it normally took twenty kills for a fighter pilot to receive the HSU. Gridnev, as noted earlier, stated that the 586th *had* qualified for Guards, but that personal vendettas against him and against the women in general were the reasons that the 586th failed to receive the highest honors: "Not one woman pilot was awarded the Hero of the Soviet Union in our regiment, on account of the prejudice and foolishness of the commander of Fighter Aviation of PVO, General Osipenko. He hated the women's 586th regiment and its commander."[94]

Gridnev had some interesting comments about the treatment of women in the military. Gridnev has repeatedly written and spoken about the outstanding combat skills of some of his women pilots, but he also noted that others were only average—as in any regiment. On the whole, he said, "our experience showed that women fighter pilots in the majority of circumstances, much better than men, endured g-loads to the body which arose during abrupt and sharp changes of aircraft attitude—in steep banking turns, combat turns [chandelles], and during abrupt exits from a dive. Also the women-pilots had greater endurance than men during high-altitude

Table 1. Breakdown of Combat Sorties of the 586th Fighter
        Aviation Regiment

Type	Number of Flights	Number of Hours
Unspecified combat missions	2,073	2,413
Escort of bomber and ground attack aircraft	49	60
Cover for battle formations of ground forces	310	296
Cover for troops in movement	174	141
Reconnaissance flights	16	18
Escort of VIP/transport aircraft	301	496
Intercept flights	337	293
Patrol over fixed targets	1,159	1,077
Total	4,419	4,794

flights without oxygen."[95] When asked whether his regiment had received any special treatment during the war, Gridnev stressed that it had not. Then he remarked, "It would be better if the women's regiment could have had some privileges. I don't mean very special privileges, but you should have more a tender attitude toward them." When asked for clarification, Gridnev replied, "For example, in food, in the place where they live. They needed different kinds of clothing, and hygienic conditions must be organized differently."[96] These practical considerations, which would be largely a matter of course in a modern military, may have been difficult for Soviet women in the Second World War.

Altogether, the 586th made more than 9,000 flights, of which 4,419 were considered combat sorties. A total of 125 air battles occurred, during which thirty-eight aircraft were shot down (twelve fighters, fourteen bombers, one transport, and eleven reconnaissance). A variety of ground targets were also destroyed (including two Ju-52 aircraft on the ground, four tanks, thirty vehicles, twenty horses, and several antiaircraft sites).[97] The breakdown of combat flights is shown in Table 1. At least ten women pilots of the 586th died during the war, or close to 30 percent of its flying personnel.[98]

6

Women at War in Mostly Male Regiments

❖ ❖ ❖ ❖ ❖ ❖ ❖ ❖ ❖ ❖ ❖ ❖ ❖ ❖ ❖

The women aviators of "Raskova's regiments" flew a variety of aircraft in a variety of places, but one thing they all had in common was that in those regiments, women were in the majority. However, these were not the only women who flew in the VVS during the war; there were a number of women aviators—pilots, navigators, and gunners—who served in regular line units. Some of them started out with Raskova's regiments, but others were never part of Raskova's group. Their experience of war was rather different from that of the women discussed in the previous chapters; they served alone, or with a handful of other women, within units that were overwhelmingly male. For example, Valentina Grizodubova (who flew with Raskova on the 1938 flight of the *Rodina* discussed in chapter 1) became the commander of the 101st Long-Range Air Regiment, a bomber-transport unit. Other women flew in dive-bomber, reconnaissance, and ground attack regiments. Most of these women had already attained military rank prior to the war. The fighter pilots from the 586th who were assigned to other regiments, either temporarily (during Stalingrad) or permanently (Liliia Litviak and Katia Budanova), are discussed here as well.

The most prominent woman to serve outside of Raskova's regiments was Valentina Grizodubova, who chose not to be associated with the women's regiments. Instead, she gained command of the 101st Aviation Regiment, a group formed early in the war from experienced civil aviation pilots. The 101st (later redesignated the 31st Guards Bomber Aviation Regiment) flew Li-2 aircraft, which were American D-3s produced in Russia, commonly referred to in Russian as the "Dooglas." The Li-2s were converted for bombing missions early in the war, but later flew primarily partisan resupply. The date when the 101st was formed is not clear, but it was flying combat missions by June 1942. It operated on the Southwestern Front, near Bryansk and Voronezh, and flew more than a thousand resupply sorties into occupied Ukraine and Belorussia.[1] Grizodubova, unlike Raskova, was not given late-model aircraft for her regiment but was forced to work with a makeshift wartime adaptation of a transport aircraft. The Li-2 was not really suited to be a bomber. Many pilots in the 101st had strong reservations about its capability; they feared that it would be unable to attain altitude or maneuver against antiaircraft fire with a load of bombs, and it would be completely defenseless against enemy fighters. Grizodubova brought in special pilots with polar and test-flying experience to help train the regiment.[2]

Soviet men did not regard a female regimental commander as part of the normal military order of things. A. Verkhozin, who became Grizodubova's chief of staff, related his reaction when he was first assigned to work for her:

> If someone had said to me, an ordinary navigator, that I would become the chief of staff of an aviation regiment which was commanded by a woman, I would have taken it for a joke and forgotten about it on the spot. But in my orders it was listed: to Grizodubova's regiment. Position: chief of staff. How could I not believe it! . . . If Grizodubova had formed a women's aviation regiment, as Marina Raskova had done, everything would have been clear. But here was a commander who was a woman, and subordinates who were men.[3]

Grizodubova was a rather enigmatic character. Verkhozin noted that the opinions of those who knew her before the war varied greatly. Some regarded her as excessively strict; others said she was concerned about people; yet others claimed she took a lot of risks. Verkhozin himself noted that "she could, when it was required, be implacably severe" and that "as a commander, when it was unavoidable, she took calculated risks." She had something of an eagle eye; Verkhozin commented that nothing got past her. She was especially strict about training and personally instructed the pilots in her regiment in flying technique. When one of her subordinates demonstrated a "gap in knowledge," such as being late to target or losing his orientation in the clouds, the mistake was held forth as a bad example to the entire regiment. But Grizodubova was always prepared to show them herself how to do things correctly—and not just in training. Unlike some regimental commanders, Grizodubova was extremely active as a pilot during the war.[4] The 101st had a long and distinguished wartime record under her command.[5]

One of the most famous women to fly in a male regiment was Anna Timofeeva-Egorova, who flew the Il-2 *shturmovik* ground attack aircraft. Egorova started the war as a pilot in a communications squadron on the Southern Front. She was unhappy flying the unarmed U-2 and requested an assignment to a combat regiment; after persistent efforts, she achieved a transfer to the 805th Ground Attack Aviation Regiment (230th Ground Attack Aviation Division, 4th Air Army). On her 277th mission, Egorova was shot down and captured by the Germans—one of the few women aviators to end up as a prisoner of war. She was in the camps for five months until she was released by a liberating Soviet tank unit on 31 January 1945. Her harrowing story is told in her memoirs; Timofeeva-Egorova was later awarded the HSU.[6] After the war, an interviewer asked her how she had learned to master the "flying tank," which not every man could fly. Egorova replied, "The Il-2, of course, is not a 'lady's' aircraft. But after all, I'm no princess, but a metal worker who helped build the Moscow subway system."[7]

Another Il-2 pilot, Tamara Konstantinova (a friend of Egorova's from before the war), flew with the 999th Ground Attack Aviation Regiment (277th Ground Attack Aviation Division). A flying instructor before the war, Konstantinova at first flew the Po-2 in a support unit, but in March 1944 she achieved a transfer to combat aviation and trained in the Il-2. Konstantinova was the only woman Il-2 pilot on the Leningrad Front; her gunner, Aleksandra Mukoseeva, was also female. Konstantinova attained the position of deputy squadron commander and was awarded the Hero of the Soviet Union in 1945 for her performance in more than sixty combat missions. Her brother, who followed in her footsteps to become a combat pilot, also received the HSU.[8] Other women who flew the Il-2 included Lidiia Ivanovna Shulaikina (Baltic Fleet) and Mariia Tolstova.[9] Nadezhda Zhurkina was a gunner on a Pe-2; she flew with HSU pilot Viktor Bogutskii in the 99th Independent Guards Reserve Aviation Regiment.[10]

Another woman who served with a men's regiment, Ekaterina Zelenko, was already a flight commander in the 135th Bomber Aviation Regiment (16th Bomber Aviation Division) based near Poltava before the war. She had been one of the few women to fly during the Soviet-Finnish War in

1939–1940. Zelenko flew the Su-2 bomber in combat from the very start of the war. On 12 September 1941, Senior Lieutenant Zelenko, now a deputy squadron commander, was attacked by a pair of Me-109s; her aircraft was badly damaged, she was wounded, and her navigator was killed. Zelenko rammed an enemy fighter and reportedly survived but was shot down by yet another German fighter. Her regiment put her name forward for the Hero of the Soviet Union, but since she had crashed in occupied territory and her body had not been recovered, the award was refused, as was nearly always the case for anyone listed as missing in action. Eventually her documents were found, but it was many years before enough eyewitness accounts were compiled to verify that she had indeed died in combat. In 1990, she was posthumously awarded the HSU.[11]

There were a number of women scattered in combat support regiments, especially those flying the Po-2. For example, the 16th Air Army history mentions the 399th Communications Regiment's work during the summer of 1943, delivering cargoes to partisans north of Polotsk at night and transporting the wounded; "there was only one woman pilot among them—JrLt M. G. Sokolova, flew as many sorties as the men."[12] There were at least two women Po-2 pilots in the 2nd Separate Air Regiment (OAP; later the 105th Guards OAP), M. S. Peshkevich and E. V. Degtiareva.[13] Cottam also discovered that at least one navigator from the 46th, Meri Avidzba, transferred to a men's night bomber regiment during the war; and pilot O. M. Lisikova, who flew U-2 ambulance planes for up to eighteen hours a day during the early days of the war, later flew heavy transports into besieged Leningrad.[14] There were probably many women flying in line regiments who are unknown to us because they did not win prestigious medals and so were not mentioned by name in published materials.[15] It remains to be determined just how many women served in support positions in combat aviation regiments. One historian believes that women constituted 12.5 percent of the personnel in Soviet aviation (including ground personnel) by the end of the war.[16]

Another group of women who flew in mostly male regiments was the squadron from the 586th Fighter Aviation Regiment that was ordered to Stalingrad on 10 September 1942.[17] This squadron arrived at Stalingrad in the worst period of the six-month battle. Soviet troops were on the defensive. The Luftwaffe had attained near complete control of the air. Hardesty noted that Soviet air operations at this time were "in no way a serious challenge to Luftwaffe supremacy." The Soviets were fighting a delaying action while their new air armies were being brought up to strength, in preparation for the counteroffensive that would begin in mid-November.[18] In other words, the women from the 586th were thrown into action with regiments that were badly outnumbered, poorly supplied, and demoralized from severe casualties.

The squadron of eight women pilots and their crews was divided into two groups that were sent to two different regiments. The first group, which was assigned to the 434th Independent Fighter Aviation Regiment, included pilots Lebedeva, Nechaeva, Blinova, and Shakhova.[19] The 434th, commanded by Major I. I. Kleshchev, had been fighting near Stalingrad since June 1942. It was reassigned to the 16th Air Army in mid-September, after being upgraded to Yak-7 and Yak-9 fighters. The women pilots must have arrived in conjunction with this reassignment, since the 434th's first combat assignment at Stalingrad was on 16 September. Klavdiia Nechaeva was killed on 17 September by German fighters while flying as wingman to Captain I. I. Izbinskii. Upon returning to the airfield after a mission, Izbinskii began to land in accordance with procedure. But during his landing approach, when he was most vulnerable, with his wheels down and unable to maneuver, he was attacked by two German fighters. Nechaeva saved his life by intervening and drawing the fire of the Germans. She was probably too inexperienced to know how to defend herself against two enemy aircraft at low altitude, and she was killed. The 434th flew sixty-five sorties on 17 September and shot down seven German aircraft; Nechaeva's loss is the only one mentioned on that day.[20] However, the regiment as a whole did incur serious losses that month; by the end of September, more than a third of its aircraft were reported damaged or destroyed.[21]

Among the most famous women to fly in men's regiments were fighter pilots Lidia (Liliia) Litviak and Ekaterina (Katia) Budanova. They were among the second group of four pilots sent to Stalingrad by the 586th. The commander of their group was Raisa Beliaeva; Maria M. Kuznetsova was also in the group. Beliaeva's group had been ordered to join the 437th Fighter Aviation Regiment at Verkhnaia Akhtuba airfield on the east bank of the Volga River. However, when they approached the runway, they noticed that the airfield was empty—there were no aircraft visible. The moment they landed, a frightened-looking mechanic ran over to Beliaeva and shouted, "Take off immediately! Our aircraft are already at Sredniaia Akhtuba. The fascist artillery has been hitting us here, there might even be an assault!"[22]

Beliaeva's group flew to Sredniaia Akhtuba, keeping at minimum altitude to avoid German fighters. The situation was grave, both in the air and on the ground. The pilots' crews (mechanics and armorers) flew to the airfield in a bomber, as transport aircraft were unavailable. "We were put in the bomb bay. Instead of bombs, there were mechanics," remembered Inna Pasportnikova, Kuznetsova's mechanic. "And as soon as we arrived, we were bombed." The plane did not even taxi to the hardstand; the pilot opened the bomb bays, and the passengers jumped out and ran for shelter.[23]

It turned out that the 437th, commanded by a Major Khvostikov, was a LaGG-3 regiment, which meant that the women's Yak fighters could not be properly maintained.[24] The assignment only made sense as some sort of administrative error—unless it was an intentional effort to endanger these women by sending them to the hottest part of the front, regardless of whether the assignment made sense in military terms. Despite the obvious difficulties of a half squadron of Yak fighters flying with a LaGG regiment, the women pilots were determined to fly. But the unit commander was skeptical of their ability: "This is combat, not a flying club! There are air battles every day. We're waiting for real pilots, and they sent us a bunch of girls."[25]

In some ways, the women pilots did not receive the sort of training a male pilot could expect.[26] They certainly were not "protected." This fact is graphically illustrated by the case of some of the women fighter pilots when they arrived at Stalingrad. One pilot who knew them recalled:

> There were four of them in our regiment. Four girl-pilots. They composed the women's flight, which was commanded by Guards Senior Lieutenant Beliaeva (I don't remember her first name). . . . Quite often one or another would ask to be wingman to the most active male fighter pilots, especially young Liliia Litviak. She appealed to many, including me. And we, every time, politely refused. Personally, to me it would have been unbelievably difficult to go through the death of such a wingman in combat. And after all, a woman! . . . The girls, however, got along without male leadership, and fought well in their own flight.[27]

In Soviet tactics, leaders had primary responsibility for attacking, while wingmen were responsible for protecting their leaders. When the women pilots flew with men, the men generally had more combat experience and flew as the leaders. Thus it was often the women who performed the role of protector. For example, Klavdiia Nechaeva died protecting her flight lead.[28]

Combat flying near Stalingrad in the fall of 1942 was dangerous and demanding. Even the ground crews were at risk from frequent strafing attacks. German fighter attacks against Soviet airfields near Stalingrad were frequent in this period. On another occasion, Pasportnikova narrowly missed being strafed. "I went to the trench and carried my gas mask for a pillow and took a nap. We never slept more than three to four hours at a time." She heard a commotion and looked up to see several people running toward her. "There were twelve holes in my aircraft. Two Messerschmitts had shot it up."[29] Soviet sources indicate that in August through October 1942, there were an average of 600 to 800 enemy flights each day within the Stalingrad Air Defense Region.[30] Pasportnikova described the living conditions at this time:

> The pilots lived in Akhtuba and the mechanics lived in a trench near their aircraft. In the morning, they brought us kasha, in the evening they brought us soup. There were no trees, no woods, no bushes. There was not a single bush here. And only stickers were around. And tumbleweeds. They brought us water on camels. . . . The ground was very hard, like cement. There was a lot of dust. Mosquitoes. The nights were cold and we sometimes even woke up covered with ice. . . . The smoke was often blown here [from] where the city was burning. Sometimes we did not know if it was a sunny day or not. The whole city was on fire.[31]

The women fighter pilots had to prove their abilities to earn the respect of the men, who did not take them seriously. Pasportnikova noted, "When we arrived at a male regiment, men did not want to fly with us, because of the responsibility, and also because they were afraid for themselves. They were afraid that the female wingmen would not cover them."[32] It was difficult enough for a woman like Budanova, who was the type that is kindly called "strapping." For Litviak, it must have been impossible; she was tiny, blonde, and stunningly beautiful. But if Litviak had trouble gaining professional respect on the ground, she quickly set the pace in the air. On 13 September, only three days after arriving at Stalingrad, Liliia Litviak scored her first two victories and became the first woman in the world to shoot down an enemy aircraft.[33] Pasportnikova remembered that day. "Liliia was the wingman to the regimental commander. They spotted three Junkers-

88s to the side of a bigger group of bombers. The leader decided to attack; Liliia followed his lead. She attacked so energetically that the bombers scattered and dropped their bombs. Taking advantage of this, her leader shot down one Ju-88, while Liliia killed a second." But the battle was not over. Liliia spotted her friend Beliaeva attacking an Me-109, but Beliaeva ran out of ammunition. Liliia engaged the Messerschmitt and damaged it severely. "The pilot had to bail out," Pasportnikova wrote. "He landed on our territory and was captured. He turned out to be a famous German ace who considered himself unbeatable. When he was questioned, he asked to be permitted to meet the pilot who had managed to bring him down. How astonished he was when he learned that the pilot turned out to be a young, twenty-year-old girl!" The German ace was a three-time winner of the Iron Cross, a member of the Richthofen Air Fleet. He refused to believe that Litviak was the pilot who had beaten him until she related a blow-by-blow description of their engagement. For a pilot newly arrived at the front to achieve two kills in a single day—one against a fighter ace—was a rarity.[34]

"We didn't stay in this regiment very long," Pasportnikova wrote. "They transferred us to the 9th Guards Fighter Regiment, which after heavy fighting and losses in Odessa had flown to Zhitkur [Kazakhstan]."[35] The 9th Guards, formerly a LaGG-3 regiment, was in the process of re-equipping with new aircraft and replenishing its personnel; new Yak-1s were received in early November.[36] What was particularly interesting about this transfer is that during this period, the 9th Guards was also being assigned a concentration of experienced pilots to create an "ace" regiment.[37] Mikhail Baranov, a celebrated pilot, was the deputy commander of the regiment. Soon afterward, several other famous fighter pilots were also transferred into the regiment, including Vladimir Lavrinenkov and Amet-Khan Sultan.[38] The women pilots were apparently happy in the 9th Guards, where they were accepted as capable pilots and had the opportunity to fly with some of the top aces in the Soviet Union. Lavrinenkov wrote the following about his first meeting with the women:

> In the dormitory, we found two girls. They were dressed in the light-weight flight suits which pilots wore then. They were gaily chatting about something, sitting on a blanket-covered mattress. Seeing the girls, we decided that we had ended up at the wrong address, and in confusion came to a stop in the doorway. "Come on in! Don't be embarrassed," said one of the pilots. "Have you only just arrived?"

"Yes," confirmed some one of us. "Us, too. Let's get acquainted. Liliia Litviak. And this is Katia Budanova."[39]

Lavrinenkov next met some of the male pilots, including three Heroes of the Soviet Union. He recognized Baranov instantly; "the famous combat deeds of Baranov were known to all pilots. . . . Baranov in those days was the most popular fighter pilot on our front." When Baranov instructed the new pilots to get settled in, Amet-Khan declared, "I've already chosen!" and tossed his suitcase on a mattress next to the one where the women were sitting. Baranov informed him that the women would be moving to other quarters.[40]

At dinner that night, the regimental commander, twenty-five-year-old HSU Lieutenant Colonel Shestakov, welcomed the new pilots and made a little speech about the women. "Watch out for the girls, and don't offend them. They came to us from a PVO regiment. The girls fly excellently and have already killed some Fritzes. Be friends with the girls, support their combat attitude. There are four of them in all in the men's regiment. And they are feeling, it is likely, not very comfortable."[41] But it was not long before someone apparently discovered the "mistake" in sending the women to Stalingrad. Pasportnikova recalled:

> An order arrived, I don't remember the date, about the return of the women's crews to the 586th. Budanova and Litviak appealed to LtCol Shestakov, the commander of the 9th Fighter Regiment, with a request to let them remain in the regiment. Armorer Valia Krasnoshchekova remained with her commander Litviak, but the aircraft mechanic decided to return to the women's regiment. And then Liliia persuaded me to remain with her crew.[42]

Kuznetsova, who had been ill, and Beliaeva returned to the 586th, but Litviak and Budanova remained with the 9th for a little over three months. Lavrinenkov described the two women as being quite different. Budanova was tall, kept her hair cut short, "and in her flightsuit hardly stood out from the fellows." Beside Budanova, the tiny Litviak "seemed like a little girl." Lavrinenkov characterized Budanova as a "cheerful, lively character," while Litviak was "thoughtful and quiet." He noted that Litviak seemed a "model of femininity and charm" and was pursued by several love-smitten pilots. But she "reacted extremely reservedly to the rapturous glances . . . she showed no preference to anyone. And this was especially impressive to us." Both, he said, were excellent pilots. When the women first arrived, they had flown together most of the time, but now Litviak and Budanova flew separately, as wingmen to male pilots.[43]

In January 1943, the 9th was once more re-equipped—this time with the P-39 "Cobra." It was suggested that the women transfer to the 296th Fighter Aviation Regiment (later the 73rd Guards Fighter Aviation Regiment), so that they could stay in the Yak. This occurred at Kotelnikov, where the 9th was based on the same airfield with the 73rd. "We only moved from one dormitory to another," Pasportnikova remembered. "We even ate at the same dining hall, since this was all at one airfield."[44] Apparently, there was some question about which regiment Litviak and Budanova would be assigned to within the division. General Eremin commanded a reconnaissance regiment in the division, and Nikolai Baranov commanded a fighter regiment.[45] At first, the division commander, Colonel Sidnev, asked Eremin to take the women, but he refused: "For some reason they wanted to fight in the ranks of our regiment precisely. About this, the more decisive and bold Liliia Litviak insisted."[46] But Eremin refused to agree. "I could not even imagine mentally, how I could send these girls into the rear of the enemy—and indeed if they landed in my regiment, they'd have to fly reconnaissance." Eremin noted that each flight was extremely dangerous, even for the most experienced pilots; he said that if the women were killed in combat, he could not have borne having their deaths on his hands. Ironically, Litviak ended up flying with Eremin's own former wingman, Alexei Solomatin, who had also transferred to the 73rd.[47]

Baranov seemed to have little trouble accepting the women pilots. Pasportnikova recalled that "Nikolai Baranov was a completely extraordinary person in all respects. He was wonderful as a person, as a commander, as a friend, as a comrade." It was in the 73rd that Litviak and Budanova found their true home; here they achieved the bulk of their combat kills. Baranov finally gave Litviak and Budanova the opportunity to prove their skill. There were many well-known fighter pilots in the regiment, such as squadron commander Alexei Solomatin, who had participated in a famous air engagement a few months earlier, when seven Soviet fighters engaged twenty-nine enemy aircraft. Solomatin took Litviak as his wingman, and Budanova was selected to fly with Baranov. In this way, the women were able to benefit from flying with highly experienced leaders.[48]

Litviak was something of a rebel. She made few concessions to conformity; even among the other women at Engels, she stood out from the crowd. Later, when she was among men, she was circumspect in her behavior but never attempted to act like "one of the guys." For example, Litviak loved flowers. She had them painted on her aircraft, she kept pictures of them above her bed, and whenever possible, she placed flowers in the cockpit of her fighter. Pasportnikova laughed when she recalled, "When men flew Liliia's plane, they sometimes found one of her little bouquets. They would pick it up between their fingers," Inna demonstrated, using her thumb and one finger, as if holding something rotten and smelly, "and shout, 'What the hell is this?' and they threw it out of the cockpit."[49]

Pasportnikova related how difficult life was for mechanics at the front. She and the crew armorer usually slept in an air-raid trench behind the aircraft:

> The trench was so narrow that we had to both turn over together at the same time, "by command." In the winter we used one of the engine covers; it was cotton-stuffed, and in the morning it would be covered with frost. One time when it was very cold, an engineer came with a canister of spirits, and he brought mugs with him. We were very much afraid, we didn't want to. He said, you'll drink or I'll shoot you! But the spirits were awful, the canister had been used for gas.[50]

The women became exceptionally close during the following months. Pasportnikova remembered:

> All of us were absolutely to some degree callused, but in the rare, brief hours and minutes of quiet and respite we invariably began to have intimate women's conversations. There were no secrets among us. We dreamed about how good and peaceful life would be when the cursed war was over. We made plans for the future, and nobody talked about death, which was lying in wait for us at every step. Everyone wanted to live until the bright day of Victory, although in our hearts, of course, we understood that in war, anything could happen.[51]

Litviak was deadly determined to prove herself as a fighter pilot—not just from personal ambition and patriotism, but also in order to redeem her family name. Her father had been among the thousands "purged" and imprisoned in 1937 for charges that were never specified. She never doubted her father's innocence and believed that she could reclaim the family's honor by gaining fame in combat. But if her father's status as an "enemy of the people" heightened her desire to fight, it was also the source of her deepest dread. More than anything else, Litviak feared that she would go missing in action. Any Soviet soldier whose body could not be found, who went "missing without a trace," was automatically suspected of desertion. Pilots often flew deep into enemy territory; they could be taken prisoner, or they might crash with their aircraft, leaving their bodies impossible to identify. Litviak was determined not to die that way but to land in friendly territory, even if it was with her dying breath.

On 11 February 1943, Litviak was involved in an air battle in which four fighters from the 73rd encountered twenty-nine enemy aircraft.[52] Flying with Baranov, Solomatin, and a fourth pilot, Litviak personally shot down a Ju-87 and shared a kill with Baranov against a Focke-Wulf 190 fighter.[53] Later that month, she was selected to join the ranks of the elite "free hunters"—fighter pilots who, because of their skill, were sent out in pairs to find and destroy the enemy.[54] She became a flight commander and was promoted from sergeant to junior lieutenant.[55] On 8 March 1943, the 296th was renamed the 73rd Guards Fighter Aviation Regiment in recognition of its combat performance.[56]

Early in her career, Litviak adopted the showy, and strictly forbidden, habit of buzzing the airfield when she returned from a kill. Approaching the airfield after a successful mission, Litviak would break from formation and perform high-speed, low-altitude passes and victory rolls. Pasportnikova said that "after her 'circus number' in the air, Liliia always asked me, 'Did Batya swear terribly?' And if I said, 'terribly!' she would hang her head and walk over to him with her post-mission report." In other words, Litviak was careful to give the appearance of being appropriately contrite after breaking the rules.

Litviak was badly wounded in air combat on 22 March 1943.[57] She was flying as part of a group of six Yak fighters when they attacked a dozen Ju-88 bombers. Litviak shot down one of the bombers, then felt a sharp pain in her leg. She was being attacked by a pair of Messerschmitts. As she evaded the attack, four more enemy fighters joined in, and Litviak found herself in a singlehanded dogfight against six Me-109 fighters. In an aerial game of "chicken," Litviak employed a tactic often used by Soviet pilots who had especially steely nerves: she pushed the throttle forward and raced directly into a group of enemy fighters. At the last minute, they veered and she was able to get into good firing position; she shot down one Messerschmitt before the fight ended. In severe pain and losing blood, Litviak managed to return to her airfield and land her plane. She stopped on the runway but could not taxi the plane to a parking spot; she lost consciousness.[58]

After receiving field treatment, Litviak was sent to a hospital in Moscow for surgery. She received permission to recuperate at home; hospital beds were in short supply. But she was restless and anxious to get back to the front; after a few days, Litviak talked her way onto a transport and returned to her regiment. Less than six weeks after her injury, Litviak was back on the scoreboard. She shot down two aircraft in March, made three kills in May, and another four in July (all personal kills). Litviak shot down Me-109 fighters on 5 and 7 May.[59] Reportedly, she had not entirely regained her strength when she first returned to flying and was so weak after her 5 May flight that Baranov refused to let her fly again that day.[60]

The month of May brought tragedy as well as victory for Litviak. On 6 May, Nikolai Baranov died when he attempted to bail out of his burning aircraft. Baranov's parachute opened, but it was already on fire. His pilots saw him plummet to his death, with the burning parachute trailing in the air. Then on 21 May, Litviak suffered an even deeper loss. Before the eyes of the entire regiment, while conducting training with a new pilot above the airfield, Alexei Solomatin crashed and was killed. Only two weeks earlier, he had received the highest military decoration, the Hero of the Soviet Union medal.

A lot has been written about the supposed romance between Litviak and Solomatin, who flew together in the 73rd. Pasportnikova believed that "Liliia understood that Solomatin was an exceptional pilot and she appreciated him. Everyone knew that he loved her, everyone knew. But she never told me she was in love with him."[61] General Eremin, who was Solomatin's flight lead early in the war, said that "Solomatin had a very high opinion of [Litviak] as a pilot. He said, 'You know, Boris Nikolaevich, she's a great pilot. She understands me perfectly.' " Eremin was asked in an interview whether he thought Solomatin's love for Litviak affected his performance; Pasportnikova, who was present, interjected, "Quite the reverse!" Eremin agreed: "On the contrary. Solomatin, Liliia—they fought well. Such friendship. They had a special friendship."[62] According to Litviak's letters, she did not realize that she loved Solomatin until after his death. She wrote a wrenching letter to her mother at the end of May, a few days after Solomatin's funeral:

Fate has snatched away my best friend Lyosha Solomatin. . . . He was everyone's favorite and he loved me very much, but at that time he was not my ideal. Because of this there was a lot of unpleasantness. I transferred to another squadron and maybe that's why I was shot down over Rostov. [Next, Litviak described a dream she had.] The river was seething, to swim across was impossible; [Solomatin] stood on the other bank and called me, he called so, simply to tears, and he said, "After all, Batya managed to get me for himself, he couldn't manage without me." And again Alyosha called me and asked: "Lilka, aren't you coming?" And I told him, "If they let me . . ." But I know that I can't swim across this river anyway. And I woke up. And now it's terrible for me to endure, and I confide, mamochka, that I valued this friendship only in the moment of his death. If he had remained alive, then it seems this friendship would have become exceptionally beautiful and strong. You see, he was a fellow not to my taste, but his persistence and his love for me compelled me to love him, and now . . . it seems to me that I will never again meet such a person.[63]

Litviak seems to have become increasingly daring—some might say reckless—after the deaths of Baranov and Solomatin. Her third kill in May 1943 is the one for which she is most remembered by her comrades, and it was not an aircraft at all, but a balloon. The Germans had placed an artillery observation balloon near the village of Troitskoe, about ten miles behind the front lines. The balloon was tethered to the ground and could be raised to permit artillery spotters to observe Soviet positions; they could then accurately direct German artillery fire. The balloon was protected by a heavy screen of antiaircraft fire and could be quickly lowered. Several attempts had already been made by Soviet pilots to destroy the balloon, but all had been turned back by German defensive fire. Litviak decided on a new tactic. First, she flew into friendly territory, far away from the front, before circling back and crossing the front lines. She then penetrated deep into enemy territory before turning to approach the balloon from the rear, behind its defenses. She destroyed it on the first pass.[64]

On 13 June 1943, Litviak was appointed flight commander in the 3rd Aviation Squadron of the 73rd Guards Fighter Aviation Regiment.[65] A few days later, she was involved in a disastrous air engagement. Litviak was flying as wingman to the new regimental commander, I. V. Golyshev, when they set out to intercept an enemy reconnaissance aircraft. They encountered four Me-109 fighters. Golyshev was wounded; Litviak managed to cover his exit from the fight, but her aircraft was badly shot up in the process. Despite ten holes in her Yak-1, Litviak was able to land the plane successfully.[66]

Litviak was wounded once more on 16 July 1943 when six Yak-1s battled against thirty Ju-88s escorted by six Me-109s.[67] She was wounded early in the battle but stayed in the fight and shot down one bomber and one fighter. She received serious damage to her aircraft and was forced to leave the area. She was attacked again during her return to base and wounded a second time. Litviak received local medical attention for her shoulder and leg but refused to be sent to a field hospital, claiming that the wounds were not serious.[68]

Nineteen July was another fateful day for Litviak. She shot down one Me-109 while escorting Il-2s. On the same day, Katia Budanova died. Pasportnikova recalled that the day was "sultry and hot, and the battles were even hotter," when Budanova took off on an escort mission:

> She spotted three Messerschmitts going on the attack against a group of bombers. Katia attacked and diverted the enemy. A desperate fight developed in the air. Katia managed to pick up an enemy aircraft in her sights and riddle him with bullets. This was the fifth aircraft she killed personally. Katia's fighter rapidly soared upward and swooped down on a second enemy aircraft. She "stitched" it with bullets, and the second Messer, streaming black smoke, escaped to the west. But Katia's red-starred fighter had been hit; tongues of flame were already licking at the wings. She managed to put out the fire and to land her aircraft on no-man's land. The local farmers found her and pulled her out, but she was already dead. They buried her on the outskirts of the village of Novokrasnovka. Lily was stunned by Katia's death.[69]

Budanova is still a little-known figure. One source credits her with having claimed six kills by June 1943 and says that during the fighting near Rostov on Don, she achieved another five kills before her death.[70] This would give her eleven kills and put her in the running for a Hero of the Soviet Union award, but apparently none has been granted. However, Pasportnikova stated that Budanova had only five personal kills at the time of her death.[71]

The next day, Litviak barely survived a fierce air battle when she and Golyshev encountered ten enemy fighters. Litviak bailed out of her burning aircraft; Golyshev was killed. Near the end of July, Litviak wrote to her mother, "I am completely absorbed in combat life. I can't seem to think of anything but the fighting."[72] Now she had the personal desire to revenge her fallen friends to add to her list of motivations.

Litviak's final flights took place on 1 August 1943. She flew a total of four times that day. On her third flight, she shared a kill against an Me-109. On her ill-fated fourth flight, she participated in a mass air battle involving six Yak-1s against twelve Me-109s and thirty Ju-88 bombers. Litviak shot down an Me-109, then flew into the clouds, trailing smoke, as she attempted to evade two more attacking German fighters.[73] She disappeared over enemy territory. When Soviet forces recaptured the area a few days later, her regiment conducted extensive searches but could find no trace of Litviak's aircraft. Her worst fear had been realized; her records were marked "missing without a trace." One of Litviak's colleagues, pilot Ivan Borisenko, later wrote: "It is difficult to imagine our grief. Everyone without exception loved her. As a person and as a pilot she was wonderful."[74]

Litviak was recommended for the Hero of the Soviet Union medal, but it was a military regulation that the medal could not be awarded to anyone who had disappeared in combat. Pasportnikova vowed that she would not rest until Litviak's body had been found and her name cleared. She worked for many years with various groups that searched for and identified victims of the war. As it turned out, Litviak did not go down where she was thought to have landed. Apparently, she flew some distance before landing; she was attempting to return to friendly territory. In 1979, the searchers discovered that an unidentified woman pilot had been buried in the village of Dmitrievka.[75] No personal identification was found, but the woman had been very short and had received a mortal head wound. She had been found dead in her aircraft. A search of military records revealed that Litviak was the only unaccounted-for woman pilot in the region at that time, and it was concluded that the body was hers. Finally, in 1988, Litviak's records were amended; rather than being listed as missing, she was now officially "killed in action." The Hero of the Soviet Union nomination went forward at last. In May 1990, Soviet Chairman Mikhail Gorbachev signed the award, which was presented to Litviak's brother Yuri Kunavin. Kunavin died soon afterward, but he had lived to see the names of both his father and his sister restored to honor.[76]

Litviak completed 268 combat flights; her personal kills included one

Ju-87 and three Ju-88 bombers, seven Me-109 fighters, and one artillery observation balloon. Her shared kills included one FW-190 and two Me-109 fighters. All her kills were accomplished in less than one year of combat flying, between 13 September 1942 and 1 August 1943.[77]

During her brief life, Litviak made her mark. She was the first woman in history to shoot down an enemy aircraft. She also holds the top rank for total number of kills among women fighter pilots; her tally of twelve personal kills is a respectable score for any fighter ace. Litviak chose a thoroughly unfeminine profession, yet maintained an almost blatant femininity even in wartime. When the other pilots were having shark's teeth painted on their aircraft, Litviak asked for flowers. She had her mechanic obtain peroxide for her so that she could continue to bleach her hair the shade of blonde she preferred. Yet her skill as a fighter pilot is indisputable. She is remembered by her male colleagues as "a remarkable girl, smart, with the true character of a fighter pilot and a daredevil."[78]

7

Demobilization and Postwar Experiences

❖ ❖ ❖ ❖ ❖ ❖ ❖ ❖ ❖ ❖ ❖ ❖ ❖ ❖ ❖

Most women serving in Soviet military aviation were demobilized after the victory over Germany. The process was relatively gradual; on the whole, women were demobilized from service when their units were deactivated as part of the general force drawdown that followed the end of the war. Soviet Air Force units in the European area ceased combat activities when the Germans surrendered in May 1945, but these units were widely deployed and had to return to Soviet territory before deactivation. For example, in May 1945, the 46th Night Bomber Aviation Regiment was in German territory, the 586th Fighter Aviation Regiment was in Hungary, and the 125th Bomber Aviation Regiment had just transferred from Prussia to the Baltic; it took days or weeks for these units to return to Soviet bases. These regiments were among the many that were completely deactivated after the war; official dates of deactivation ranged from the fall of 1945 (the 586th and 46th) to February 1947 (the 125th). By the fall of 1945, within months of the war's end, a decree was issued demobilizing all women from military service except for a few specialists.[1] Most male combat pilots remained in military service, pursuing study at military academies and upgrading to new equipment.[2]

A few women were permitted to continue on active duty in the Soviet Air Force after the war. However, for the most part, women were discharged from the Soviet military very quickly after the war and were subsequently banned from service academies (virtually the only way to become a military pilot or officer in the Soviet Union).[3] A tendency to revert to old hierarchies is common throughout history, and that is precisely what happened in the Soviet Union.[4] There was no change in the cultural perception that, except during emergencies, war (and therefore military service) was simply not women's work.

The rapid demobilization of women from military service and their virtual exclusion thereafter was due largely to pro-natalist policies in the Soviet government and the need for workers in the civilian sector. Because of heavy wartime casualties and because women were already an essential portion of the workforce before the war, Soviet women had a dual obligation in 1945. Although the government stressed that women were "first and foremost wives and mothers," they were also workers; in late 1945, even after many men had been demobilized from service, women made up 63 percent of the workforce in Moscow.[5] One former 46th pilot told an interviewer that she did not miss her flying days. "How could I explain . . . that peace was the only thing we cared about? Not one girl in our regiment chose to remain in the forces. We just wanted to return to a normal life."[6] Such generalizations must be taken as representative, not authoritative. Pilot Mariia Smirnova, also a veteran of the 46th, said that "after the war our regiment was released, and we all wanted to fly in civil aviation."[7] And some personnel from the 46th did stay in the service.[8]

Information on the postwar fate of women veterans is difficult to obtain. References are scattered throughout memoirs, unit histories, and interviews, but there is no authoritative documentary source. At least 400 women served in the three "women's" regiments, plus an undetermined number in the rest of the Soviet Air Force. In their regimental photo albums, the 46th listed 240 personnel, and the 125th listed 289. The 586th would have been slightly smaller, since fighters were single-crew aircraft. There were approximately one-third male personnel in the 125th and 586th.[9] I was able to compile information on seventy-seven women veterans of aviation (twenty-eight pilots, fifteen navigators, two gunners, two engineers, twenty-four mechanics and armorers, and six staff officers). This group is a completely random sample and represents between 10 and 18 percent of women veterans of aviation who survived the war. If it cannot be considered truly representative, it should at least be indicative of what happened to the larger group of women veterans.[10]

The women veterans of aviation were a varied group with widely differing levels of education. Most of the pilots and many of the navigators had been involved in aviation before the war began; most were air club–qualified pilots, and many were full- or part-time instructor pilots in air

Left to right: Ekaterina Batukhtina, Mariia Dolina, Praskov'ia Zueva, Aleksandra Votintseva, Olga Sholokhova, and Mariia Kirillova participate in a Moscow parade in 1945. (Reprinted from Kazarinova, Kravtsova, and Poliantseva, V nebe frontovom, *2nd ed., 153.)*

Pilot Tamara Pamiatnykh of the 586th IAP. (Courtesy Aleksandr Gridnev.)

Pilot Raisa Surnachevskaia of the 586th IAP. (Courtesy Aleksandr Gridnev.)

Pilots of the 586th (left to right) Raisa Beliaeva, Valentina Khomiakova, Evgeniia Prokhorova. (Courtesy Aleksandr Gridnev.)

Nina Slovokhotova (left), chief of chemical services, 586th IAP. Pilot Valeriia Khomiakova (right) of the 586th IAP. (Reprinted from Kazarinova and Poliantseva, V nebe frontovom, *1st ed., 192, 194.)*

Valeriia Khomiakova (center) being congratulated by Tamara Kazarinova (right) and commissar O. P. Kulikova (left). (Reprinted from Kazarinova and Poliantseva, V nebe frontovom, *1st ed., 195.)*

Aleksandr Gridnev, 1943. (Courtesy Aleksandr Gridnev.)

Pilot Evgeniia Prokhorova of the 586th IAP. (Reprinted from Kazarinova and Poliantseva, V nebe frontovom, *1st ed., 260.)*

Pilots of the 586th at Anisovka. Left to right: Ol'ga Shakhova, Zinaida Solomatina, Aleksandra Akimova, Mariia Batrakova. (Courtesy Aleksandr Gridnev.)

Mechanics at work on a Yak fighter. (Courtesy Aleksandr Gridnev.)

Klavdiia Terekhova, armorer with the 586th IAP. (Courtesy Aleksandr Gridnev.)

Pilot Raisa Beliaeva of the 586th IAP. (Reprinted from Kazarinova and Poliantseva, V nebe fron-tovom, *1st ed., 272.)*

The 586th IAP at Zhitomir in 1944. Aleksandr Gridnev is seated in the front row, third from the right. (Courtesy Aleksandr Gridnev.)

Pilot Klavdiia Nechaeva of the 586th IAP. (Reprinted from Kazarinova and Poliantseva, V nebe frontovom, *1st ed., 218.)*

From left to right: pilots Liliia Litviak, Ekaterina Budanova, and Mariia Kuznetsova of the 586th IAP and 437th IAP. (Courtesy Inna Vladimirovna Pasportnikova.)

Mechanic Inna Pasportnikova of the 586th IAP and 73rd GvIAP. (Courtesy Inna Vladimirovna Pasportnikova.)

Liliia Litviak, pilot with the 73rd GvIAP. (Courtesy Inna Vladimirovna Pasportnikova.)

Pilot Ekaterina Budanova of the 73rd GvIAP. (Reprinted from Kazarinova and Poliantseva, V nebe frontovom, *1st ed., 226.)*

Pilot Aleksei Solomatin of the 73rd GvIAP.
(Courtesy Inna Vladimirovna
Pasportnikova.)

Members of the 73rd GvIAP: Regimental Commander Nikolai Baranov (seat-
ed), Liliia Litviak (second from right), Aleksei Solomatin (leaning on roof).
(Courtesy Inna Vladimirovna Pasportnikova.)

Liliia Litviak in flight gear, standing on the wing of a Yak fighter. (Courtesy Vladimirovna Pasportnikova.)

Funeral of Aleksei Solomatin, May 1943. Liliia Litviak is to the right of the coffin. (Courtesy Inna Vladimirovna Pasportnikova.)

Boris Eremin of the 31st
GvIAP. (Courtesy Inna
Vladimirovna Pasportnikova.)

Left to right: Aleksandr Gridnev, the author, and Vladimir Ravkin in 1993.
(Courtesy the author.)

Inna Pasportnikova and the author in 1993, standing in front of a portrait of Liliia Litviak. (Courtesy the author.)

clubs or at aviation schools. Most pilots and navigators, and some mechanics, had been university-level students at the outbreak of the war. Most of the mechanics were drawn from factories and technical schools. Nearly all these women hoped to return to their old jobs or complete their education once the war was over. Many also felt a strong desire to start families, as was usual for Soviet women in their early twenties.

WOMEN WHO WERE MEDICALLY DISCHARGED

The war took a toll on the health of all veterans. Health problems resulting from wounds, injuries, illnesses, and stress accounted for many women being denied permission to continue in military service after the war. In some ways, the veterans of the 46th appear to have suffered most due to their length of uninterrupted service at the front, compounded by continual night flying. One of the "night witches" noted that although the women refused to report health problems during the war, they suffered in the long term. Senior Lieutenant Serafima Amosova-Taranenko noted that "after the war we had a lot of headaches, could not relax, and had very severe problems with our sleeping, because for nearly three years we had reversed day and night . . . for the first year after the war everyone had problems with sleeping."[11]

Some women who were wounded late in the war were still recovering when the war ended and quickly received medical discharges. Pilot Klavdiia Serebriakova of the 46th had been seriously wounded in March 1945 and was only released from the hospital in late 1946; she became a high school history teacher.[12] Pilot Mariia Smirnova, who hoped to fly in civil aviation, failed the medical examination. "I had undermined my physical and mental health at the front; I was completely exhausted by the four years of war and combat."[13] Navigator Antonina Pavlova suffered multiple fractures in a March 1945 crash; she left the service at the end of the war, married a pilot she had met in the hospital, and became a teacher.[14] Navigator Anastasiia Sharova showed incredible determination to serve despite repeated bouts of illness. She fell ill in 1943 with brucellosis and meningitis, spent several months in the hospital, then was demobilized from the army for half a year. Sharova was reinstated and returned to the 46th; she was too weak to fly but served as adjutant until the end of the war. She left the service and suffered continual health problems after the war but became a teacher. In April 1951, Sharova returned to active duty as a senior instructor at an academy; she was demobilized again in 1955.[15]

Fighter pilot Olga Yakovleva was wounded in one arm in 1943; after a lengthy rehabilitation, she was permitted to fly the Po-2 in a communications squadron until the end of the war but apparently was forced to stop flying afterward.[16] Anna Timofeeva-Egorova, who flew the Il-2 *shturmovik* in an all-male regiment, spent five months in a German prisoner of war (POW) camp at the end of the war. She suffered extensive injuries when she was shot down—broken arms, a broken leg, back and head injuries, and burns—and received no medical treatment from the Germans. She was invalided out of the service at the end of the war after suffering extensive questioning by the Soviet secret police, who suspected her, as they did all POWs, of being a German collaborator. After the war, she married her division commander, had two sons, and completed advanced degrees in history and aviation technology.[17]

In addition to the women who were medically discharged at the end of the war, there were a number of women who were allowed to continue flying in either military or civil aviation for a brief time (a year or two) after the war but then were declared medically unfit (see below).

WOMEN WHO REMAINED IN THE MILITARY

Only twelve of the seventy-seven veterans I studied (about 15 percent) remained in military service: nine pilots, one navigator, an engineer, and a staff officer. Of the flying personnel who continued in the military, half were discharged by 1950. Two former pilots from the 46th Guards remained in the service. Night bomber pilot Serafima Amosova-Taranenko continued flying for two years after the war, apparently in military service, but was then medically discharged.[18] Pilot and HSU Irina Sebrova, who flew more than a thousand combat missions, also remained in the military as a test pilot; after a serious accident in 1948, she was medically retired.[19]

Interviews and memoirs of veterans of the 125th are somewhat contradictory. Pilot Antonina Skoblikova wrote in 1962 that only two female pilots remained in the regiment after the war: herself and Tamara Rusakova.[20] Skoblikova continued flying, upgrading to the Tu-2 bomber and qualifying as pilot first class before transferring to the reserve in 1954.[21] However, pilot Klavdiia Fomicheva also stayed in the service after the war, telling her friends, "I can't think of anything else I would rather do. I plan to stay with the regiment, but if and when it is disbanded—well, there are other units. I can't live without flying."[22] Fomicheva apparently was sent to the Zhukovskii Academy, where she served as a flight instructor until a serious illness caused her death.[23] Navigator Galina Dzhunkovskaia, who married 125th regimental commander Valentin Markov after the war, also stayed in the service. It was apparently unusual for women to remain in the military; Dzhunkovskaia described a 1949 reunion where she told Fomicheva, "It seems that you and I are the last Mohicans." Fomicheva told her that Skoblikova and Rusakova were also still flying, in naval aviation.[24] In 1950, Dzhunkovskaia retired as chief navigator of an air division and transferred to the reserves.[25]

Yet another pilot from the 125th, Antonina Bondareva-Spitsina, continued serving after the war. Bondareva-Spitsina told an interviewer that "there were only three women pilots in my unit who wished to remain in the active air force; we were retrained to fly the Tu-2 aircraft and were assigned to a male regiment. I flew until 1950."[26] And Elena Kulkova-Maliutina, despite having suffered grievous abdominal wounds during the war, also stayed on in military aviation, transferring to a male Tu-2 regiment; she retired in 1949 when she got pregnant.[27] Apparently, then, at least five pilots from the 125th (Skoblikova, Rusakova, Fomicheva, Bondareva-Spitsina, and Kulkova-Maliutina) plus one navigator (Dzhunkovskaia-Markova) remained in the service for at least a few years after the war.

At least two fighter pilots from the 586th remained in the service. Zoya Pozhidaeva married a fighter pilot during the war, and after the war ended, she transferred to his regiment. She flew only until 1946; when she became pregnant, she was apparently discharged.[28] Olga Yamshchikova had been a flying instructor before the war and graduated from the Zhukovskii Academy as an engineer soon after the war started. She remained in military aviation as a test pilot and is often credited in Soviet sources as the first woman to fly a jet (Ann Baumgartner of the United States was actually first). She is credited with flying more than fifty different aircraft types in over thirty years of flying.[29]

Women who had the best chance of remaining in military service for long-term careers seem to be those who had prewar service in nonflying positions. Aviation engineer Klavdiia Iliushina was transferred to the 46th during the war and remained in the air force for a total of thirty-two years, retiring in 1968.[30] Communications officer Marta Meriuts was commissioned in 1933, served with the 125th during the war, and retired in 1956 as a lieutenant colonel.[31] Unfortunately, many of the women with the greatest prewar experience—such as Raskova (who set several world records) and the members of the women's aerobatic team (Raisa Beliaeva, Valeriia Khomiakova, and Evgeniia Prokhorova)—were killed during the war, perhaps because they undertook some of the most dangerous assignments.

WOMEN WHO JOINED CIVIL AVIATION

Many of the women veterans had held positions in civil aviation before the war, and many hoped to obtain postwar employment there. However, only a few managed to find positions—ten out of the seventy-seven in this survey (eight pilots, one navigator, and one mechanic). There may have been a preference for women who flew aircraft most similar to those in civil aviation (the Po-2, flown by the 46th, was widely used in civil aviation, and the Pe-2 twin-engine bomber flown by the 125th was similar to civilian transports). Fighter pilot Klavdiia Pankratova echoed the common belief that fighter pilots were usually rejected by Aeroflot.[32]

Night bomber pilot Mariia Tepikina-Popova, despite having married in 1945, was anxious to continue flying. Although she had flown for two years in civil aviation before the war, she was not automatically allowed to return to Aeroflot. She says, "In 1947 I managed to get a position as a copilot in civil aviation, flying cargo aircraft. I flew only one year, and then the doctors refused to let me fly anymore."[33] Pilot Raisa Zhitova-Yushina, with 535 combat missions, managed a slightly longer career; she flew with the Ministry of Geology as a pilot until 1951, when a Yak-12 crash ended her flying days.[34] Pilot Mariia Akilina, who was shot down during the war, spent months in the hospital; her jaw was smashed, she lost all her lower teeth, her ribs were broken, and she had a spinal injury. Akilina recovered from her injuries and returned to flying. After the war, she flew for nearly twenty years in civil aviation as a crop duster and ambulance pilot.[35] Pilot Vera Tikhomirova, who had been an instructor pilot in civil aviation before the war, also completed a twenty-year postwar career in civil aviation, despite the fact that a serious illness in the last half of 1944 terminated her military career. She returned to flying in 1949 and flew the Li-2 and Il-14.[36]

Pilot Aleksandra Krivonogova and navigator Aleksandra Eremenko, who were crewed together in the 125th, both continued flying in airline jobs. Krivonogova became an aircraft captain and flew more than 4 million kilometers during twenty-five years as a pilot with the Latvian civil aviation administration. Eremenko flew as a navigator in the Riga Group of Civil Aviation, accumulating more than 8,000 flying hours and participating in rescue missions in the Gulf of Riga in the Il-14, which earned her the Order of Lenin.[37] Irina Osadze also went to civil aviation.[38] Krivonogova, Eremenko, and Osadze are described in most sources as "returning" to civil aviation or "resuming" flying civilian aircraft, indicating that they had served with Aeroflot before the war.[39]

At least two former fighter pilots found civil aviation jobs. Zinaida Solomatina went to civil aviation after the war, graduating from flying light ambulance aircraft to heavier twin-engine aircraft. She eventually became an aircraft captain and, in more than twenty years of flying, accumulated 2 million kilometers of air miles and 10,000 hours of flying time.[40] Galina Burdina, who once provided a fighter escort for Nikita Khrushchev during the war, also became an ambulance pilot after the war and continued flying until sometime in the 1960s.[41]

WOMEN WHO ENTERED OTHER AVIATION-RELATED FIELDS

A number of women who were unable to remain in the military or to find flying positions in civil aviation ended up in other sorts of aviation-related work. Since some of these women had been combat pilots during the war, it appears that they loved aviation so much that they were willing to accept low-prestige, low-paying jobs rather than switch careers. Others, like mechanics, simply continued in the same line of work. For example, former 46th mechanic Tatiana Alekseeva, who had trained as a civil aviation mechanic in the early 1930s, returned to civil aviation after the war; she worked for more than thirty years in an unspecified position at Kherson Airfield.[42] Former 125th mechanic Iuliia Tiuliakova worked after the war as chief of an aircraft plant's labor and wages department.[43] Mechanic Ekaterina Kirillova of the 586th returned to the aircraft factory in Saratov where she had worked before the war.[44] Inna Pasportnikova had served as a mechanic with the 586th and later in all-male regiments. Near the end of the war, she says, "I got scarlatina. They thought I would die. They cut off all my hair because they said it would fall out anyway. I had to rest for a whole year. I started working at [an aviation] institute in December 1945. Simultaneously I attended evening classes. My diploma was classified; my adviser was a famous Soviet designer. I designed a jet fighter aircraft. When I graduated, the designer started a design bureau." Pasportnikova worked for many years as an engineer at this bureau, where she met her future husband.[45]

A 1975 article on the women fighter pilots of the 586th mentions that some of the pilots remained in aviation after the war, but the three women it names all became aircraft controllers. These included Surnachevskaia and Pamiatnykh, the pilots who once took on forty-two German bombers and shot down four in a single engagement.[46] Tamara Pamiatnykh had married a fighter pilot in 1944 and flew with his regiment for the remainder of the war; he survived a stint in Buchenwald and went on to complete a long military career before retiring as a colonel. Pamiatnykh apparently became an aircraft controller because it allowed her to remain connected with aviation while raising three children and following her husband's military career.[47] The third pilot named in the article is Zinaida Solomatina, mentioned earlier as a civil aviation pilot. Apparently, she flew for some twenty years and then became an air traffic controller.[48] Former fighter pilot Valentina Petrochenkova became a senior test technician in a parachute center; she also trained female cosmonauts in parachute work.[49] M. S. Pashkevich, who served as a pilot in a male Po-2 regiment during the war, is simply described as working at the Minsk Airport after the war.[50]

WOMEN WHO ENTERED SCIENCE AND ENGINEERING

Some of the women who returned to university studies took advanced degrees in science and engineering. Former 46th Guards chief of staff Irina Rakobolskaia became a senior professor of physics at Moscow State University.[51] Gunner Ira Minakova of the 125th also became an assistant professor of physics.[52] The 125th's regimental navigator Antonina Zubkova returned to Moscow State University and completed postgraduate work in engineering; she later became an instructor at the Zhukovskii Air Engineering Academy.[53] Tamara Meshcheriakova and Sonya Mosolova graduated from Moscow Aviation Institute and became engineers; Meshcheriakova stayed on as an instructor.[54] Former 46th mechanic Matriona Yurodeeva-Samsonova returned to aviation technical school and then worked as an engineer in central Asia.[55] Former 586th armorer Nina Yermakova remained a mechanic of armament for an aviation plant after the war, she says, "because I didn't want to give up aviation." Although the work was "very hard" and "mostly manual labor," she worked for fifty years until her retirement.[56]

Many former armorers and mechanics completed science degrees after the war. From the 125th, these included Lara Belova (geology), Irina Monakhova, Galina Zhidiaevskaia, and Galina Volova.[57] Former 125th navigator Polina Zueva became a senior scientific associate, and Valentina Kravchenko was a senior process engineer.[58] From the 586th, mechanic Valentina Kislitsa completed a university degree and worked at the Central Aerohydrodynamic Research Institute for more than forty years, and mechanic Karelia Zarinia also obtained an engineering degree and worked in Latvia.[59] Former Komsomol organizer Nina Ivakina became chief engineer of "one of Moscow's biggest trolleybus depots."[60] Chemical officer Nina Slovokhotova obtained a doctorate in chemistry.[61]

WOMEN WHO ENTERED PROFESSIONAL FIELDS AND PARTY WORK

From the 46th, navigator and HSU Polina Gelman returned to Moscow State University, taking degrees in history and military interpreting; later she completed postgraduate work in economics.[62] The party organizer of the 46th, Mariia Runt, returned to party work in her native city of Kuibyshev and later completed postgraduate studies.[63] The regiment's Komsomol organizer, Aleksandra Khoroshilova-Arkhangelskaia, went to Moscow to complete her studies at a pedagogical institute at the end of war (leaving behind her husband); she later defended her dissertation while seven months' pregnant with her third child.[64] Navigator Tatiana Sumarokova had been studying to become a surgeon before the war; afterward, she held a long-term position as an editor at Progress Publishers.[65] Navigator Lidiia Demeshova joined the police after the war. She hoped to work as a detective but was refused on account of her war injuries; she ended up in the internal passport bureau.[66]

Former 586th mechanic Marina Muzhikova became a lawyer and continued working for more than thirty-five years.[67] Former radio operator and gunner Anna Popova, who had flown on C-47s with a male transport unit, completed postgraduate work in languages.[68] The former regimental navigator of the 586th, Azerbaijani Zuleika Seidmamedova, was demobilized after the war, even though she had been a military navigator before the war. Seidmamedova returned to Baku, became involved in party work, and in 1952 became Azerbaijan's Minister of Social Security.[69]

From the 125th, navigator Galina Brok-Beltsova worked for the KGB after the war; she completed a history degree in 1960 and then taught, eventually becoming head of the Moscow Engineering Institute's history department.[70] Navigator Mariia Dolina became a Party worker.[71] Natalia Alferova became an instructor of literature at the Friendship of Peoples University.[72] Zina Vasil'eva went to a financial technical school, and Anya Artem'eva became a pediatrician.[73] Former mechanic Olga Vorontsova became a legal investigator in Volgograd.[74]

WOMEN IN FACTORIES

Former 586th armorer Anna Shibaeva returned to the medical equipment plant where she had worked before the war and remained there until her retirement. Mechanic Galina Drobovich worked at a nuclear research institute and later as a telephone station master.[75] Former 125th armorer Evgeniia Zapol'nova had been a student at the Moscow Aviation Institute before the war; she returned there afterward but left before graduation when her father died and she was forced to work to help support her family. Armorer Anna Kirilina returned to her prewar occupation in textiles, saying, "As a pilot loves her aircraft, I loved my instrument very much, and when I returned to the plant, entered the room, and saw my textile instrument standing there, I rushed up to it. I was extremely happy that I had returned to peaceful labor."[76]

DEMOBILIZATION OF WOMEN: WHY IT HAPPENED

Cultural Ideas of Gender Roles

One of the most important factors in the exclusion of women from the postwar military was the simple fact that gender roles had changed very little. Whatever the reasons for allowing women to fight, the Soviets did not see wartime integration of women into the military as a catalyst for fostering long-range changes in gender roles in society. Gender roles were firmly entrenched in Soviet culture. Many women reported problems they had faced even before the war, when flying was widely seen as "not a job for the women."[77] And if aviation was seen as being outside the scope of acceptable women's work, then military aviation was even less acceptable. Many Soviets believed that women should serve in the military only in the most desperate circumstances. Even then, only the persistence of the women themselves forced a temporary expansion of gender roles—one that was doomed to snap back and even produce postwar backlash. For example, despite her fame and influence, Raskova met strong resistance over forming the women's regiments.

Most women who learned to fly before the war, like Raskova, contended that women could and should fly in combat aviation. These include many like 125th pilot HSU Klavdiia Fomicheva, who said after the war, "I can't live without flying."[78] Former 46th pilot and HSU Marina Chechneva recalled that even before the war, she wanted more than anything to be a fighter pilot. She feared that she had missed her chance to ever fly in combat after the battles of Lake Khasan and Khalkin-Gol, which occurred during the late 1930s, while she was still in training.[79]

One can assume that the women who remained in military flying after the war (Amosova-Taranenko, Bondareva-Spitsina, Dzhunkovskaia-Markova, Fomicheva, Kulkova-Maliutina, Pozhidaeva, Rusakova, Sebrova, Skoblikova, Yamshchikova) supported the idea that women should continue to perform combat duties. Pilot Petrochenkova of the 586th noted that she was "eager to fly more" but acceded to her husband's and family's demands.[80] Fighter pilot Klavdiia Pankratova, who flew in her husband's regiment during the war but was forced to retire afterward, said, "I have the strong belief that it doesn't matter whether it is a woman at the controls; a woman can be a military pilot, she can fulfill combat missions."[81] In a speech in 1979, former 46th pilot and HSU Nina Raspopova said, "It is necessary to fight for peace not only with words. I also fight physically. I fight as a communist, as a mother of two sons, as a person who knows well what war is like."[82]

Some women veterans, however—especially among support and former enlisted personnel—espouse essentialist arguments that it is simply not in "women's nature" to participate in war. They often invoke women's role as childbearer and "nurturer" as contradictory to any role as soldier. Former mechanic Zoya Malkova, despite volunteering for service, claimed that "at that time and now, my position is that war is not for women; women shouldn't participate. In a way it's against their nature, because women's first purpose is to preserve peace."[83] Navigator Akimova of the 46th said that "the very nature of a woman rejects the idea of fighting. A woman is born to give birth to children, to nurture. Flying combat missions is against our nature." Navigator Liudmila Popova of the 125th believes that "war is not a normal thing for any country, for any state, for any man, and especially for a woman."[84] Former 586th chief of staff Aleksandra Makunina stated that while "it was proper to be at the front" and that military service was "the duty of all the men and the women too . . . I don't think women should make combat flights at all; I think a woman should remain a woman. Combat is not for a woman."[85] Fighter pilot Valentina Volkova-Tikhonova changed her opinion during the war. "When I was young during the war, I was convinced it was a job for a woman to fly combat. . . . I had become a pilot before the war, and it was only natural for me to become a military pilot. Now I realize that the stress was very great and that it is not a female job."[86]

However, even those who hold such attitudes do not necessarily believe that women should never fight. Former 46th pilot and HSU Mariia Smirnova remarked in 1990, "Was the war a woman's business? Of course not." Yet Smirnova stressed that the 46th had outperformed a male Po-2 regiment with which it was based, and she supported women's role in civil aviation.[87] And Akimova proudly pointed out that "at the cornerstones of our history, women were together with men." She objected primarily to the idea that women should *want* to fight: "To be in the army in crucial periods is one thing, but to want to be in the military is not quite natural for a woman."[88]

The women's attitudes were of course shaped by the culture in which they lived and by which they were educated. Performance was not the issue for these women; none said that women should not be in the military because they cannot do the job. Most of the objections were practical. In the Soviet Union, military life was extremely difficult—more so than in many other countries. In a country where the men do notoriously little household work and rarely assist with child care, the women might find it difficult to imagine combining a military career with a family. It was not enough for the women to change; men must change too.

In her study of sexual equality in later Soviet policy, Gail Lapidus found that despite legal and political equalities, there was no evidence that the Soviet government systematically sought to change the social status of women. Lapidus believed that many people were misled by the authoritarian nature of the Soviet state into believing that all important developments in society were centrally planned:

> Soviet efforts to alter the position of women have lacked the centrality, coherence, and deliberateness that are often assumed by admirers. Particularly since the 1930s, the position of women in Soviet society has been shaped in fundamental ways by economic and political choices in which a concern for sexual equality has been negligible.[89]

Even in fiction, there was an increasing tendency to minimize the role of the women participants in the postwar years. One study of Soviet fiction written about World War II found "the contrast between a woman's gentleness and the brutality of war continues to be stressed, as well as the incongruity of her effort when pitched against the enemy's power. But unlike the heroes of Civil War fiction, men of this period often disapprove in principle of female participation in the war."[90] The same author noted that Soviet fiction did not denigrate women's combat performance: "In action, female soldiers are as brave as men."[91] Even so, women soldiers are rarely protagonists but almost always secondary characters, "bringing a ray of happiness into the life of a brave officer who is the protagonist in the story."[92] Twenty years after the war, although war novels continued to be popular, the role of women receded further into the background.[93]

Pro-Natalism and Family Choices

One specific aspect of gender roles that affected women veterans was the traditional Russian stress on motherhood. Stalin's pro-natalist policies of the 1930s were evident in the reduced availability of abortion, the virtual absence of birth control aids, and the existence of laws making divorce more difficult and costly. Pro-natalist policies were even more pervasive in the postwar years, undoubtedly accelerated by the need to replace the tens of millions of people lost during collectivization, the purges, and the war.

Moreover, traditional views of women's role in the family were always strong in the Soviet Union, and perhaps especially so among those who survived the war. Gregory Smith concluded that although the image of women was one of independence early in the war, it changed back to one stressing the importance of motherhood and family by 1944–1945.[94] Most Russians still believe that motherhood takes precedence over career and precludes military work. Even Aleksandr Gridnev, who gave the highest assessment of the skills of the women fighter pilots of his regiment, told me that "the main calling of a woman is the preservation and increase of the human race" and stated that this was "obviously" the reason there were so few women in the Soviet military after the war.[95] Rakobolskaia commented, "I think that during the war, when the fate of our country was being decided, the bringing in of women into aviation was justified. But in peacetime a woman can only fly for sport. That's how it seems to me. Otherwise how can one combine a career with a family and with maternal happiness?"[96] Rakobolskaia, a senior faculty member in physics at Moscow State University for many years, did not seem to find an academic career incompatible with having a family; her son is now a physics professor at Stanford University.

In the 1940s, most Soviet men believed that women were morally obligated to give up a career when it came time to bear children. Some women, like Valentina Petrochenkova, were forced by their husbands to choose between family and career. In 1946, Petrochenkova's husband—a test pilot—gave her an ultimatum: give up flying, or get divorced.[97] Another former fighter pilot, Klavdiia Pankratova, was also forced to give up flying for her husband's sake. Pankratova married another fighter pilot during the war, transferred to his regiment, and flew there for the last year of the war; she shot down a German aircraft and flew the American P-39 and the British Spitfire. But after the war, she says, "it came to who should retire. It was not the men, of course; I was made to retire, and I didn't want to. Later I tried to go into civil aviation, but they hated fighter pilots, they didn't take me. So I had to quit flying."[98]

Nina Raspopova, a veteran of the night bomber regiment, survived not only being shot down twice in her 857 missions but also a 1937 arrest during the purges before the war; she was demobilized in 1946, got married, had two sons, and "did not fly anymore."[99] Mechanic Nina Karaseva-Buzina married a military pilot and could not work because of frequent transfers. She also noted the concern that wartime work might affect her ability to bear children. "There was some question as to whether we mechanics could bear children after the heavy work and the overstraining of our strength during the war, but it didn't affect us [even though] we had bad nutrition, never enough sleep, and very hard work."[100] Night bomber pilot Nadia Popova contradicted herself. In one interview she said, "Most of us got married immediately and began to have children," but she told another interviewer that many veterans of her regiment never married.[101]

Not all women believed that flying and family were mutually exclusive; many of those who continued flying also had children. A few of the women veterans, including Raskova herself, had started families before the war. Former 46th pilot Mariia Akilina married and had two children before the war. Her husband, a bomber pilot, was sent to the front on the first day of the war; Akilina immediately volunteered and was eventually assigned to the 46th. She was not informed until after the war ended that both her children and her husband had perished during the war.[102] Pilot Olga Lisikova had flown in civil and military aviation since 1937; she flew many missions in subzero temperatures during the Soviet-Finnish War in 1939–1940, stopping only when she was eight months' pregnant. She then became a military pilot after the war began and tells many proud stories of how she accomplished missions at which men had failed.[103] Nevertheless, an overwhelming number of the women veterans believe that flying must stop when childbearing begins, and that a woman cannot remain in the military and have a family at the same time.

War-weariness

It might seem odd that the women themselves did not protest their exclusion from the military after their wartime contributions. Gregory Smith provided one explanation: simple war-weariness. Smith noted that "the overwhelming sadness of the era is the most salient feature of the wartime psyche of the Soviet Union, and perhaps this is why people desperately clung to tradition, to something comfortable, to the desire to retreat into a solid world, a world of home, family, and personal comfort."[104] This "consuming sorrow at the horrible losses and suffering of the war, and fatigue at the endless work, drudgery and sacrifice," limited the development of a feminist consciousness in the postwar Soviet Union.[105] Most of the women I interviewed stressed that by the end of the war, they were tired and ready to return home, even if it meant leaving the service. Some women veterans were eager to leave the service; 586th mechanic Zoya Malkova, who became a teacher, says that "after the war I was fed up with aviation."[106]

Night bomber pilot Nadia Popova stressed that there was not just warweariness but fatigue at the mere thought of the overwhelming tasks of postwar reconstruction. "We came home to face all the destruction and severe food shortages. We worked eighteen hours a day to reconstruct. Maybe that is why we didn't have much postcombat stress—we didn't have time to reflect on our personal experiences in the war, we were too occupied by the present."[107]

Planned Exclusion of Women from the Postwar Military

Some women wanted to continue flying but simply found it too difficult. If they had faced obstacles in their pursuit of aviation careers before the war, the impediments became entrenched after the war. More than a simple reversion to old societal structures, there seems to have been a retrenchment, even a backlash, against women who sought nontraditional careers. For example, whereas women had been discouraged from attending academies before the war, after the war they were officially prohibited from enrolling. Griesse and Stites note that Stalin's prewar policies had already set the tone for the military's attitudes toward women: "Along with the still officially held doctrine of equality of the sexes . . . arose a kind of conservative reaction in the Stalinist thirties to *actual* equality of the sexes."[108] These sorts of attitudes accelerated in the postwar period.

A number of stories illustrate that even before the war ended, there were plans to dismantle the women's regiments as soon as the war was over and policies within the military to oust most women from the service. As previously discussed, medical reasons were frequently used to prevent otherwise highly qualified women from continuing in service. For example, in March 1945, the regimental commander of the 46th Guards Night Bombers decided to send two pilots—Ekaterina Riabova and Mariia Smirnova, both winners of the Hero of the Soviet Union medal—to the Zhukovskii Military Aviation Academy in Moscow. Upon their arrival, they were called in by the commanding general for a "chat." He told them, "You are real heroes of our Motherland. You have already proved what Soviet women are capable of when their help is essential. But the conditions of study in a military academy take a heavy toll on the female body. You lost a lot of strength and health in the war. We must protect you. Enroll to study in a civilian university instead." The girls understood, according to one author, that the friendly general was politely turning them away. Riabova's husband, an Il-2 pilot who won the HSU twice, was sent to the Zhukovskii Academy immediately after the war; apparently, his health was not questioned.[109] One might "logically" assume that the women's health had indeed been undermined by the hardships of war. Yet Riabova was strong enough to complete her undergraduate studies; travel to Italy, Finland, Germany, Korea, and Bulgaria on speaking engagements; give birth to a daughter; and enroll in graduate school—all by the end of 1947.[110]

Aleksandr Gridnev, former commander of the 586th, noted several examples that indicate a plan to diminish the achievements of his regiment and relegate it to postwar obscurity.[111] Gridnev told the story of how the 586th had been promised Guards designation, only to have it withdrawn without explanation: "The war ended and we never became Guards. The regiment was dismantled as soon as possible, and I was simply expelled from the army."[112]

Gregory Smith noted that "in striking contrast to the US and Britain, where women left the work force in great numbers after the end of the war, more Soviet women than ever started to work in the immediate postwar era."[113]

The overwhelming message of Soviet propaganda was that although women could fulfill combat roles when duty called, they were not to expect permanent careers in the military. Their achievements were acknowledged during the war but then quickly forgotten or even obscured. Griesse noted that "what women accomplished earned them credit from other women or in women's journals, and in a once-a-year splash on International Communist Women's Day." In the 1980s, Tatyana Mamonova, former editor of the samizdat (underground) publication *Woman and Russia*, wrote that "the heroism of Soviet women in World War II, when they distinguished themselves as snipers, fliers, and parachutists, is forgotten."[114] In a study of Soviet education, a Western scholar confirmed the fact that the Soviets did not discuss the role of women in combat or even remember their women heroes: "Most of the 'celebration of women' is essentially a eulogizing of motherhood . . . female heroes are, in large measure, absent. . . . One is led to suspect that the failure to honor female heroes . . . is not an oversight but a deliberate policy."[115]

It was a policy not readily accepted by every Soviet woman. Some of the veterans—particularly the pilots—clearly regretted being forced to leave their flying careers after the war. As late as 1988, former fighter pilot Klavdiia Terekhova said, "My flying was the best thing I've had in life."[116] And bomber pilot Bondareva-Spitsina, who was forced to quit flying in 1950, said in 1990 that "I often have dreams about aircraft—of flying. It is my favorite dream."[117]

Conclusion

In evaluating the performance of the women, it is first important to consider whether these regiments flew the same type and number of missions as did other regiments that were comparable. A statistical analysis, based on detailed comparisons of sortie rates per pilot or aircrew, sorties per aircraft, air engagements or bombs on target as a percentage of total combat sorties, and percentages of successful missions, is not yet feasible. Eventually, a comparison of the archival combat records of the women's regiments with those of similar male regiments will be possible. Such a comparison would require extensive archival research, however, since these are the sorts of statistics that the Russians have not yet made available or possibly even compiled. Hardesty has noted the difficulties of assessing the combat performance of the Soviet air forces in general. Published Soviet sources often stress achievements, while failures are minimized or omitted.[1] New information is only beginning to surface, although recent interviews have been enlightening. The evaluations here are necessarily subjective and preliminary, but they provide a basis for further discussion and research, and some general conclusions are possible.

TYPE AND NUMBER OF MISSIONS

There appears to be little or no difference in the numbers and types of missions flown by the women's aviation regiments and other Soviet Air Force regiments. Vladimir Lavrinenkov, general-colonel of aviation and twice HSU, confirmed that the women flew the same type of missions and performed as well as the men:

> The women pilots served at the airfield on an equal footing with the men. And they even fought as well as the men. . . . It wasn't easy for

the girls at the front. Especially for women fighter-pilots: air combat demanded from them unusual physical strength and endurance. And the fact that the girls without complaining bore all the difficulties is a credit to them, and evoked tremendous respect from those around them.[2]

Another way to evaluate combat performance is to study cases in which the women flew under severe stress—with damaged aircraft, while wounded, or after the loss of a neighboring aircraft. Most of the wounds received by the women were from machine guns and cannon shells from enemy fighters, from antiaircraft guns, or from shrapnel. Like any soldiers remembering their days in combat, the women veterans tell a lot of "war stories" about occasions when they or their comrades were wounded. A number of examples of self-sacrifice, when women gave their lives to save others, have been cited in previous chapters. In the context of the ability to endure stress, it is interesting to note that in the United States, the high incidence of stress among fliers had such a negative effect on morale that a tour of duty of twenty-five combat missions was instituted for bomber crews in Europe in the spring of 1943.[3] Allied missions into Germany entailed a high casualty rate, and many crew members did not survive even twenty-five missions; many others returned to combat duty after their initial tour was up. Nevertheless, the United States was able to provide a concrete measure of hope to its aircrews, a luxury that the Soviet Union could not afford. Units such as the 46th Guards Night Bomber Aviation Regiment were at the front lines for three straight years and at times encountered conditions nearly as severe as those the Americans faced in Germany. The crews of the 46th flew at night and often encountered heavy antiaircraft fire and even enemy night fighters. In their wooden, open-cockpit biplanes, with no parachutes, they were even more vulnerable than American bomber crews. Yet many Soviet women aviators accumulated hundreds of combat missions; one woman in the 46th had more than 1,000 combat flights. Their ability to endure stress was demonstrably equal to that of male aircrews.

EFFECTS ON MALE ATTITUDES AND PERFORMANCE

In general, Soviet men were unaccustomed to seeing women in combat; their first reaction was skeptical or hostile. However, once the women's regiments demonstrated acceptable performance in combat, they were assimilated into wartime forces with apparently little difficulty. A number of examples of this have already been given. A key factor seems to have been exposure. Men who were assigned to the women's regiments or who flew with women in other regiments adjusted fastest, while men who remained segregated (such as those in other regiments that shared bases with the women's regiments) were slower to adapt. Interestingly, a similar pattern was observed fifty years later by U.S. Army psychologists who studied sexual harassment of women soldiers during the Gulf War; "most of the overt forms of harassment were conducted by men outside a woman's unit."[4] Men who worked with women adjusted very quickly.

But some men who resisted the idea of women in combat eventually changed their views. A good example is that of Boris Eremin (later lieutenant general of aviation), who was a regimental commander in the division to which Litviak and Budanova were assigned. He admitted that he "felt alarm" when the women arrived and that he refused to have them in his regiment. "The division commander said to me, 'Comrade commander, why don't you want to take these girls into your regiment?' and I was ashamed to answer, because the girls were right there. But Liliia Litviak was a very aggressive person and she said, 'He's afraid of us, that's all. He's young, a regimental commander, a bachelor—he's afraid.' "[5] However, he credited the women for their performance:

> Liliia Litviak and Katia Budanova were assigned to the 296th regiment of Nikolai Baranov. I heard that in the regiment they were well accepted, that they successfully began to fight, and from the first of their combat flights, proved themselves quite well. Not much later, I was hearing about the successes of Liliia Litviak.[6]

General Eremin confirmed in a 1993 interview that this was his true attitude, and not something that had been imposed by an editor. He emphasized even more strongly that the women were exceptional pilots, especially Litviak, who was "a born fighter pilot."[7] The late Marshal of Aviation K. A. Vershinin, commander of the 4th Air Army, rated the women's performance quite highly, as did Marshals Novikov and Chuikov. Men who actually flew with the women also have given them high marks.[8] Lavrinenkov made the following comments on the women's performance:

> I value highly the courage of the women pilots of the 46th Guards Aviation Regiment of night bombers, who flew in the Po-2, and with

pleasure read the vast literature about their famous military victories. But each time, I involuntarily think: how rarely do we recall the names of the women fighter pilots! There weren't many of them, but their combat actions deserve the very highest appraisal. Precisely they disproved the erroneous opinion, that the profession of air combat is unacceptable for women. Katia Budanova and Liliia Litviak were, for us, dependable comrades-in-arms in the skies of the front. I am deeply convinced that they deserve to have a book written about them.[9]

One question that is frequently raised about mixed-gender combat units is whether emotional involvement of women and men affects military performance. Some believe that the men in the unit might become "protective" of the women and neglect their duties. Others think that romantic and sexual relationships would have a negative effect. There were certainly some wartime romances in the Soviet mixed-gender aviation units; at least a few marriages resulted. However, there is no evidence that these relationships negatively affected combat performance.[10] Another issue is that of battle protection—the idea that in mixed-gender units, some men might jeopardize the mission because of their attempts to protect the women more than they would protect other men.[11] Some Soviet pilots who refused to fly with women claimed that it was to protect them. General Eremin refused to take Litviak and Budanova into his regiment because he could not bear the idea of their deaths. Several male pilots are quoted in various sources as refusing to fly with women for the same reason. To view this as wishing to protect the women does not make sense, however. The women were not prevented from flying; they were simply prevented from flying with the experienced pilots who turned them down.[12] In all these cases, the women flew anyway—with one another, rather than on the wing of a seasoned veteran. Many men who refused to fly with women probably sought to protect themselves, and not the women at all.[13] This attitude would be consistent with the findings of Charles Moskos, which indicate that one's own survival is usually a more compelling motivation in combat than protecting someone else.[14]

In any event, it would be difficult to determine how much of male pilots' reluctance to fly with newly arrived women was due to their gender rather than to the men's fears about the capability of the relatively inexperienced pilots. British pilots during the Battle of Britain often regarded rookies as "cannon fodder," not to be relied on. The Soviets had the same attitude;

General Eremin commented, "It was more difficult with young pilots. Young, good-looking Russian kids. They lacked experience. They were killed very often. Sometimes we didn't even remember their names."[15]

In any event, these sorts of reactions were evident only when the women were newly arrived in a regiment; I did not find examples of men who continued to refuse to fly with women once they had flown a few combat sorties in the regiment. And although some male pilots initially refused to take the women as wingmen, there was usually someone in the squadron who agreed—often a senior pilot who felt that it was his duty.

The greatest difficulty with male attitudes was initial acceptance. The women working in mostly male units had to prove their abilities to their colleagues; the experiences of Litviak and Budanova are a case in point. But the women in the 46th did not escape this problem. All the women had to prove themselves—to men in their own regiments, to their commanders, to other regiments, to the higher command.[16] Rakobolskaia claimed that "after the first six months of the war we always felt that the male pilots and the commanders treated us with respect."[17] But the initial problems with attitude appear to have been relatively minor. The combat performance of the regiments was apparently unimpaired. It appears that emotional involvement and overprotectiveness rarely, if ever, had a negative impact on combat performance in mixed-gender regiments. This conclusion is consistent with recent studies of gender integration in work and peacetime military settings.[18]

STYLES OF LEADERSHIP

Whether women have distinctively different styles of leadership from men, and whether there are advantages or disadvantages to those styles, has also been debated. The Soviet case does not resolve this issue. Of the three women who served as regimental commanders—Raskova, Kazarinova, and Bershanskaia—only the last served in combat. But even in peacetime, the three women were quite different from one another. Evdokiia Bershanskaia of the 46th had what might be considered the most "feminine" style of leadership. Her innovative and unorthodox style enabled the 46th to become one of the top-performing Po-2 night bomber regiments in the Soviet military. By contrast, the first female commander of the 586th, Tamara Kazarinova, was strict, harsh, and cold—traditionally "masculine" in her style. She did not evoke the sort of loyalty that Raskova received, but some veterans of the 586th still credit Kazarinova with trying her best. It seems obvious that Kazarinova was lacking in military judgment and would not have made a good wartime commander, but this is more reasonably attributed to personality defects than to gender. After all, she was not at all typical of Russian women in her approach. Her successor, Gridnev, was warm and known for his humor and storytelling ability; he is fondly remembered by the women who served in his regiment.

The experience of the 125th is almost the reverse of that of the 586th. The first commander, Raskova, was soft-spoken, though firm, and was beloved by her subordinates to the point of idolization. One of her deputies described her as "gentle and tactful" and said, "I don't remember a single case when she yelled or even raised her voice, or rudely interrupted a subordinate. Her method of education was persuasion. She never punished anyone in a fit of temper. . . . Her self-control was enviable. Not every leader had such capability and talent."[19] Raskova died before she could test her skills as a leader in combat, but based on her performance in the 122nd, she would have been a capable leader. Not only did her devoted subordinates turn in an impressive performance in training, but her superiors also gave her strong support. Her successor, Valentin Markov, was stern and demanding, at least for the first few months, but his navigator believed that he succeeded in the regiment because he adapted his style, becoming more persuading than demanding.[20]

Aleksandr Gridnev was an outspoken critic of the women commanders in one regard: he believed that they had insufficient military training and experience. "We had a strict rule in aviation. In order to become a commander of a regiment, you were supposed to advance through a particular chain of positions: flight commander, then squadron commander . . . through twelve positions, altogether." Gridnev thought that this background was absolutely essential to a military commander. He believed that Raskova died because "she had no experience to be a regimental commander," and he noted:

> She could have lived and she could have done great things. In my own opinion she was killed by the higher commanders. . . . She wasn't prepared to be regimental commander. She could have been preserved. I and people who thought like me thought it would have been

better to organize a special department to deal with women's combat units. We thought it would be better to appoint her there so that she could watch the combat activities of all three regiments.[21]

Although Gridnev's belief is debatable (Raskova's death is clearly attributable at least as much to bad weather as to her lack of experience as a pilot or a commander), his criticism has validity. It would almost certainly have been better had the leaders of the women's regiments all been experienced commanders. Yet Tamara Kazarinova, the least capable of the commanders, had the most formal experience in the military and had risen through at least some of the positions that Gridnev described as obligatory. Command experience probably would have been beneficial but in itself was no guarantee of skill or judgment.

Gridnev's criticism also provokes the question of how the commanders of the women's regiments were selected. Raskova herself chose them and was obviously determined to keep her newly formed women's regiments as much in women's hands as possible. It probably would have been better, in purely military terms, had her pilots simply been assimilated into line regiments in the way other pilots joined their units. But if Raskova had not created women's regiments, most of the women pilots would never have been given the chance to join a military unit at all. And once the units were created as women's regiments, Raskova was probably psychologically incapable of turning them over to male commanders. After all, she took command of one regiment herself, despite her complete lack of operational military experience and her inexperience as a pilot. In this area, Raskova's judgment may not have been "rational." The question cannot be resolved, since Raskova never had the chance to prove herself in combat. In contrast, Bershanskaia—who probably would have been voted least likely to succeed in military terms—proved herself a capable and innovative commander.

Gridnev's suggestion that Raskova would have been better used on the VVS staff, overseeing all three regiments, might seem logical—if the regiments had continued to be treated as women's regiments, somehow different from the usual aviation unit. But they were not. Although the initial recruitment was handled in an unusual manner, the combat regiments were always part of the regular chain of command. Even before Raskova's death, men were integrated into two of the regiments.

All the commanders of the women's regiments were able to train their squadrons effectively, although their leadership styles varied drastically. The least effective was clearly Kazarinova's traditional approach—perhaps because she simply did not have the skill to back up her perfectionistic demands. Markov and Gridnev, both men, had very different personalities, but both were accepted and effective. Raskova and Bershanskaia were somewhat similar in approach but quite different in terms of experience and willingness to command, yet both were successful leaders. In purely objective terms, Bershanskaia—the least experienced and most unorthodox of the commanders—could be judged the most effective; her regiment won the most honors, produced the most Heroes, and flew the most combat flights. As noted in chapter 3, Bershanskaia was singled out for mention as one of twelve "remarkable air regiment commanders" in the VVS.[22]

MORALE AND UNIT COHESION

The literal definition of *cohesion* is the tendency to stick together. In military terms, this elusive term refers to the overall state of relationships within a unit, or the effects of morale and bonding. It is difficult to study empirically, but it is generally regarded as an important factor in combat performance.[23] Some military sociologists, influenced by the works of sociobiologists such as Edward Wilson and Lionel Tiger, postulate that the presence of women in a combat unit would impede male-male bonding, which is considered essential to good cohesion.[24] Obviously, such studies do not consider what cohesion might be like in an all-female combat unit. In any event, M. C. Devilbiss speculates that the bonding studied in the past was as much due to commonality of experience as to commonality of gender.[25]

Both female and male veterans in the Soviet Union have expressed perceived gender differences in attitudes, though not in overall performance. Devilbiss has identified a similar phenomenon in the U.S. military, which she identifies as "gender consciousness."[26] The women veterans freely voiced their opinions about the similarities and differences of men and women in combat service. Polina Gelman believes that "women in general are, by their nature, more organized" and that "the women, in contrast to the men, were very scrupulous about the fulfillment of each mission."[27] A common theme of many women veterans was that women were more disciplined, more organized, more reliable. Even General Eremin repeated this view.[28] Kravchenko said, "How were we different from the men's regiments? We were more disciplined. In the men's regiments someone might get drunk and go AWOL [absent without leave]."[29] Gelman emphasized the same point: "We weren't drunkards, and we didn't go running after girls." She noted that the division records in Podolsk state that the 46th "took first place in combat work and in discipline."[30]

The women often emphasized the close emotional connection they felt with their colleagues; veterans of the 46th are especially vocal in this regard. "Our regiment was very harmonious and close-knit," wrote Gelman. "We were like sisters. So we have passed through our entire lives. Right to the present we rely on one another as if we were family."[31] Regimental engineer Iliushina noted that even though she had resisted being sent to an all-female regiment, eventually "we all became like sisters. Up to the present day we call all members of our regiment sisters."[32] Armorer Nina Egorova-Arefieva worked in a male fighter regiment before transferring to the 46th and noted that in the all-female unit, "I found the conditions there much more favorable. Everyone was so nice and open."[33]

Many women stressed the fact that they were volunteers. "Even in the most difficult times, women in the army weren't conscripted, only volunteers went into service."[34] The women volunteered because their country had been invaded. It would be difficult to overstress patriotism as a motivation. "There is some kind of magical force in the word 'homeland,'" wrote Aronova. "That force enters into a person, evidently, at birth, and grows together with them."[35] But patriotism and the will to fight are not the same thing. Those who took up factory labor and other support tasks such as medical service were also patriots. The women in this study did not simply support their country in its time of need; they were willing to kill to do it. They fought for the right to fight, insisting on using their special skills in aviation. Rakobolskaia also stressed the importance of voluntary duty. "The women flew as well as men, and in many respects better, more emotionally, with imagination. After all, they were not required to serve in the Air Force. It was their free will, and that which is done at the call of the heart is always done better than that which is done out of obligation."[36]

The women faced not only the test of combat but also the task of continually proving themselves to their own people. The women were very aware that they had to measure up to, or even surpass, the standards set by male aviators. Gelman noted, "We were always trying to prove that we were as good as men. This of course was one of the incentives."[37] The women could hardly fail to recognize that many men questioned their abilities, that they were constantly being judged and tested. There were a number of concrete examples of this, most often occurring when one of the women's regiments arrived at a new base. For example, there was the incident when male fighter pilots staged a fake attack against the inbound (and defenseless) Po-2s—then denigrated the rookie women pilots for scattering out of formation.[38]

An interesting comparison to the Soviet experience is a study conducted in 1942–1943 by U.S. Army Chief of Staff George Marshall, in which units that were half male and half female not only performed better than all-male units but also were judged to have a high level of unit cohesion.[39] The experience of the Soviet mixed-gender units seems to validate Marshall's conclusions.

COMBAT PERFORMANCE

Based on an extensive examination of the sources available—considering mainly primary sources, such as the women's memoirs and a variety of men's eyewitness accounts—two preliminary conclusions about combat performance are possible. First, it appears that the women's regiments did perform the same type and number of missions as did other regiments. This would be consistent with the way in which other Soviet women in combat roles were assigned—snipers, sappers, and tank drivers, for example.[40] Second, the regiments seem to have performed at least as well as the average male regiment. Supporting evidence is the fact that two of the three regiments became Guards regiments, that all the personnel of all three regiments were decorated; and that at least thirty-three female pilots and navigators became Heroes of the Soviet Union. Both these conclusions are supported in the available primary sources. It is particularly interesting that the male eyewitnesses who often admitted to initial doubts about the women's capabilities later praised their skills.

In her book *Soviet Airwomen*, Jean Cottam concluded that the all-female 46th exhibited the best combat performance and that women in all-male or mostly male regiments also fared well; the 125th and 586th, which were "diluted" with men, had higher casualties and did not perform quite as well.[41] Her conclusion is apparently based on a comparison of HSU medals awarded, and from that objective standpoint, the 46th certainly exceeded all the others. But I believe that Cottam erred. The achievements of the 46th, though very real, are better known because they received much more attention in the press and memoir literature; there is no evidence that the women of the other regiments exhibited any less courage, ability, or dedication. As mentioned in chapter 3, the possibility that the 46th received a disproportionate number of HSUs, either because of the influence of its commissar or because it was more culturally acceptable to recognize the women flying "frail" aircraft, cannot be discounted. If the HSU was awarded based partly on the number of combat flights made, then the 46th had a distinct advantage over the other regiments; the Po-2 could simply fly many more sorties per day due to both logistics and basing. The Pe-2 flew much longer missions, and the 586th was limited to combat patrols over fixed targets. Furthermore, Cottam's conclusion that casualties were lower in the 46th is not supported by my research, which shows that the 46th actually had a higher casualty rate than the 125th.[42] The 46th did have a very high level of morale and camaraderie. This was in large part due to the obvious pride of the women in maintaining their regiment's all-female status, but it also was at least partly due to other factors such as consistency of command. The 46th served under a single, beloved commander for the entire war, while the 125th suffered Raskova's death at the outset, and the 586th was plagued with problems in its chain of command.

There is also little basis to conclude that individual women flying in men's regiments had a better chance to excel than did women in mixed or all-female regiments. The primary factor was far more likely that women such as Egorova and Konstantinova, flying in all-male regiments, happened to be in the thick of combat. Similarly, Litviak and Budanova certainly distinguished themselves in the 73rd; they would probably never have had the opportunity in the 586th. Moreover, we do not know how many women served in all-male regiments who did not distinguish themselves sufficiently to make the history books. We know of several women in all-male or mostly male regiments who received the HSU medal, while others did not. In short, these cases reveal little relation between women's combat performance and either gender integration or segregation. Women aviators exhibited exemplary performance in all-female units (the 46th), as well as in situations where they were virtually alone among men. But women and men in mixed regiments such as the 125th and 586th also demonstrated respectable performance in combat.

Griesse and Stites's conclusion regarding the women aviators is validated by my more detailed examination of the combat performance of the women's regiments: "The composite picture suggested by the sources— even when allowing for piousness and hyperbole—is one of several thousand dedicated and brave women risking their lives daily and nightly and having a tactical, if not strategic, significance out of proportion to their numbers."[43] Pilot Alexei Maresiev, a Hero of the Soviet Union who lost both feet early in the war and returned to fly with artificial limbs, said that "in fighters and bombers, [the women] destroyed the enemy just as well as men did. They demonstrated that young Soviet women have an iron character, a steady hand, and an accurate eye."[44]

OVERALL CONCLUSIONS

Of the three main factors in the formation of the women's aviation regiments—personnel shortages, propaganda, and Marina Raskova's influence—Raskova's role was the most important. At the time the regiments were formed, there was not a sufficient shortage of pilots to induce the formation of women's regiments as a "desperation measure"; in any event, the total personnel of the regiments was too small to be militarily significant. When the women's aviation units were formed in October 1941, the situation in the Soviet Union was indeed desperate. Whether that desperation was the primary reason for the units' creation is doubtful. The VVS faced severe shortages of aircraft and parts, but no shortage of pilots. Did it alleviate any military desperation to dedicate scarce resources to untested women pilots, and to do so at the height of the evacuation from Moscow? The desperation argument is not compelling. Neither is the idea that the regiments were merely an exercise in public relations. Although propaganda and morale benefits were derived from the existence of the women's regiments, there is little evidence that publicity was the main factor behind their formation. Top Soviet leaders did not propagandize these regiments in any significant way, and little information was given to the foreign press or to important Soviet war correspondents on the women aviators.

There is a great deal of evidence, however, to support the conclusion that it was Marina Raskova who was the driving force behind the regiments' formation. This view is supported not only by the women who flew in the regiments but also by male veterans and by contemporary and modern Soviet journalists. Raskova had the fame, the skill, and the personal connections that enabled her to pursue her idea, and she had strong popular backing from the women who appealed to her and to the Soviet government.

In April 1942, a new commander took over the VVS and implemented a massive reorganization. If the women's regiments had been created merely in desperation, or through some bureaucratic error, it would have been an opportune time for the VVS to rethink that move. The women could easily have been relegated to support and training duties, demoted to nonflying jobs, or even demobilized altogether. But no such actions were taken, then or later. The regiments continued to fight, and the most likely explanation is that they were found to be effective and useful.

The rapid postwar demobilization of women from military service and their virtual exclusion thereafter was due largely to pro-natalist policies in the Soviet government and the need for workers in the civilian sector. Because of heavy wartime casualties and because women were already an essential portion of the workforce before the war, Soviet women had a dual obligation in 1945. Although the government stressed that women were "first and foremost wives and mothers," they were also workers; in late 1945, even after many men had been demobilized from service, women made up 63 percent of the workforce in Moscow.[45] In addition to these practical considerations, there was no change in the cultural perception that, except during emergencies, war (and therefore military service) was simply not women's work.

Despite their well-documented performance in combat, women were never received as part of the Soviet military elite. It is clear that the Soviets regarded the use of women in combat as a temporary measure. Even while women were at the front, the Soviets instituted gender segregation in the educational system and excluded women from the newly created Suvorov cadet schools. In 1943, the groundwork was already laid for the exclusion of women from the postwar military. It seems apparent that no matter how well the women performed in nontraditional combat roles, they could not change ingrained societal ideas of gender roles. Performance was irrelevant to Soviet decision making about whether to allow women to remain in military service, and there is strong evidence that during the postwar period, the Soviet government deliberately obscured women's wartime achievements.

There is evidence that the performance of Soviet women in combat has been forgotten by the general Soviet public (in much the same way that the combat performance of the racially segregated combat units in U.S. forces is virtually unknown to Americans). Griesse and Stites noted that "for the most part public recognition of women's sacrifices and experiences in war was not played up very much. What was stressed in the postwar years were the new crucial roles for women, for instance, motherhood and the labor force."[46] This phenomenon of selective amnesia is not unique to the Soviets. Sharon Macdonald points out that because war is traditionally defined as masculine, women in combat disrupt the social order by their very existence. They are outside the social framework of understanding, and when history is written after the war, their experiences are usually explained away or simply forgotten.[47]

This situation is not unique to the Soviet Union. Nancy Loring Goldman believes that this is "a phenomenon that was almost universal in the twentieth-century utilization of women." She points out "the willingness of the military to use women for the most dangerous missions in the emergency of a desperate struggle and then to demobilize them after the emergency is over." However, "even maximum participation in quantity and quality in a combat war situation does not guarantee equality in the service, in other walks of life, or in the postwar society."[48] This situation is evident not only in the Soviet experience but also in Yugoslavia, Israel, and Vietnam. Ellen Jones noted that servicewomen in all countries were demobilized after the end of the war.[49]

The reason the Soviets excluded women from the postwar military is at least partly related to a wider phenomenon. The United States passed combat exclusion laws against women in 1948, despite the fact that women had not been used in combat during World War II. Although the Soviets were willing to use women in combat on a much wider scale than were other countries when the situation demanded it, they also reverted to traditional role models and behaviors as soon as the crisis ended. A tendency to revert to old hierarchies is common throughout history.[50]

Even if Soviet military women had not already been consigned to planned obscurity by the Soviet government, the fact that gender roles had not changed would almost certainly have forced a snapping back of their roles. Any image of the new Soviet woman as military officer and pilot that resulted from wartime experience was far outweighed by the overwhelming official emphasis on the Soviet woman as mother, wife, and builder of society. Where the Americans had Uncle Sam, the Soviets had Mother Russia. Soviet women were constantly reminded—and many believed—that their true place was on the home front, not the battlefront.

Appendix A:

Lists of Regimental Personnel

An asterisk denotes those killed during the war. Women's married surnames appear in brackets after their maiden names.

46TH GUARDS NIGHT BOMBER AVIATION REGIMENT
(ALL FEMALE)

Pilots

(last name)	*(first name)*	*(patronymic)*
Akilina	Mariia	
Altsibeeva	Nina	
Amosova	Anna	
Amosova [Taranenko]	Serafima	Tarasovna
Aronova	Raisa	Ermolaevna
Bekarevich	Nina	
Belkina*	Pelageia	Grigor'evna
Belkina	Praskov'ia	
Bershanskaia	Evdokiia	Davydovna
Chechneva	Marina	Pavlovna
Dudina	Anna	
Ezhova	Nadezhda	
Fokina	Taisia	
Gorbacheva	Liudmila	
Iushina [Zhitova]	Raisa	
Kazberuk	Elizaveta	
Khudiakova [Agusheva]	Antonina	Fedorovna
Klopkova	Liudmila	
Kokosh	Sof'ia	
Kornienko	Akulina	
Krutova*	Evgeniia	
Makarova*	Tat'iana	Petrovna

Makogon*	Polina	Aleksandrovna
Malakhova*	Anna	
Meklin [Kravtsova]	Natal'ia	Fedorovna
Nikitina	Mariia	
Nikulina	Evdokiia	Andreevna
Nosal'*	Evdokiia	Ivanovna
Ol'khovskaia*	Liubov'	
Oleinik	Ekaterina	
Osokina	Tat'iana	
Parfenova [Akimova]	Zoia	Ivanovna
Paromova	Mira	
Pashkova*	Iuliia	Fedorovna
Perepecha	Valentina	
Piskareva	Ekaterina	Ivanovna
Polunina*	Valentina	
Popova	Anastasiia	Vasil'evna
Popova	Evgeniia	
Popova	Nadezhda	Vasil'evna
Prasolova	Praskov'ia	
Prokop'eva	Panna	
Putina	Anna	
Raspopova	Nina	Maksimovna
Rogova*	Sof'ia	
Rukavitsina	Mariia	
Ryl'skaia	Kaleriia	
Ryzhkova	Klavdiia	
Sanfirova*	Ol'ga	Aleksandrovna
Sebrova	Irina	Fedorovna
Serebriakova	Klavdiia	
Smirnova	Mariia	Vasil'evna
Solov'eva	Zoia	
Syrtlanova	Maguba	G.
Tepikina [Popova]	Mariia	
Tikhomirova	Vera	Ivanovna
Tormosina*	Liliia	
Troparevskaia	Nadezhda	Evgen'evna
Volodina*	Taisia	
Vysotskaia*	Anna	Grigor'evna
Zhigulenko	Evgeniia	Andreevna

Navigators

Avidzba	Meri	
Belik*	Vera	Luk'ianovna
Bespalova	Galina	
Bondareva*	Anna	
Burzaeva	Sof'ia	Ivanovna
Danilova	Nina	
Demeshova	Lidiia	Konstantinovna
Dokutovich*	Galina	
Dospanova	Khivaz	

Efimova*	Antonina	Grigor'evna
Frolova*	Tamara	
Gasheva	Rufina	Sergeevna
Gel'man	Polina	Vladimirovna
Glamazdina	Evgeniia	
Glatman	Irina	
Golubeva	Lidiia	
Golubeva [Teres]	Ol'ga	Timofeeva
Iakovleva	Ol'ga	
Kashirina*	Irina	
Khurtina	Vera	
Kliueva	Ol'ga	Aleksandrovna
Komogortsova*	Nadezhda	
Kostina	Tat'iana	
Lavrent'eva	Lidiia	
Loshmanova	Lidiia	
Luchinkina	Valentina	
Maslennikova	Tat'iana	
Mesniankina	Ekaterina	
Nikitina	Elena	
Pas'ko	Evdokiia	Borisovna
Pavlova	Antonina	Vasil'evna
Pavlova	Evgeniia	
Penchuk	Mariia	
Petkileva	Polina	
Petrova	Anna	
Petrova	Zinaida	
Popova	Aleksandra	
Pustovoitenko	Valentina	
Rachkevich	Evdokiia	Iakovlevna
Radchikova	Larisa	
Reutskaia	Nina	
Riabova	Ekaterina	Vasil'evna
Rozanova [Litvinova]	Larisa	Nikolaevna
Rozova	Antonina	
Rudneva*	Evgeniia	Maksimovna
Salikova*	Elena	
Sharova	Anastasiia	Ivanovna
Shevchenko	Liubov'	
Startseva	Klavdiia	
Studilina	Nadezhda	
Sukhorukova*	Evgeniia	
Sumarokova	Tat'iana	Nikolaevna
Svistunova*	Lidiia	Aleksandrovna
Tarasova*	Vera	
Timchenko	Ekaterina	Pavlovna
Tseloval'nikova	Lidiia	
Tsuranova	Anastasiia	
Ul'ianenko	Nina	Zakharovna
Ul'ianova	Polina	

Vinogradova*	Mariia	
Vodianik	Sof'ia	
Volosiuk	Anna	
Zhdanova	Lidiia	

Staff, Political Officers, and Others

Artem'eva	Anna	
Driagina	Irina	Viktorovna
Dushina	Anna	
Elenina	Anna	Pavlovna
Fetisova	Ol'ga	Spiridonovna
Gorman	Zinaida	
Gumilevskaia	Tamara	Anatol'evna
Karpunina	Kseniia	Pavlovna
Khoroshilova [Arkhangelskaia]	Aleksandra	Vladimirovna
Khudiakova	Nina	
Kolbasina	Nina	
Makhova	Lidiia	
Maksimova	Valentina	
Martynova	Nadezhda	
Mazdrina	Raisa	
Rakobolskaia	Irina	Viacheslavna
Runt	Mariia	Ivanovna
Serdiuk	Nina	
Smirnova	Anna	
Stupina*	Valentina	Sergeevna
Tkachenko	Ekaterina	
Volkova	Nina	Vasil'evna
Zhukovskaia	Olga	Isaakovna

Mechanics, Armorers, Engineers

Eidlina	F.	
Ermakova	Liubov'	
Erokhina [Averianova]	Ol'ga	
Evpolova	Elena	
Fedotova	Mariia	
Glazkova	E.	
Glebova	Klavdiia	
Glinina	A.	
Gogina	Lidiia	
Golovko		
Golovkova	M.	
Gorelkina	N.	
Grosheva	L.	
Guseva	Nina	
Il'ina	Iuliia	
Iliushina	Klavdiia	Alekseevna
Irlina	Anzhelika	

Iurod'eva [Samsonova]	Matrena	
Ivanova	Antonina	
Kalinkina	Antonina	Tikhonovna
Karaseva [Buzina]	Nina	
Kas'ianova	A.	
Kazantseva	Alla	
Kharitonova	Raisa	
Khlapova		
Khotina	Liubov'	
Kirilenko	Anna	
Klimova	G.	
Kniazeva	V.	
Kolokol'nikova*	Anna	
Komkova	Galina	
Kondrat'eva	Aleksandra	
Korobeinikova	Taisia	
Korotchenko	Evdokiia	
Korsun	Galina	
Kosova	Polina	
Kropina	Mariia	
Kuz'menko	Zinaida	
Kuznetsova	I.	
Lapteva	Anna	
Larina	Nadezhda	
Lavrent'eva	Sof'ia	
Liadskaia	Galina	
Logacheva	Mariia	
Lomakina	Tat'iana	
Lopukhina	K.	
Mal'tseva	N.	
Mamenko	Vera	
Marina	Mariia	
Mashchenko	L.	
Maslennikova*	Liudmila	
Medvedeva	Anna	
Meluzova	Tamara	
Mironenko	Mariia	
Mishchenko	L.	
Nikitina	Mariia	Grigor'evna
Nikolaeva	Lidiia	
Ogii	Vera	
Ol'khovskaia	M.	
Orlova	Rakhime	
Osmantseva	Aleksandra	
Ozerkova	Sof'ia	
Paklina	Elena	
Parshina	A.	
Pilipenko	Galina	
Platonova	Aleksandra	
Ponomarenko	G.	
Popusheva		
Prudnikova	Rimma	
Rad'ko	Aleksandra	

Radina	Zinaida	
Romanova	Zinaida	
Rudakova	Antonina	
Rumiantseva	Valentina	
Rybal'chenko	Elizaveta	
Sapronova	Evgeniia	
Serebrianova		
Sergeeva	Anna	
Serova	G.	
Sharoevskaia	Zinaida	
Shchelkanova	Mariia (Masha)	
Shcherbinina	Tat'iana	
Sheiankina	Valentina	
Shepturova	Anna	
Sherstneva	Anna	
Stolbikova	Anna	
Strelkova	Nadezhda	Aleksandrovna
Svetlanova	Maguba	
Titova	Ekaterina	
Tuchina	Polina	
Turianskaia	E.	
Vakhromeeva	Antonina	
Varakina	Liubov'	
Vasil'eva	Vera	
Vasil'eva	Zoia	
Vishneva	Zinaida	
Zarubina	A.	
Zhukovitskaia	Mariia	
Zhuravleva	Evgeniia	

❖ ❖ ❖

125TH GUARDS BOMBER AVIATION REGIMENT

Pilots: Female

Dolina [Mel'nikova]	Mariia	Iosifovna
Egorova*	Aleksandra	Stepanovna
Fedotova	Ekaterina	Petrovna
Fedutenko	Nadezhda	Nikiforovna
Fomicheva	Klavdiia	Iakovlevna
Gubina*	Liubov'	Mikhailovna
Iazovskaia*	Anna	Maksimovna
Kirillova	Mariia	Andreevna
Krivonogova	Aleksandra	Ivanovna
Kuzenkova*	Vera	Ivanovna
Lapunova*	Mariia	Mikhailovna
Lomanova [Tenueva]	Galina	Dmitrievna
Maliutina [Kulkova]	Elena	Mironovna
Malkova	Nina	Fedorovna

Maslova	Tamara	Nikolaevna
Matiukhina*	Valentina	Alekseevna
Melashvili	Tamara	Davydovna
Nikitina [Chapligina]	Galina	Konstantinovna
Osadze	Irina	Sergeevna
Pogorelova	Mariia	Konstantinovna
Rusakova	Tamara	Ivanovna
Shiriaeva	Zinaida	Fedorovna
Shishkova	Anna	Aleksandrovna
Sholokhova	Ol'ga	Mitrofanovna
Skoblikova	Antonina	Andriianovna
Spitsina [Bondareva]	Antonina	Grigor'evna
Tarasenko	Mariia	Terent'evna
Timofeeva*	Elena	Pavlovna
Timofeeva	Evgeniia	Dmitrievna
Tret'iakova	Zinaida	Ivanovna

Pilots: Male

Liakh	F.	I.
Markov	Valentin	Vasil'evich
Titenko	Semen	Moiseevich

Navigators: Female

Azarkina	Elena	Vladimirovna
Batukhtina	Ekaterina	Iakovlevna
Brok [Beltsova]	Galina	Pavlovna
Dubkova	Klara	Fedorovna
Dzhunkovskaia [Markova]	Galina	Ivanovna
Eremenko	Aleksandra	Davydovna
Guruleva	Evgeniia	Vasil'evna
Iushina	Elena	Vasil'evna
Karaseva	Nina	Dmitrievna
Kezina*	Anna	Ivanovna
Konkina	Valentina	Ivanovna
Kravchenko [Savitskaia]	Valentina	Flegontovna
Ol'khovskaia	Galina	Fedorovna
Orlova	Zinaida	Dmitrievna
Ponomareva*	Elena	Nikolaevna
Popova	Liudmila	Leonidovna
Pugacheva	Antonina	Iosifovna
Sergeeva	Evgeniia	Prokof'evna
Stepanova	Zinaida	Nikolaevna
Tsvetkova	Ekaterina	Vasil'evna
Turabelidze	Galina	Prokof'evna
Vasil'eva	Galina	Sergeevna
Vasil'eva*	Nadezhda	Grigor'evna
Vatintseva	Aleksandra	Semenovna
Volkova	Valentina	Georgievna

Vozhakova*	Mariia	Fedoseevna
Zubkova	Antonina	Leont'evna
Zueva	Praskov'ia	Grigor'evna

Navigators: Male

Khil'*	Kirill	Il'ich
Nikitin	Nikolai	Aleksandrovich

Gunners: Female

Absoliamova	Elizaveta	Fedorovna
Chernova	Margarita	Konstantinovna
Firsova	Mariia	Vasil'evna
Khokhlova [Dubkova]	Antonina	Tikhonovna
Mil'dzikhova	Madina	Khazbievna
Panferova	Taisia	Sergeevna
Ratkevich	Raisa	Stepanovna
Severina	Klavdiia	Ivanovna
Smirnova	Natal'ia	Alekseevna
Sycheva	Aleksandra	Vasil'evna
Zhukovitskaia*	Ida	Iosifovna

Gunners: Male

Abibulaev	Raif	
Aleksandrov		
Bagirov	Magerram	Abasauli-Ogly
Erofeev*	Nikolai	Nikolaevich
Gorbachev	Petr	Alekseevich
Gorskii	Stepan	Petrovich
Grishko*	Grigorii	Ivanovich
Iuska*	Nikolai	Dmitrievich
Khotov	Valentin	Prokhorovich
Kochugin	Anatolii	Mikhailovich
Kotov	Valentin	Prokhorovich
Krymskii*	Kvintel'ian	Efimovich
Krysa*	Nikolai	Stepanovich
Kudriavtsev	Aleksandr	Prokop'evich
Kurkin	Ivan	Semenovich
Levit	Mikhail	Mikhailovich
Maniakin	Aleksandr	Semenovich
Mil'man	Boris	Borisovich
Nazarov		
Omel'chenko	Aleksei	Ivanovich
Papusha*	Nikolai	Moiseevich
Seliutin	Dmitrii	Vasil'evich
Shatkovskii	Petro	Nikiforovich

Solenov	Ivan	Grigor'evich
Stepanov	Viacheslav	Petrovich
Taziev	Nazid	Tazievich
Tikhii	Vasilii	Ivanovich
Tsimbal	Grigorii	Anisimovich
Tsitrikov	Stepan	Illarionovich
Vasil'ev	Dmitrii	Vasil'evich

Staff, Political Officers, and Others: Female

Abramova	Mariia	Borisovna
Arkharova	Nina	Vasil'evna
Bereznitskaia	Antonina	Mikhailovna
Eliseeva	Lina	Iakovlevna
Izvoshikova	Irina	Aleksandrovna
Kazarinova	Militsiia	Aleksandrovna
Lukina	Elena	Ivanovna
Meriuts	Marta	Pimenovna
Migunova	Ekaterina	Aleksandrovna
Molokova	Zinaida	Nikolaevna
Monakhova	Irina	
Nikiforova	Tat'iana	Sergeevna
Novikova	Faina	Mikhailovna
Ponomareva	Mariia	Ivanovna
Raskova*	Marina	Mikhailovna
Sanchuk	Kseniia	Apolinar'evna
Semenova	Elena	Andreevna
Shchegrova	Mariia	Illarionovna
Tsar'kova	Nina	Semenovna
Tsar'kova	Polina	Semenovna
Tusnolobova		
Vorontsova	Ol'ga	Ivanovna
Zhidiaevskaia	Galina	

Staff, Political Officers, and Others: Male

Bukin	Semen	Fedorovich
Mazurin*		
Svetil'nikov	Vitalii	Fedorovich
Zagainyi	Pavel	Alekseevich
Zarutskii	Vladimir	Ivanovich

Mechanics, Armorers, Engineers: Female

Abramova	Liubov'	Vasil'evna
Abramova	Mariia	
Alferova	Natal'ia	Vasil'evna
Artem'eva	Anna	Vasil'evna

Artem'eva	Ol'ga	Nikolaevna
Baidiuk	Eva	Alekseevna
Baikova	Valentina	
Bakotina	Mariia	Ivanovna
Belova	Larisa	Nikolaevna
Bondarenko	Mariia	Il'inichna
Bulatova	Rimma	Mikhailovna
Bulycheva	Valeriia	Viacheslavna
Chalaia	Dar'ia	Andreevna
Chuikova	Ekaterina	Petrovna
Dmitrienko	Varvara	Sidorovna
Gorelkina	Nina	
Gracheva	Tat'iana	Ivanovna
Gromova	Ekaterina	Vasil'evna
Guseva	Liubov'	
Iudina*	Antonina	Vasil'evna
Ivanova	Zinaida	Fedorovna
Kaloshina	Mariia	Ivanovna
Khmeleva	Antonina	Ivanovna
Kiseleva	Mariia	
Kobiakova	Galina	Alekseevna
Kolesnik	Vera	Terent'evna
Kriuchkova	Evgeniia	Semenovna
Krugliakova	Mariia	Petrovna
Kutarkina*	Nadezhda	Aleksandrovna
Larkina	Klara	Prokof'evna
Lepilina	Antonina	Dmitrievna
Litvinova	Anna	Ivanovna
Lukovikhina	Antonina	Grigor'evna
Maksiushina	Vera	Pavlovna
Matveeva	Aleksandra	Borisovna
Meshcheriakova	Tamara	Pavlovna
Minakova	Irina	Il'inichna
Morozova	Evdokiia	Nikolaevna
Mosolova	Sof'ia (Sonya)	Stepanovna
Ozimina	Mariia	Petrovna
Paramonova	Klavdiia	Vasil'evna
Polezhaeva	Taisia	
Riabinina	Adelina	Sergeevna
Romanova	Anna	Ivanovna
Rumiantseva	Viktoriia	Vasil'evna
Samoilova	Valentina	Kupriianovna
Sedova	Iuliia	Illarionovna
Sever'ianova	Mariia	Gerasimovna
Smakhtina	Raisa	Nikolaevna
Sokolova*	Anna	Aleksandrovna
Stepanova	Polina	Viktorovna
Studenova	Agrafena	Petrovna
Sukhovilova	Liudmila	Vasil'evna
Teteriatnikova	Ialevtina	Pavlovna
Tiuliakova	Iuliia	Petrovna
Trifonova	Anna	Vasil'evna
Ulanova	Elena	Grigor'evna

Vargina	Ol'ga	Filippovna
Vasil'eva	Zinaida	Ivanovna
Vinokurova	Zoia	Nikolaevna
Volova	Galina	Mikhailovna
Zapol'nova	Evgeniia	Nikitichna
Zarembo	Anastasiia	Kondrat'evna
Zhbankova	Valentina	Antonovna
Zhediaevskaia	Galina	Dmitrievna
Zhirkova	Mariia	Emel'ianovna
Zubova	Irina	Stepanovna

Mechanics, Armorers, Engineers: Male

Ageev	Evgenii	Mikhailovich
Alent'ev	Fedor	Georgievich
Alferchik	Nikolai	Nikolaevich
Baidarov	Petr	Ivanovich
Bakunov	Sergei	Vasil'evich
Barsukov	Aleksandr	Ivanovich
Beliaev	Mikhail	Ivanovich
Belkin	Semen	Semenovich
Bezliudnyi	Ivan	Fedorovich
Blizniuk	Vasilii	Danilovich
Bondarev	Petr	
Borisov	Aleksei	Alekseevich
Bychkov	Konstantin	Leont'evich
Chumirenko		
Dal'nov	Mikhail	Ivanovich
Drachenko	Leonid	
Erofeev	Fedor	Vasil'evich
Evchenko	Kuz'ma	Evdokimovich
Feshchenko	Zakhar	Antonovich
Glazunov	Vasilii	Afanas'evich
Golovkin	Vasilii	Ivanovich
Golubev	Vasilii	Maksimovich
Grichukhin	Nikolai	Vasil'evich
Grishunin	Nikolai	Stepanovich
Gromov	Iosif	Matveevich
Grushevskii		
Ibragimov	Nurgalei	Nurmykhametovich
Igant'ev		
Il'in	Nikolai	Vasil'evich
Iurochka	Vladimir	Iakovlevich
Ivanov	Ivan	Vasil'evich
Kakama	Aleksei	Gavrilovich
Kalduzov	Vladimir	Alekseevich
Kaplan		
Karp	Boris	Shlemovich
Karputin	Nikolai	Sergeevich
Kindiukhin	Ivan	Nikitich
Kiselev	Terentii	Romanovich

Kobriakov		
Kolotilov	Aleksei	Dmitrievich
Korenkov		
Korpilov	Mikhail	Ivanovich
Korshynov	Mikhail	
Kostromin	Aleksandr	Leont'evich
Kovtun*	Grigorii	Ivanovich
Kruglov*	Vladimir	Ivanovich
Kuchkarov	Shody	Mirzoevich
Kulashnikov*	Pavel	Nikolaevich
Kurcherenko	Evgenii	Trofimovich
Kuroptev	Nikolai	Mikhailovich
Laletin	Anatolii	Efimovich
Levin	Iosif	Grigor'evich
Litosh	Vasilii	Leont'evich
Mal'shev	Leonid	Aleksandrovich
Martyniuk	Nikolai	Moiseevich
Moldovanchuk	Ivan	Ivanovich
Nalivaiko	Andrei	Egorovich
Neskoblinov	Mikhail	Dmitrievich
Nuridinov	Abdyganpar	Dosankulovich
Obukhov	Mikhail	Ivanovich
Oleshagin	Viktor	Ivanovich
Osipov	Nikolai	
Panteliat	Il'ia	Iudovich
Piatkov	Petr	Ivanovich
Piatyshev	Kornelii	Ivanovich
Plotnir	Ivan	Ivanovich
Poliakov		
Polovykh	Aleksandr	Kharlampievich
Pristavka	Iosif	Ignat'evich
Prokopenko	Nikolai	Andreevich
Reztsov	Viktor	Vasil'evich
Riza-Ogly	Aleksei	Vladimirovich
Romanov	Petr	Nikolaevich
Rubtsov	Andrei	Ivanovich
Rybin	Viktor	Ivanovich
Rybnikov		
Sapronov	Aleksandr	Timofeevich
Senkovskii	Evgenii	Vasil'evich
Sergeev	Iurii	Grigor'evich
Sevost'ianov	Pavel	Petrovich
Shcherbakov	Mikhail	Alekseevich
Sherman	Leonid	Artem'evich
Shilin	Boris	Grigor'evich
Shilov	Boris	Vasil'evich
Shinkarenko	Nikolai	Il'ich
Shumarin*	Aleksei	Maksimovich
Slobodianiuk	Vladimir	Iakovlevich
Smirnov	Aleksandr	Petrovich
Sofin	Vikentii	Ivanovich
Solodovnikov	Nikolai	
Stepanov	Aleksandr	Vasil'evich

Sukhinov	Georgii	Georgievich
Teterin	Semen	Vasil'evich
Ushakov	Ivan	Grigor'evich
Usmanov	Abdugani	
Varenik	Vladimir	Serafimovich
Vertousov	Vladimir	Nikolaevich
Volgushkin	Pavel	Ivanovich
Vstrechevskii	Valentin	Aleksandrovich
Zaitsev	Vasilii	Konstantinovich
Zhernosenko	Ivan	Iakovlevich

586TH FIGHTER AVIATION REGIMENT

Pilots: Female

Akimova	Aleksandra	
Batrakova*	Mariia	Semenovna
Beliaeva*	Raisa	Vasil'evna
Blinova	Klavdiia	
Budanova*	Ekaterina	Vasil'evna
Burdina	Galina	Pavlovna
Demchenko	Anna	Nikolaevna
Golysheva*	Ol'ga	Andreevna
Gvozdikova	Anna	
Iakovleva	Antonina	
Iakovleva	Ol'ga	Andreevna
Iamshchikova	Ol'ga	Nikolaevna
Kazarinova	Tamara	Aleksandrovna
Khomiakova	Valeriia	Dmitrievna
Kuznetsova	Mariia	Sergeevna
Kuznetsova [Zhukotskaia]	Mariia	Mikhailovna
Lebedeva*	Antonina	
Lisitsyna	Valentina	Mikhailovna
Litviak*	Lidiia	Vladimirovna
Lomako	Vera	Fedorovna
Nechaeva*	Klavdiia	Andreevna
Ol'kova	Iraida	Ivanovna
Pamiatnykh	Tamara	Ustinovna
Pankratova	Klavdiia	Luk'ianovna
Petrochenkova [Neminushchaia]	Valentina	Abramovna
Poliantseva	Agnia	
Pozhidaeva	Zoia	Mikhailovna
Prokhorova*	Evgeniia	Filippovna
Seid-Mamedova	Zuleika	Gabibovna
Shakhova	Ol'ga	Ivanovna
Smirnova*	Lina	Ivanovna
Smirnova	Taisia	Dmitrievna
Solomatina	Zinaida	Fedorovna

Studenetskaia	Ol'ga	Il'inichna
Surnachevskaia	Raisa	Nefedovna
Volkova-Tikhonova	Valentina	
Voronova	Tamara	

Pilots: Male

Beliakov		
Borisov		
Chulochnikov		
Durakov	Nikolai	Konstantinovich
Gridnev	Aleksandr	Vasil'evich
Ivanov		
Kokovikhin	Aleksei	Fedorovich
Korolev*	Nikolai	
Malakhov	Vasilii	Ivanovich
Mordosevich		
Pakhomov	K.	
Tsokaev	German	Konstantinovich
Tubalov		

Staff, Political Officers, and Others: Female

Andreeva	Nina	Nikolaevna
Budkareva [Ermolaeva]	Zinaida	Alekseevna
Bystrova	Lidiia	Aleksandrovna
Drobovich	Galina	
Fedorova	Ekaterina	
Gorelova	Anastasiia	Nikolaevna
Khrul'kova	Tat'iana	Nikolaevna
Krasnoshchekova	Valentina	
Kul'vits	Anastasiia	Aleksandrovna
Kulikova	O.	P.
Litviak	Lidiia	Vladimirovna
Makunina	Aleksandra	Aleksandrovna
Muzhikova	Marina	
Nikulina	Mariia	Andreevna
Shibaeva	Anna	
Slovokhotova	Nina	Arkad'evna
Tikhomirova	Vera	Ivanovna
Zariniia	Kareliia	

Staff, Political Officers, and Others: Male

Baurin	Aleksei	Timofeevich
Bokaev	M.	K.
Kashirtsev	Pavel	Maksimovich
Kirov	Rodion	Il'ich

Markov	Vladimir	
Nozhkin*		
Podruzhko	Stepan	Aleksandrovich
Reznik	Iurii	Grigor'evich
Rozhkov	Aleksandr	Kuz'mich

Mechanics, Armorers, Engineers: Female

Aban'kina	Valentina	Ivanovna
Berekhova	Elizaveta	Andreevna
Borok	Evgeniia	Dmitrievna
Bosiakova	Mariia	Vasil'evna
Bratsilova	Liublina	Arkad'evna
Buivolova	Galina	Ivanovna
Buzinova	Lina	Petrovna
Davydova	Ol'ga	Ivanovna
Emel'ianova [Danilova]	Irina	Ivanovna
Ermakova	Nina	Sergeevna
Eskina	Aleksandra	Antonovna
Favorskaia [Luneva]	Irina	Maksimovna
Fedosova	Anastasiia	Dmitrievna
Gazizov	Khamit	Garievich
Girich	Lidiia	Pavlovna
Golubeva	Ol'ga	Afanas'evna
Gorbunova	Antonina	Aleksandrovna
Goreninova	Galina	Ivanovna
Gubareva	Tat'iana	Sergeevna
Gushina	Vera	Sergeevna
Indichenko	Ivan	Afanas'evich
Ivakina	Nina	
Ivanchuk	Tat'iana	Mikhailovna
Kachurina	Antonina	Fedorovna
Karakorskaia	Elena	Nikolaevna
Kireeva	Mariia	Ivanovna
Kirillova	Ekaterina	Pavlovna
Kislitsa	Valentina	Vladimirovna
Kokina	Margarita	Vasil'evna
Konkina	Mariia	Kapitonovna
Kovaleva [Sergeicheva]	Valentina	Vasil'evna
Kudishina	Pelageia	Vladimirovna
Liamina	Valentina	Nikolaevna
Lysogorskaia	Tat'iana	Ianovna
Malkova	Zoia	Alekseevna
Mamaeva	Klavdiia	Aleksandrovna
Mebalina	Nina	Nikolaevna
Miagkikh [Anashina]	Zinaida	Ivanovna
Mironova	Vera	Timofeevna
Mutikova	Mariia	Mikhailovna
Osipova	Sof'ia	Vladimirovna
Piatrovskaia	Antonina	Iaroslavna
Pleshchevtseva [Pasportnikova]	Inna	Vladimirovna

Polunina	Ekaterina	Kuz'minichna
Prokhoda	Zoia	Vasil'evna
Rad'ko	Praskov'ia	Andreevna
Radzivon	Kaleriia	Evgen'evna
Saltykova	Antonina	Pavlovna
Shchatova	Matrena	Lukinichna
Shcherbakova	Vera	Stepanovna
Shcherbatiuk	Mariia	Dmitrievna
Shebalina	Anna	Iakovlevna
Shebalina	Nina	Nikolaevna
Shmatova	Matrena	Luk'ianovna
Skachkova	Valentina	Il'inichna
Skvortsova	A.	K.
Smykova	Ekaterina	Nikolaevna
Sokolova	Polina	Vasil'evna
Starova	Polina	Gerasimovna
Terekhova [Kasatkina]	Klavdiia	I.
Tishurova	Sof'ia	Sidorovna
Tkachenko	Fedos'ia	Grigor'evna
Volkova	Klavdiia	Semenovna

Mechanics, Armorers, Engineers: Male

Abramov	Mikhail	Konstantinovich
Artemov	Ivan	Mikhailovich
Bobkov	Mikhail	Tikhonovich
Bogdanov	Evgenii	Valer'ieevich
Chekushenko	Aleksandr	Ivanovich
Dronov	Konstantin	Vasil'evich
Drozd	Ivan	Vasil'evich
Emel'ianov	Fedor	Fedorovich
Gordienko	Ivan	Tarasovich
Gorelov	Aleksei	Lazarevich
Kazanin	Viktor	Nikolaevich
Klimov	Petr	Petrovich
Klochkovskii	Leontii	Ivanovich
Konokhov	Mikhail	Osipovich
Krichevtsov	Nikolai	Aleksandrovich
Kurapeev	Lev	Il'ich
Kurdin	Nikolai	Stepanovich
Kuz'min	Anatolii	Petrovich
Laptev	Lavrentii	Vasil'evich
Latyshev	Arkadii	Ivanovich
Lebedev	Andrei	Nikiforovich
Lunev	Fedor	Fedorovich
Lutsenko	Mikhail	Sergeevich
Malen'kov		
Morshnev	Pavel	Ivanovich
Nazarchuk	Georgii	L'vovich
Nizin	Semen	Grigor'evich
Pokusaev	Timofei	Ivanovich

Poliakov	Aleksandr	Naumovich
Povstianoi	Dorf	Artem'evich
Pshenichnikov	Petr	Petrovich
Razdobreev	Ivan	Petrovich
Reutskii	Anatolii	Sergeevich
Saninsky	Sergei	Stepanovich
Shcherbakov		
Shpoltakov	Egor	Petrovich
Sokolov	Dmitrii	Alekseevich
Sushchenko	Vasilii	Prokorovich
Suzikov	Aleksei	Petrovich
Tkachenko	Dmitrii	Dmitrievich
Voronov	Ivan	Maksimovich
Zviagin	Petr	Vasil'evich

ALPHABETICAL LISTING OF ALL PERSONNEL

Aban'kina, Valentina, Ivanovna, armorer, 586th IAP, female

Abibulaev, Raif, gunner, 587th/125th GvBAP, male

Abramov, Mikhail, Konstantinovich, engine mechanic, 586th IAP, male

Abramova, Liubov', Vasil'evna, instrument mechanic, 587th/125th GvBAP, female

Abramova, Mariia, instrument mechanic, 587th/125th GvBAP, female

Abramova, Mariia, Borisovna, staff, 587th/125th GvBAP, female

Abrosimova, Valentina, mechanic, 588th/46th GvBAP, female

Absoliamova, Elizaveta, Fedorovna, gunner, 587th/125th GvBAP, female

Ageev, Evgenii, Mikhailovich, armorer, 587th/125th GvBAP, male

Akilina, Mariia, pilot, 588th/46th GvBAP, female

Akimova, Aleksandra, pilot, 586th IAP, female

Akimova, Aleksandra, Fedorovna, mechanic, 588th/46th GvBAP, female

Aleksandrov, gunner, 587th/125th GvBAP, male

Alekseeva, Tat'iana, Timofeevna, engineer, 588th/46th GvBAP, female

Alent'ev, Fedor, Georgievich, technical services, 587th/125th GvBAP, male

Alferchik, Nikolai, Nikolaevich, technical services, 587th/125th GvBAP, male

Alferova, Natal'ia, Vasil'evna, armorer, 587th/125th GvBAP, female

Altsibeeva, Nina, pilot, 588th/46th GvBAP, female

Amet-Khan, Sultan, pilot, 9th GvIAP, male

Amosova, Anna, pilot, 588th/46th GvBAP, female

Amosova [Taranenko], Serafima, Tarasovna, pilot, 588th/46th GvBAP, female

Andreeva, Nina, Nikolaevna, staff, 586th IAP, female

Andrusenko, Valentina, armorer, 588th/46th GvBAP, female

Arkharova, Nina, Vasil'evna, staff, 587th/125th GvBAP, female

Aronova, Raisa, Ermolaevna, pilot, 588th/46th GvBAP, female

Artem'eva, Anna, staff, 588th/46th GvBAP, female

Artem'eva, Anna, Vasil'evna, armorer, 587th/125th GvBAP, female
Artem'eva, Avgustina, armorer, 588th/46th GvBAP, female
Artem'eva, Ol'ga, Nikolaevna, mechanic, 587th/125th GvBAP, female
Artemov, Ivan, Mikhailovich, mechanic, 586th IAP, male
Avidzba, Meri, navigator, 588th/46th GvBAP, female
Azarkina, Elena, Vladimirovna, navigator, 587th/125th GvBAP, female
Bagirov, Magerram, Abasauli-Ogly, gunner, 587th/125th GvBAP, male
Baidarov, Petr, Ivanovich, technical services, 587th/125th GvBAP, male
Baidiuk, Eva, Alekseevna, technical services, 587th/125th GvBAP, female
Baikova, Valentina, armorer, 587th/125th GvBAP, female
Bakotina, Mariia, Ivanovna, instrument mechanic, 587th/125th GvBAP, female
Bakunov, Sergei, Vasil'evich, technical services, 587th/125th GvBAP, male
Baranov*, Nikolai, pilot, 296th/73rd GvIAP, male
Barsukov, Aleksandr, Ivanovich, technical services, 587th/125th GvBAP, male
Batrakova*, Mariia, Semenovna, pilot, 586th IAP, female
Batukhtina, Ekaterina, Iakovlevna, navigator, 587th/125th GvBAP, female
Baurin, Aleksei, Timofeevich, staff, 586th IAP, male
Bekarevich, Nina, pilot, 588th/46th GvBAP, female
Beliaev, Mikhail, Ivanovich, technical services, 587th/125th GvBAP, male
Beliaeva*, Raisa, Vasil'evna, pilot, 586th IAP, 437th IAP, female
Beliakov, pilot, 586th IAP, male
Belik*, Vera, Luk'ianovna, navigator, 588th/46th GvBAP, female
Belkin, Semen, Semenovich, armorer, 587th/125th GvBAP, male
Belkina*, Pelageia, Grigor'evna, pilot, 588th/46th GvBAP, female
Belkina, Praskov'ia, pilot, 588th/46th GvBAP, female
Belova, Larisa, Nikolaevna, instrument mechanic, 587th/125th GvBAP, female
Berekhova, Elizaveta, Andreevna, armorer, 586th IAP, female
Bereznitskaia, Antonina, Mikhailovna, staff, 587th/125th GvBAP, female
Bershanskaia, Evdokiia, Davydovna, pilot, 588th/46th GvBAP, female
Bespalova, Galina, navigator, 588th/46th GvBAP, female
Bezliudnyi, Ivan, Fedorovich, instrument mechanic, 587th/125th GvBAP, male
Blinova, Klavdiia, pilot, 586th IAP, female
Blizniuk, Vasilii, Danilovich, armorer, 587th/125th GvBAP, male
Bobkov, Mikhail, Tikhonovich, technical services, 586th IAP, male
Bogdanov, Evgenii, Valer'ieevich, mechanic, 586th IAP, male
Bokaev, M. K., 586th IAP, male
Bondarenko, Mariia, Il'inichna, armorer, 587th/125th GvBAP, female
Bondarenko, Vera, instrument mechanic, 588th/46th GvBAP, female
Bondarev, Petr, armorer, 587th/125th GvBAP, male
Bondareva*, Anna, navigator, 588th/46th GvBAP, female
Borisenko, Ivan, I., pilot, 73rd GvIAP, male
Borisov, pilot, 586th IAP, male
Borisov, Aleksei, Alekseevich, armorer, 587th/125th GvBAP, male
Borisov, Ivan, pilot, 9th GvIAP, male

Borisova, 588th/46th GvBAP, female

Borisova, E., 588th/46th GvBAP, female

Borok, Evgeniia, Dmitrievna, mechanic, 586th IAP, female

Bosiakova, Mariia, Vasil'evna, instrument mechanic, 586th IAP, female

Bratsilova, Liublina, Arkad'evna, mechanic, 586th IAP, female

Broiko, Ekaterina, mechanic, 588th/46th GvBAP, female

Brok [Beltsova], Galina, Pavlovna, navigator, 587th/125th GvBAP, female

Budanova*, Ekaterina, Vasil'evna, pilot, 586th IAP, 437th IAP, 296th/73rd GvIAP, female

Budkareva [Ermolaeva], Zinaida, Alekseevna, staff, 586th IAP, female

Buivolova, Galina, Ivanovna, mechanic, 586th IAP, female

Bukin, Semen, Fedorovich, staff, 587th/125th GvBAP, male

Bulatova, Rimma, Mikhailovna, instrument mechanic, 587th/125th GvBAP, female

Bulycheva, Valeriia, Viacheslavna, technical services, 587th/125th GvBAP, female

Burdina, Galina, Pavlovna, pilot, 586th IAP, female

Burzaeva, Sof'ia, Ivanovna, navigator, 588th/46th GvBAP, female

Butenko, Liubov', armorer, 588th/46th GvBAP, female

Butkareva, Klavdiia, Pavlovna, staff, 586th IAP, female

Buzina [Karaseva], Nina, armorer, 588th/46th GvBAP, female

Buzinova, Lina, Petrovna, engine mechanic, 586th IAP, female

Bychkov, Konstantin, Leont'evich, technical services, 587th/125th GvBAP, male

Bystrova, Lidiia, Aleksandrovna, staff, 586th IAP, female

Chalaia, Dar'ia, Andreevna, armorer, 587th/125th GvBAP, female

Chechneva, Marina, Pavlovna, pilot, 588th/46th GvBAP, female

Chekushenko, Aleksandr, Ivanovich, armorer, 586th IAP, male

Chernova, Margarita, Konstantinovna, gunner, 587th/125th GvBAP, female

Chuikova, Ekaterina, Petrovna, armorer, 587th/125th GvBAP, female

Chulochnikov, pilot, 586th IAP, male

Chumirenko, technical services, 587th/125th GvBAP, male

Dal'nov, Mikhail, Ivanovich, technical services, 587th/125th GvBAP, male

Danilova, Nina, navigator, 588th/46th GvBAP, female

Davydova, Ol'ga, Ivanovna, instrument mechanic, 586th IAP, female

Demchenko, Anna, Nikolaevna, pilot, 586th IAP, female

Demeshova, Lidiia, Konstantinovna, navigator, 588th/46th GvBAP, female

Dmitrienko, Varvara, Sidorovna, technical services, 587th/125th GvBAP, female

Dmitrienko, Vera, mechanic, 588th/46th GvBAP, female

Dmitrieva, U., 588th/46th GvBAP, female

Dokutovich*, Galina, navigator, 588th/46th GvBAP, female

Dolina [Mel'nikova], Mariia, Iosifovna, pilot, 587th/125th GvBAP, female

Dospanova, Khivaz, navigator, 588th/46th GvBAP, female

Drachenko, Leonid, armorer, 587th/125th GvBAP, male
Dranishchev, Evgenii, P. [Petrovich?], 9th GvIAP, male
Driagina, Irina, Viktorovna, staff, 588th/46th GvBAP, female
Drobovich, Galina, 586th IAP, female
Dronov, Konstantin, Vasil'evich, instrument mechanic, 586th IAP, male
Drozd, Ivan, Vasil'evich, armorer, 586th IAP, male
Dubkova, Klara, Fedorovna, navigator, 587th/125th GvBAP, female
Dudina, Anna, pilot, 588th/46th GvBAP, female
Durakov, Nikolai, Konstantinovich, pilot, 586th IAP, male
Dushina, Anna, staff, 588th/46th GvBAP, female
Dzhunkovskaia [Markova], Galina, Ivanovna, navigator, 587th/125th GvBAP, female
Efimova*, Antonina, Grigor'evna, navigator, 588th/46th GvBAP, female
Egorova*, Aleksandra, Stepanovna, pilot, 587th/125th GvBAP, female
Egorova, Anna, mechanic, 588th/46th GvBAP, female
Egorova [Timofeeva], Anna, Aleksandrovna, pilot, 805th ShAP, female
Egorova [Arefeeva], Nina, mechanic, 588th/46th GvBAP, female
Eidlina, F., 588th/46th GvBAP, female
Elenina, Anna, Pavlovna, staff, 588th/46th GvBAP, female
Eliseeva, Lina, Iakovlevna, staff, 587th/125th GvBAP, female
Emel'ianov, Fedor, Fedorovich, mechanic, 586th IAP, male
Emel'ianova [Danilova], Irina, Ivanovna, engineer, 586th IAP, female
Eremenko, Aleksandra, Davydovna, navigator, 587th/125th GvBAP, female
Eremin, Boris, Nikolaevich, 8th VA, male
Ermakova, Liubov', armorer, 588th/46th GvBAP, female
Ermakova, Nina, Sergeevna, armorer, 586th IAP, female
Erofeev, Fedor, Vasil'evich, technical services, 587th/125th GvBAP, male
Erofeev*, Nikolai, Nikolaevich, gunner, 587th/125th GvBAP, male
Erokhina [Averianova], Ol'ga, armorer, 588th/46th GvBAP, female
Eskina, Aleksandra, Antonovna, mechanic, 586th IAP, female
Evchenko, Kuz'ma, Evdokimovich, technical services, 587th/125th GvBAP, male
Evdokimov, A., 73rd, male
Evpolova, Elena, mechanic, 588th/46th GvBAP, female
Ezhova, Nadezhda, pilot, 588th/46th GvBAP, female
Favorskaia [Luneva], Irina, Maksimovna, engine mechanic, 586th IAP, female
Fedorova, Ekaterina, 586th IAP, female
Fedosova, Anastasiia, Dmitrievna, engine mechanic, 586th IAP, female
Fedotova, Ekaterina, Petrovna, pilot, 587th/125th GvBAP, female
Fedotova, Mariia, armorer, 588th/46th GvBAP, female
Fedutenko, Nadezhda, Nikiforovna, pilot, 587th/125th GvBAP, female
Feshchenko, Zakhar, Antonovich, technical services, 587th/125th GvBAP, male
Fetisova, Ol'ga, Spiridonovna, staff, 588th/46th GvBAP, female
Firsova, Mariia, Vasil'evna, gunner, 587th/125th GvBAP, female

Fokina, Taisia, pilot, 588th/46th GvBAP, female
Fomicheva, Klavdiia, Iakovlevna, pilot, 587th/125th GvBAP, female
Frolova*, Tamara, navigator, 588th/46th GvBAP, female
Gasheva, Rufina, Sergeevna, navigator, 588th/46th GvBAP, female
Gazizov, Khamit, Garievich, mechanic, 586th IAP, female
Gel'man, Polina, Vladimirovna, navigator, 588th/46th GvBAP, female
Girich, Lidiia, Pavlovna, mechanic, 586th IAP, female
Glamazdina, Evgeniia, navigator, 588th/46th GvBAP, female
Glatman, Irina, navigator, 588th/46th GvBAP, female
Glazkova, E., 588th/46th GvBAP, female
Glazunov, Vasilii, Afanas'evich, technical services, 587th/125th GvBAP, male
Glebova, Klavdiia, mechanic, 588th/46th GvBAP, female
Glinina, A., 588th/46th GvBAP, female
Gogina, Lidiia, armorer, 588th/46th GvBAP, female
Golovachev, Pavel, Iakovlevich, 73rd, male
Golovkin, Vasilii, Ivanovich, technical services, 587th/125th GvBAP, male
Golovko, 588th/46th GvBAP, female
Golovkova, M., 588th/46th GvBAP, female
Golubev, Vasilii, Maksimovich, technical services, 587th/125th GvBAP, male
Golubeva, Lidiia, navigator, 588th/46th GvBAP, female
Golubeva, Ol'ga, Afanas'evna, engine mechanic, 586th IAP, female
Golubeva [Teres], Ol'ga, Timofeeva, navigator, 588th/46th GvBAP, female
Golyshev, Ivan, Vasil'evich, pilot, 73rd, male
Golysheva*, Ol'ga, Andreevna, pilot, 586th IAP, female
Gorbachev, Petr, Alekseevich, gunner, 587th/125th GvBAP, male
Gorbacheva, Liudmila, pilot, 588th/46th GvBAP, female
Gorbunova, Antonina, Aleksandrovna, mechanic, 586th IAP, female
Gordienko, Ivan, Tarasovich, mechanic, 586th IAP, male
Gorelkina, N., 588th/46th GvBAP, female
Gorelkina, Nina, armorer, 587th/125th GvBAP, female
Gorelov, Aleksei, Lazarevich, armorer, 586th IAP, male
Gorelova, Anastasiia, Nikolaevna, staff, 586th IAP, female
Goreninova, Galina, Ivanovna, engine mechanic, 586th IAP, female
Gorkhiver, Simon, 73rd, male
Gorman, Zinaida, staff, 588th/46th GvBAP, female
Gorskii, Stepan, Petrovich, gunner, 587th/125th GvBAP, male
Gracheva, Tat'iana, Ivanovna, instrument mechanic, 587th/125th GvBAP, female
Grichukhin, Nikolai, Vasil'evich, engine mechanic, 587th/125th GvBAP, male
Gridnev, Aleksandr, Vasil'evich, pilot, 586th IAP, male
Grishko*, Grigorii, Ivanovich, gunner, 587th/125th GvBAP, male
Grishunin, Nikolai, Stepanovich, technical services, 587th/125th GvBAP, male
Gromov, Iosif, Matveevich, technical services, 587th/125th GvBAP, male
Gromova, Ekaterina, Vasil'evna, armorer, 587th/125th GvBAP, female

Grushevskii, technical services, 587th/125th GvBAP, male
Gubareva, Tat'iana, Sergeevna, armorer, 586th IAP, female
Gubina*, Liubov', Mikhailovna, pilot, 587th/125th GvBAP, female
Gumilevskaia, Tamara, Anatol'evna, staff, 588th/46th GvBAP, female
Guruleva, Evgeniia, Vasil'evna, navigator, 587th/125th GvBAP, female
Guseva, Liubov', armorer, 587th/125th GvBAP, female
Guseva, Nina, instrument mechanic, 588th/46th GvBAP, female
Gushina, Vera, Sergeevna, armorer, 586th IAP, female
Gvozdikova, Anna, pilot, 586th IAP, female
Iakovleva, Antonina, pilot, 586th IAP, female
Iakovleva, Ol'ga, navigator, 588th/46th GvBAP, female
Iakovleva, Ol'ga, Andreevna, pilot, 586th IAP, female
Iamshchikova, Ol'ga, Nikolaevna, pilot, 586th IAP, female
Iazovskaia*, Anna, Maksimovna, pilot, 587th/125th GvBAP, female
Ibragimov, Nurgalei, Nurmykhametovich, technical services, 587th/125th GvBAP, male
Igant'ev, technical services, 587th/125th GvBAP, male
Il'in, Nikolai, Vasil'evich, technical services, 587th/125th GvBAP, male
Il'ina, Iuliia, instrument mechanic, 588th/46th GvBAP, female
Iliushina, Klavdiia, Alekseevna, engineer, 588th/46th GvBAP, female
Indichenko, Ivan, Afanas'evich, mechanic, 586th IAP, female
Irlina, Anzhelika, mechanic, 588th/46th GvBAP, female
Iudina*, Antonina, Vasil'evna, technical services, 587th/125th GvBAP, female
Iurochka, Vladimir, Iakovlevich, technical services, 587th/125th GvBAP, male
Iurod'eva [Samsonova], Matrena, mechanic, 588th/46th GvBAP, female
Iushina, Elena, Vasil'evna, navigator, 587th/125th GvBAP, female
Iushina [Zhitova], Raisa, pilot, 588th/46th GvBAP, female
Iuska*, Nikolai, Dmitrievich, gunner, 587th/125th GvBAP, male
Ivakina, Nina, staff, 586th IAP, female
Ivanchuk, Tat'iana, Mikhailovna, mechanic, 586th IAP, female
Ivanov, pilot, 586th IAP, male
Ivanov, Ivan, Vasil'evich, technical services, 587th/125th GvBAP, male
Ivanova, Antonina, mechanic, 588th/46th GvBAP, female
Ivanova, Zinaida, Fedorovna, armorer, 587th/125th GvBAP, female
Izvoshikova, Irina, Aleksandrovna, staff, 587th/125th GvBAP, female
Kachurina, Antonina, Fedorovna, engine mechanic, 586th IAP, female
Kakama, Aleksei, Gavrilovich, technical services, 587th/125th GvBAP, male
Kalduzov, Vladimir, Alekseevich, technical services, 587th/125th GvBAP, male
Kalinkina, Antonina, Tikhonovna, mechanic, 588th/46th GvBAP, female
Kaloshina, Mariia, Ivanovna, armorer, 587th/125th GvBAP, female
Kaplan, technical services, 587th/125th GvBAP, male
Karakorskaia, Elena, Nikolaevna, mechanic, 586th IAP, female
Karaseva [Buzina], Nina, armorer, 588th/46th GvBAP, female
Karaseva, Nina, Dmitrievna, navigator, 587th/125th GvBAP, female

Karp, Boris, Shlemovich, technical services, 587th/125th GvBAP, male

Karpunina, Kseniia, Pavlovna, staff, 588th/46th GvBAP, female

Karputin, Nikolai, Sergeevich, technical services, 587th/125th GvBAP, male

Kashirina*, Irina, navigator, 588th/46th GvBAP, female

Kashirtsev, Pavel, Maksimovich, staff, 586th IAP, male

Kas'ianova, A., 588th/46th GvBAP, female

Kazanin, Viktor, Nikolaevich, engineer, 586th IAP, male

Kazantseva, Alla, mechanic, 588th/46th GvBAP, female

Kazarinova, Militsiia, Aleksandrovna, staff, 587th/125th GvBAP, female

Kazarinova, Tamara, Aleksandrovna, pilot, 586th IAP, female

Kazberuk, Elizaveta, pilot, 588th/46th GvBAP, female

Kezina*, Anna, Ivanovna, navigator, 587th/125th GvBAP, female

Kharitonova, Raisa, mechanic, 588th/46th GvBAP, female

Khil'*, Kirill, Il'ich, navigator, 587th/125th GvBAP, male

Khlapova, 588th/46th GvBAP, female

Khmeleva, Antonina, Ivanovna, technical services, 587th/125th GvBAP, female

Khokhlova [Dubkova], Antonina, Tikhonovna, gunner, 587th/125th GvBAP, female

Khomiakova, Valeriia, Dmitrievna, pilot, 586th IAP, female

Khoroshilova [Arkhangelskaia], Aleksandra, Vladimirovna, staff, 588th/46th GvBAP, female

Khotina, Liubov', armorer, 588th/46th GvBAP, female

Khotov, Valentin, Prokhorovich, gunner, 587th/125th GvBAP, male

Khriukin, Timofei, Timofeevich, 8th VA, male

Khrul'kova, Tat'iana, Nikolaevna, staff, 586th IAP, female

Khudiakova [Agusheva], Antonina, Fedorovna, pilot, 588th/46th GvBAP, female

Khudiakova, Nina, staff, 588th/46th GvBAP, female

Khurtina, Vera, navigator, 588th/46th GvBAP, female

Kindiukhin, Ivan, Nikitich, technical services, 587th/125th GvBAP, male

Kireeva, Mariia, Ivanovna, engine mechanic, 586th IAP, female

Kirilenko, Anna, mechanic, 588th/46th GvBAP, female

Kirillova, Ekaterina, Pavlovna, engine mechanic, 586th IAP, female

Kirillova, Mariia, Andreevna, pilot, 587th/125th GvBAP, female

Kirov, Rodion, Il'ich, staff, 586th IAP, male

Kiselev, Terentii, Romanovich, technical services, 587th/125th GvBAP, male

Kiseleva, Mariia, armorer, 587th/125th GvBAP, female

Kislitsa, Valentina, Vladimirovna, mechanic, 586th IAP, female

Klimov, Petr, Petrovich, mechanic, 586th IAP, male

Klimova, G., 588th/46th GvBAP, female

Kliueva, Ol'ga, Aleksandrovna, navigator, 588th/46th GvBAP, female

Klochkovskii, Leontii, Ivanovich, mechanic, 586th IAP, male

Klopkova, Liudmila, pilot, 588th/46th GvBAP, female

Kniazeva, V., 588th/46th GvBAP, female

Kobiakova, Galina, Alekseevna, technical services, 587th/125th GvBAP, female

Kobriakov, technical services, 587th/125th GvBAP, male

Kochugin, Anatolii, Mikhailovich, gunner, 587th/125th GvBAP, male

Kokina, Margarita, Vasil'evna, armorer, 586th IAP, female

Kokosh, Sof'ia, pilot, 588th/46th GvBAP, female

Kokovikhin, Aleksei, Fedorovich, pilot, 586th IAP, male

Kolbasina, Nina, staff, 588th/46th GvBAP, female

Kolesnik, Vera, Terent'evna, armorer, 587th/125th GvBAP, female

Kolokol'nikova*, Anna, instrument mechanic, 588th/46th GvBAP, female

Kolotilov, Aleksei, Dmitrievich, technical services, 587th/125th GvBAP, male

Komkova, Galina, armorer, 588th/46th GvBAP, female

Komogortseva*, Nadezhda, navigator, 588th/46th GvBAP, female

Kondrat'eva, Aleksandra, armorer, 588th/46th GvBAP, female

Konkina, Mariia, Kapitonovna, armorer, 586th IAP, female

Konkina, Valentina, Ivanovna, navigator, 587th/125th GvBAP, female

Konokhov, Mikhail, Osipovich, armorer, 586th IAP, male

Konstantinova, Tamara, F., pilot, other, female

Korenkov, engine mechanic, 587th/125th GvBAP, male

Kornienko, Akulina, pilot, 588th/46th GvBAP, female

Korobeinikova, Taisia, mechanic, 588th/46th GvBAP, female

Korolev*, Nikolai, pilot, 586th IAP, male

Korotchenko, Evdokiia, mechanic, 588th/46th GvBAP, female

Korpilov, Mikhail, Ivanovich, technical services, 587th/125th GvBAP, male

Korshynov, Mikhail, technical services, 587th/125th GvBAP, male

Korsun, Galina, mechanic, 588th/46th GvBAP, female

Kosova, Polina, mechanic, 588th/46th GvBAP, female

Kostina, Tat'iana, navigator, 588th/46th GvBAP, female

Kostromin, Aleksandr, Leont'evich, technical services, 587th/125th GvBAP, male

Kotov, Valentin, Prokhorovich, gunner, 587th/125th GvBAP, male

Kovaleva [Sergeicheva], Valentina, Vasil'evna, mechanic, 586th IAP, female

Kovtun*, Grigorii, Ivanovich, technical services, 587th/125th GvBAP, male

Krasnoshchekova, Valentina, 586th IAP, female

Kravchenko [Savitskaia], Valentina, Flegontovna, navigator, 587th/125th GvBAP, female

Krichevtsov, Nikolai, Aleksandrovich, mechanic, 586th IAP, male

Kriuchkova, Evgeniia, Semenovna, instrument mechanic, 587th/125th GvBAP, female

Krivonogova, Aleksandra, Ivanovna, pilot, 587th/125th GvBAP, female

Kropina, Mariia, mechanic, 588th/46th GvBAP, female

Krugliakova, Mariia, Petrovna, technical services, 587th/125th GvBAP, female

Kruglov*, Vladimir, Ivanovich, technical services, 587th/125th GvBAP, male

Krutova*, Evgeniia, pilot, 588th/46th GvBAP, female

Krymskii*, Kvintel'ian, Efimovich, gunner, 587th/125th GvBAP, male

Krysa*, Nikolai, Stepanovich, gunner, 587th/125th GvBAP, male
Kuchkarov, Shody, Mirzoevich, technical services, 587th/125th GvBAP, male
Kudishina, Pelageia, Vladimirovna, mechanic, 586th IAP, female
Kudriavtsev, Aleksandr, Prokop'evich, gunner, 587th/125th GvBAP, male
Kul'vits, Anastasiia, Aleksandrovna, staff, 586th IAP, female
Kulashnikov*, Pavel, Nikolaevich, technical services, 587th/125th GvBAP, male
Kulikova, O. P., staff, 586th IAP, female
Kurapeev, Lev, Il'ich, engineer, 586th IAP, male
Kurcherenko, Evgenii, Trofimovich, technical services, 587th/125th GvBAP, male
Kurdin, Nikolai, Stepanovich, mechanic, 586th IAP, male
Kurkin, Ivan, Semenovich, gunner, 587th/125th GvBAP, male
Kuroptev, Nikolai, Mikhailovich, instrument mechanic, 587th/125th GvBAP, male
Kutarkina*, Nadezhda, Aleksandrovna, instrument mechanic, 587th/125th GvBAP, female
Kuz'menko, Zinaida, mechanic, 588th/46th GvBAP, female
Kuz'min, Anatolii, Petrovich, armorer, 586th IAP, male
Kuzenkova*, Vera, Ivanovna, pilot, 587th/125th GvBAP, female
Kuznetsova, I., 588th/46th GvBAP, female
Kuznetsova [Zhukotskaia], Mariia, Mikhailovna, pilot, 586th IAP, female
Kuznetsova , Mariia, Sergeevna, pilot, 586th IAP, female
Laletin, Anatolii, Efimovich, engine mechanic, 587th/125th GvBAP, male
Laptev, Lavrentii, Vasil'evich, armorer, 586th IAP, male
Lapteva, Anna, instrument mechanic, 588th/46th GvBAP, female
Lapunova*, Mariia, Mikhailovna, pilot, 587th/125th GvBAP, female
Larina, Nadezhda, armorer, 588th/46th GvBAP, female
Larkina, Klara, Prokof'evna, armorer, 587th/125th GvBAP, female
Latyshev, Arkadii, Ivanovich, armorer, 586th IAP, male
Lavrent'eva, Lidiia, navigator, 588th/46th GvBAP, female
Lavrent'eva, Sof'ia, mechanic, 588th/46th GvBAP, female
Lebedev, Andrei, Nikiforovich, armorer, 586th IAP, male
Lebedeva*, Antonina, pilot, 586th IAP, female
Lepilina, Antonina, Dmitrievna, armorer, 587th/125th GvBAP, female
Levin, Iosif, Grigor'evich, technical services, 587th/125th GvBAP, male
Levit, Mikhail, Mikhailovich, gunner, 587th/125th GvBAP, male
Liadskaia, Galina, mechanic, 588th/46th GvBAP, female
Liakh, F., I., pilot, 587th/125th GvBAP, male
Liamina, Valentina, Nikolaevna, mechanic, 586th IAP, female
Lisitsyna, Valentina, Mikhailovna, pilot, 586th IAP, female
Litosh, Vasilii, Leont'evich, technical services, 587th/125th GvBAP, male
Litviak*, Lidiia, Vladimirovna, pilot, 586th IAP, 296th/73rd GvIAP, female
Litvinova, Anna, Ivanovna, instrument mechanic, 587th/125th GvBAP, female
Logacheva, Mariia, armorer, 588th/46th GvBAP, female

Lomakina, Tat'iana, armorer, 588th/46th GvBAP, female

Lomako, Vera, Fedorovna, pilot, 586th IAP, female

Lomanova [Tenueva], Galina, Dmitrievna, pilot, 587th/125th GvBAP, female

Lopukhina, K., 588th/46th GvBAP, female

Loshmanova, Lidiia, navigator, 588th/46th GvBAP, female

Luchinkina, Valentina, navigator, 588th/46th GvBAP, female

Lukina, Elena, Ivanovna, staff, 587th/125th GvBAP, female

Lukovikhina, Antonina, Grigor'evna, armorer, 587th/125th GvBAP, female

Lunev, Fedor, Fedorovich, engineer, 586th IAP, male

Lutsenko, Mikhail, Sergeevich, mechanic, 586th IAP, male

Lysogorskaia, Tat'iana, Ianovna, mechanic, 586th IAP, female

Makarova*, Tat'iana, Petrovna, pilot, 588th/46th GvBAP, female

Makhova, Lidiia, staff, 588th/46th GvBAP, female

Makogon*, Polina, Aleksandrovna, pilot, 588th/46th GvBAP, female

Maksimova, Valentina, staff, 588th/46th GvBAP, female

Maksiushina, Vera, Pavlovna, technical services, 587th/125th GvBAP, female

Makunina, Aleksandra, Aleksandrovna, staff, 586th IAP, female

Mal'shev, Leonid, Aleksandrovich, armorer, 587th/125th GvBAP, male

Mal'tseva, N., 588th/46th GvBAP, female

Malakhov, Vasilii, Ivanovich, pilot, 586th IAP, male

Malakhova*, Anna, pilot, 588th/46th GvBAP, female

Malen'kov, mechanic, 586th IAP, male

Maliutina [Kulkova], Elena, Mironovna, pilot, 587th/125th GvBAP, female

Malkova, Nina, Fedorovna, pilot, 587th/125th GvBAP, female

Malkova, Zoia, Alekseevna, mechanic, 586th IAP, female

Mamaeva, Klavdiia, Aleksandrovna, instrument mechanic, 586th IAP, female

Mamenko, Vera, mechanic, 588th/46th GvBAP, female

Maniakin, Aleksandr, Semenovich, gunner, 587th/125th GvBAP, male

Marina, Mariia, armorer, 588th/46th GvBAP, female

Markov, Valentin, Vasil'evich, pilot, 587th/125th GvBAP, male

Markov, Vladimir, 586th IAP, male

Martyniuk, Nikolai, Moiseevich, technical services, 587th/125th GvBAP, male

Martynova, Nadezhda, staff, 588th/46th GvBAP, female

Mashchenko, L., 588th/46th GvBAP, female

Maslennikova*, Liudmila, mechanic, 588th/46th GvBAP, female

Maslennikova, Tat'iana, navigator, 588th/46th GvBAP, female

Maslova, Tamara, Nikolaevna, pilot, 587th/125th GvBAP, female

Matiukhina*, Valentina, Alekseevna, pilot, 587th/125th GvBAP, female

Matveeva, Aleksandra, Borisovna, instrument mechanic, 587th/125th GvBAP, female

Mazdrina, Raisa, staff, 588th/46th GvBAP, female

Mazurin*, 587th/125th GvBAP, male

Mebalina, Nina, Nikolaevna, mechanic, 586th IAP, female

Medvedeva, Anna, armorer, 588th/46th GvBAP, female

Meklin [Kravtsova], Natal'ia, Fedorovna, pilot, 588th/46th GvBAP, female

Melashvili, Tamara, Davydovna, pilot, 587th/125th GvBAP, female

Meluzova, Tamara, mechanic, 588th/46th GvBAP, female

Meriuts, Marta, Pimenovna, staff, 587th/125th GvBAP, female

Meshcheriakova, Tamara, Pavlovna, armorer, 587th/125th GvBAP, female

Mesniankina, Ekaterina, navigator, 588th/46th GvBAP, female

Miagkikh [Anashina], Zinaida, Ivanovna, engine mechanic, 586th IAP, female

Migunova, Ekaterina, Aleksandrovna, staff, 587th/125th GvBAP, female

Mil'dzikhova, Madina, Khazbievna, gunner, 587th/125th GvBAP, female

Mil'man, Boris, Borisovich, gunner, 587th/125th GvBAP, male

Minakova, Irina, Il'inichna, armorer, 587th/125th GvBAP, female

Minkov, Ivan, Nikolaevich, 73rd, male

Mironenko, Mariia, mechanic, 588th/46th GvBAP, female

Mironova, Vera, Timofeevna, instrument mechanic, 586th IAP, female

Mishchenko, L., 588th/46th GvBAP, female

Moldovanchuk, Ivan, Ivanovich, technical services, 587th/125th GvBAP, male

Molokova, Zinaida, Nikolaevna, staff, 587th/125th GvBAP, female

Monakhova, Irina, 587th/125th GvBAP, female

Mordosevich, pilot, 586th IAP, male

Morozova, Evdokiia, Nikolaevna, armorer, 587th/125th GvBAP, female

Morshnev, Pavel, Ivanovich, engineer, 586th IAP, male

Mosolova, Sof'ia, Stepanovna, armorer, 587th/125th GvBAP, female

Mutikova, Mariia, Mikhailovna, mechanic, 586th IAP, female

Muzhikova, Marina, mechanic, 586th IAP, female

Nalivaiko, Andrei, Egorovich, technical services, 587th/125th GvBAP, male

Nazarchuk, Georgii, L'vovich, instrument mechanic, 586th IAP, male

Nazarov, gunner, 587th/125th GvBAP, male

Nechaeva*, Klavdiia, Andreevna, pilot, 586th IAP, 434th IAP, female

Neskoblinov, Mikhail, Dmitrievich, technical services, 587th/125th GvBAP, male

Nikiforova, Tat'iana, Sergeevna, staff, 587th/125th GvBAP, female

Nikitin, Nikolai, Aleksandrovich, navigator, 587th/125th GvBAP, male

Nikitina, Elena, navigator, 588th/46th GvBAP, female

Nikitina [Chapligina], Galina, Konstantinovna, pilot, 587th/125th GvBAP, female

Nikitina, Mariia, pilot, 588th/46th GvBAP, female

Nikitina, Mariia, Grigor'evna, mechanic, 588th/46th GvBAP, female

Nikolaeva, Lidiia, 588th/46th GvBAP, female

Nikulina, Evdokiia, Andreevna, pilot, 588th/46th GvBAP, female

Nikulina, Mariia, Andreevna, staff, 586th IAP, female

Nizin, Semen, Grigor'evich, mechanic, 586th IAP, male

Nosal'*, Evdokiia, Ivanovna, pilot, 588th/46th GvBAP, female

Novikova, Faina, Mikhailovna, staff, 587th/125th GvBAP, female

Nozhkin*, 586th IAP, male

Nuridinov, Abdyganpar, Dosankulovich, technical services, 587th/125th GvBAP, male

Obukhov, Mikhail, Ivanovich, technical services, 587th/125th GvBAP, male

Ogii, Vera, instrument mechanic, 588th/46th GvBAP, female

Ol'khovskaia, Galina, Fedorovna, navigator, 587th/125th GvBAP, female

Ol'khovskaia*, Liubov', pilot, 588th/46th GvBAP, female

Ol'khovskaia, M., 588th/46th GvBAP, female

Ol'kova, Iraida, Ivanovna, pilot, 586th IAP, female

Oleinik, Ekaterina, pilot, 588th/46th GvBAP, female

Oleshagin, Viktor, Ivanovich, technical services, 587th/125th GvBAP, male

Omel'chenko, Aleksei, Ivanovich, gunner, 587th/125th GvBAP, male

Orlova, Rakhime, instrument mechanic, 588th/46th GvBAP, female

Orlova, Zinaida, Dmitrievna, navigator, 587th/125th GvBAP, female

Osadze, Irina, Sergeevna, pilot, 587th/125th GvBAP, female

Osipov, Nikolai, technical services, 587th/125th GvBAP, male

Osipova, Sof'ia, Vladimirovna, mechanic, 586th IAP, female

Osmantseva, Aleksandra, mechanic, 588th/46th GvBAP, female

Osokina, Tat'iana, pilot, 588th/46th GvBAP, female

Ozerkova, Sof'ia, engineer, 588th/46th GvBAP, female

Ozimina, Mariia, Petrovna, armorer, 587th/125th GvBAP, female

Pakhomov, K., pilot, 586th IAP, male

Paklina, Elena, mechanic, 588th/46th GvBAP, female

Pamiatnykh, Tamara, Ustinovna, pilot, 586th IAP, female

Panferova, Taisia, Sergeevna, gunner, 587th/125th GvBAP, female

Pankratova, Klavdiia, Luk'ianovna, pilot, 586th IAP, female

Panteliat, Il'ia, Iudovich, technical services, 587th/125th GvBAP, male

Papusha*, Nikolai, Moiseevich, gunner, 587th/125th GvBAP, male

Paramonova, Klavdiia, Vasil'evna, armorer, 587th/125th GvBAP, female

Parfenova [Akimova], Zoia, Ivanovna, pilot, 588th/46th GvBAP, female

Paromova, Mira, pilot, 588th/46th GvBAP, female

Parshina, A., 588th/46th GvBAP, female

Pas'ko, Evdokiia, Borisovna, navigator, 588th/46th GvBAP, female

Pashkova*, Iuliia, Fedorovna, pilot, 588th/46th GvBAP, female

Pavlova, Antonina, Vasil'evna, navigator, 588th/46th GvBAP, female

Pavlova, Evgeniia, navigator, 588th/46th GvBAP, female

Penchuk, Mariia, navigator, 588th/46th GvBAP, female

Perepecha, Valentina, pilot, 588th/46th GvBAP, female

Petkileva, Polina, navigator, 588th/46th GvBAP, female

Petrochenkova [Neminushchaia], Valentina, Abramovna, pilot, 586th IAP, female

Petrova, Anna, navigator, 588th/46th GvBAP, female

Petrova, Zinaida, navigator, 588th/46th GvBAP, female

Piatkov, Petr, Ivanovich, technical services, 587th/125th GvBAP, male

Piatrovskaia, Antonina, Iaroslavna, armorer, 586th IAP, female

Piatyshev, Kornelii, Ivanovich, technical services, 587th/125th GvBAP, male

Pilipenko, Galina, mechanic, 588th/46th GvBAP, female

Piskareva, Ekaterina, Ivanovna, pilot, 588th/46th GvBAP, female

Platonova, Aleksandra, mechanic, 588th/46th GvBAP, female

Pleshchevtseva [Pasportnikova], Inna, Vladimirovna, mechanic, 586th IAP, 296th/73rd GvIAP, female

Plotnir, Ivan, Ivanovich, technical services, 587th/125th GvBAP, male

Podruzhko, Stepan, Aleksandrovich, staff, 586th IAP, male

Pogorelova, Mariia, Konstantinovna, pilot, 587th/125th GvBAP, female

Pokusaev, Timofei, Ivanovich, engine mechanic, 586th IAP, male

Polezhaeva, Taisia, armorer, 587th/125th GvBAP, female

Poliakov, technical services, 587th/125th GvBAP, male

Poliakov, Aleksandr, Naumovich, mechanic, 586th IAP, male

Poliantseva, Agnia, pilot, 586th IAP, female

Polovykh, Aleksandr, Kharlampievich, technical services, 587th/125th GvBAP, male

Polunina, Ekaterina, Kuz'minichna, mechanic, 586th IAP, female

Polunina*, Valentina, pilot, 588th/46th GvBAP, female

Ponomarenko, G., 588th/46th GvBAP, female

Ponomareva*, Elena, Nikolaevna, navigator, 587th/125th GvBAP, female

Ponomareva, Mariia, Ivanovna, staff, 587th/125th GvBAP, female

Popova, Aleksandra, navigator, 588th/46th GvBAP, female

Popova, Anastasiia, Vasil'evna, pilot, 588th/46th GvBAP, female

Popova, Evgeniia, pilot, 588th/46th GvBAP, female

Popova, Liudmila, Leonidovna, navigator, 587th/125th GvBAP, female

Popova, Nadezhda, Vasil'evna, pilot, 588th/46th GvBAP, female

Popusheva, 588th/46th GvBAP, female

Povstianoi, Dorf, Artem'evich, mechanic, 586th IAP, male

Pozhidaeva, Zoia, Mikhailovna, pilot, 586th IAP, female

Prasolova, Praskov'ia, pilot, 588th/46th GvBAP, female

Pristavka, Iosif, Ignat'evich, technical services, 587th/125th GvBAP, male

Prokhoda, Zoia, Vasil'evna, staff, 586th IAP, female

Prokhorova*, Evgeniia, Filippovna, pilot, 586th IAP, female

Prokop'eva, Panna, pilot, 588th/46th GvBAP, female

Prokopenko, Nikolai, Andreevich, technical services, 587th/125th GvBAP, male

Prudnikova, Rimma, mechanic, 588th/46th GvBAP, female

Pshenichnikov, Petr, Petrovich, mechanic, 586th IAP, male

Pugacheva [Makarova], Antonina, Iosifovna, navigator, 587th/125th GvBAP, female

Pustovoitenko, Valentina, navigator, 588th/46th GvBAP, female

Putina, Anna, pilot, 588th/46th GvBAP, female

Rachkevich, Evdokiia, Iakovlevna, navigator, 588th/46th GvBAP, female

Rad'ko, Aleksandra, mechanic, 588th/46th GvBAP, female

Rad'ko, Praskov'ia, Andreevna, mechanic, 586th IAP, female

Radchikova, Larisa, navigator, 588th/46th GvBAP, female

Radina, Zinaida, mechanic, 588th/46th GvBAP, female

Radzivon, Kaleriia, Evgen'evna, engine mechanic, 586th IAP, female

Rakobolskaia, Irina, Viacheslavna, staff, 588th/46th GvBAP, female

Raskova*, Marina, Mikhailovna, 587th/125th GvBAP, 587th/125th GvBAP, female

Raspopova, Nina, Maksimovna, pilot, 588th/46th GvBAP, female

Ratkevich, Raisa, Stepanovna, gunner, 587th/125th GvBAP, female

Razdobreev, Ivan, Petrovich, armorer, 586th IAP, male

Reutskaia, Nina, navigator, 588th/46th GvBAP, female

Reutskii, Anatolii, Sergeevich, engineer, 586th IAP, male

Reznik, Iurii, Grigor'evich, staff, 586th IAP, male

Reztsov, Viktor, Vasil'evich, technical services, 587th/125th GvBAP, male

Riabinina, Adelina, Sergeevna, instrument mechanic, 587th/125th GvBAP, female

Riabova, Ekaterina, Vasil'evna, navigator, 588th/46th GvBAP, female

Riza-Ogly, Aleksei, Vladimirovich, technical services, 587th/125th GvBAP, male

Rogova*, Sof'ia, pilot, 588th/46th GvBAP, female

Romanov, Petr, Nikolaevich, technical services, 587th/125th GvBAP, male

Romanova, Anna, Ivanovna, armorer, 587th/125th GvBAP, female

Romanova, Zinaida, armorer, 588th/46th GvBAP, female

Rozanova [Litvinova], Larisa, Nikolaevna, navigator, 588th/46th GvBAP, female

Rozhkov, Aleksandr, Kuz'mich, staff, 586th IAP, male

Rozova, Antonina, navigator, 588th/46th GvBAP, female

Rubtsov, Andrei, Ivanovich, technical services, 587th/125th GvBAP, male

Rudakova, Antonina, mechanic, 588th/46th GvBAP, female

Rudneva*, Evgeniia, Maksimovna, navigator, 588th/46th GvBAP, female

Rukavitsina, Mariia, pilot, 588th/46th GvBAP, female

Rumiantseva, Valentina, instrument mechanic, 588th/46th GvBAP, female

Rumiantseva, Viktoriia, Vasil'evna, armorer, 587th/125th GvBAP, female

Runt, Mariia, Ivanovna, staff, 588th/46th GvBAP, female

Rusakova, Tamara, Ivanovna, pilot, 587th/125th GvBAP, female

Rybal'chenko, Elizaveta, mechanic, 588th/46th GvBAP, female

Rybin, Viktor, Ivanovich, technical services, 587th/125th GvBAP, male

Rybnikov, technical services, 587th/125th GvBAP, male

Ryl'skaia, Kaleriia, pilot, 588th/46th GvBAP, female

Ryzhkova, Klavdiia, pilot, 588th/46th GvBAP, female

Salikova*, Elena, navigator, 588th/46th GvBAP, female

Saltykova, Antonina, Pavlovna, instrument mechanic, 586th IAP, female

Samoilova, Valentina, Kupriianovna, technical services, 587th/125th GvBAP, female

Sanchuk, Kseniia, Apolinar'evna, staff, 587th/125th GvBAP, female

Sanfirova*, Ol'ga, Aleksandrovna, pilot, 588th/46th GvBAP, female

Saninsky, Sergei, Stepanovich, mechanic, 586th IAP, male

Sapronov, Aleksandr, Timofeevich, technical services, 587th/125th GvBAP, male

Sapronova, Evgeniia, instrument mechanic, 588th/46th GvBAP, female

Sebrova, Irina, Fedorovna, pilot, 588th/46th GvBAP, female

Sedova, Iuliia, Illarionovna, technical services, 587th/125th GvBAP, female

Seid-Mamedova, Zuleika, Gabibovna, pilot, 586th IAP, female

Seliutin, Dmitrii, Vasil'evich, gunner, 587th/125th GvBAP, male

Semenova, Elena, Andreevna, staff, 587th/125th GvBAP, female

Senkovskii, Evgenii, Vasil'evich, instrument mechanic, 587th/125th GvBAP, male

Serdiuk, Nina, staff, 588th/46th GvBAP, female

Serebriakova, Klavdiia, pilot, 588th/46th GvBAP, female

Serebrianova, 588th/46th GvBAP, female

Sergeev, Iurii, Grigor'evich, technical services, 587th/125th GvBAP, male

Sergeeva, Anna, armorer, 588th/46th GvBAP, female

Sergeeva, Evgeniia, Prokof'evna, navigator, 587th/125th GvBAP, female

Serova, G., 588th/46th GvBAP, female

Sever'ianova, Mariia, Gerasimovna, instrument mechanic, 587th/125th GvBAP, female

Severina, Klavdiia, Ivanovna, gunner, 587th/125th GvBAP, female

Sevost'ianov, Pavel, Petrovich, technical services, 587th/125th GvBAP, male

Shakhova, Ol'ga, Ivanovna, pilot, 586th IAP, female

Sharoevskaia, Zinaida, mechanic, 588th/46th GvBAP, female

Sharova, Anastasiia, Ivanovna, navigator, 588th/46th GvBAP, female

Shatkovskii, Petro, Nikiforovich, gunner, 587th/125th GvBAP, male

Shchatova, Matrena, Lukinichna, engine mechanic, 586th IAP, female

Shchegrova, Mariia, Illarionovna, staff, 587th/125th GvBAP, female

Shchelkanova, Mariia, mechanic, 588th/46th GvBAP, female

Shcherbakov, mechanic, 586th IAP, male

Shcherbakov, Mikhail, Alekseevich, technical services, 587th/125th GvBAP, male

Shcherbakova, Vera, Stepanovna, engineer, 586th IAP, female

Shcherbatiuk, Mariia, Dmitrievna, armorer, 586th IAP, female

Shcherbinina, Tat'iana, armorer, 588th/46th GvBAP, female

Shebalina, Anna, Iakovlevna, armorer, 586th IAP, female

Shebalina, Nina, Nikolaevna, mechanic, 586th IAP, female

Sheiankina, Valentina, mechanic, 588th/46th GvBAP, female

Shepturova, Anna, armorer, 588th/46th GvBAP, female

Sherman, Leonid, Artem'evich, technical services, 587th/125th GvBAP, male

Sherstneva, Anna, mechanic, 588th/46th GvBAP, female

Shevchenko, Liubov', navigator, 588th/46th GvBAP, female

Shibaeva, Anna, 586th IAP, female

Shilin, Boris, Grigor'evich, technical services, 587th/125th GvBAP, male

Shilov, Boris, Vasil'evich, armorer, 587th/125th GvBAP, male

Shinkarenko, Nikolai, Il'ich, technical services, 587th/125th GvBAP, male

Shiriaeva, Zinaida, Fedorovna, pilot, 587th/125th GvBAP, female

Shishkova, Anna, Aleksandrovna, pilot, 587th/125th GvBAP, female

Shmatova, Matrena, Luk'ianovna, engine mechanic, 586th IAP, female

Sholokhova, Ol'ga, Mitrofanovna, pilot, 587th/125th GvBAP, female

Shpoltakov, Egor, Petrovich, armorer, 586th IAP, male

Shumarin*, Aleksei, Maksimovich, technical services, 587th/125th GvBAP, male

Skachkova, Valentina, Il'inichna, mechanic, 586th IAP, female

Skoblikova, Antonina, Andriianovna, pilot, 587th/125th GvBAP, female

Skvortsova, A., K., engineer, 586th IAP, female

Slobodianiuk, Vladimir, Iakovlevich, technical services, 587th/125th GvBAP, male

Slovokhotova, Nina, Arkad'evna, staff, 586th IAP, female

Smakhtina, Raisa, Nikolaevna, instrument mechanic, 587th/125th GvBAP, female

Smirnov, Aleksandr, Petrovich, technical services, 587th/125th GvBAP, male

Smirnova, Anna, staff, 588th/46th GvBAP, female

Smirnova*, Lina, Ivanovna, pilot, 586th IAP, female

Smirnova, Mariia, Vasil'evna, pilot, 588th/46th GvBAP, female

Smirnova, Natal'ia, Alekseevna, gunner, 587th/125th GvBAP, female

Smirnova, Taisia, Dmitrievna, pilot, 586th IAP, female

Smykova, Ekaterina, Nikolaevna, instrument mechanic, 586th IAP, female

Sofin, Vikentii, Ivanovich, technical services, 587th/125th GvBAP, male

Sokolov, Dmitrii, Alekseevich, engineer, 586th IAP, male

Sokolova*, Anna, Aleksandrovna, armorer, 587th/125th GvBAP, female

Sokolova, Polina, Vasil'evna, engine mechanic, 586th IAP, female

Solenov, Ivan, Grigor'evich, gunner, 587th/125th GvBAP, male

Solodovnikov, Nikolai, technical services, 587th/125th GvBAP, male

Solomatin, Aleksei, Frolovich, 73rd GvIAP, male

Solomatina, Zinaida, Fedorovna, pilot, 586th IAP, female

Solov'eva, Zoia, pilot, 588th/46th GvBAP, female

Spitsina [Bondareva], Antonina, Grigor'evna, pilot, 587th/125th GvBAP, female

Starova, Polina, Gerasimovna, instrument mechanic, 586th IAP, female

Startseva, Klavdiia, navigator, 588th/46th GvBAP, female

Stepanov, Aleksandr, Vasil'evich, engineer, 587th/125th GvBAP, male

Stepanov, Viacheslav, Petrovich, gunner, 587th/125th GvBAP, male

Stepanova, Polina, Viktorovna, technical services, 587th/125th GvBAP, female

Stepanova, Zinaida, Nikolaevna, navigator, 587th/125th GvBAP, female

Stolbikova, Anna, mechanic, 588th/46th GvBAP, female

Strelkova, Nadezhda, Aleksandrovna, engineer, 588th/46th GvBAP, female

Studenetskaia, Ol'ga, Il'inichna, pilot, 586th IAP, female

Studenova, Agrafena, Petrovna, instrument mechanic, 587th/125th GvBAP, female

Studilina, Nadezhda, navigator, 588th/46th GvBAP, female

Stupina*, Valentina, Sergeevna, staff, 588th/46th GvBAP, female

Sukhinov, Georgii, Georgievich, technical services, 587th/125th GvBAP, male

Sukhorukova*, Evgeniia, navigator, 588th/46th GvBAP, female

Sukhovilova, Liudmila, Vasil'evna, technical services, 587th/125th GvBAP, female

Sumarokova, Tat'iana, Nikolaevna, navigator, 588th/46th GvBAP, female

Surnachevskaia, Raisa, Nefedovna, pilot, 586th IAP, female

Sushchenko, Vasilii, Prokorovich, engineer, 586th IAP, male

Suzikov, Aleksei, Petrovich, armorer, 586th IAP, male

Svetil'nikov, Vitalii, Fedorovich, staff, 587th/125th GvBAP, male

Svetlanova, Maguba, 588th/46th GvBAP, female

Svistunova*, Lidiia, Aleksandrovna, navigator, 588th/46th GvBAP, female

Sycheva, Aleksandra, Vasil'evna, gunner, 587th/125th GvBAP, female

Syrtlanova, Maguba, G., pilot, 588th/46th GvBAP, female

Tarasenko, Mariia, Terent'evna, pilot, 587th/125th GvBAP, female

Tarasova*, Vera, navigator, 588th/46th GvBAP, female

Taziev, Nazid, Tazievich, gunner, 587th/125th GvBAP, male

Tepikina [Popova], Mariia, pilot, 588th/46th GvBAP, female

Terekhova [Kasatkina], Klavdiia, I., armorer, 586th IAP, female

Teteriatnikova, Ialevtina, Pavlovna, instrument mechanic, 587th/125th GvBAP, female

Teterin, Semen, Vasil'evich, technical services, 587th/125th GvBAP, male

Tikhii, Vasilii, Ivanovich, gunner, 587th/125th GvBAP, male

Tikhomirova, Vera, Ivanovna, staff, 586th IAP, female

Tikhomirova, Vera, Ivanovna, pilot, 588th/46th GvBAP, female

Timchenko, Ekaterina, Pavlovna, navigator, 588th/46th GvBAP, female

Timofeeva*, Elena, Pavlovna, pilot, 587th/125th GvBAP, female

Timofeeva, Evgeniia, Dmitrievna, pilot, 587th/125th GvBAP, female

Tishurova, Sof'ia, Sidorovna, armorer, 586th IAP, female

Titenko, Semen, Moiseevich, pilot, 587th/125th GvBAP, male

Titova, Ekaterina, mechanic, 588th/46th GvBAP, female

Tiuliakova, Iuliia, Petrovna, technical services, 587th/125th GvBAP, female

Tkachenko, Dmitrii, Dmitrievich, mechanic, 586th IAP, male

Tkachenko, Ekaterina, staff, 588th/46th GvBAP, female

Tkachenko, Fedos'ia, Grigor'evna, instrument mechanic, 586th IAP, female

Tormosina*, Liliia, pilot, 588th/46th GvBAP, female

Tret'iakova, Zinaida, Ivanovna, pilot, 587th/125th GvBAP, female

Trifonova, Anna, Vasil'evna, instrument mechanic, 587th/125th GvBAP, female

Troparevskaia, Nadezhda, Evgen'evna, pilot, 588th/46th GvBAP, female

Tsar'kova, Nina, Semenovna, staff, 587th/125th GvBAP, female

Tsar'kova, Polina, Semenovna, staff, 587th/125th GvBAP, female
Tseloval'nikova, Lidiia, navigator, 588th/46th GvBAP, female
Tsimbal, Grigorii, Anisimovich, gunner, 587th/125th GvBAP, male
Tsitrikov, Stepan, Illarionovich, gunner, 587th/125th GvBAP, male
Tsokaev, German, Konstantinovich, pilot, 586th IAP, male
Tsuranova, Anastasiia, navigator, 588th/46th GvBAP, female
Tsvetkova, Ekaterina, Vasil'evna, navigator, 587th/125th GvBAP, female
Tubalov, pilot, 586th IAP, male
Tuchina, Polina, armorer, 588th/46th GvBAP, female
Turabelidze, Galina, Prokof'evna, navigator, 587th/125th GvBAP, female
Turianskaia, E., 588th/46th GvBAP, female
Tusnolobova, 587th/125th GvBAP, female
Ul'ianenko, Nina, Zakharovna, navigator, 588th/46th GvBAP, female
Ul'ianova, Polina, navigator, 588th/46th GvBAP, female
Ulanova, Elena, Grigor'evna, instrument engineer, 587th/125th GvBAP, female
Ushakov, Ivan, Grigor'evich, technical services, 587th/125th GvBAP, male
Usmanov, Abdugani, technical services, 587th/125th GvBAP, male
Vakhromeeva, Antonina, mechanic, 588th/46th GvBAP, female
Varakina, Liubov', mechanic, 588th/46th GvBAP, female
Varenik, Vladimir, Serafimovich, technical services, 587th/125th GvBAP, male
Vargina, Ol'ga, Filippovna, instrument mechanic, 587th/125th GvBAP, female
Vasil'ev, Dmitrii, Vasil'evich, gunner, 587th/125th GvBAP, male
Vasil'eva, Galina, Sergeevna, navigator, 587th/125th GvBAP, female
Vasil'eva*, Nadezhda, Grigor'evna, navigator, 587th/125th GvBAP, female
Vasil'eva, Vera, armorer, 588th/46th GvBAP, female
Vasil'eva, Zinaida, Ivanovna, armorer, 587th/125th GvBAP, female
Vasil'eva, Zoia, instrument mechanic, 588th/46th GvBAP, female
Vatintseva, Aleksandra, Semenovna, navigator, 587th/125th GvBAP, female
Vertousov, Vladimir, Nikolaevich, engine mechanic, 587th/125th GvBAP, male
Vinogradova*, Mariia, navigator, 588th/46th GvBAP, female
Vinokurova, Zoia, Nikolaevna, technical services, 587th/125th GvBAP, female
Vishneva, Zinaida, armorer, 588th/46th GvBAP, female
Vodianik, Sof'ia, navigator, 588th/46th GvBAP, female
Volgushkin, Pavel, Ivanovich, technical services, 587th/125th GvBAP, male
Volkova, Klavdiia, Semenovna, instrument engineer, 586th IAP, female
Volkova, Nina, Vasil'evna, staff, 588th/46th GvBAP, female
Volkova [Tikhonova], Valentina, pilot, 586th IAP, female
Volkova, Valentina, Georgievna, navigator, 587th/125th GvBAP, female
Volodina*, Taisia, pilot, 588th/46th GvBAP, female
Volosiuk, Anna, navigator, 588th/46th GvBAP, female
Volova, Galina, Mikhailovna, engineer, 587th/125th GvBAP, female
Voronov, Ivan, Maksimovich, engine mechanic, 586th IAP, male
Voronova, Tamara, pilot, 586th IAP, female
Vorontsova, Ol'ga, Ivanovna, staff, 587th/125th GvBAP, female

Vozhakova*, Mariia, Fedoseevna, navigator, 587th/125th GvBAP, female

Vstrechevskii, Valentin, Aleksandrovich, technical services, 587th/125th GvBAP, male

Vysotskaia*, Anna, Grigor'evna, pilot, 588th/46th GvBAP, female

Zagainyi, Pavel, Alekseevich, staff, 587th/125th GvBAP, male

Zaitsev, Vasilii, Konstantinovich, technical services, 587th/125th GvBAP, male

Zapol'nova, Evgeniia, Nikitichna, armorer, 587th/125th GvBAP, female

Zarembo, Anastasiia, Kondrat'evna, instrument mechanic, 587th/125th GvBAP, female

Zariniia, Kareliia, 586th IAP, female

Zarubina, A., 588th/46th GvBAP, female

Zarutskii, Vladimir, Ivanovich, staff, 587th/125th GvBAP, male

Zelenko, Ekaterina, Ivanovna, pilot, 135th BAP, female

Zhbankova, Valentina, Antonovna, instrument mechanic, 587th/125th GvBAP, female

Zhdanova, Lidiia, navigator, 588th/46th GvBAP, female

Zhediaevskaia, Galina, Dmitrievna, technical services, 587th/125th GvBAP, female

Zhernosenko, Ivan, Iakovlevich, technical services, 587th/125th GvBAP, male

Zhidiaevskaia, Galina, 587th/125th GvBAP, female

Zhigulenko, Evgeniia, Andreevna, pilot, 588th/46th GvBAP, female

Zhirkova, Mariia, Emel'ianovna, technical services, 587th/125th GvBAP, female

Zhukovitskaia*, Ida, Iosifovna, gunner, 587th/125th GvBAP, female

Zhukovitskaia, Mariia, 588th/46th GvBAP, female

Zhukovskaia, Olga, Isaakovna, staff, 588th/46th GvBAP, female

Zhuravleva, Evgeniia, mechanic, 588th/46th GvBAP, female

Zubkova, Antonina, Leont'evna, navigator, 587th/125th GvBAP, female

Zubova, Irina, Stepanovna, armorer, 587th/125th GvBAP, female

Zueva, Praskov'ia, Grigor'evna, navigator, 587th/125th GvBAP, female

Zviagin, Petr, Vasil'evich, armorer, 586th IAP, male

Appendix B:

Female Heroes of the Soviet Union

The title Hero of the Soviet Union (HSU) was first awarded in 1934, and pilots were the first recipients. Later the title included the Gold Star Medal and was the highest military award given in the Soviet Union during the Second World War. A total of 181 pilots received the HSU prior to the war.[1] During the war, 11,635 people received the HSU (including 895 fighter pilots and 840 ground attack pilots), with another 115 recipients designated "Twice Hero of the Soviet Union" and three men designated as three-time HSU recipients (two fighter pilots and Marshal Zhukov).[2] A total of 2,420 aviation personnel received the HSU.[3] The Order of Lenin was the next highest military decoration and was automatically awarded in conjunction with the HSU. There were 41,000 Order of Lenin recipients during the war.[4] The Order of the Red Banner was the most common military decoration and was given to more than 13 million people during the war.

A total of ninety women received the HSU for their service during the Second World War, including thirty-eight aviators. Among all women who served, aviators and partisans received awards far out of proportion to their numbers—perhaps indicating that these women were more likely to find themselves in positions to display conspicuous individual bravery than were women in air defense or the army. K. Jean Cottam's book *Women in War and Resistance* provides information on most of the women recipients of the HSU, as well as additional background on the award itself. Following is a list of women in aviation who have received the HSU award.

Prewar and Postwar HSU Recipients

1938 flight of *Rodina*	3	(Grizodubova, Osipenko, Raskova)
Cosmonauts	2	(Tereshkova and Savitskaia)

Wartime HSU Recipients by Regiment

46th GvBAP	24	(18 pilots, 6 navigators)[5]
125th GvBAP	5	(3 pilots, 2 navigators)
805th BAP	2	(Timofeeva-Egorova, Konstantinova)
135th BAP	1	(Zelenko)
73rd GvIAP	1	(Livtiak)
Total	38	(33 World War II)

Appendix C:

Thoughts on Sources and Historiography

A study of the Soviet women who flew during the war must be positioned at the intersection of Russian history, military history, and women's history—and this is probably the reason it has not been undertaken in the past. Specialists in military history rarely address "women's issues," and those who write the history of women seldom have an interest in military history; Russian historians often ignore both. The challenge of this book, then, was to analyze the history of one particular group of women in combat, taking into account the concerns of both military and women's history. The case of the women who flew in combat aviation in the Soviet Union during the Second World War provides a singular opportunity for such a study. What is lacking, in both English and Russian, is an attempt to systematically analyze the reasons for the formation of women's regiments and to examine issues of gender integration, unit cohesion, and combat performance within the context of the war, the military, and Soviet society. This demands a comprehensive study of the history of the regiments that incorporates memoir literature with interviews, unit histories, and archival documents.

Despite the advent of the "new military history," with its increased emphasis on social and cultural history, military historians have been slow to examine the question of women's participation and the broader issue of gender in military history. Authors such as Paul Fussell and J. Glenn Gray have examined issues of the masculine imagery of war, but the soldiers themselves are always assumed to be male.[1] Military historians have assumed, like John Keegan, that the role of women in military history has been trivial or even nonexistent. When their participation in combat is acknowledged, it is generally dismissed as "historically insignificant," "anomalous," or "more at the symbolic level than the real."[2] Some military historians are increasingly interested in the behaviors, perceptions, and reactions of men in combat—but, as M. C. Devilbiss argues, even when women were present in combat, their presence has often been overlooked.[3] There are many possible reasons for the failure of military history to examine the role of women. A Western bias that dismisses the relevance of foreign experience is one probable explanation, and the gender bias of male historians who have written most military history has certainly been a factor. Yet the new recognition of the importance of the experience of the common soldier, the "history from below" approach (so admirably accomplished by Keegan in *The Face of Battle* and other books), makes an examination of the experience of women combatants more imperative than ever. This has been recognized by some military historians, such as Richard Kohn, but has not yet been integrated into mainstream military history.[4]

Kohn has suggested some of the questions that should be asked when writing the social history of male soldiers, and similar questions should be posed regarding women's military experience.[5] Who were these women? What do we really know of their experience? Why did they enlist? Where did they come from? What did their leaving and their returning mean to their communities? What did they think? Why did they fight? How did they behave? What impact did service have on them, and they on the nation? Kohn also suggests three overriding "lines of inquiry" that must be pursued in constructing a history of military service (he specifies the United States, but the same questions apply to any nation):

1. Who served (age, ethnic background, economic status, occupation, and so forth)?
2. What was military service like (the life and environment of military personnel)? (In this area, Kohn suggests that "startling new material might emerge on such topics as the large and important role of women in military organization and war before the twentieth century.")
3. What was the interaction between the military and the rest of society?[6]

These are excellent questions, but they have rarely been applied specifically to women.

The history of women in combat has also been neglected by those studying women's history. The first major impetus in women's history was to fill in the gaps by redressing omissions in traditional work—to make women "visible." This study contributes to that effort, as it provides basic documentation of the activities of women in military aviation. Another important aspect of women's history is an emphasis on the importance of women's voices, focusing on sources such as diaries, letters, and memoirs that reveal the women's own perception of their experience. This approach coincides with the trend in military history toward history from below. The experiences of women in combat have sometimes been recorded in their own words but—like the letters of Rosetta Wakeman, who fought in the Civil War—have been hidden or overlooked until recently.[7] Another important approach in women's history was the theory of a public-private dichotomy, or separate spheres of influence and activity, in which women were seen as universally associated with private (domestic) spheres.[8] Theorists today question the universality of this dichotomy;[9] this study examines one historical arena in which women were not confined to the private sphere. Recent trends also favor moving beyond women's history toward a broader approach of studying gender or the creation of sex roles and the relations between women and men.[10] Yet another recent trend is the examination of ways in which women have had power; women's experiences in combat provide one basis for assessing how and when women have been powerful in a wartime setting. Furthermore, some writers have suggested that the exclusion of women from ruling elites was due to and justified by their exclusion from the military.[11]

There have been multiple approaches to women's history, including social, class, and economic perspectives. However, feminist approaches to history have virtually ignored the issue of women in combat; history lags behind sociology, anthropology, and literature in this respect. For example, it is anthropologist Sharon Macdonald who notes that women's experience of warfare is a still relatively uncharted area.[12] D'Ann Campbell observes that "the question of women in combat has generated a vast literature that draws from law, biology, and psychology, but seldom from history."[13] The literature on military women includes many works by sociologists and political scientists, as well as by amateur historians; professional historians are sadly underrepresented.

The overall neglect of the history of military women is so marked that in many ways the topic is a historiographical no-man's land, situated in a region between the differing concerns of military history and women's history, at times ignored and at times contested. Those who venture forth are subject to fire from the opposite side; those who dodge bullets successfully might still trip on barbed wire or wander into a historiographical minefield. Despite the risks, it is a necessary endeavor. Miriam Cooke has suggested that "the challenge that gender studies present to the analysis of war is to narrow the gap between reality and myth," the myth being that men fought while women remained at home. The way to break the myth is to make outsiders privy to women's "atypical" war experiences; placing gender at the center of an analysis of war allows us to examine the myth.[14] If it can be demonstrated that, when given the opportunity, women performed as well as men in military roles and even in combat, new avenues of historical questioning can be opened regarding the interconnection among gender roles, military service, and power. The study of military women offers an excellent opportunity to examine the interaction and integration of women and men in a combat situation, which speaks to many of the concerns mentioned earlier.

Even though women in aviation made up a small percentage of the total number of women who served, there are several reasons for focusing on this particular group. The three women's regiments provide a basis for a manageable case study. They were direct participants in combat, so questions of women's experience and performance can be examined. Two of these women's regiments had at least one-third male personnel by the end of the war, and the other regiment remained entirely female; thus, issues of unit cohesion, gender segregation, and integration can be addressed. Furthermore, the study of these aviators might provide special insights. One analyst believes that "while combat pilots are only a very small minority of all service veterans, their impact, in terms of the outcome of modern war, is extraordinarily disproportionate."[15]

The difficulty in acquiring and disseminating hard evidence on the role of women in combat has been a major factor in delaying its study as a legitimate topic for scholarly work. However, even before the opening of the archives in the 1990s, it was possible to piece together a great deal of relatively accurate information from published sources. For example, Smithsonian curator and historian Von Hardesty noted in the early 1980s that "given the floodtide since 1960 of Soviet historical literature on the subject of the air war, much of it excellent in quality, Westerners can no longer justify their silence with lamentations over the paucity of historical materials."[16] Soviet sources naturally provide the most information about the women's aviation units. John Erickson cogently addressed the reliability of these sources in his introduction to Michael Parrish's *The USSR in World War II:* "The cry that all Soviet sources are 'unreliable' or, as mere extravagant propaganda, devoid of value must fall flat when the sources have never even been examined: to dismiss them or to ignore them *tout court* is patently absurd and self-defeating."[17]

Two excellent overviews of the current state of Soviet historical materials are contained in the preface to John and Ljubica Erickson's *The Soviet Armed Forces, 1918–1992,* and in the "Archival Sources" appendix to *When Titans Clashed* by David Glantz and Jonathan M. House.[18] These scholars explain the challenges and utility of Soviet sources such as memoirs and archival documents, and readers should refer to these excellent works for general information on Soviet military sources.

Most documents pertaining to the women's regiments are located in the Central Archive of the United Armed Forces of the Commonwealth of Independent States in Podolsk *(Tsentral'nyi arkhiv Ob'edinennykh Vooruzhennykh Sil Soiuza Nezavisimykh Gosudarstv,* or TsAOVS-SNG; formerly the Central Archive of the Ministry of Defense, or TsAMO-SSSR), commonly referred to as TsAMO. Additional documents can be found in the archives of the Engels Aviation School. Bureaucratic difficulties and lack of time prevented me from personally conducting research in the archives; my sponsors at the Military Historical Institute in Moscow provided me with a number of photocopies of documents from TsAMO (unfortunately, they failed to provide precise archival references for some of these documents). As Glantz explains in *When Titans Clashed,* foreign scholars have not yet been granted free access to the military archives, and documents are customarily brought to researchers, so my frustrating experience in depending on the Military Historical Institute is not uncommon.

Friends subsequently helped me track down additional archival materials, which are referenced herein.

The published sources that cover Soviet women's participation in wartime aviation include the following. The official history of the Soviet Air Forces in World War II mentions the existence of the women's combat regiments, although only in passing.[19] The women pilots are mentioned in a number of unit histories, such as those of the air armies.[20] The women's regiments or the divisions to which they were subordinated are listed in the published order of battle for the war.[21] Many high-ranking military officers, including Marshal V. I. Chuikov (commander of the 62nd Army at Stalingrad), Marshal of Aviation Novikov (former commander of the Soviet Air Forces), and Generals of Aviation Eremin and Lavrinenkov, mention them in their memoirs.[22] The names of the women aviators who received the Hero of the Soviet Union medal for wartime valor appear in lists of medal recipients (these lists are often included as appendices in unit histories and memoirs).[23] Many of the women's names, and brief notes on their combat records, can be found in the *Soviet Military Encyclopedia*, the *Military Encyclopedic Dictionary*, and the *Great Encyclopedia*.[24]

Major newspapers such as *Pravda* and *Krasnaia zvezda* featured occasional stories and photographs about the women aviators during the war; other publications, such as the youth-oriented *Ogonek* and women's journals like *Rabotnitsa*, gave more frequent coverage. In the fifty years since the war, other journalistic publications, particularly aviation-oriented magazines such as *Aviatsiia i kosmonavtika* and *Krylia rodiny*, have published a small but continual series of articles on the subject.[25] The authoritative *Voenno-istoricheskii zhurnal* has also published articles on the women pilots.[26] A few Soviet scholars have published articles and books on women in combat that include sections on women in aviation. Vera Semenova Murmantseva stands out, with at least two books and articles in *Voprosy istorii* and *Voenno-istoricheskii zhurnal*.[27]

The combat albums of the women's regiments have been published in very limited circulation and include information on wartime bases, total sorties flown, and significant achievements, such as total bombs dropped or enemy aircraft destroyed.[28] Numerous photographs and even some wartime film footage are available. At least one movie has been made about the night bombers, directed by a woman who flew with that regiment.[29] There are many memoirs written by the women pilots themselves, which include specific information on the technical aspects of their aircraft and missions, the organization of their units, and detailed descriptions of combat sorties. Although many of the memoirs recall the achievements of fellow pilots who died during the war, they describe both the heroic qualities and the shortcomings of their comrades.[30] In general, there is about the same amount of information on the women's regiments as on any given aviation regiment.

The most important single source in Russian are the two editions of *V nebe frontovom*.[31] This collection includes numerous short memoirs written primarily by veterans of the women's regiments, and each regiment is well represented in the second (1971) edition. Both editions have been translated by K. J. Cottam and are available in English (see below). There were substantial changes between the two editions, both in the distribution of articles covering the three regiments and in the deletion and addition of articles. This source must be used judiciously, especially regarding the 586th regiment. The motivations and credibility of its chief editor, Militsa Kazarinova, have been questioned by some veterans. There is evidence that Kazarinova censored and edited materials on several occasions to glorify her sister (and possibly herself) at the expense of other veterans. Some veterans accuse her of vengeful and vindictive actions after the war. For example, the work of Aleksandr Gridnev, who commanded the 586th for two and a half years, is omitted, whereas Tamara Kazarinova, who commanded the regiment for only six months (and was the sister of Militsa), receives a great deal of attention. On the whole, however, it is a useful reference.

There has been little written in English about the Soviet women aviators, and the quality of those materials is uneven. During the war, some Western magazines and newspapers printed stories about the women pilots (though it could be argued that these publications merely repeated Soviet sources).[32] There were few Western observers on the Eastern Front who could corroborate the existence of the women's regiments firsthand. One French fighter squadron that flew with the Soviet Air Force was based with the 587th and observed its performance in combat.[33] There is at least one German report of a woman pilot who was found dead after her aircraft had been shot down by the Luftwaffe.[34] Soviets who immigrated to the West after the war, including at least one fighter pilot, have provided firsthand accounts of the women combat pilots.[35]

The best known and most frequently cited English-language book is Bruce Myles's *Night Witches,* based on interviews conducted in the late 1970s. Myles's book is flawed by appalling transliteration that distorts many names in the book; this brings into question the ability of Myles's interpreters and the accuracy of their translations.[36] Furthermore, there are many factual errors that result from Myles's reliance on interviews and his unfamiliarity with Soviet sources. This defect is compounded by the depiction of several episodes in a manner inconsistent with the facts.[37] Several veterans whom I interviewed in 1992 and 1993 held very poor opinions of the book; they said that Myles used "unknown names," that he "mixed up the facts," and so on. They were also disturbed that he used the same title as a book of memoirs by a veteran of the 46th.[38] Polina Gelman said, "I saw a copy of *Night Witches* in English. . . . It is a falsification. Everything that is written in it is a forgery. Different names, different events."[39] In short, Myles's book can be regarded as little better than fiction; indeed, it is worse because of the confusion it creates by masquerading as historical fact.

More recently, photographer and former Women's Airforce Service Pilot (WASP) Anne Noggle conducted numerous interviews with veterans of the women's regiments. Noggle's book on the Soviet women aviators is patterned on her earlier book about the WASPs, *For God, Country, and the Thrill of It All.* Both books feature a series of wartime photographs of women aviators followed by present-day portraits taken during unit reunions. *A Dance with Death,* published in 1994, also includes interviews and is an important documentary work about the Soviet regiments; it is a valuable resource but does not provide a complete history.[40] The major shortcomings are a lack of context and consistency; neither the interviewer nor the Russian translator were familiar with published materials or the basic histories of the regiments, and they failed to cross-check dates and events. Military titles are translated haphazardly; for example, "flight commander" *(komandir zvena)* is rendered "commander of the formation." The firsthand accounts are vivid and gripping, but there are inconsistencies. For example, Nina Raspopova's intense account of being wounded in combat near the Terek River is given as occurring on 9 December 1942 in Noggle's book, but archival materials relate what is apparently the same incident as occurring on 10–11 September 1942.[41] The lack of an index makes it very difficult to use the book as a reference; the interviews are not organized in any particular order, except by regiment, making it arduous to locate individuals by name. Noggle provided an exceptional service in tracking down a large number of Soviet women veterans of aviation who were still alive in the early 1990s and capturing their stories before they were lost to history altogether. However, *A Dance with Death* does not stand alone as a historical source.

The most important work to date in English is by Kazimiera Jean Cottam, a Canadian researcher and defense analyst (recently retired). For many years, Cottam was virtually the only scholar publishing on Soviet military women. Her 1983 book *Soviet Airwomen in Combat in World War II* included a thirty-seven-page history of the women's regiments, followed by a short essay about fighter pilot Liliia Litviak and an abridged translation of the memoirs of a female navigator.[42] Her 1984 *The Golden-Tressed Soldier* is another collection of translated memoir excerpts, including one chapter from the memoirs of a female night bomber pilot.[43] In 1984, Cottam translated the 1962 Soviet collection of memoirs mentioned above, and more recently, she translated the second and expanded edition of the same collection.[44] Cottam has also provided an outstanding reference work in her study of women Heroes of the Soviet Union.[45] Cottam's translations, supported by extensive footnoting of hard-to-find magazine and newspaper articles, are an excellent resource. One weakness of these publications is that although most of the translations are edited, they retain much of the phrasing of the Russian originals; a more critical tone and more familiarity with military aviation would have been welcome. Nevertheless, Cottam deserves credit for almost single-handedly keeping alive interest in this much-neglected field (an effort she continues to this day).

In addition to all these sources, I was able to locate and interview many veterans of the women's regiments, as well as some of the men who flew with them during the war. In the summer of 1992, I began an ongoing correspondence with these veterans, and in April–May 1993, I went to Russia to conduct personal interviews and to make a preliminary examination of the archives. While there, I attended the annual 2 May reunion of the veterans of the women's aviation regiments in front of the Bolshoi Theater in Moscow. I traveled to Volgograd (formerly Stalingrad) with Inna Pasportnikova, a former mechanic in the 586th, and visited one of the airfields where she served during the Battle of Stalingrad. In Volgograd I also met with Aleksandr Gridnev, former commander of the 586th, who provided me with a copy of his memoir (previously unpublished in either Russian or English), which I hope to translate and have published.[46]

Many veterans kindly allowed me to copy letters, photographs, regimental histories, and unpublished memoirs. Irina Rakobolskaia, former chief of staff of the 46th GvBAP, and Valentina Kravchenko, former navigator of the 125th GvBAP, allowed me to copy their regimental albums. Ekaterina Polunina, unofficial historian of the 586th, gave me copies of a number of biographies of regimental personnel. Inna Pasportnikova and her husband, Vladimir Stepanovich Pasportnikov, gave me a large collection of materials primarily about pilot Liliia Litviak. Lieutenant Colonel Anatoly Kanevsky also gave me some materials and copies of archival documents about Litviak. I also had access to tapes of interviews conducted by Anne Noggle in 1990–1992. Noggle, a former WASP, interviewed nearly seventy veterans in connection with her book *A Dance with Death*. She had far more material than she was able to have translated and include in her book, and she graciously allowed me access to the original tapes. Although I did not use this material in this book, relying instead on my own interviews or published material, it provided me with important background information.

The data are extensive and persuasive and leave no doubt that the women's aviation regiments did indeed exist and fly in combat. The quantity and diversity of sources, primary and secondary, published at the time of the events and afterward provide a credible basis for research. Recently obtained archival documents, combined with interviews of the veterans of these regiments, confirm basic facts, reveal certain omissions and errors, and add new information, particularly concerning wartime problems.

Notes

Introduction

1. John Keegan, *A History of Warfare* (New York: Knopf, 1993), 76.

2. John Keegan, *The Face of Battle: A Study of Agincourt, Waterloo and the Somme* (New York: Penguin, 1978), 30.

3. D'Ann Campbell, "Women in Combat: The World War II Experience in the United States, Great Britain, Germany, and the Soviet Union," *Journal of Military History* 57, no. 2 (1993): 301.

4. Only rough estimates of the number of women involved are possible. Available figures indicate that 5,000 to 6,000 women fought in World War I, and around 80,000 women fought in the civil war (including medical personnel). See Anne Eliot Griesse and Richard Stites, "Russia: Revolution and War," in *Female Soldiers—Combatants or Noncombatants? Historical and Contemporary Perspectives,* ed. Nancy Loring Goldman (Westport, Conn.: Greenwood, 1982), 67.

5. Nancy Loring Goldman, ed., *Female Soldiers—Combatants or Noncombatants? Historical and Contemporary Perspectives* (Westport, Conn.: Greenwood, 1982), 7.

6. Vera Semenova Murmantseva, *Zhenshchiny v soldatskikh shineliakh* (Moscow: Voenizdat, 1971), 9. See also Griesse and Stites, "Revolution and War," 73. The Soviets have given these figures for the past fifty years; however, precise statistical breakdowns are not available. Some corroboration is possible through examination of Komsomol histories (the Komsomol claims to have mobilized 500,000 women in five major mobilization drives) and through extensive reading of memoir literature. Even the opening of Soviet archives has not permitted an accurate count. Most recently, G. F. Krivosheev, *Soviet Casualties and Combat Losses in the Twentieth Century,* trans. Christine Barnard (London and Mechanicsburg, Pa.: Greenhill Books and Stackpole Books, 1997), gives a figure of 490,235 women who were "called up" during the war, based on archival research (xi, 230). This is consistent with the Komsomol mobilization figure and may not include women who entered military service outside of Komsomol channels. Half a million women is still an impressive figure, far outweighing the participation of women in any other country.

7. A typical regiment consisted of three squadrons of ten aircraft each.

8. In contrast, the United States' Women's Airforce Service Pilots (WASPs), who performed noncombat ferry and target-towing duties, were deactivated in December 1944—against their bitter protests—to open up jobs for male pilots who were no longer needed to train replacement pilots for the front. See Deborah G. Douglas, *United States Women in Aviation 1940–1985*, Smithsonian Studies in Air and Space No. 7 (Washington, D.C.: Smithsonian, 1990), 55.

9. This figure includes two fighter pilots who began their careers in the 586th but made their kills with other regiments (Liliia Litviak and Ekaterina Budanova). An "ace" is usually defined as a fighter pilot who has five or more kills.

10. George H. Quester, "Women in Combat," *International Security* (spring 1977): 80–91; Jeff M. Tuten, "The Argument Against Female Combatants," in *Female Soldiers—Combatants or Noncombatants? Historical and Contemporary Perspectives,* ed. Nancy Loring Goldman (Westport, Conn.: Greenwood, 1982), 237–66.

CHAPTER 1
Before the War

1. Tadeusz Sulimirski, *The Sarmatians* (New York: Praeger, 1970), 33–34, 48, 105–6; Jeannine Davis-Kimball, "Warrior Women of the Eurasian Steppes," *Archaeology* (January–February 1997): 44–48. Although most historians trace the name *Amazon* to a Greek origin (from the Greek *a* [without], *mazos* [breast]), at least one Russian writer claims that the word is a Greek adaptation of the Slavic name *omuzhony* (masculine women). See Dorothy Atkinson, "Society and Sexes in the Russian Past," in *Women in Russia,* ed. Dorothy Atkinson, Alexander Dallin, and Gail Warshofsky Lapidus (Stanford, Calif.: Stanford University Press, 1977), 3, citing V. K. Tred'iakovskii, *Sochineniia* (SPb, 1849), 3:351.

2. Atkinson, "Society and Sexes," 10.

3. Svetlana Alexiyevich, *War's Unwomanly Face,* trans. Keith Hammond and Lyudmila Lezhneva (Moscow: Progress Publishers, 1988), 63. The same commander admitted that he refused to accept women sappers in his battalion during the war—not because he believed that they could not do the job, but because he could not bear to think of them dead and "considered it unnecessary for women to go to the front line. There were enough of us men for that." He also seemed to resent his interviewer's interest in women, telling her, "War is a man's business. And there are more than enough men worthy of being written about."

4. Mary Zirin, introduction to *The Cavalry Maiden: Journals of a Female Russian Officer in the Napoleonic Wars,* by Nadezhda Durova, trans. Mary Fleming Zirin (London: Angel, 1988), xv–xxviii.

5. Alfred G. Meyer, "The Impact of World War I on Russian Women's Lives," in *Russia's Women: Accommodation, Resistance, Transformation*, ed. Barbara Evans Clements et al. (Berkeley: University of California Press, 1991), 219.

6. Her name is pronounced "Boch-kar-YO-va." It is spelled in various ways in English due to a lack of consistent transliteration in the journalistic sources. In the translation of her memoir, her name is given as "Botchkareva," but Bochkareva is more correct.

7. Maria Botchkareva, *Yashka: My Life as Peasant, Officer and Exile* (New York: Stokes, 1919), 73–75. Bochkareva says that she was told by the clerk at the 25th Reserve Battalion in Tomsk that "the regulations do not permit us to enlist women. It is against the law." The unit commander suggested that she send a telegram to the tsar, which she did; the commander later received a return telegram with the tsar's authorization for Bochkareva to enlist. The best overview of Bochkareva is Richard Abraham, "Mariia L. Bochkareva and the Russian Amazons of 1917," in *Women and Society in Russia and the Soviet Union*, ed. Linda Edmondson (Cambridge: Cambridge University Press, 1992), 124–44. See also Mariia Bocharnikova, "Boi v zimnem dvortse," *Novyi zhurnal* 68 (1962): 215–27 (Bocharnikova was a veteran of the 1st Petrograd Women's Battalion); A. S. Senin, "Zhenskie batal'ony i voennye komandy v 1917 godu," *Voprosy Istorii* 10 (1987): 176–82; and Richard Stites, *The Women's Liberation Movement in Russia: Feminism, Nihilism and Bolshevism, 1860–1930* (Princeton, N.J.: Princeton University Press, 1978), 295–300.

8. Botchkareva, *My Life*, 149–51.

9. Ibid., 157.

10. Ibid., 159. Griesse and Stites note that "it was certainly the first instance in modern history in which women were used in all-female fighting units as models of military valor and performance in order to check desertion and fraternization with the enemy." Anne Eliot Griesse and Richard Stites, "Russia: Revolution and War," in *Female Soldiers—Combatants or Noncombatants? Historical and Contemporary Perspectives*, ed. Nancy Loring Goldman (Westport, Conn.: Greenwood, 1982), 64.

11. Botchkareva, *My Life*, 159–60; Griesse and Stites, "Revolution and War," 64. Other Women's Battalions of Death were formed in Moscow, Odessa, Ekaterinodar, and Perm, but only the Perm unit and Bochkareva's in Petrograd were used in combat or police actions. See also Bessie Beatty's *The Red Heart of Russia* (New York: N.p., 1918).

12. See Barbara Evans Clements, Barbara Alpern Engel, and Christine D. Worobec, eds., *Russia's Women: Accommodation, Resistance, Transformation* (Berkeley and Los Angeles: University of California Press, 1991), illustration 14, for a photo in which the patriarch of the Russian Orthodox Church is blessing the Women's Battalion of Death before its departure for the front.

13. Botchkareva, *My Life*, 208–18.

14. Ibid., 203.

15. According to Richard Abraham, *Alexander Kerensky: The First Love of the*

Revolution (New York: Columbia University Press, 1987), 321: "It was widely alleged that several of the women soldiers were raped, and one young woman did commit suicide. Less well-known was the fact that British diplomatic intervention was successful in protecting the women. The allegation of rape increased revulsion against Kerensky in many circles. His own silence on the women soldiers of 1917 is part of the familiar pattern of patriarchal erasure, the product of collective 'masculine' shame." Abraham notes that "neither Rodzianko nor Kerensky found it worth mentioning the women in their memoirs" (440), but he cites a number of eyewitness accounts from both Soviet and British sources regarding Bochkareva and the Women's Battalion of Death. Interestingly, Abraham also states that "Kerensky's first wife was astonished at his omission of his favorite sister, Nadia from his memoirs, perhaps as an example of his tendency to repress unhappy incidents" (390). If Kerensky did have such a tendency, it would support Abraham's statement regarding "patriarchal erasure" and "masculine shame."

16. Richard Stites, "Women and the Russian Intelligentsia: Three Perspectives," in *Women in Russia,* ed. Dorothy Atkinson et al. (Stanford, Calif.: Stanford University Press, 1977), 60–61.

17. Alfred G. Meyer, "Marxism and the Women's Movement," in *Women in Russia,* ed. Dorothy Atkinson et al. (Stanford, Calif.: Stanford University Press, 1977), 85. Clara Zetkin defined the relationship between women's liberation and communism: "The female workers' movement is an integral part of the total workers' movement. It is not a fight of women against men, because proletarian women work side by side with their men." Zetkin discussed these issues with Lenin and is believed to have influenced his views. See Meyer, "Marxism," 111.

18. Gail Warshofsky Lapidus, "Sexual Equality in Soviet Policy: A Developmental Perspective," in *Women in Russia,* ed. Dorothy Atkinson et al. (Stanford, Calif.: Stanford University Press, 1977), 115–19. The Soviet concept of citizenship included the condition of work "as both a right and an obligation," and women were subject to labor conscription. Lapidus explains that "the Labor Code of 1918 treated work as a form of service to society."

19. Ellen Jones, *Red Army and Society* (Boston: Allen and Unwin, 1985), 98–99.

20. Meyer, "Marxism," 112. Meyer notes that Luxemburg also denied the existence of the Jewish question, the Polish question, and the national question.

21. Griesse and Stites, "Revolution and War," 66.

22. Ibid., 62.

23. Jones, *Red Army,* 99.

24. Griesse and Stites, "Revolution and War," 68.

25. Kazimiera J. Cottam, ed., *Women in War and Resistance: Selected Biographies of Soviet Women Soldiers* (Nepean, Ontario: New Military Publishing, 1998), xix.

26. *Flying* (June 1913): 25.

27. Paper marked "LB71768" from Smithsonian Air and Space Museum collection; photocopy given to the author by Dr. Von Hardesty; Meyer, "Impact of World War I," 219–220.

28. Valerie Moolman, *Women Aloft,* Epic of Flight Series (Alexandria, Va.: Time-Life Books, 1981), 157–64; paper marked "Robertson, Russian Women in WWI," p. 160, from Smithsonian Air and Space Museum collection; photocopy given to the author by Dr. Von Hardesty.

29. "Robertson, Russian Women in WWI," 160.

30. Ibid.

31. K. Jean Cottam, *Soviet Airwomen in Combat in World War II* (Manhattan, Kans.: Sunflower University Press, 1983), 1.

32. Ibid., 8; V. Mitroshenkov, "They Were First," *Soviet Military Review* (March 1969): 20–22.

33. Marina Chechneva, *Nebo ostaetsia nashim* (Moscow: Voenizdat, 1976), 9–10. The astronaut Yuri Gagarin reportedly claimed that he was inspired by the example of Chechneva, who after the war led an aerial acrobatic team and set numerous sports records. See Cottam, *Soviet Airwomen,* 15–16.

34. Anne Noggle, *A Dance with Death: Soviet Airwomen in World War II* (College Station: Texas A&M University Press, 1994), 22.

35. Alexiyevich, *War's Unwomanly Face,* 29.

36. Mitroshenkov, "They Were First," 20–22; Cottam, *Soviet Airwomen,* 1.

37. Mitroshenkov, "They Were First," 20–22. Valery Chkalov, who later became the most famous Soviet test pilot, was also a member of the Egorevsk school at that time.

38. Mitroshenkov, "They Were First," 20–22.

39. Raisa E. Aronova, *Nochnye ved'my,* 2nd ed. (Moscow: Sovetskaia Rossiia, 1980), 8.

40. V. Grizodubova, "Doch' naroda," in *Geroini: ocherki o zhenshchinakh—Geroiakh Sovetskogo Soiuza,* 2 vols., ed. L. F. Toropov (Moscow: Politizdat, 1969), 2:103–4.

41. "Marina Raskova," *Voennii entsiklopedicheskii slovar',* 1983 ed.; "Marina Raskova," *Bolshaia Sovetskaia Entsiklopediia,* 3rd ed.; Heinrich E. Schulz, Paul K. Urban, and Andrew I. Lebed, eds., *Who Was Who in the USSR* (Metuchen, N.J.: Scarecrow Press, 1972), 472.

42. Lazar Konstantinovich Brontman and L. Khvat, *The Heroic Flight of the Rodina* (Moscow: Foreign Languages Publishing House, 1938), 101.

43. Brontman and Khvat, *Heroic Flight,* 103.

44. V. I. Tarasov, A. Ya. Zotov, et al., *Akademiia imeni M. V. Frunze* [The M. V. Frunze Academy] (Moscow: Voenizdat, 1973), 126.

45. William Odom identifies the propagandization of aviation as one of the organizational goals of the Osoaviakhim in his book *The Soviet Volunteers: Modernization and Bureaucracy in a Public Mass Organization* (Princeton, N.J.: Princeton University Press, 1973), 302. It is interesting to note that Odom be-

lieves that Osoaviakhim's "goals were not synchronically established but rather worked out in a political struggle beginning several years before Osoaviakhim was founded and continuing through most of the period of the study."

46. Brontman and Khvat, *Heroic Flight*, 15; emphasis added.

47. Robert C. Tucker, *Stalin in Power: The Revolution from Above, 1928–1941* (New York: Norton, 1990), 565.

48. Kenneth R. Whiting, "Soviet Aviation and Air Power Under Stalin, 1928–1941," in *Soviet Aviation and Air Power: A Historical View*, ed. Robin Higham and Jacob W. Kipp (Boulder, Colo.: Westview, 1977), 54.

49. Seweryn Bialer, ed., *Stalin and His Generals: Soviet Military Memoirs of World War II* (New York: Pegasus, 1969), 166–71.

50. On the glorification of aviation heroes, see Katerina Clark, "The Aviation Hero as the Paradigmatic New Man," in *The Soviet Novel: History as Ritual* (Chicago: University of Chicago Press, 1981), 124–29. On the uses of aviation as justification for the Stalinist regime, see Kenneth E. Bailes, "Technology and Legitimacy: Soviet Aviation and Stalinism in the 1930s," *Technology and Culture* 17, no. 1 (1976): 55–81. Regarding Soviet women in aviation during this period, Clark never mentions the existence of aviation *heroines*. Bailes focuses entirely on the male pilots, except for a passing reference to Stalin giving a Kremlin reception for women pilots in 1938 (see his note 37).

51. Brontman and Khvat, *Heroic Flight*, 22.

52. Madelin Blitzstein, "How Women Flyers Fight Russia's Air War," *Aviation Magazine* (July 1944): 116ff; K. Jean Cottam, "Soviet Women in Combat in World War II: The Ground/Air Defense Forces," in *Women in Eastern Europe and the Soviet Union*, ed. Tova Yedlin (New York: Praeger, 1980), 1.

53. Brontman and Khvat, *Heroic Flight*, 22.

54. Ibid., 20.

55. See Robin Higham and Jacob Kipp, *Soviet Aviation and Air Power: A Historical View* (Boulder, Colo.: Westview, 1977), 54.

56. Amelia Earhart set the women's record in 1932 with a 3,939-kilometer flight from Los Angeles to New York; in May 1938, the French pilot Elisabeth Lyon beat Earhart's record by 124 kilometers; two days later, another Frenchwoman, Dupeyron, set a new distance record with a 4,360-kilometer flight. This was the record that Raskova and her copilots hoped to break.

57. Brontman and Khvat, *Heroic Flight*, 28–29.

58. Ibid., 32–33.

59. Ibid., 38–39.

60. The equipment failure was aggravated by the fact that the ground communications expert on the team had been arrested a week before the flight; Cottam, *Women in War and Resistance*, 5; Kazimiera J. Cottam, "Soviet Women Soldiers in World War II: Three Biographical Sketches," *Minerva: Quarterly Report on Women and the Military* 18, nos. 3–4 (2001).

61. Cottam, *Women in War and Resistance*, 5.

62. Brontman and Khvat, *Heroic Flight*, 18; Cottam, *Women in War and Resistance*, 5.

63. See *Pravda* during the period 24 September through 28 October 1938.

64. Marina Raskova, *Zapiski Shturmana* (Moscow: Molodaia Gvardiia, 1939), 220–25; Brontman and Khvat, *Heroic Flight*, 104.

65. Alexander Boyd, *The Soviet Air Force Since 1918* (New York: Stein and Day, 1977), 66. It is interesting to note that the Hero of the Soviet Union title was first devised for another group of pilots—those who rescued the crew of a trapped icebreaker in the Chukchi Sea in February 1934 (see Higham and Kipp, *Soviet Aviation*, 53). During World War II, the HSU became the most important military award.

66. As examples of the publicity surrounding Stalin's interest in aviation, Bailes in "Technology and Legitimacy" cited contemporary sources, including works by the pilots themselves, such as I. Gromov, "Letchiki novogo tipa" [Pilots of a New Type], in *Vstrechi tovarishchem Stalinym* [Meetings with Comrade Stalin], ed. A. Fadeev (Moscow: Politizdat, 1939), 38–40, and Valerii Pavlovich Chkalov, "Nash otets" [Our Father], in *Letchik nashego vremeni* [A Pilot of Our Time] (Moscow: 1938), 315: "The aviators of the Soviet Union call Soviet aviation, Stalinist aviation." See also a large number of newspaper articles, such as the piece in *Grazhdanskaia aviatsiia* [Civil Aviation], 7 November 1933, in which Stalin charges Soviet aviation with the task of "flying farther than anyone, faster than anyone, and higher than anyone."

67. Bailes, "Technology and Legitimacy," 55, 80.

68. On Stalin's personal interest in the women aviators, see the reprint of his telegram to the crew of the *Rodina*, congratulating them on setting a new world record ("Ekipazhu samoleta 'Rodina,'" *Pravda*, 8 October 1938, 1); see *Pravda*, 28 October 1938, 1, for reports of Stalin's Kremlin reception for the same women pilots. See "Smert' A. K. Serovo i P. D. Osipenko" [The Death of A. K. Serov and P. D. Osipenko], *Literaturnaia gazeta*, 15 May 1939, 1, for a report of Stalin's participation in Polina Osipenko's funeral.

69. Alexander Werth, *Russia at War: 1941–45*, 3rd ed. (New York: Carroll and Graf, 1988), 7–8.

70. Ibid., 48.

71. Helene Keyssar and Vladimir Pozner, *Remembering War: A U.S.-Soviet Dialogue* (New York: Oxford University Press, 1990), 39–40; interview with Evgeniia Zhigulenko.

72. Raskova, *Zapiski Shturmana*.

73. Raisa E. Aronova, *Nochnye ved'my*, 1st ed. (Moscow: Sovetskaia Rossiia, 1969), 13.

74. Valentina Flegontovna Kravchenko-Savitskaia, tape-recorded interview by author, Moscow (Kravchenko's apartment), 7 May 1993.

75. Raskova, *Zapiski Shturmana*, 3.

76. Blitzstein, "How Women Flyers Fight," 116; Grizodubova, "Doch' naroda," 107.

77. Evgeniia Zhigulenko, "Those Magnificent Women in Their Flying Machines," *Soviet Life* (May 1990): 12.

78. Kravchenko-Savitskaia interview by author, 7 May 1993; Inna Vladimirovna Pasportnikova, tape-recorded interview by author, Zhukovsky, Russia (Pasportnikova's apartment), 8 May 1993.

79. Alexei Flerovsky, "Women Flyers of Fighter Planes," *Soviet Life* (May 1975): 28.

80. Natalia Kravtsova, *Ot zakata do rassveta* [From Sunset to Dawn] (Moscow: Voenizdat, 1968).

81. S. Gribanov, "Ognennaia Liliia," in *Geroi i podvigi,* 1st ed., 4 vols., ed. M. F. Loshchits (Moscow: Voenizdat, 1966), 4:154; also S. Gribanov, "Liliia," in *V nebe frontovom: sbornik vospominaniy sovetskikh letchits-uchastnits Velikoi Otechestvennoi voiny,* 2nd ed., ed. M. A. Kazarinova et al. (Moscow: Molodaia Gvardiia, 1971), 331.

CHAPTER 2
Recruitment and Training of Aviation Group 122

1. Shelley Saywell, *Women in War* (Markham, Ontario: Viking, 1985), 136.

2. Evgeniia Zhigulenko, "Those Magnificent Women in Their Flying Machines," *Soviet Life* (May 1990): 12. Zhigulenko later became a film director and made a well-known 1981 movie, *Night Witches in the Sky,* about the 588th.

3. K. Jean Cottam, "Soviet Women in Combat in World War II: The Rear Services, Resistance Behind Enemy Lines, and Military Political Workers," *International Journal of Women's Studies* 5, no. 4 (1982): 363.

4. Ibid., 363–64.

5. Anne Eliot Griesse, "Soviet Women and World War II: Mobilization and Combat Policies" (master's thesis, Georgetown University, 1980), 40–41.

6. Alexander Samoilovich Magid, *Gvardeiskii Tamanskii aviatsionnyi polk* [Guards Taman Aviation Regiment], 2nd ed. (Moscow: DOSAAF, 1956), 3; emphasis added.

7. V. Mitroshenkov, "They Were First," *Soviet Military Review* (March 1969): 22.

8. One historian who read an early version of this manuscript expressed his opinion that in the Soviet system, a single individual could not have had such influence.

9. A source that I have been unable to examine might shed light on this question. According to Roma Simons, a civilian historian working for the air force, a small booklet entitled *Rasskazy o Stalina,* published in 1943 in Erevan, contains the memoirs and reminiscences of three women who met with Stalin in 1941. Raskova is one of the women; perhaps this booklet contains the text of her conversation with Stalin on the formation of the 122nd. Unfortunately, the only copy of the booklet that has been located is in the Lenin Library in a special collection and could not be examined.

10. Richard E. Lauterbach, *These Are the Russians*, 3rd ed. (New York: Harper, 1945), 107.

11. Lauterbach is the only reference I have been able to find regarding an affair between Stalin and Raskova. Since he states that the gossip was "mostly foreign," this rumor probably originated among Westerners, who perhaps found it difficult to believe that Raskova's fame rested solely on her flying skill.

12. A. Beliakov, foreword to *Zapiski shturmana/Prodolzheniie podviga*, 2nd ed., ed. Marina Raskova and Ekaterina Migunova (Moscow: DOSAAF, 1976), 3–11.

13. General Major of Aviation A. Nikitin, "M. M. Raskova," *Krasnaia zvezda*, 12 January 1943, 4.

14. Saywell, *Women in War*, 136–37.

15. Zhigulenko, "Those Magnificent Women in Their Flying Machines," 12.

16. A. Skopintseva, "Knigi o ratnykh podvigakh sovetskikh zhenshchin," *Vestnik protivovozdushnoi oborony* (1978): 89.

17. William E. Odom, *The Soviet Volunteers: Modernization and Bureaucracy in a Public Mass Organization* (Princeton, N.J.: Princeton University Press, 1973), 304–5: "It is possible that Osoaviakhim could have been producing an adequate manpower base that the military squandered in the early stages of the war."

18. Valentina Flegontovna Kravchenko-Savitskaia, tape-recorded interview by author, Moscow (Kravchenko's apartment), 7 May 1993.

19. Anne Noggle, *A Dance with Death: Soviet Airwomen in World War II* (College Station: Texas A&M University Press, 1994), 132.

20. Alexei Flerovsky, "Women Flyers of Fighter Planes," *Soviet Life* (May 1975): 28.

21. Polina Gelman, letter to author, 11 August 1992.

22. Some Soviet women believe that it is possible, in isolated cases, for Soviet women to demand concessions by pressure from below. A parallel case is discussed by Mamonova, who said that the space flight of Valentina Tereshkova is now "a distant memory of the short liberalization of the sixties." She went on to comment that the astronaut Savitskaia was permitted to fly in 1982 as "a direct response to our feminist movement's demands for more participation by women in the space program." Tatyana Mamonova, *Russian Women's Studies: Essays on Sexism in Soviet Culture* (New York: Pergamon, 1989).

23. Helene Keyssar and Vladimir Pozner, *Remembering War: A U.S.-Soviet Dialogue* (New York: Oxford University Press, 1990), 39–40, interview with Evgeniia Zhigulenko.

24. Walter Laqueur, *The Fate of the Revolution: Interpretations of Soviet History*, rev. and updated ed. (New York: Macmillan, 1987), 247.

25. D. A. Zhuravlev, *Ognevoi Shchit Moskvy* (Moscow: Voenizdat, 1972), 125–27, cited in K. Jean Cottam, "Soviet Women in Combat in World War II:

The Ground/Air Defense Forces," in *Women in Eastern Europe and the Soviet Union,* ed. Tova Yedlin (New York: Praeger, 1980), 117.

26. Aleksandr Vasilevich Gridnev, "Memuary," trans. Reina Pennington (typescript, n.d.).

27. Galina I. Markova, "Youth Under Fire: The Story of Klavdiya Fomicheva, a Woman Dive Bomber Pilot," in *Soviet Airwomen in Combat in World War II,* trans. and ed. K. J. Cottam (Manhattan, Kans.: Sunflower University Press, 1983), 91; Evgeniia Timofeeva, "Pervyi boi," in *V nebe frontovom,* 2nd ed., ed. M. A. Kazarinova, N. F. Kravtsova, and A. A. Poliantseva (Moscow: Molodaia Gvardiia, 1971), 26. Hereafter, *VNF* (2nd ed.).

28. "Pamiati Geroia Sovetskogo Soiuza Mariny Raskovoi," *Krasnaia zvezda,* 9 January 1943, 3.

29. Svetlana Alexiyevich, *War's Unwomanly Face,* trans. Keith Hammond and Lyudmila Lezhneva (Moscow: Progress Publishers, 1988), 91.

30. M. A. Kazarinova, "Rodina zovet!" in *VNF* (2nd ed.), 9.

31. V. F. Kravchenko, ed., *125 Gvardeiskii Bombardirovochnyi Aviatsionnyi Borisovskii ordenov Suvorova i Kutuzova polk imeni Geroia Sovetskogo Soiuza Mariny Raskovoi* (Moscow: privately published, 1976), 28.

32. E. A. Migunova, "Prodolzheniie podviga," in *Zapiski shturmana prodolzheniie podviga* (Moscow: DOSAAF, 1976), 86.

33. Liudmila Zabavskaia, "Not a Job for the Women," *Soviet Military Review* (March 1989): 20.

34. Migunova, "Prodolzheniie podviga," 244; Galina I. Markova, *Vzlet: O Geroe Sovetskogo Soiuza M. M. Raskovoi* (Moscow: Politizdat, 1986), 66–67; emphasis added.

35. Migunova, "Prodolzheniie podviga," 246.

36. Ibid., 246–47.

37. Ibid., 251.

38. Ibid., 252.

39. Von Hardesty, *Red Phoenix: The Rise of Soviet Air Power, 1941–1945* (Washington, D.C.: Smithsonian, 1982), 55.

40. V. F. Kravchenko, ed., *125 Gvardeiskii Bombardirovochnyi Aviatsionnyi Borisovskii ordenov Suvoroba i Kutuzova polk imeni Geroia Sovetskogo Soiuza Mariny Raskovoi* (Moscow: privately published, 1976), 3. The U-2 was the training variant of the Po-2.

41. Hardesty, *Red Phoenix,* 68.

42. Gelman, letter to the author, 28 July 1992. Smith concluded that as many as 200,000 Muscovites, mostly women, were involved in digging antitank ditches during this time. Gregory Malloy Smith, "The Impact of World War II on Women, Family Life, and Mores in Moscow, 1941–1945" (Ph.D. diss., Stanford University, 1989), 79–80.

43. See A. M. Bereznitskaia, "Pervye Dni," in *V nebe frontovom,* 1st ed., ed. M. A. Kazarinova and A. A. Poliantseva (Moscow: Molodaia Gvardiia, 1962), 21. Hereafter, *VNF* (1st ed.).

44. Raisa E. Aronova, *Nochnye ved'my*, 2nd ed. (Moscow: Sovetskaia Rossiia, 1980), 21.

45. Inna Vladimirovna Pasportnikova, tape-recorded interview by author, Zhukovsky, Russia (Pasportnikova's apartment), 8 May 1993. Pasportnikova's maiden name was Pleshchevtseva.

46. Ellen Jones, *Red Army and Society* (Boston: Allen and Unwin, 1985), 101.

47. Hubert Griffith, *R.A.F. in Russia* (London: Hammond, 1942), 29–30.

48. I have been unable to discover what became of the other two pilots, O. Popova and M. Glukhovtseva.

49. Kravchenko-Savitskaia, interview by author, 7 May 1993; Pasportnikova, interview by author, 8 May 1993.

50. Noggle, *Dance with Death*, 49.

51. Migunova, "Prodolzheniie podviga," 261–62; Galina Ol'khozovskaia, "Otvazhnaia eskadril'ia," in *VNF* (2nd ed.), 37–38.

52. Magid, *Gvardeiskii Tamanskii*, 56.

53. Irina Ivanovna Danilova-Emel'ianova, tape-recorded interview by author, Moscow, 3 May 1993.

54. Ol'ga Yamshchikova, "Druzhba," in *VNF* (2nd ed.), 341–53.

55. Aleksandra Eremenko, "Zhizn' za tovarishcha," in *VNF* (2nd ed.), 102.

56. Valentina Abramovna Petrochenkova-Neminushchaia, interview by author, Chkalovsk, Russia (Petrochenkova's apartment), 9 May 1993.

57. Ibid.

58. Gelman, letter to author, 11 August 1992.

59. Pasportnikova, interview by author, 8 May 1993.

60. Cottam, *Soviet Airwomen*, 2.

61. Migunova, "Prodolzheniie podviga," 254–55; Markova, *Vzlet*, 66–67.

62. Markova, *Vzlet*, 86.

63. Ibid., 69.

64. Migunova, "Prodolzheniie podviga," 319–20.

65. Ibid., 320.

66. Aleksandra Aleksandrovna Makunina, tape-recorded interview by author, Moscow (Favorskaia's apartment), 10 May 1993.

67. Migunova, "Prodolzheniie podviga," 319–20.

68. Hardesty, *Red Phoenix*, 69.

69. Migunova, "Prodolzheniie podviga," 255.

70. Aronova, *Nochnye ved'my* (2nd ed.), 22; Bereznitskaia, "Pervye Dni," 23.

71. Migunova, "Prodolzheniie podviga," 256.

72. Ibid., 255–56.

73. Aronova, *Nochnye ved'my* (2nd ed.), 22–23.

74. Kravchenko-Savitskaia, interview by author, 7 May 1993; Migunova, "Prodolzheniie podviga," 257.

75. Migunova, "Prodolzheniie podviga," 256.

76. Bereznitskaia, "Pervye Dni," 23.

77. Aronova, *Nochnye ved'my* (2nd ed.), 24.

78. Ibid.; Magid, *Gvardeiskii Tamanskii*, 33.

79. Bereznitskaia, "Pervye Dni," 23. Favorskaia told me that when the women finally received uniforms, there were still problems. "In 1943 we got skirts for parades and for attending dances. But we had no stockings. Another problem was how to hold up the stockings. Should we try to pin them or use rubber bands?" Irina Favorskaia-Luneva, personal interview, 10 May 1993. Migunova, "Prodolzheniie podviga," 258, recalls the date as being the sixteenth. Perhaps the uniforms were distributed on two days.

80. Migunova, "Prodolzheniie podviga," 258.

81. Markova,*Vzlet*, 70.

82. Ibid., 71.

83. Smith, "Impact of World War II," 74.

84. Sources vary in saying the departure was on 16 or 17 October and on whether it began late at night or early in the morning. Migunova and Magid agree on 17 October, late at night.

85. Aronova, *Nochnye ved'my* (2nd ed.), 25–26; Magid, *Gvardeiskii Tamanskii*, 37.

86. M. A. Kazarinova, "Rodina zovet!" in *VNF* (1st ed.), 10.

87. Aronova, *Nochnye ved'my* (2nd ed.), 24.

88. Bereznitskaia, "Pervye Dni," 23; Saywell, *Women in War*, 138.

89. Konstantin Vershinin, *Chetvertaia Vozdushnaia* (Moscow: Voenizdat, 1973), 137; Irina Rakobolskaia, interview by author, Moscow (Rakobolskaia's apartment), 10 May 1993.

90. Raskova knew that she was preparing for one fighter and two bomber regiments. Most regiments at the time consisted of two squadrons with ten aircraft each. For a bomber squadron, this would require a minimum of one pilot, navigator, mechanic, and armorer for each aircraft, plus staff personnel, or a minimum of 100 people. The fighter regiment would need pilots but only one or two staff navigators, giving a minimum figure of 80 personnel. Altogether, a bare minimum of about 300 people would have been required, and this probably underestimates the number of support personnel. In their regimental photo albums, the 46th listed 240 personnel, and the 125th listed 289. Evodokia Bershanskaia et al., eds., *46 Gvardeiskii Tamanskii zhenskii aviatsionyi polk* (n.p.: Tsentral'nyi Dom Sovetskoi Armii imeni M. v. Frunze, n.d.); V. F. Kravchenko, ed., *125 Gvardeiskii Bombardirovochnyi Aviatsionnyi Borisovskii ordenov Suvoroba i Kutuzova polk imeni Geroia Sovetskogo Soiuza Mariny Raskovoi* (Moscow: privately published, 1976). My own database includes these totals of personnel for each unit (including casualties and replacements): 46th, 261; 125th, 300; 586th, 184.

91. Migunova, "Prodolzheniie podviga," 259.

92. Kazarinova, "Rodina zovet!" 14.

93. Migunova, "Prodolzheniie podviga," 259.

94. Ibid., 260.

95. Kazarinova, "Rodina zovet!" 14–15.

96. Migunova, "Prodolzheniie podviga," 260.

97. Kravchenko-Savitskaia, interview by author, 7 May 1993.

98. Kazarinova, "Rodina zovet!" 10–11.

99. Migunova, "Prodolzheniie podviga," 260; Aronova, *Nochnye ved'my* (2nd ed.), 26–27.

100. Aronova, *Nochnye ved'my* (2nd ed.), 28.

101. Migunova, "Prodolzheniie podviga," 262.

102. Ibid.

103. Kazarinova, "Rodina zovet!" 15.

104. Migunova, "Prodolzheniie podviga," 265.

105. Markova, *Vzlet*, 74; Migunova, "Prodolzheniie podviga," 262.

106. Aronova, *Nochnye ved'my* (2nd ed.), 37. Several women whom I interviewed mentioned the poem by Iuliia Drunina (who was often quoted to me) that begins, "No, it's not the huts that are burning— / it's my youth in the fire. / Young girls are going off to war / looking like young fellows."

107. Aronova, *Nochnye ved'my* (2nd ed.), 37.

108. Ibid., 38.

109. Migunova, "Prodolzheniie podviga," 271.

110. Aronova, *Nochnye ved'my* (2nd ed.), 49.

111. Saywell, *Women in War*, 138.

112. Hans D. Seidl, *Stalin's Eagles: An Illustrated Study of the Soviet Aces of World War II and Korea* (Atglen, Pa.: Schiffer Military History, 1998), 7, as noted by V. I. Popkov, Twice Hero of the Soviet Union.

113. Migunova, "Prodolzheniie podviga," 262.

114. Gridnev, "Memuary."

115. Migunova, "Prodolzheniie podviga," 301–2.

116. Ibid., 268.

117. Marina Chechneva, *Nebo ostaetsia nashim* (Moscow: Voenizdat, 1976), 40.

118. Markova, *Vzlet*, 82.

119. Migunova, "Prodolzheniie podviga," 313.

120. Chechneva, *Nebo*, 41.

121. Ekaterina Fedotova, "Batia," in *VNF* (2nd ed.), 33–36.

122. Migunova, "Prodolzheniie podviga," 266.

123. Markova, *Vzlet*, 82.

124. Migunova, "Prodolzheniie podviga," 266–67.

125. Ibid., 313.

126. Kravchenko-Savitskaia, interview by author, 7 May 1993.

127. Migunova, "Prodolzheniie podviga," 267–68.

128. Aronova, *Nochnye ved'my* (2nd ed.), 23.

129. Inna Vladimirovna Pasportnikova, *Moi komandir* (typescript in author's collection, 1989).

130. Aronova, *Nochnye ved'my* (2nd ed.), 36.

131. Ibid., 39.

132. Markova, *Vzlet*, 80.

133. Ibid., 81–82; Migunova, "Prodolzheniie podviga," 278–82.

134. Markova, *Vzlet,* 81.

135. Ibid., 86. Migunova also provides no details on Kazarinova's selection, simply noting that she was designated to the position.

136. "Vypuska iz istoricheskogo formuliara 586 IAP," TsAMO, Podolsk, Russia (n.d.), f. 586 IAP, op., d., l. not recorded; N. A. Kirsanov and V. F. Cheremisov, "Zhenshchiny v voiskakh protivo-vozdushnoi oborony v gody Velikoi Otechestvennoi voiny," *Istoriia SSSR* 3 (1975): 64.

137. Migunova, "Prodolzheniie podviga," 283–87.

138. [No title; designation of the 588th NLBP, 218 AD, 4 VA, Zakavakasky Front as a Guards Aviation Regiment], TsAMO, Podolsk, Russia (11 February 1943), f. 46 GvBAP, op. 143370c, d. 1, l. 1–3.

139. Markova, *Vzlet,* 87–88; Aronova, *Nochnye ved'my* (2nd ed.), 43.

140. Ekaterina Kuzminichna Polunina and Valentina Vasilevna Kovaleva, interview by author, Moscow (Polunina's apartment), 1 May 1993.

141. Magid, *Gvardeiskii Tamanskii,* 80–83.

142. Aronova, *Nochnye ved'my* (2nd ed.), 44; see also Magid, *Gvardeiskii Tamanskii,* 80.

143. "Vypuska iz istoricheskogo formuliara 586 IAP," f. 586 IAP, op., d., l. unknown, citing telegram no. 363 from the commander of IA/PVO.

144. Aronova, *Nochnye ved'my* (2nd ed.), 50–51.

145. Polunina and Kovaleva, interview by author, 1 May 1993.

146. I. S. Levin, *Groznye gody* (Saratov: Privolzhskoe, 1984), "K chitateliu."

147. Ibid., 28.

148. Hardesty, *Red Phoenix,* 30, 59–61.

149. Levin, *Groznye gody,* 29–30.

150. Gridnev, "Memuary."

151. "Vypuska iz istoricheskogo formuliara 586 IAP."

152. Levin, *Groznye gody,* 29–30.

153. Irina Ivanovna Danilova-Emel'ianova, tape-recorded interview by author, Moscow, 3 May 1993. For an interesting discussion of the importance and development of the use of radios in aircraft, see B. B. Lariokhin and I. A. Tretiak, "Improved Radio Communications for Radar Support Air Operations in the Great Patriotic War," *Voenno-istoricheskii zhurnal* 9 (1986): 68–73.

154. Hardesty, *Red Phoenix,* 115.

155. Noggle, *Dance with Death,* 106.

156. Markova, *Vzlet,* 84; Migunova, "Prodolzheniie podviga," 293, 299.

157. Markova, *Vzlet,* 92–93.

158. The order is reprinted in Kravchenko, *125 Gvardeiskii,* 5.

159. Markova, *Vzlet,* 93; Migunova, "Prodolzheniie podviga," 293.

160. Migunova, "Prodolzheniie podviga," 299.

161. Kravchenko-Savitskaia, interview by author, 7 May 1993.

162. Kazarinova, "Rodina zovet!" 17–18. Interestingly, this paragraph did not appear in the 1962 version of Kazarinova's article.

163. Migunova, "Prodolzheniie podviga," 302–3.

164. Noggle, *Dance with Death*, 114.

165. Kravchenko, *125 Gvardeiskii*, 4; Markova, *Vzlet*, 94–95.

166. Kravchenko, *125 Gvardeiskii*, 4; Markova, *Vzlet*, 94–95; Migunova, "Prodolzheniie podviga," 302.

167. Markova, *Vzlet*, 94.

168. Kazarinova, "Rodina zovet!" 18; Migunova, "Prodolzheniie podviga," 307–8.

169. Kazarinova, "Rodina zovet!" 17.

170. Migunova, "Prodolzheniie podviga," 303–4.

171. Ibid., 307.

172. Noggle, *Dance with Death*, 147.

173. Kravchenko, *125 Gvardeiskii*, 6. Besides the Pe-2, other training aircraft included the U-2, Su-2, and TB-3. Migunova, "Prodolzheniie podviga," 338.

174. Gail Warshovsky Lapidus, "Sexual Equality in Soviet Policy: A Developmental Perspective," in *Women in Russia,* ed. Dorothy Atkinson, Alexander Dallin, and Gail Warshovsky Lapidus (Stanford, Calif.: Stanford University Press, 1977), 125.

175. Anne Eliot Griesse and Richard Stites, "Russia: Revolution and War," in *Female Soldiers—Combatants or Noncombatants? Historical and Contemporary Perspectives,* ed. Nancy Loring Goldman (Westport, Conn.: Greenwood, 1982), 69.

176. Ibid.

177. Zhuravlev, *Ognevo: Shchit Moskvy,* 117.

178. Cottam, "Ground/Air Defense Forces," 117.

179. See M. C. Devilbiss, *Women and Military Service: A History, Analysis, and Overview of Key Issues* (Maxwell Air Force Base, Ala., 1990) and Goldman, *Female Soldiers,* for examinations of necessity as a factor. Campbell is among those who concludes the aviation units were formed for the same reasons as other women's units: "It was not feminism but fear of the lack of sufficient 'manpower' to fight World War II, which served as the catalyst for . . . the Soviet Night Witches" (D'Ann Campbell, "Women in Combat: The World War II Experience in the United States, Great Britain, Germany, and the Soviet Union," *Journal of Military History* 57, no. 2 [1993]: 323).

180. Hardesty, *Red Phoenix,* 30, 59–61. Interestingly, even some Germans have commented on the "unexpectedly quick recovery of the Soviet Air Forces around the end of 1941 and the beginning of 1942 in spite of the annihilating blows it had received during the previous summer" (D. W. Schwabedissen, *The Russian Air Force in the Eyes of German Commanders* [New York: Arno Press, 1968], 52).

181. Levin, *Groznye gody,* 30.

182. Gridnev, "Memuary."

183. Goldman, *Female Soldiers,* 6. In Germany, the women auxiliaries were "strongly cautioned against using firearms even as a last resort" when capture

was imminent (55). The German rationale was that the women should avoid giving their captors an excuse for retribution. One wonders why the concept of a woman shooting at an enemy in self-defense was apparently so abhorrent.

184. To most Westerners, the very word *propaganda* is pejorative. We think of something covert, an appeal to the emotions rather than to the mind. Kenez, however, suggests a broader definition: "propaganda is nothing more than the attempt to transmit social and political values in the hope of affecting people's thinking, emotions, and thereby behavior." It is important to understand that the primary goal of propaganda in the Soviet state was education. See Peter Kenez, *The Birth of the Propaganda State: Soviet Methods of Mass Mobilization, 1917–1929.* (Cambridge: Cambridge University Press, 1985). This excellent study is highly recommended.

185. George H. Quester, "Women in Combat," *International Security* (spring 1977): 90–91; emphasis added.

186. Margaret Bourke-White, *Shooting the Russian War* (New York: Simon and Schuster, 1942); Erskine Caldwell, *All-Out on the Road to Smolensk* (New York: Duell, Sloan and Pearce, 1942).

187. Raskova's prewar career is mentioned in Alexander Werth, *Russia at War: 1941–45,* 3rd ed. (New York: Carroll and Graf, 1988), 8, 48.

188. Ibid., 176–77.

189. Smith, "Impact of World War II," 127.

190. Werth, *Russia at War,* 233.

191. Cottam, *Soviet Airwomen,* 35–36.

192. I examined wartime issues of newspapers such as *Pravda* and *Krasnaia Zvezda,* as well as the following collections of wartime works or memoirs, and found no references to the women aviators (and few, if any, to women in combat): Ilya Ehrenburg, *Russia at War* (London: Hamilton, 1943); *The Tempering of Russia,* trans. Alexander Kaun (New York: Knopf, 1944); and *The War: 1941–45,* Men, Years—Life Series, trans. Tatiana Shebunina, in collaboration with Yvonne Kapp (London: MacGibbon and Kee, 1964); Ilya Ehrenburg and Konstantin Simonov, *V odnoi gazete* (Moscow: Novosti, 1979); Vasily Grossman, *Life and Fate,* trans. Robert Chandler (London: Collins Harvill, 1985); Konstantin Simonov, *Always a Journalist* (Moscow: Progress, 1989); *Days and Nights,* trans. Joseph Barnes (New York: Simon and Schuster, 1945); *Ot Chernogo do Barentseva Moria: Zapiski Voennogo Korrespondenta* [From the Black Sea to the Barents] (Moscow: Sovetskii Pisatel', 1944); and *Ot Nashego Voennogo Korrespondenta* [From Our Military Correspondent] (Moscow: Voenizdat, 1948).

193. Werth, *Russia at War,* 411–12.

194. On Soviet pilots in Spain, see Ilya Ehrenburg, *Eve of War: 1933–1941,* Men, Years—Life Series, trans. Tatiana Shebunina, in collaboration with Yvonne Kapp (London: MacGibbon and Kee, 1963), 152; on the French pilots, see Ehrenburg, *The War,* 67–68, 132.

195. Werth, *Russia at War,* 249.

196. Joseph Stalin, *The Great Patriotic War of the Soviet Union* (New York: In-

ternational Publishers, 1945), 9, 34–35, 47, 55, 70–71, 73, 75, 150; emphasis added. Checked against Joseph Stalin, *Sochineniia* [Works] (Stanford, Calif.: Stanford University Press, 1967).

197. Many studies have shown that in Russian, as in English, supposedly gender-neutral masculine nouns are perceived as male unless women are specifically included in the phrase.

198. Stalin, *Great Patriotic War*, 134–35.

199. "Nasha boevaia zhizn'," *Izvestiia*, March 8, 1945, 3. Smith also notes that there was a decrease in emphasis on nontraditional roles of women in International Women's Day coverage as early as 1943 ("Impact of World War II," 147).

200. Edgar S. Meos, "Russian Women Fighter Pilots," *Flight International* (December 27, 1962): 1019–20; Meos was a Soviet fighter pilot during the war. See also Alexei Flerovsky, "Women Flyers of Fighter Planes," *Soviet Life* (May 1975): 28–29; Liudmila Zabavskaia, "Women Fighter Pilots," *Soviet Military Review* (March 1977): 61–62. Some sources imply that Khomiakova was the first woman to shoot down an enemy aircraft of any kind. That honor, however, goes to Liliia Litviak and Raisa Beliaeva. Litviak was the first woman to achieve a personal kill, a Ju-88, at Stalingrad on 13 September 1942 with the 437th IAP; Litviak and Beliaeva shared a kill against an Me-109 on the same day.

201. L. Lodgauz, "Boevoi pochin Valerii Khomiakovoi," *Ogonek* 46, no. 807 (1942): 5.

202. "Liubimaia doch' sovetskogo naroda." *Ogonek* 4, no. 817 (31 January 1943): 7.

203. "Vozdushnykh pobed,"*Ogonek* 15–16, nos. 828–29 (1943): cover, 1.

204. Raskova perished with her entire crew when her Pe-2 crashed during a snowstorm in January 1943. Litviak was killed in action on 1 August 1943, during an air engagement; Budanova was also killed in action in 1943.

205. Although the 586th and 587th received some male personnel, especially in support positions such as technicians, they also received additional women during the war. Unfortunately, available sources do not provide exact personnel figures, so a breakdown of gender percentages is not possible. The 586th had one squadron of male pilots and two of women.

206. I owe thanks for this idea to the Canadian historian K. Jean Cottam; in her letter to me of 9 April 1991, she suggests that "praise was heaped and still is almost exclusively on the Po-2 pilots. Is it because they flew more 'feminine' aircraft?"

207. B. Tseilin, "Orliata," *Ogonek* 27 (1943): 4.

208. Sharon Macdonald, "Drawing the Lines—Gender, Peace and War: An Introduction," in *Images of Women in Peace and War*, ed. Sharon Macdonald, Pat Holden, and Shirley Ardener (London: Macmillan, 1987), 7.

209. Photographs in author's personal collection.

210. Rakobolskaia, letter to author, 10 August 1992.

211. Gelman, letter to author, 11 August 1992.

212. Kravchenko-Savitskaia, interview by author, 7 May 1993.

213. Noggle, *Dance with Death,* 105.

214. Griesse and Stites, "Revolution and War," 68.

215. Cottam, "Ground/Air Defense Forces," 121–22.

216. Mary Zirin, introduction to *The Cavalry Maiden,* by Nadezhda Durova (London: Angel, 1988), xxix. *The Cavalry Maiden* was not reprinted for more than 100 years after its initial publication in 1836. Zirin noted that "one striking characteristic of the bibliography of works about Durova is the total absence of any interest in this uncomfortably loyal subject of Alexander I during the first twenty-five years of Soviet power. Her story surfaced only in World War II, as the propaganda machine began cranking out patriotic exhortations. Durova became a model of female heroism."

217. Ibid., xxx–xxxi. Zirin writes that "judging from the timid, heavily expurgated edition of *The Cavalry Maiden* . . . that appeared four times in the USSR from 1960 to 1979, it was not easy for the Soviets to come to terms with her addiction to a wandering life and the preference she expresses for foreign lands; her independent, even insubordinate, spirit . . . her skeptical attitudes toward masculine prerogatives; and her defiance of the stereotype of oppressed womanhood." The complete text of Durova's 1836 book was finally published on the 200th anniversary of her birth, in 1983.

218. According to Zirin, "it is a reflection of the tragedy of the Stalin epoch, and the haste to get Durova's example before the Soviet public, that the authors of *Kama Foundling* did not work closer to the known historical record," and that both works "betray the haste of [their] conception to fulfill the urgent needs of propaganda" (ibid., xxx). The play twisted the tsar's sponsorship of Durova into a confrontation, in which Tsar Alexander I "reproaches her with violating the religiously ordained subordination of women" (a form of subordination that the Soviets claimed to have ended). General Kutuzov (only recently rehabilitated himself in the Second World War as a useful propaganda hero) was inaccurately portrayed as Durova's protector rather than the tsar, whom the Soviets could not show in a good light.

219. Ibid., xxx. Zirin also notes that the introduction to a 1984 reprinting of Durova's work continues to stress the hardship and isolation of her life in the military.

220. Zirin also says, "Durova would seem to be a natural precursor of the Communist heroine who sacrifices her personal life to the greater good of country and party in so many Soviet novels" (ibid., xxx).

221. Kazarinova, "Liubimyi Komandir," 216. See also Chechneva, *Nebe,* 41; Kazarinova, "Rodina zovet!"

222. Richard Abraham, *Alexander Kerensky: The First Love of the Revolution* (New York: Columbia University Press, 1987), 202.

223. Cited in Cottam, "Rear Services," 375.

224. *Iskusstvo v boevom stroiu* (Moscow: 1985).

225. Cottam, "Ground/Air Defense Forces," 122.

226. Goldman, *Female Soldiers*, 7.

227. Grigorii A. Tokaev, *Comrade X* (London: Harvill, 1956), 176–77.

228. Ibid., 195–96. Tokaev says that Grizodubova turned him down, telling him that it was only a rumor that she was being given a regiment. Grizodubova did go on to command the 101st Long-Range Aviation Regiment; one can only speculate whether she knew that she would actually get the regiment when she refused Tokaev.

229. Alexiyevich, *War's Unwomanly Face*, 244. This book offers many other examples of the bad reputation and unfair postwar treatment that Soviet women war veterans believe they received.

230. Leila Rupp, *Mobilizing Women for War: German and American Propaganda, 1939–1945* (Princeton, N.J.: Princeton University Press, 1978), 4. Rockwell's famous painting of Rosie the Riveter for the cover of the *Saturday Evening Post* (29 May 1943) is remarkably reminiscent of Soviet propaganda posters of the same period.

231. Griesse, "Soviet Women," 33.

232. Smith, "Impact of World War II," 133–34.

233. Olga Mishakova, "Sovetskaia zhenshchina velikaia sila," *Pravda*, 8 March 1945, 3; emphasis added. This was a distinct change in tone from some of her earlier works. For example, in *Sovetskaia zhenshchina v Velikoi Otechestnnoi voine* [Soviet Woman in the Great Patriotic War] (Moscow: Voenizdat, 1943), she extolls only the bravery and combat skill of the women; see pp. 28–29 for an account of fighter pilot Katia Budanova. In *Sovetskie devushki v Otechestnnoi voine* [Soviet Girls in the Great Patriotic War] (Moscow: Voenizdat, 1944), Mishakova compares the exploits of Nadezhda Durova with the brave deeds of Soviet women like night bomber pilot Dusia Nosal' (40–41).

234. Smith, "Impact of World War II," 164.

235. Carol R. Berkin and Clara M. Lovett, eds., *Women, War and Revolution* (New York: Holmes and Meier, 1980), 212.

236. M. I. Kalinin, *On Communist Education: Selected Speeches and Articles* (Moscow: Foreign Languages Publishing House, 1953), 428.

237. Marina Raskova and Ekaterina Migunova, *Zapiski shturmana/Prodolzheniie podviga* [Notes of a Navigator/Continuation of a Brave Deed] (Moscow: DOSAAF, 1976); see photo of Raskova and Kalinin on p. 238.

238. Griesse, "Soviet Women," 61.

239. Gelman, letter to author, 11 August 1992.

240. John Erickson, *The Road to Berlin: Continuing the History of Stalin's War with Germany* (Boulder, Colo.: Westview Press, 1983) and *The Road to Stalingrad: Stalin's War with Germany* (Boulder, Colo.: Westview Press, 1984); David M. Glantz and Jonathan M. House, *When Titans Clashed: How the Red Army Stopped Hitler*, Modern War Studies Series (Lawrence: University Press of Kansas, 1995).

241. Hardesty, *Red Phoenix*, 214.

242. Ibid.

243. Von Hardesty, "Roles and Missions: Soviet Tactical Air Power in the Second Period of the Great Patriotic War," in *Transformation in Russian and Soviet Military History* (Washington, D.C.: U.S. Government Printing Office, 1986), 154.

244. Hardesty, *Red Phoenix,* 213.

CHAPTER 3
The 46th Guards Night Bomber Aviation Regiment

1. Cottam notes that regiments always received these orders in the III class; higher units received II class, and only armies and fronts received the I class. K. Jean Cottam, ed., *In the Sky Above the Front: A Collection of Memoirs of Soviet Air Women Participants in the Great Patriotic War* (Manhattan, Kans.: Sunflower University Press, 1984), 20.

2. A. N. Grylev, *Boevoi sostav Sovetskoi armii,* vol. 2 (Ianvar'-dekabr' 1942 goda) (Moskva: Voenizdat, 1966), 74, 127, 150, 174, 196, 217, 242; vol. 3 (Ianvar'-dekabr' 1943 goda) (Moskva: Voenizdat, 1972), 20, 43, 68, 90, 115, 141, 168, 199, 227, 255, 284, 312; vol. 4 (Ianvar'-dekabr' 1944 goda) (Moskva: Voenizdat, 1988), 22, 51, 81, 111, 131, 192, 253. See also Evodokia Bershanskaia et al., eds., *46 Gvardeiskii Tamanskii zhenskii aviatsionyi polk* (n.p.: Tsentral'nyi Dom Sovetskoi Armii imeni M. v. Frunze, n.d.).

3. Ann Noggle, *A Dance with Death* (College Station: Texas A&M University Press, 1994), 23; "[no title; designation of the 588th NLBP, 218 AD, 4 VA, Zakavakasky Front as a Guards Aviation Regiment]," TsAMO, Podolsk, Russia (11 February 1943), f. 46 GvBAP, op. 143370c, d. 1, l. 2. The date is given as 9 December 1942 in Noggle's book, but archival materials relate what is apparently the same incident as occurring on 10–11 September 1942.

4. Noggle, *Dance with Death,* 23.

5. Ibid., 24.

6. [No title; designation of the 588th NLBP, 218 AD, 4 VA, Zakavakasky Front as a Guards Aviation Regiment]," TsAMO, Podolsk, Russia (11 February 1943), f. 46 GvBAP, op. 143370c, d. 1, l. 2.

7. Ibid.

8. Polina Gelman, letter to author, 15 July 1992.

9. Irina Rakobolskaia, letter to author, 10 August 1992.

10. N. Chaika, "Na nochnom bombardirovshchike," in *Geroini: ocherki o zhenshchinakh—Geroiakh Sovetskogo Soiuza,* 2 vols., ed. L. F. Toropov (Moscow: Politizdat, 1969), 2:152–53.

11. Irina Rakobolskaia, "Dni Minuvshiie," in *V nebe frontovom: sbornik vospominaniy sovetskikh letchits-uchastnits Velikoi Otechestvennoi voiny,* 2nd ed., ed. M. A. Kazarinova et al. (Moscow: Molodaia Gvardiia, 1971), 162. The mechanic had a "neutral" last name, Purshan, so it would not have been clear whether he was a man or a woman.

12. Alexander Samilovich Magid, *Gvardeiskii Tamanskii aviatsionnyi polk*, 3rd ed. (Moscow: DOSAAF, 1960), 66ff. She received the orders on 7 October 1941, but for some reason, her transfer was delayed. Instead of joining the women in Moscow, Bershanskaia went directly to Engels on 15 November.

13. Gelman, letter to author, 11 August 1992.

14. M. N. Kozhevnikov, *Komandovanie i shtab VVS Sovetskoi Armii v Velikoi Otechestvennoi voine 1941–1945 gg* (Moscow: Nauka, 1977), 248. Generals Eremin and Kutakhov (later VVS commander) are among the other names mentioned.

15. Svetlana Alexiyevich, *War's Unwomanly Face,* trans. Keith Hammond and Lyudmila Lezhneva (Moscow: Progress Publishers, 1988), 153.

16. Ibid.

17. Galina I. Markova, *Vzlet: o Geroe Sovetskogo Soiuza M. M. Raskovoi* (Moscow: Politizdat, 1986), 90.

18. Raisa E. Aronova, *Nochnye ved'my,* 2nd ed. (Moscow: Sovetskaia Rossia, 1980), 52–53. Many of the veterans recall this incident. Magid's 1960 history, however, glosses over it, mentioning only that the Po-2s were met by friendly fighters (*Gvardeiskii Tamanskii,* 85).

19. Aronova, *Nochnye ved'my* (2nd ed.), 53; Magid, *Gvardeiskii Tamanskii,* 87; Polina Vladimirovna Gelman, personal interview, 3 May 1993.

20. Konstantin Andreevich Vershinin, *Chetvertaia Vozdushnaia* (Moscow: Voenizdat, 1975), 137.

21. Aronova, *Nochnye ved'my* (2nd ed.), 60; Magid, *Gvardeiskii Tamanskii,* 87–88. Magid goes on to claim that the ice was soon broken, and Popov warmed up to the regiment, but memoir sources do not bear this out.

22. Aronova, *Nochnye ved'my* (2nd ed.), 59–60.

23. For additional accounts of Popov's attitude, see Natal'ia Kravtsova, *Ot zakata do rassveta* (Moscow: Voenizdat, 1968), 30; Mariia Smirnova's interview in Noggle, *Dance with Death.*

24. Vershinin, *Chetvertaia Vozdushnaia,* 137.

25. Aronova, *Nochnye ved'my* (2nd ed.), 60.

26. Ibid., 53. This sort of flying is called *breiushchii polet,* literally, "shaving." In English it is often called "nap of the earth," "contour flying," or sometimes "hedge hopping."

27. Rakobolskaia, "Dni Minuvshiie," 163.

28. [No title; designation of the 588th NLBP, 218 AD, 4 VA, Zakavakasky Front as a Guards Aviation Regiment]," TsAMO, Podolsk, Russia (11 February 1943), f. 46 GvBAP, op. 143370c, d. 1, l. 2.

29. Aronova, *Nochnye ved'my* (2nd ed.), 60–61; Kravtsova, *Ot zakata,* 30–31; Vershinin, *Chetvertaia Vozdushnaia,* 142. Aronova gives the date of this flight as 12 June, but Vershinin says it was 9 June.

30. Aronova, *Nochnye ved'my* (2nd ed.), 61.

31. Vershinin, *Chetvertaia Vozdushnaia,* 167.

32. Gelman, personal interview, 3 May 1993.

33. Vershinin, *Chetvertaia Vozdushnaia*, 190.

34. Von Hardesty, *Red Phoenix: The Rise of Soviet Air Power, 1941–1945* (Washington, D.C.: Smithsonian, 1982), 65.

35. D. W. Schwabedissen, *The Russian Air Force in the Eyes of German Commanders* (New York: Arno Press, 1968), 139.

36. Shelley Saywell, *Women in War* (Markham, Ontario: Viking, 1985), 144; Evgeniia Zhigulenko, "Those Magnificent Women in Their Flying Machines," *Soviet Life* (May 1990): 13. Some women from the other regiments are skeptical of these numbers. Ekaterina Polunina, a mechanic in the 586th, told me that she doubted anyone could fly so many missions. Yet the veterans of the 46th whom I interviewed were adamant that on certain nights, some pilots and navigators did indeed fly as many as fifteen or seventeen sorties.

37. [No title; designation of the 588th NLBP, 218 AD, 4 VA, Zakavakasky Front as a Guards Aviation Regiment]," TsAMO, Podolsk, Russia (11 February 1943), f. 46 GvBAP, op. 143370c, d. 1, l. 2.

38. Rakobolskaia, interview by author, 10 May 1993.

39. Rakobolskaia, letter to author, 10 August 1992.

40. Rakobolskaia, "Dni Minuvshiie," 164.

41. Gelman, letter to the author, 28 July 1992.

42. Rakobolskaia, letter to author, 10 August 1992.

43. Gelman, letter to author, 15 July 1992.

44. Noggle, *Dance with Death*, 55.

45. Ibid., 68.

46. Rakobolskaia, "Dni Minuvshiie," 167.

47. Aronova, *Nochnye ved'my* (2nd ed.), 36.

48. Noggle, *Dance with Death*, 32.

49. Ibid., 68.

50. Rakobolskaia, personal interview, 10 May 1993.

51. Rakobolskaia, "Dni Minuvshiie," 164.

52. Bershanskaia et al., *46th Gvardeiskii*, 3.

53. Rakobolskaia, interview by author, 10 May 1993.

54. Rakobolskaia, letter to author, 10 August 1992.

55. Vershinin, *Chetvertaia Vozdushnaia*, 268; "Ukaz prezidiuma verkhovnogo soveta SSSR a prosvoenii zvaniia Geroia Sovetskogo Soiuza nachal; stvui-ushchemu, sostavu VVS KA," *Krasnaia zvezda*, 24 May 1943, 1; "Nagradnoi list (Evdokiia Ivanovna Nosal')," TsAMO, Podolsk, Russia (24 April 1943), f. 33, op. 793756, d. 34, l. 168, 168 ob. 169.

56. Noggle, *Dance with Death*, 75.

57. Rakobolskaia, personal interview, 10 May 1993.

58. Rakobolskaia, letter to author, 10 August 1992.

59. Rakobolskaia, letter to author, 10 August 1992; personal interview, 10 May 1993.

60. Noggle, *Dance with Death*, 65.

61. Ibid., 66–67.

62. Natal'ia Kravtsova, "Shturman polka," in *Geroini: ocherki o zhenshchinakh—Geroiakh Sovetskogo Soiuza*, 2 vols., ed. L. F. Toropov (Moscow: Politizdat, 1969), 2:249.

63. "Prikaz verkhovnogo Glavnokomanduiushchego General-pokovniku Petrovu," *Krasnaia zvezda*, 10 October 1943, 1.

64. Rakobolskaia, letter to author, 10 August 1992. The three-minute spacing is also mentioned by other pilots; see Smirnova's interview in Noggle, *Dance with Death*, 31.

65. Vershinin, *Chetvertaia Vozdushnaia*, 320.

66. Noggle, *Dance with Death*, 51.

67. Ibid., 56–57.

68. Ibid., 57.

69. Larisa Nikolaevna Litvinova, *Letiat Skovz' Gody* (Moscow: Voenizdat, 1983), 155.

70. Rakobolskaia, interview by author, 10 May 1993.

71. Rakobolskaia, letter to author, 10 August 1992. It is interesting that Rakobolskaia seems to consider Sanfirova's death as much the fault of the parachute as the mine.

72. Bershanskaia et al., *46 Gvardeiskii*. Aronova quotes a figure of thirty-three casualties (*Nochnye ved'my* [1st ed.], 161).

73. Gelman, letter to author, 15 July 1992.

74. Gelman, letter to author, 11 August 1992. This claim should be easy to verify in the proper archives.

75. Gelman, letter to author, 28 July 1992.

76. Gelman, letter to author, 15 July 1992.

77. Noggle, *Dance with Death*, 47.

78. Bershanskaia et al., *46 Gvardeiskii*, 4, cites the usual number of twenty-three (eighteen pilots and five navigators), but Cottam notes that navigator Tat'iana Sumarokova was posthumously awarded the HSU (redesignated the Hero of the Russian Federation) in 1995. K. Jean Cottam, *Women in War and Resistance: Selected Biographies of Soviet Women Soldiers* (Nepean, Ontario: New Military Publishing, 1998), xxiii.

79. Irina Favorskaia-Luneva, tape-recorded interview by author, Moscow (Favorskaia's apartment), 10 May 1993.

80. Gelman, letter to author, 28 July 1992.

81. Hardesty, *Red Phoenix*, 65.

82. Rakobolskaia, letter to author, 10 August 1992.

CHAPTER 4
The 125th Guards Bomber Aviation Regiment

1. V. F. Kravchenko, ed., *125 Gvardeiskii Bombardirovochnyi Aviatsionnyi Borisovskii ordenov Suvorova i Kutuzova polk imeni Geroia Sovetskogo Soiuza Mariny Raskovoi* (Moscow: privately published, 1976), 26.

2. Cottam notes that regiments always received these orders in the III class; higher units received II class, and only armies and fronts received the I class. K. Jean Cottam, ed., *In the Sky Above the Front: A Collection of Memoirs of Soviet Air Women Participants in the Great Patriotic War* (Manhattan, Kans.: Sunflower University Press, 1984), 20.

3. A. N. Grylev, *Boevoi sostav Sovetskoi armii,* vol. 2 (Ianvar'-dekabr' 1942 goda) (Moskva: Voenizdat, 1966), 36, 74, 94, 115, 225, 241, 250; vol. 3 (Ianvar'-dekabr' 1943 goda) (Moskva: Voenizdat, 1972), 115, 168, 189, 276; vol. 4 (Ianvar'-dekabr' 1944 goda) (Moskva: Voenizdat, 1988), 13, 28, 57, 87, 118, 148, 161, 191, 220, 252; "Otchet a rabote 587 BBAP za period dekabr'-ianvar' 43 g.," TsAMO, Podolsk, Russia (1943), f. 125 GvBAP, op. 224259c, d. 4, l. 1–5; "Uchastie v pokhodax i boiakh [125 GvBAP]," TsAMO, Podolsk, Russia (13 January 1947), f. 125 GvBAP, op. 518876, d. 1, l. 5–7; "Istoricheskii formuliar, IX: Izmeneniia v dislokatsii chasti [125 GvBAP]," f. 125 GvBAP, op. 518876, d. 1, l. 20–27. See also Kravchenko, *125 Gvardeiskii.*

4. See chapter 2 for details.

5. Anne Noggle, *A Dance with Death* (College Station: Texas A&M University Press, 1994), 134.

6. M. Kazarinova, "Liubimyi Komandir," in *Geroini: ocherki o zhenshchinakh—Geroiakh Sovetskogo Soiuza,* 2 vols., ed. L. F. Toropov (Moscow: Politizdat, 1969), 2:214; E. A. Migunova, "Prodolzheniie podviga," in *Zapiski Shturmana/Prodolzheniie Podviga* (Moscow: DOSAAF, 1976), 302.

7. Kravchenko, *125 Gvardeiskii,* 28.

8. Ibid.

9. "Istoricheskii formuliar, I: Istoriia stroitel'stva chasti [125 GvBAP]," f. 125 GvBAP, op. 518876, d. 1, l. 2–4, 59–60; this document states that the 125th had thirty-eight pilots, thirty-nine navigators, and forty-three gunners at the end of the war, which was reduced to twenty-one pilots, twenty-three navigators, and ten gunners by the beginning of 1946. See also Kravchenko, *125 Gvardeiskii,* 44–45; Noggle, *Dance with Death,* 155.

10. Noggle, *Dance with Death,* 123.

11. Ibid., 111.

12. Migunova, "Prodolzheniie podviga," 322–27.

13. Galina I. Markova, *Vzlet: o Geroe Sovetskogo Soiuza M. M. Raskovoi* (Moscow: Politizdat, 1986), 102–6; Migunova, "Prodolzheniie podviga," 328–45.

14. "Otchet a rabote 587 BBAP," f. 125 GvBAP, op. 224259c, d. 4, l. 1.

15. Migunova, "Prodolzheniie podviga," 346–48.

16. Alexander Vasilevich Gridnev, "Memuary"; Migunova, "Prodolzheniie podviga," 355–57.

17. Kazarinova, "Liubimyi Komandir," 220–21; Kravchenko, *125 Gvardeiskii,* 7.

18. Markova, *Vzlet,* 109; Migunova, "Prodolzheniie podviga," 348–55.

19. I. S. Levin, *Groznye gody* (Saratov: Privolzhskoe, 1984), 110–11.

20. See, for example, "Pamiati Geroia Sovetskogo Soiuza Mariny Rasko-

voi," *Krasnaia zvezda,* 9 January 1943, 3; "Traurnyi miting na Krasnoi plo-shchadi, posviashchennyi pamiati M. M. Raskovoi," *Krasnaia zvezda,* 13 January 1943, 3; General Major of Aviation A. Nikitin, "M. M. Raskova," *Krasnaia zvezda,* 12 January 1943, 4.

21. Madelin Blitzstein, "How Women Flyers Fight Russia's Air War," *Aviation Magazine* (July 1944): 116.

22. Migunova, "Prodolzheniie podviga," 346–48.

23. Kravchenko-Savitskaia, interview by author, 7 May 1993.

24. Evgeniia Timofeeva, "Pervyi boi," in *V nebe frontovom,* 2nd ed., ed. M. A. Kazarinova et al. (Moscow: Molodaia Gvardiia, 1971), 25; hereafter, *VNF* (2nd ed.). To this day, some of the veterans can hardly bear to recall Raskova's death and break down in tears when asked to talk about their reaction to the news.

25. "Otchet a rabote 587 BBAP," f. 125 GvBAP, op. 224259c, d. 4, l. 1.

26. Ibid., l. 2.

27. Timofeeva, "Pervyi boi," 25–27.

28. Kravchenko, *125 Gvardeiskii,* 8; Timofeeva, "Pervyi boi," 26.

29. Kravchenko-Savitskaia, interview by author, 7 May 1993.

30. Ibid. Most of the veterans remained cold or even hostile regarding Grizodubova. Grizodubova died during my visit to Russia, on the day before the annual reunion in May 1993. I asked many of the veterans at the reunion whether they planned to attend the funeral, and the common response was, "What for? She had nothing to do with us." Only Nadia Popova of the 46th, long a public figure of the Soviet veterans' committee, announced that she would "of course" be at the funeral.

31. Kravchenko, *125 Gvardeiskii,* 9.

32. Timofeeva, "Pervyi boi," 26.

33. Galina Ol'khovskaia, "Otvazhnaia eskadril'ia," in *VNF* (2nd ed.), 40.

34. Kravchenko, *125 Gvardeiskii,* 8.

35. "Otchet a rabote 587 BBAP," f. 125 GvBAP, op. 224259c, d. 4, l. 3.

36. Ol'khovskaia, "Otvazhnaia eskadril'ia," 40; Timofeeva, "Pervyi boi," 27–28.

37. Kravchenko, *125 Gvardeiskii,* 9.

38. This is the same Nikitin who informed I. S. Levin about the formation of the women's regiments in October 1941 and was a pallbearer at Raskova's funeral.

39. V. V. Markov, "Gorzhus' boevymi druz'iami," in *VNF* (2nd ed.), 29.

40. Noggle, *Dance with Death,* 102.

41. Markov, "Gorzhus' boevymi druz'iami," 30.

42. Kravchenko-Savitskaia, interview by author, 7 May 1993.

43. Ekaterina Fedotova, "Batia," in *VNF* (2nd ed.), 34–35; Noggle, *Dance with Death,* 103.

44. Fedotova, "Batia," 34–35.

45. Noggle, *Dance with Death,* 105.

46. Markov, "Gorzhus' boevymi druz'iami," 30.

47. Ibid., 31.

48. Kravchenko-Savitskaia, interview by author, 7 May 1993.

49. Noggle, *Dance with Death*, 106.

50. Ibid., 115.

51. Markov, "Gorzhus' boevymi druz'iami," 32.

52. Kravchenko-Savitskaia, interview by author, 7 May 1993.

53. Markov, "Gorzhus' boevymi druz'iami," 32.

54. Ibid.

55. Noggle, *Dance with Death*, 105.

56. Ibid., 122.

57. Ibid.

58. "Uchastie v pokhodax i boiakh [125 GvBAP]," TsAMO, Podolsk, Russia (13 January 1947), f. 125 GvBAP, op. 518876, d. 1, l. 5–7.

59. Noggle, *Dance with Death*, 103.

60. Ibid., 103, 112. Markov specifies two hours, although it is not clear whether this applied only to the first mission of the day; an armorer, Evgeniia Zapolnova-Ageeva, said that turn time was one hour.

61. Ibid.

62. Ibid., 124.

63. Kravchenko, *125 Gvardeiskii*, 14.

64. Ibid., 15.

65. Ibid., 10.

66. Ibid., 11–12; Konstantin Andreevich Vershinin, *Chetvertaia Vozdushnaia* (Moscow: Voenizdat, 1975), 269.

67. Kravchenko, *125 Gvardeiskii*, 16–18.

68. Ibid., 19.

69. Ibid., 21.

70. Ibid., 22.

71. Noggle, *Dance with Death*, 107.

72. "Istoricheskii formuliar, VI: Nagrady i otlichiia chasti [125 GvBAP]," TsAMO, Podolsk, Russia (1947), f. 125 GvBAP, op. 518876, d. 1 (Istoricheskii formuliar), l. 13, citing "Prikaz NKO/SSSR No. 265, 3 Sep 43"; "Istoricheskii formuliar, IX: Izmeneniia v dislokatsii chasti [125 GvBAP]," f. 125 GvBAP, op. 518876, d. 1, l. 20; Kravchenko, *125 Gvardeiskii*, 26, gives a date of 23 September 1943, which may have been when the ceremony occurred.

73. Kravchenko-Savitskaia, interview by author, 7 May 1993.

74. "Istoricheskii formuliar, IX: Izmeneniia v dislokatsii chasti [125 GvBAP]," f. 125 GvBAP, op. 518876, d. 1, l. 20–27.

75. Aleksandra Eremenko, "Zhizn' za tovarishcha," in *VNF* (2nd ed.), 102–6.

76. Noggle, *Dance with Death*, 139.

77. Kravchenko-Savitskaia, interview by author, 7 May 1993.

78. Chapligina, comment made to author, 125th reunion luncheon, 2 May 1993.

79. Kravchenko, *125 Gvardeiskii*, 28.

80. Ibid., 31.

81. Ibid., 33.

82. Ibid., 34.

83. G. K. Prussakov et al., *16'aia vozdushnaia: voenno-istoricheskii ocherk o boevom puti 16-i vozdushnoi armii* (Moscow: Voenizdat, 1973), 123, 141.

84. Noggle, *Dance with Death*, 111.

85. Ibid., 145.

86. Ibid., 115–16.

87. Kravchenko, *125 Gvardeiskii*, 35; Prussakov, *16'aia vozdushaia*, 151–52.

88. Kravchenko, *125 Gvardeiskii*, 36; "Istoricheskii formuliar, II: Uchastie v pokhodax i boiakh v 1945 g. [125 GvBAP]," f. 125 GvBAP, op. 518876, d. 1, l. 36–37.

89. Kravchenko, *125 Gvardeiskii*, 37.

90. "Istoricheskii formuliar, II: Uchastie v pokhodax i boiakh v 1945 g. [125 GvBAP]," f. 125 GvBAP, op. 518876, d. 1, l. 36–37.

91. "Istoricheskii formuliar, VII: Nagrady lichnogo sostava chasti [125 GvBAP]," f. 125 GvBAP, op. 518876, d. 1 (Istoricheskii formuliar), l. 65. The award recipients included a new regimental commander, Semen Titenko, along with Bukin, Timofeeva, Fedutenko, Fomicheva, and Dolina.

92. Kravchenko, *125 Gvardeiskii*, 38.

93. Ibid., 41.

94. Noggle, *Dance with Death*, 105.

95. "Istoricheskii formuliar, III: Boevaia podgotovka chasti v 1945 [125 GvBAP]," f. 125 GvBAP, op. 518876, d. 1, l. 37–38.

96. "Istoricheskii formuliar, I: Istoriia stroitel'stva chasti [125 GvBAP]," f. 125 GvBAP, op. 518876, d. 1, l. 59–60, 65; Noggle, *Dance with Death*, 101.

97. "Istoricheskii formuliar, I: Istoriia stroitel'stva chasti [125 GvBAP]," f. 125 GvBAP, op. 518876, d. 1, l. 2–4, 59–60; this document states that the 125th had thirty-eight pilots, thirty-nine navigators, and forty-three gunners at the end of the war, which was reduced to twenty-one pilots, twenty-three navigators, and ten gunners by the beginning of 1946. See also Kravchenko, *125 Gvardeiskii*, 44–45; Noggle, *Dance with Death*, 155.

98. "Istoricheskii formuliar, I: Istoriia stroitel'stva chasti [125 GvBAP]," f. 125 GvBAP, op. 518876, d. 1, l. 59–60, 65; Noggle, *Dance with Death*, 101.

99. Kravchenko-Savitskaia, interview by author, 7 May 1993.

100. Noggle, *Dance with Death*, 105.

CHAPTER 5
The 586th Fighter Aviation Regiment

1. "Istoricheskii formuliar, IX: Izmeneniia v dislokatsii chasti [586 IAP]," TsAMO, Podolsk, Russia (n.d.), f. 586 IAP, op., d. 1, l. not recorded; A. N.

Grylev, *Boevoi sostav Sovetskoi armii,* vol. 2 (Ianvar'-dekabr' 1942 goda) (Moskva: Voenizdat, 1966), 132, 155, 178, 200, 222, 247; vol. 3 (Ianvar'-dekabr' 1943 goda) (Moskva: Voenizdat, 1972), 24, 48, 71, 94, 118–19, 144, 170, 201, 230, 258, 286, 314; vol. 4 (Ianvar'-dekabr' 1944 goda) (Moskva: Voenizdat, 1988), 24, 53, 83, 113, 144, 174, 204, 235, 267. See also "Rol' 586 Istrebitel'nogo aviastionnogo zhenskogo polka v Otechestvennoi voine," TsAMO, Podolsk, Russia (n.d.), f. 586 IAP, op., d., l. not recorded.

2. Jean Alexander, *Russian Aircraft Since 1940* (London: Putnam, 1975), 436.

3. "Rol' 586"; Alexei Flerovsky, "Women Flyers of Fighter Planes," *Soviet Life* (May 1975): 28–29; A. Poliantseva, "Dvoe protiv soroka dvukh," in *V nebe frontovom,* 2nd ed. ed. M. A. Kazarinova et al. (Moscow: Molodaia Gvardiia, 1971), hereafter, *VNF* (2nd ed.); Aleksandr Vasilevich Gridnev, letter to author, 18 August 1992. Some sources say the date was 19 March 1943.

4. Aleksandr Vasilevich Gridnev, tape-recorded interview by author, Volgograd, Russia (Gridnev's apartment), 12 May 1993. Many veterans mentioned these famous women pilots who flew aerobatics at Tushino before the war.

5. Litviak was posthumously awarded the HSU, but she was assigned to the 73rd Guards Fighter Aviation Regiment at the time she made most of her kills.

6. *VNF* (2nd ed.), 276; Vera Semenova Murmantseva, *Zhenshchiny v soldat-skikh shineliakh* (Moscow: Voenizdat, 1971), 49.

7. Ibid.; "Rol' 586."

8. Steven J. Zaloga, "Soviet Air Defense Radar in the Second World War," *Journal of Soviet Military Studies* 2, no. 3 (1988): 104–16.

9. "Vypuska iz istoricheskogo formuliara 586 IAP," TsAMO, Podolsk, Russia (n.d.), f. 586 IAP, op., d., l. not recorded.

10. Aleksandra Aleksandrovna Makunina, tape-recorded interview by author, Moscow (Favorskaia's apartment), 10 May 1993.

11. Elena Nikolaevna Karakorskaia et al., tape-recorded interview by author, Moscow (Karakorskaia's apartment), 4 May 1993.

12. Ibid.

13. Aleksandra Aleksandrovna Makunina, "Pervyi komandir polka," in *VNF* (2nd ed.).

14. Makunina, interview by author, 10 May 1993.

15. Gridnev, interview by author, 12 May 1993; letter to author, May 1993. Osipenko was the husband of Polina Osipenko; some of the veterans say that he was envious of his wife's accomplishments.

16. "Vypuska iz istoricheskogo formuliara 586 IAP."

17. Gridnev, interview by author, 12 May 1993. Many veterans mentioned these famous women pilots who flew aerobatics at Tushino before the war.

18. Gridnev, letter to author, May 1993.

19. Karakorskaia noted, "Lebedeva was also very interesting. When the war started, she was flying Yaks in a men's regiment. She was the party orga-

nizer in the regiment, and she used her position to stay in that regiment. But later she was transferred to the 586th. You know that she crashed during the war, and only thirty years later, her body was found and dug up. . . . Lebedeva was killed during the Battle of Kursk." Karakorskaia et al., interview by author, 4 May 1993.

20. Beliaeva's group was sent to a LaGG regiment, which meant that there were no spare parts or proper tools for their Yak fighters; the women were reassigned within two weeks. Inna Vladimirovna Pasportnikova, tape-recorded interview by author, Sredniaia Akhtuba airfield, Russia (near Volgograd), 15 May 1993.

21. Gridnev, letter to author, May 1993.

22. Gridnev, interview by author, 12 May 1993.

23. "Vypuska iz istoricheskogo formuliara 586 IAP"; Edgar S. Meos, "Russian Women Fighter Pilots," *Flight International* (27 December 1962): 1019–20; Meos was a Soviet fighter pilot during the war. See also Flerovsky, "Women Flyers," 28–29; Liudmila Zabavskaia, "Women Fighter Pilots," *Soviet Military Review* (March 1977): 61–62.

24. This is sometimes credited with being the first kill ever by a woman pilot, but that honor belongs to Liliia Litviak and Raisa Beliaeva, who scored kills on 13 September 1942 at Stalingrad, after their transfer to the 437th IAP. Kills scored by the women pilots at Stalingrad are credited to the regiments to which they were assigned.

25. Raisa E. Aronova, *Nochnye ved'my*, 2nd ed. (Moscow: Sovetskaia Rossiia, 1980), 31.

26. Polunina and Kovaleva, interview by author, 1 May 1993.

27. Ibid.; Irina Favorskaia-Luneva, tape-recorded interview by author, Moscow (Favorskaia's apartment), 10 May 1993; Karakorskaia et al., interview by author, 4 May 1993; Makunina, interview by author, 10 May 1993.

28. Gridnev, interview by author, 12 May 1993.

29. Ibid.

30. Ibid.

31. Makunina, "Pervyi komandir," 281.

32. Karakorskaia et al., interview by author, 4 May 1993. Polunina remarked that the women disliked both their commissars. "In the first years after the war, pilots did not want to associate with either Kulikova or Tikhomirova. Many years passed and they later forgave [Kulikova]."

33. Makunina, "Pervyi komandir," 281.

34. Alexander Vasilevich Gridnev, "Memuary" (typescript, n.d.).

35. Danilova-Emel'ianova, interview by author, 3 May 1993.

36. Alexander Vasilevich Gridnev, letter to Klavdia Ivanovna Terekhova-Kasatkina, n.d. Gridnev makes special note of Nikolai Korolev, who was killed ramming an enemy air reconnaissance aircraft, and the deputy commander of the regiment Vitaly Ivanovich Beliakov, who later became a general. Korolev is briefly mentioned by Klavdiia Pankratova, "Razvedchik unichtozhen," in *VNF* (2nd ed.), 313–17.

37. Gridnev, "Memuary."

38. Ibid.

39. Makunina, interview by author, 10 May 1993.

40. Gridnev, "Memuary."

41. Ibid.

42. Ibid.

43. Ibid. The Russian term is *kartavit'*, to "burr" or pronounce gutturally.

44. Ibid. The original quotes are "konchil delo—guliai smelo" and "konchil delo—pomogi tovarishcham." Interestingly, Gridnev also cited "the Leninist slogan 'all for one and one for all' " as the basis of his philosophy; one wonders whether Lenin read Dumas.

45. Gridnev, "Memuary."

46. Pasportnikova, interview by author, 8 May 1993.

47. Danilova-Emel'ianova, interview by author, 3 May 1993.

48. Favorskaia-Luneva, interview by author, 10 May 1993.

49. "Rol' 586."

50. Ekaterina Polunina, the unofficial regimental historian who compiles short biographical sketches of the veterans, is especially vociferous in her opposition to Gridnev's assessment that the deaths cannot be considered combat losses. Polunina and Kovaleva, interview by author, 1 May 1993.

51. Ekaterina Kuzminichna Polunina, "Evgeniia Filippovna Prokhorova" and "Valeriia Dmitrievna Khomiakova" (typescript, n.d.). Most of Polunina's sketches are only two to three pages long; she sometimes supplies more detail about the circumstances in which a pilot died, as in the cases of Nechaeva and Litviak.

52. Gridnev, interview by author, 12 May 1993.

53. Ibid.

54. "Rol' 586"; "Vypuska iz istoricheskogo formuliara 586 IAP."

55. "Rol' 586"; "Eto bylo pod Voronezhem," in *VNF* (2nd ed.), 361; "Iz soobshcheniia ot Sovetskogo informbiuro za 26 iiunia 1943," *Pravda*, 27 June 1943, 1.

56. "Rol' 586"; "Vypuska iz istoricheskogo formuliara 586 IAP."

57. "Rol' 586."

58. Ibid.

59. Ekaterina Kuzminichna Polunina, "Raisa Vasil'evna Beliaeva" (typescript, n.d.).

60. Gridnev, interview by author, 12 May 1993.

61. Ol'ga Yamshchikova, "Druzhba," in *VNF* (2nd ed.), 341–53.

62. Gridnev, interview by author, 12 May 1993.

63. Ibid.

64. Ibid.

65. Gridnev, "Memuary."

66. Polunina, "Raisa Vasil'evna Beliaeva."

67. Yamshchikova, "Druzhba."

68. Ibid.

69. Gridnev, interview by author, 12 May 1993.

70. Yamshchikova, "Druzhba." In this second edition of her memoir, Yamshchikova notes that she received many letters about Beliaeva from people who had read the first edition. She learned that one of Beliaeva's two sisters and three of four brothers (including one fighter pilot) had also been killed during the war.

71. Gridnev, interview by author, 12 May 1993; "Memuary."

72. Ibid.

73. Ibid. Gridnev showed me photographs, pointing out the differences between Guards uniforms and the standard issue.

74. Gridnev, letter to Terekhova-Kasatkina.

75. Gridnev, interview by author, 12 May 1993; "Memuary."

76. Karakorskaia et al., interview by author, 4 May 1993.

77. "Rol' 586"; "Vypuska iz istoricheskogo formuliara 586 IAP."

78. "Rol' 586."

79. Ibid.; "Vypuska iz istoricheskogo formuliara 586 IAP."

80. "Istoricheskii formuliar, IX: Izmeneniia v dislokatsii chasti [586 IAP]," TsAMO, Podolsk, Russia (n.d.), f. 586 IAP, op., d. 1, l. not recorded.

81. "Rol' 586"; "Vypuska iz istoricheskogo formuliara 586 IAP."

82. "Istoricheskii formuliar, IX."

83. Ibid.

84. "Rol' 586"; "Vypuska iz istoricheskogo formuliara 586 IAP."

85. "Istoricheskii formuliar, IX."

86. "Rol' 586"; "Vypuska iz istoricheskogo formuliara 586 IAP."

87. "Istoricheskii formuliar, IX"; "Rol' 586."

88. Gridnev told me that he wrote the first manuscript of his memoirs soon after the war. When he took it to a publishing house, he was told that both he and the editors could be arrested if they agreed to publish it. Later, Gridnev's son took the manuscript away and burned it. A few years later, Gridnev rewrote his memoirs, leaving out the more controversial material in the hope that they still might be published; they never were. He gave me a copy and told me that another copy has been deposited in an archive in Volgograd.

89. Gridnev, interview by author, 13 May 1993.

90. Ibid.

91. Fighter pilot Liliia Litviak was part of the 73rd Guards Fighter Regiment when she died, so neither her kills nor her Hero medal are credited to the 586th. See A. Kanevskii, "Ia Samaia Schastlivaia . . ." ["I'm the Luckiest . . ."] *Aviatsiia i Kosmonavtika* (1990): 36–38.

92. Zaloga, "Soviet Air Defense Radar," 104–16.

93. K. Jean Cottam, *Soviet Airwomen in Combat in World War II* (Manhattan, Kans.: Sunflower University Press, 1983), 8.

94. Gridnev, letter to author, 19 August 1992.

95. Ibid.

96. Gridnev, interview by author, 14 May 1993.

97. "Rol' 586"; "Vypuska iz istoricheskogo formuliara 586 IAP."

98. These include Batrakova, Beliaeva, Khomiakova, and Prokhorova (all killed in crashes) and four women who transferred from the 586th to male regiments and were killed in combat (Budanova, Lebedeva, Litviak, and Nechaeva).

CHAPTER 6
Women at War in Mostly Male Regiments

1. A. Verkhozin, "Komandir polka," in *Geroini: ocherki o zhenshchinakh—Geroiakh Sovetskogo Soiuza*, 2 vols., ed. L. F. Toropov (Moscow: Politizdat, 1969), 1:133–42. See also A. Verkhozin, "Polkom komanduet zhenshchina," *Kryl'ia Rodiny* (1966): 7–9; this article is supposed to be an excerpt from a book, *Samolety letiat k partizanam*, which I have been unable to locate. Another book that mentions Grizodubova's role in partisan resupply is Petro P. Vershigora, *Liudi s chistoi sovets'iu* (Moscow: Sovetskii pisatel', 1952), 76, 315. Oddly, these passages are omitted in the Soviet-produced English translation of this book; perhaps it was thought that English speakers would not understand references to "Grizodubova's regiment."

2. Verkhozin, "Komandir polka," 136.

3. Ibid., 133.

4. Ibid., 134–35, 142; V. Mitroshenkov, "They Were First," *Soviet Military Review* (March 1969): 22. For more information on Grizodubova, see K. Jean Cottam, *Women in War and Resistance: Selected Biographies of Soviet Women Soldiers* (Nepean, Ontario: New Military Publishing, 1998).

5. I. G. Inozemtsev, *Pod Krylom—Leningrad: Boevoi put's VVS Leningradskogo Voennogo Okruga, Leningradskogo fronta i 13-i vozdushnoi armii v gody velikoi otechestvennoi voiny* (Moscow: Voenizdat, 1978), 189.

6. Tamara Krol, "Zvezdy ishchut liudei," in *Geroini: ocherki o zhenshchinakh—Geroiakh Sovetskogo Soiuza*, 2 vols., ed. L. F. Toropov (Moscow: Politizdat, 1969) 2:329–33; Vera Semenova Murmantseva, *Zhenshchiny v soldatskikh shineliakh* (Moscow: Voenizdat, 1971), 88–91;Anna Aleksandrovna Timofeeva-Egorova, *Derzhis', Sestrenka!* (Moscow: Voenizdat, 1983). Konstantin Andreevich Vershinin, *Chetvertaia Vozdushnaia* (Moscow: Voenizdat, 1975), 253, also mentions Egorova; her picture appeared on the front page of *Krasnaia zvezda* on 1 July 1943. The 277 combat missions include both Po-2 and Il-2 flights. An English translation is reportedly being prepared by Texas A&M University Press.

7. D. Vlasov, "Krylataia sem'ia," in *Pamiat' ognennykh let*, ed. M. F. Loshchits et al. (Moscow: Voenizdat, 1975), 193–98; Cottam, *Women in War and Resistance*, 160–68.

8. Inozemtsev, *13-i vozdushnoi armii*, 223; A. Morozov, "Vospitannitsa komsomola," in *Geroini: ocherki o zhenshchinakh—Geroiakh Sovetskogo Soiuza*, 2

vols., ed. L. F. Toropov (Moscow: Politizdat, 1969), 1:274–82; Murmantseva, *Zhenshchiny v soldatskikh shineliakh*, 88; Cottam, *Women in War and Resistance,* 157–59.

9. Murmantseva, *Zhenshchiny v soldatskikh shineliakh*, 86–87; Vera Semenova Murmantseva, *Sovetskiie zhenshchiny y Velikoi Otechestvennoi voine 1941–1945* (Moscow: Mysl', 1974), 135; K. Jean Cottam, *Soviet Airwomen in Combat in World War II* (Manhattan, Kans.: Sunflower University Press, 1983), 32.

10. F. Selivanov, "Tri stranitsy iz zhizni" [Three pages from a life], *Kryl'ia rodiny* 10 (1965): 14–15; Murmantseva, *Zhenshchiny v soldatskikh shineliakh*, 91–93; Murmantseva, *Sovetskiie zhenshchiny*, 136; Cottam, *Women in War and Resistance,* 157–59.

11. A. Man'ko, "S komsomol'skim biletom u serdtsa" [With a Komsomol Card by Her Heart], *Aviatsiia i kosmonavtika* (March 1983): 18–19; Murmantseva, *Sovetskiie zhenshchiny*, 135–36; "Nagradi za myzhestvo," *Pravda*, 6 May 1990, 1; "Podvig ostaetsia podvigom," *Komsomolskaia pravda*, 6 May 1990, 1; Cottam, *Women in War and Resistance*, 30–35.

12. G. K. Prussakov et al., *16'aia vozdushnaia: voenno-istoricheskii ocherk o boevom puti 16-i vozdushnoi armii* (Moscow: Voenizdat, 1973), 77.

13. Ibid., 72.

14. Cottam, *Soviet Airwomen*, 29–35.

15. Von Hardesty, *Red Phoenix: The Rise of Soviet Air Power, 1941–1945* (Washington, D.C.: Smithsonian, 1982), 223.

16. Cottam, *Soviet Airwomen*, 7.

17. L. P. Ovchinnikova, *Zhenshchiny v soldatskikh shineliakh* (Volgograd: Nizhne-Volzhskoe, 1987), 5–47. A record of Litviak's transfers during this period is given in Lt. Col. Nikolai Baranov, "Kharakteristika (Lidiia Vladimirovna Litviak)" [Personal Record of Lidiia Vladimirovna Litviak], VVS (5 February 1943), courtesy of Inna Pasportnikova.

18. Hardesty, *Red Phoenix*, 92.

19. For a firsthand account, see Klavdiia Blinova, "Kogda druz'ia riadom" [When friends are near], in *V nebe frontovom*, 1st ed., ed. M. Kazarinova and A. A. Poliantseva (Moscow: Molodaia Gvardiia, 1962), 263–65. Blinova's account was cut from the 1971 edition.

20. Prussakov et al., *16'aia vozdushnaia*, 11–12.

21. Ibid., 31–32.

22. Ekaterina Kuzminichna Polunina, "Raisa Vasil'evna Beliaeva" (typescript, n.d.).

23. Inna Vladimirovna Pasportnikova, tape-recorded interview by author, Sredniaia Akhtuba airfield, Russia (near Volgograd), 15 May 1993.

24. Inna Vladimirovna Pasportnikova, letter to author, 27 August 1992; personal interview, 15 May 1993.

25. Ovchinnikova, *Zhenshchiny v soldatskikh shineliakh*, 11.

26. In today's terminology, we would say they were not "mentored." This situation applied almost exclusively to the women who fought with mostly

male regiments. In the primarily female regiments, such as the 586th and 125th, there are no reports that men ever refused or even resisted flying with women. Obviously, this was less of a problem for the all-female 46th.

27. P. Golovachev, "My ikh lyubili," in *Geroi i Podvigi*, 4 vols., ed. M. F. Loshchits (Moscow: Voenizdat, 1963), 1:111–13.

28. Inna Vladimirovna Pasportnikova, letter to author, 3 September 1992.

29. Pasportnikova, interview by author, 8 May 1993.

30. Col. Gen. S. Romanov, "Protivovozdushnye oborony strany," *Voenno-istoricheskii zhurnal* 11 (1982): 29–35.

31. Pasportnikova, interview by author, 15 May 1993.

32. Pasportnikova, interview by author, 8 May 1993.

33. B. N. Eremin, "Nagradnoi list (Lidiia Vladimirovna Litviak)" [List of Awards of Lidiia Vladimirovna Litviak], Komitet veteranov VOV (25 May 1989), courtesy of Lt. Col. Anatoly Kanevsky. The history of the 8th Air Army erroneously describes this engagement as occurring on 27 September, after Litviak had transferred to the 287th Fighter Aviation Division; see B. A. Gubin and V. A. Kiselev, *Vos'maia Vozdushnaia: boevoi put' 8-i vozdushnoi armii* (Moscow: Voenizdat, 1986), 78–79. All the personal documents and archival records that I examined have the 13 September date.

34. Pasportnikova, letter to author, 27 August 1992; "Rol' 586 Istrebitel'-nogo aviastionnogo zhenskogo polka v Otechestvennoi voine," TsAMO, Podolsk, Russia (n.d.), f. 586 IAP, op., d., l. not recorded. The fact that the kills by Litviak and Beliaeva were the first kills ever scored by women pilots went completely unrecognized and unremarked—probably because they were no longer flying with a "women's" regiment. The commander of the 437th probably had no incentive to make their achievements known, since the women flew with his unit for only two weeks.

35. Pasportnikova, letter to author, 27 August 1992.

36. Vladimir Dmitrievich Lavrinenkov, *Vozvrashchenie v nebo*, 2nd ed. (Moscow: Voenizdat, 1983), 42–43; Tomas Polak and Christopher Shores, *Stalin's Falcons: The Aces of the Red Star, a Tribute to the Notable Fighter Pilots of the Soviet Air Forces, 1918–1953* (London: Grub Street, 1999), 48.

37. Hans D. Seidl, *Stalin's Eagles: An Illustrated Study of the Soviet Aces of World War II and Korea* (Atglen, Pa.: Schiffer Military History, 1998), 20.

38. Lavrinenkov, *Vozvrashchenie v nebo*, 42–43.

39. Ibid.

40. Ibid., 43.

41. Ibid.

42. Pasportnikova, letter to author, 27 August 1992.

43. Lavrinenkov, *Vozvrashchenie v nebo*, 57.

44. Pasportnikova, letter to author, 27 August 1992.

45. The activities of Eremin (pronounced "Yer-YO-min") are discussed throughout the history of the 8th Air Army; see Gubin and Kiselev, *Vos'maia Vozdushnaia*.

46. Boris Nikolaevich Eremin, *Vozdushnye boitsy* (Moscow: Voenizdat, 1987), 182–84; personal interview, 10 May 1993.

47. Ibid., 183–84; personal interview, 10 May 1993.

48. Inna Vladimirovna Pasportnikova, ''Moi komandir'' (typescript in author's collection, 1989); Pasportnikova, letter to author, 3 September 1992.

49. Pasportnikova, interview by author, 8 May 1993.

50. Ibid.

51. Pasportnikova, ''Moi komandir.''

52. *Nagradnoi list: Litviak, Lidiia Vladimirovna,* Sovetskoi komitet veteranov voiny, 1989; Pasportnikova, ''Moi komandir.''

53. *Khronika boevykh pobed gv. mladshchego leitenanta Litviak Lidii Vladimirovny,* TsAMO, 1989.

54. *Nagradnoi list: Litviak, Lidiia Vladimirovna.*

55. Pasportnikova, ''Moi komandir.''

56. *Nagradnoi list: Litviak, Lidiia Vladimirovna.*

57. Ibid.

58. Pasportnikova, ''Moi komandir.''

59. *Khronika boevykh pobed gv. mladshchego leitenanta Litviak Lidii Vladimirovny; Nagradnoi list: Litviak, Lidiia Vladimirovna.*

60. A. Kanevskii, ''Ia samaia schastlivaia . . .'' *Aviatsiia i Kosmonavtika* (March 1990): 36–38.

61. Pasportnikova, interview by author, 8 May 1993.

62. Eremin, interview by author, 10 May 1993.

63. Pasportnikova, ''Moi komandir.''

64. Ibid.

65. *Nagradnoi list: Litviak, Lidiia Vladimirovna.*

66. Ibid.

67. *Khronika boevykh pobed gv. mladshchego leitenanta Litviak Lidii Vladimirovny; Nagradnoi list: Litviak, Lidiia Vladimirovna.*

68. Ibid.

69. Pasportnikova, ''Moi komandir.''

70. Polak and Shores, *Stalin's Falcons,* 97.

71. Pasportnikova, ''Moi komandir.''

72. Ibid.

73. *Khronika boevykh pobed gv. mladshchego leitenanta Litviak Lidii Vladimirovny.*

74. Pasportnikova, ''Moi komandir.''

75. Ibid.

76. Kanevskii, ''Ia samaia schastlivaia . . . ,'' 36–38; Pasportnikova, ''Moi komandir.''

77. *Khronika boevykh pobed gv. mladshchego leitenanta Litviak Lidii Vladimirovny.*

78. Eremin, *Vozdushnye boitsy,* 182–84.

CHAPTER 7
Demobilization and Postwar Experiences

1. Ann Eliot Griesse and Richard Stites, "Russia: Revolution and War," in *Female Soldiers—Combatants or Noncombatants? Historical and Contemporary Perspectives,* ed. Nancy Loring Goldman (Westport, Conn.: Greenwood, 1982), 78.

2. Hans D. Seidl, *Stalin's Eagles: An Illustrated Study of the Soviet Aces of World War II and Korea* (Atglen, Pa.: Schiffer Military History, 1998), 7.

3. The women veterans sometimes note, with irony, that they have given speeches about their combat service to all-male audiences. When Aronova returned to speak to the cadets of the Engels Aviation School in 1964, she noted that in the audience there was "hardly a single girl." Raisa E. Aronova, *Nochnye ved'my,* 2nd ed. (Moscow: Sovetskaia Rossiia, 1980), 36.

4. Sharon Macdonald, "Drawing the Lines—Gender, Peace and War: An Introduction," in *Images of Women in Peace and War,* ed. Sharon Macdonald, Pat Holden, and Shirley Ardener (London: Macmillan, 1987), 9.

5. Gregory Malloy Smith, "The Impact of World War II on Women, Family Life, and Mores in Moscow, 1941–1945" (Ph.D. diss., Stanford University, 1989), 333.

6. Shelley Saywell, *Women in War* (Markham, Ontario: Viking, 1985), 157–58.

7. Anne Noggle, *A Dance with Death* (College Station: Texas A&M University Press, 1994), 33.

8. Pilot Serafima Amosova-Taranenko stayed until she was medically retired in 1947 (Noggle, *Dance with Death,* 47). Pilot Mariia Tepikina-Popova flew in civil aviation but was medically discharged in 1948 (ibid., 63).

9. Evodokia Bershanskaia et al., *46 Gvardeiskii Tamanskii zhenskii aviatsionyi polk* (n.p.: Tsentral'nyi Dom Sovetskoi Armii M. v. Frunze, n.d.); V. F. Kravchenko, ed., *125 Gvardeiskii* (Moscow: privately published, 1976).

10. The distribution by regiment was as follows: 46th, twenty-two; 125th, twenty-nine; 586th, twenty-three; other, three.

11. Noggle, *Dance with Death,* 47.

12. Tat'iana Sumarokova, "Volia k zhizni," in *V nebe frontovom,* 1st ed., ed. M. A. Kazarinova et al. (Moscow: Molodaia Gvardiia, 1962), 157–59; hereafter, *VNF* (1st ed.).

13. Noggle, *Dance with Death,* 37.

14. Marina Chechneva, *"Lastochki" nad frontom* (Moscow: DOSAAF, 1984), 117–18.

15. Ibid., 129–35.

16. Olga Yakovleva, "Na istrebitele," in *VNF* (1st ed.), 209–10. Yakovleva recalled that she worked for eight months to regain the use of her hand and elbow; one surgeon refused to certify her for flying duty on the grounds that she had already flown for eight years, which in his opinion was "enough" for a woman.

17. Noggle, *Dance with Death,* 220.

18. Ibid., 47.

19. Ibid., 77.

20. Antonina Skoblikova, "Neravnyi boi," in *VNF* (1st ed.), 102.

21. Ibid.

22. Galina I. Markova, "Youth Under Fire: The Story of Klavdiya Fomicheva, a Woman Dive Bomber Pilot," in *Soviet Airwomen in Combat in World War II,* ed. and trans. K. Jean Cottam (Manhattan, Kans.: Sunflower University Press, 1983), 126–27.

23. Galina Dzhunkovskaia, "Vyderzhka i khladnokrovie," in *VNF* (1st ed.), 75; Galina Dzhunkovskaia, "Komesk," in *V nebe frontovom,* 2nd ed., ed. M. A. Kazarinova et al. (Moscow: Molodaia Gvardiia, 1971), 124–32; hereafter, *VNF* (2nd ed.).

24. Markova, "Youth Under Fire," 126–27.

25. Ibid., 131.

26. Noggle, *Dance with Death,* 109. Unfortunately, she does not name the other women.

27. Ibid., 131.

28. Ibid., 217.

29. Nina Slovokhotova, "Ot motorista do letchika-ispytatelia," in *VNF* (1st ed.), 218; Alexei Flerovsky, "Women Flyers of Fighter Planes," *Soviet Life* (May 1975); Liudmila Zabavskaia, "Women Fighter Pilots," *Soviet Military Review* (March 1977). See K. Jean Cottam, ed., *In the Sky Above the Front: A Collection of Memoirs of Soviet Air Women Participants in the Great Patriotic War* (Manhattan, Kans.: Sunflower University Press, 1984), 270 n. 28; Noggle, *Dance with Death,* 170.

30. Noggle, *Dance with Death,* 52; Chechneva, *"Lastochki" nad frontom,* 163–69.

31. Noggle, *Dance with Death,* 135–37.

32. Ibid., 184.

33. Ibid., 63.

34. Ibid., 90–91. Crashes are always a risk in aviation; Zhitova-Yushina's husband, an Aeroflot navigator, was killed in a 1956 Tu-114 crash in the Congo.

35. Ibid., 97–98.

36. Chechneva, *"Lastochki" nad frontom,* 93, 106.

37. P. S. Anishchenkov and V. Ye. Shurinov, *Tret'ia vozdushnaia: Voenno-istoricheskii ocherk o boevom puti VVS Kalininskogo fronta i 3-i vozdushnoi armii v gody Velikoi Otechestvennoi voiny* (Moscow: Voenizdat, 1984), 179; A. M. Bereznitskaia, "Snaiperskii ekipazh," in *VNF* (1st ed.), 48–49.

38. Skoblikova, "Neravnyi boi," 102.

39. L. Ya. Eliseeva, "Sila sovetskogo patriotizma," in *VNF* (1st ed.), 114.

40. Flerovsky, "Women Flyers of Fighter Planes"; *VNF* (1st ed.), 276–77; Zabavskaia, "Women Fighter Pilots."

41. Nina Potapova, "Pilot Galina Burdina," in *VNF* (1st ed.), 285; Noggle, *Dance with Death,* 208.

42. Chechneva, *"Lastochki" nad frontom*, 84–92.

43. Anishchenkov and Shurinov, *Tret'ia vozdushnaia*, 178.

44. I. S. Levin, *Groznye gody* (Saratov: Privolzhskoe, 1984).

45. Pasportnikova, interview by author, 8 May 1993.

46. Flerovsky, "Women Flyers of Fighter Planes," 28–29.

47. Noggle, *Dance with Death*, 162.

48. Flerovsky, "Women Flyers of Fighter Planes," 29.

49. Petrochenkova-Neminushchaia, interview by author, 9 May 1993; Noggle, *Dance with Death*, 178.

50. Anishchenkov and Shurinov, *Tret'ia vozdushnaia*, 181.

51. Rakobolskaia, interview by author, 10 May 1993.

52. Eliseeva, "Sila sovetskogo patriotizma," 114.

53. Anishchenkov and Shurinov, *Tret'ia vozdushnaia*, 178.

54. Ibid.; Evgeniia Zapol'nova, "Neziraia na trudnosti," in *VNF* (1st ed.), 87.

55. Noggle, *Dance with Death*, 79.

56. Ibid., 171–72.

57. Anishchenkov and Shurinov, *Tret'ia vozdushnaia*, 178; Eliseeva, "Sila sovetskogo patriotizma," 114.

58. Ibid.

59. Noggle, *Dance with Death*, 200, 215.

60. Flerovsky, "Women Flyers of Fighter Planes," 29.

61. Slovokhotova, interview by author, 10 May 1993.

62. Gelman, interview by author, 3 May 1993.

63. Chechneva, *"Lastochki" nad frontom*, 44.

64. Ibid., 55–56.

65. Ibid., 72, 75.

66. Ibid., 136–43.

67. Noggle, *Dance with Death*, 213.

68. Ibid., 236.

69. Valentina Endakova, "Letchik-ministr," in *VNF* (2nd ed.), 363–67.

70. Anishchenkov and Shurinov, *Tret'ia vozdushnaia*, 178; Galina Brok, "Vospitannye na boevykh traditsiiakh," in *VNF* (1st ed.), 108; Noggle, *Dance with Death*, 134.

71. Maria Dolina, "Pryzhok iz plameni," in *VNF* (1st ed.), 80; Eliseeva, "Sila sovetskogo patriotizma," 114.

72. Anishchenkov and Shurinov, *Tret'ia vozdushnaia*, 114.

73. Zapol'nova, "Neziraia na trudnosti," 87; Eliseeva, "Sila sovetskogo patriotizma," 114.

74. Eliseeva, "Sila sovetskogo patriotizma," 114.

75. Noggle, *Dance with Death*, 181, 190.

76. Ibid., 113, 125.

77. Svetlana Alexiyevich, *War's Unwomanly Face*, trans. Keith Hammond and Lyudmila Lezhneva (Moscow: Progress Publishers, 1988), 29; Marina Chechneva, *Nebo ostaetsia nashim* (Moscow: Voenizdat, 1976), 9–10.

78. Markova, "Youth Under Fire," 126–27.
79. Chechneva, *"Lastochki" nad frontom*, 7.
80. Noggle, *Dance with Death*, 178.
81. Ibid., 184.
82. Chechneva, *"Lastochki" nad frontom*, 72.
83. Noggle, *Dance with Death*, 217.
84. Ibid., 147.
85. Ibid., 166.
86. Ibid., 201–2.
87. Ibid., 36–37.
88. Ibid., 94.
89. Gail Warshofsky Lapidus, "Sexual Equality in Soviet Policy: A Developmental Perspective," in *Women in Russia*, ed. Dorothy Atkinson et al. (Stanford, Calif.: Stanford University Press, 1977), 117.
90. Xenia Gasiorowska, *Women in Soviet Fiction 1917–1964* (Madison: University of Wisconsin Press, 1968), 159. See also Vera Dunham, *In Stalin's Time: Middleclass Values in Soviet Fiction* (Cambridge: Cambridge University Press, 1976). For an example of the way women combatants were portrayed in civil war fiction, see Peter Kenez, *The Birth of the Propaganda State: Soviet Methods of Mass Mobilization, 1917–1929* (Cambridge: Cambridge University Press, 1985), 214–15: "The argument that class interest supersedes other causes and other human feelings was also expressed in one of the most popular revolutionary films, Protazanov's *Forty First*, made in 1927. This is a Civil War love story with fable-like qualities. A Bolshevik woman soldier and a White officer are stranded on a desert island. They fall in love. When an enemy ship appears on the horizon, the class-conscious woman realizes that the ship would rescue the officer, and to avoid helping the enemy, she shoots her man. He is her forty-first kill."
91. Gasiorowska, *Women in Soviet Fiction*, 160.
92. Ibid. In nearly five years of research, I have identified only one novel about the women pilots: Klara Larionova's *Povesti* (Moscow: Sovetskii Pisatel', 1973).
93. Gasiorowska, *Women in Soviet Fiction*, 243.
94. Smith, "Impact of World War II," iv.
95. Gridnev, letter to author, 19 August 1992.
96. Rakobolskaia, letter to author, 10 August 1992.
97. Petrochenkova-Neminushchaia, interview with author, 9 May 1993.
98. Noggle, *Dance with Death*, 184.
99. Ibid., 26.
100. Ibid., 86.
101. Saywell, *Women in War*, 157; Noggle, *Dance with Death*, 85.
102. Noggle, *Dance with Death*, 97–98.
103. Ibid., 236–45.
104. Smith, "Impact of World War II," 342.

105. Ibid., 335.

106. Noggle, *Dance with Death,* 218; Flerovsky, "Women Flyers of Fighter Planes," 29.

107. Saywell, *Women in War,* 137.

108. Griesse and Stites, "Revolution and War," 68.

109. Tat'iana Sumarokova, *Proleti nado mnoi posle boia* [Fly over me after the battle], 1st ed. (Moscow: Politizdat, 1988), 89–91. Smirnova was so determined to fly that she apparently applied to civil aviation, which also rejected her for health reasons (see the earlier section "Women who were medically discharged").

110. Ibid., 94–95.

111. Gridnev, interview with author, 12 May 1993.

112. Gridnev, interview with author, 13 May 1993.

113. Smith, "Impact of World War II," 333.

114. Anne Eliot Griesse, "Soviet Women and World War II: Mobilization and Combat Policies" (master's thesis, Georgetown University, 1980), 81; Tatyana Mamonova, *Russian Women's Studies: Essays on Sexism in Soviet Culture* (New York: Pergamon, 1989), 150.

115. Mollie Schwartz Rosenhan, "Images of Male and Female in Children's Readers," in *Women in Russia,* ed. Dorothy Atkinson, Alexander Dallin, and Gail Warshofsky Lapidus (Stanford, Calif.: Stanford University Press, 1977), 302–3.

116. Alexiyevich, *War's Unwomanly Face,* 50.

117. Noggle, *Dance with Death,* 109.

Conclusion

1. See Von Hardesty's *Red Phoenix: The Rise of Soviet Air Power, 1941–1945* (Washington, D.C.: Smithsonian, 1982), 217–25, for an evaluation of VVS performance.

2. Vladimir Lavrinenkov, *Vozvrashchenie v nebo,* 2nd ed. (Moscow: Voenizdat, 1983), 56–57.

3. Stanley D. Rosenberg, "The Threshold of Thrill: Life Stories in the Skies over Southeast Asia," in *Gendering War Talk,* ed. Miriam Cooke and Angela Woollacott (Princeton, N.J.: Princeton University Press, 1993), 49.

4. D'Ann Campbell, "Combating the Gender Gulf," *Minerva* 10, no. 3/4 (1992): 24.

5. Boris Nikolaevich Eremin, personal interview, 10 May 1993.

6. Eremin, *Vozdushnye boitsy,* 182–85.

7. Boris Nikolaevich Eremin, interview by author, 10 May 1993.

8. See appendix C for complete references.

9. Lavrinenkov, *Vozvrashchenie,* 57.

10. This is not the sort of problem that is addressed in official literature or

in most memoirs. But none of the veterans I interviewed believed that there were detrimental effects. Some of my interviewees had married people they met at the front, such as Galina Brok-Beltsova, whose husband (whom I also met) had been an instructor pilot for the 125th, and Irina Favorskaia-Luneva, who married another mechanic in the 586th.

11. This issue has frequently been raised in debates about the American military but is based on assumption rather than fact. Devilbiss noted that "we can find little empirical evidence to support the contention of battle protection at all," and it would be difficult to determine whether instances of protecting a comrade were gender related or simply an aspect of cohesion and camaraderie. M. C. Devilbiss, "Gender Integration and Unit Deployment: A Study of GI Jo," *Armed Forces and Society* 11, no. 4 (1985): 529. Devilbiss noted that concern for fellow combatants is probably independent of gender distinctions; she cites J. Glenn Gray, *The Warriors: Reflections on Men in Battle* (New York: Harper, 1970), 88–95. See also Judith Hicks Stiehm, "The Protected, the Protector, the Defender," *Women's Studies International Forum* 5, no. 3/4 (1982): 367–76.

12. This is an interesting parallel to Devilbiss's observations of an Air National Guard exercise in which some men "tended to share neither their knowledge . . . nor their tools," which "exposed the women to danger since access to knowledge and tools are keys to survival under such circumstances" ("Gender Integration and Unit Deployment," 539–40).

13. Pasportnikova noted, "When we arrived at a male regiment, men did not want to fly with us, because of the responsibility, and also because they were afraid for themselves. They were afraid that the female wingmen would not cover them." Inna Vladimirovna Pasportnikova, personal interview, 8 May 1993.

14. Charles C. Moskos, *The American Enlisted Man: The Rank and File in Today's Military* (New York: Russel Sage, 1970), 145, cited in Devilbiss, "Gender Integration and Unit Deployment," 540.

15. Eremin, interview with author, 10 May 1993.

16. This is consistent with Devilbiss's observations, which showed that most cases of harassment were practiced by men against women with whom they did not work directly; few cases occurred within work groups.

17. Irina Rakobolskaia, letter to author, 10 August 1992.

18. Devilbiss, "Gender Integration and Unit Deployment," 529–30.

19. E. A. Migunova, "Prodolzheniie podviga," in *Zapiski Shturmana/Prodolzheniie Podviga* (Moscow: DOSAAF, 1976), 320.

20. Valentina Flegontovna Kravchenko-Savitskaia, interview by author, 7 May 1993.

21. Aleksandr Vasilevich Gridnev, interview by author, 13 May 1993.

22. M. N. Kozhevnikov, *Komandovanie i shtab VVS Sovetskoi Armii v Velikoi Otechestvennoi voine 1941–1945 gg.* (Moscow: Nauka, 1977), 248. Generals Eremin and Kutakhov (later VVS commander) are among the other names mentioned.

23. Elliot P. Chodoff, "Ideology and Primary Groups," *Armed Forces and Society* 9 (1983): 569–93; Sam C. Sarkesian, ed., *Combat Effectiveness: Cohesion, Stress, and the Volunteer Military* (Beverly Hills, Calif.: Sage, 1980); H. Wallace Sinaiko, Mady Wechsler Segal, and Robert L. Goldich, "Cohesion in Military Forces" (Smithsonian Institution, November 1984), cited by Devilbiss, "Gender Integration and Unit Deployment," 529–30.

24. Ibid.

25. Ibid., 540–41.

26. Ibid., 533.

27. Gelman, letter to author, 28 July 1992.

28. Eremin, interview by author, 10 May 1993.

29. Kravchenko-Savitskaia, interview by author, 7 May 1993.

30. Gelman, interview by author, 3 May 1993.

31. Gelman, letter to author, 11 August 1992.

32. Anne Noggle, *A Dance with Death* (College Station: Texas A&M University Press, 1994), 49.

33. Ibid., 64.

34. Gelman, letter to author, 28 July 1992.

35. Raisa E. Aronova, *Nochnye ved'my*, 2nd ed. (Moscow: Sovetskaia Rossiia, 1980), 29. Patriotic sentiments were not just inserted into memoirs by Soviet editors; all my interviewees talked of their love for their country. Even today in Russia, women express these feelings. A friend of mine in Moscow, an interpreter, had the chance to marry a Russian man and move to America. Although she has made several visits to America, she told me that she could never leave Russia permanently. "I want to be rooted here, with my dearest soil and trees, my culture and language, my family and friends. I will suffer with it, but it is only natural, because I am its integral part, I am Russia's daughter" (Margarita Ponomareva, letter to author, October 1993).

36. Rakobolskaia, letter to author, 10 August 1992.

37. Gelman, letter to author, 28 July 1992.

38. Aronova, *Nochnye ved'my* (2nd ed.), 52–53.

39. Campbell, "Combating the Gender Gulf," 14.

40. Alexei Flerovsky, "Women Flyers of Fighter Planes," *Soviet Life* (May 1975): 28; K. Jean Cottam, "Soviet Women in Combat in World War II: The Ground Forces and the Navy," *International Journal of Women's Studies* 3, no. 4 (1980): 345–57; K. Jean Cottam, "Soviet Women in Combat in World War II: The Ground/Air Defense Forces," in *Women in Eastern Europe and the Soviet Union*, ed. Tova Yedlin (New York: Praeger, 1980); K. Jean Cottam, ed., *The Golden-Tressed Soldier* (Manhattan, Kans.: Sunflower University Press, 1984).

41. K. Jean Cottam, *Soviet Airwomen in Combat in World War II* (Manhattan, Kans.: Sunflower University Press, 1983), 34.

42. Cottam probably based her conclusion about casualties on opinions expressed in the memoirs on whether casualties were heavy or bearable; or perhaps she simply believed that there were more survivors in the 46th be-

cause of the larger volume of memoirs. Cottam did not have access to the regimental albums I examined, which provided more concrete information. This issue must ultimately be resolved by the archival records.

43. Ann Eliot Griesse and Richard Stites, "Russia: Revolution and War," in *Female Soldiers—Combatants or Noncombatants? Historical and Contemporary Perspectives,* ed. Nancy Loring Goldman (Westport, Conn.: Greenwood, 1982), 70.

44. Alexei Maresiev, introduction to M. Kazarinova et al., eds., *V nebe frontovom,* 2nd ed. (Moscow: Molodaia Gvardiia, 1971), 4. Interestingly, Maresiev was originally in the unit that became the 73rd Guards Fighter Regiment and flew under the same commander, Nikolai Baranov, as did Litviak and Budanova later in the war. Maresiev's own fascinating story was fictionalized by Boris Polevoi, *Povest' o nastoiashchem cheloveke* [Story of a real man] (Moscow: Detskaia Literatura, 1984). The book was also made into a popular movie.

45. Gregory Mallory Smith, "The Impact of World War II on Women, Family Life, and Mores in Moscow, 1941–1945" (Ph.D. diss., Stanford University, 1989), 333.

46. Griesse and Stites, "Revolution and War," 79.

47. Sharon Macdonald, "Drawing the Lines—Gender, Peace and War: An Introduction," in *Images of Women in Peace and War,* ed. Sharon Macdonald, Pat Holden, and Shirley Ardener (London: Macmillan, 1987), 6.

48. Goldman, *Female Soldiers—Combatants or Noncombatants?* 8–9.

49. Ellen Jones, *Red Army and Society* (Boston: Allen and Unwin, 1985), 101. Dr. Paul Mackenzie notes that in Britain, the Auxiliary Territorial Service lived on as a volunteer force, as did the American Women's Army Corps, though both were greatly reduced in scale.

50. Macdonald, "Drawing the Lines," 9.

APPENDIX B
Female Heroes of the Soviet Union

1. Tomas Polak and Christopher Shores, *Stalin's Falcons: The Aces of the Red Star, a Tribute to the Notable Fighter Pilots of the Soviet Air Forces, 1918–1953* (London: Grub Street, 1999), 19.

2. Ibid.

3. M. N. Kozhevnikov, *Komandovanie i shtab VVS* (Moscow: Nauka, 1977), 252.

4. Polak and Shores, *Stalin's Falcons,* 19.

5. Evdokiia Bershanskaia et al., eds., *46 Gvardeiskii Tamanskii zhenskii aviatsionyi polk* (n.p.: Tsentral'nyi Dom Sovetskoi Armii imeni M. v. Frunze, n.d.), 4 cites the usual number of twenty-three (eighteen pilots, five navigators), but Cottam notes that navigator Tat'iana Sumarokova was posthumously awarded the HSU (redesignated the Hero of the Russian Federation) in 1995. K. Jean

Cottam, *Women in War and Resistance* (Nepean, Ontario: New Military Publishing, 1998), xxiii.

APPENDIX C
Thoughts on Sources and Historiography

1. Paul Fussell, *Wartime: Understanding and Behavior in the Second World War* (New York: Oxford University Press, 1989); J. Glenn Gray, *The Warriors: Reflections on Men in Battle* (New York: Harper, 1970).

2. Edd D. Wheeler, "Women in Combat: A Demurrer," *Air University Review* 30, no. 1 (1978): 62–68.

3. M. C. Devilbiss, "Gender Integration and Unit Deployment: A Study of GI Jo," *Armed Forces and Society* 11, no. 4 (1985): 526.

4. Kohn suggests that new research will reveal "the large and important role of women in military organization and war before the twentieth century." Richard E. Kohn, "The Social History of the American Soldier: A Review and Prospectus for Research," *American Historical Review* 86, no. 3 (1981): 566.

5. Ibid.

6. Ibid., 564–66.

7. Lauren Cook Burgess, ed., *An Uncommon Soldier: The Civil War Letters of Sarah Rosetta Wakeman, Alias Pvt. Lyons Wakeman, 153rd Regiment, New York State Volunteers, 1862–1864* (Pasadena, Md.: Minerva, 1994).

8. Michelle Zimbalist Rosaldo, "Women, Culture and Society: A Theoretical Overview," in *Women, Culture and Society*, ed. Michelle Zimbalist Rosaldo and Louise Lamphere (Stanford, Calif.: Stanford University Press, 1974), 17–42.

9. Dorothy O. Helly and Susan M. Reverby, eds., *Gendered Domains: Rethinking Public and Private in Women's History* (Ithaca, N.Y.: Cornell University Press, 1991), xi, 6.

10. Pauline Schmitt Pantel, ed., *A History of Women in the West* (Cambridge, Mass.: Belknap, 1992), 465.

11. Elise Boulding, "Public Nurturance and the Man on Horseback," in *Face to Face: Fathers, Mothers, Masters, Monsters: Essays for a Nonsexist Future*, ed. Meg Murray (Westport, Conn.: Greenwood, 1983), 273–92.

12. Sharon Macdonald, "Drawing the Lines—Gender, Peace and War: An Introduction," in *Images of Women in Peace and War*, ed. Sharon Macdonald, Pat Holden, and Shirley Ardener (London: Macmillan, 1987), 1.

13. D'Ann Campbell, "Women in Combat: The World War II Experience in the United States, Great Britain, Germany, and the Soviet Union," *Journal of Military History* 57, no. 2 (1993): 322.

14. Miriam Cooke, "Wo-man, Retelling the War Myth," in *Gendering War Talk*, ed. Miriam Cooke and Angela Woollacott (Princeton, N.J.: Princeton University Press, 1993), 177–78.

15. Stanley D. Rosenberg, "The Threshold of Thrill: Life Stories in the Skies

over Southeast Asia," *Gendering War Talk*, ed. Miriam Cooke and Angela Wool-lacott (Princeton, N.J.: Princeton University Press, 1993), 43.

16. Von Hardesty, *Red Phoenix: The Rise of Soviet Air Power, 1941–1945*, 1st ed. (Washington, D.C.: Smithsonian Institution Press, 1982), 7.

17. John Erickson, introduction to *The USSR in World War II, an Annotated Bibliography of Books Published in the Soviet Union, 1945–1975; with an Addenda for the Years 1975–1980*, by Michael Parrish (New York: Garland, 1981), xviii.

18. John Erickson and Ljubica Erickson, *The Soviet Armed Forces, 1918–1992: A Research Guide to Soviet Sources* (Westport, Conn.: Greenwood, 1996); David Glantz and Jonathan M. House, *When Titans Clashed: How the Red Army Stopped Hitler* (Lawrence: University Press of Kansas, 1995).

19. *Sovetskie Voenno-vozdushnye sily v Velikoi Otechestvennoi voine 1941–1945* (Moscow: Voenizdat, 1968); available in English translation in Ray Wagner, ed., *The Soviet Air Force in World War II: The Official History*, trans. Leland Fetzer (Garden City, N.Y.: Doubleday, 1973). In the original, the 587th (125th Guards) is mentioned on p. 169; the 588th (46th Guards) is mentioned on pp. 163–64 and 296–97. In the translation, the women's regiments are discussed in a long footnote written by the American editor. The 586th, which belonged to the PVO rather than the VVS, is not mentioned. The women's regiments are mentioned only in connection with their involvement in particular battles or offensives; their formation and recruitment are not covered. This is consistent with the scope of the book; individual regiments are rarely discussed. Such treatment tends to support the view that the women's regiments were not seen as exceptional—except by the American translator.

20. P. S. Anishchenkov and V. Ye. Shurinov, *Tret'ia vozdushnaia: Voenno-isto-richeskii ocherk o boevom puti VVS Kalininskogo fronta i 3-i vozdushnoi armii v gody Velikoi Otechestvennoi voiny* [The Third Air Army: a military-historical essay of the campaign record of the air forces of the Kalinin Front and the Third Air Army during the Great Patriotic War] (Moscow: Voenizdat, 1984), 72, 77, 123, 141, 151–52, 165, 178–80; B. A. Gubin and V. A. Kiselev, *Vos'maia Vozdushnaia: boevoi put' 8-i vozdushnoi armii* [The Eighth Air (Army): combat history] (Moscow: Voenizdat, 1986), 78–79, 126–29; I. G. Inozemtsev, *Pod Krylom—Leningrad: Boevoi put' VVS Leningradskogo Voennogo Okruga, Leningradskogo fronta i 13-i vozdushnoi armii v gody velikoi otechestvennoi voiny* [Under the wings—Leningrad: the combat record of the air forces of the Leningrad Military District, the Leningrad Front and the 13th Air Army during the years of the Great Patriotic War] (Moscow: Voenizdat, 1978), 189, 223; M. N. Kozhevnikov, *Komandovanie i shtab VVS Sovetskoi Armii v Velikoi Otechestvennoi voine 1941–1945 gg.* [Command and staff of the air forces of the Soviet army in the Great Patriotic War 1941–1945] (Moscow: Nauka, 1977), 178, 248, 252; G. K. Prussakov et al., *16'aia vozdushnaia: voenno-istoricheskii ocherk o boevom puti 16-i vozdushnoi armii* [The 16th Air Army: a military historical essay on the campaign record of the 16th Air Army (1942–1945)] (Moscow: Voenizdat, 1973), 11–12; Konstantin Andreevich Vershinin, *Chetvertaia Vozdushnaia* [Fourth Air (Army)] (Moscow: Voenizdat, 1975), 137–38, 142, 167, 190, 253, 267–69, 320.

21. A. N. Grylev, *Boevoi sostav Sovetskoi armii* (Moskva: Voenno-nauchnoe upravlenie General'nogo shtaba Voenno-istoricheskii otdel, 1963–1990).

22. V. I. Chuikov, *Vystoiav, my pobedili: zapiski komandarma 62-y* [By enduring, we won: notes of the 62nd Army commander] (Moscow: Sovetskaia Rossiia, 1960), 88, and *Battle for Stalingrad* (New York: Holt, 1964), 222; Boris Nikolaevich Eremin, *Vozdushnye boitsy* [Air warriors] (Moscow: Voenizdat, 1987), 182–85; Vladimir Dmitrievich Lavrinenkov, *Vozvrashchenie v nebo* [Return to the sky], 2nd ed. (Moscow: Voenizdat, 1983), 41–45, 55–60; A. A. Novikov, *V nebe Leningrada: zapiski komanduiushchego aviatsiei* [In the sky of Leningrad: notes of an air commander] (Moscow: Nauka, 1970).

23. B. Bashkirov and N. Semenkevich, "Geroini Sovetskogo neba" [Heroines of the Soviet sky], *Kryl'ia rodiny* [Wings of the Homeland] (March 1969), features a four-page photo spread of the thirty-four women aviators who had received the HSU medal up to that time (including three women who received the award before the war and one female astronaut).

24. Additional information can be found in Western sources such as the *Modern Encyclopedia of Russian and Soviet History, The Biographical Dictionary of the Soviet Union,* and *Who Was Who in the Soviet Union.*

25. These articles usually appear in connection with International Women's Day (18 March). For example, *Soviet Military Review* published articles about the women pilots in March 1969, 1972, 1976, and 1977; *Aviation and Cosmonautics* in March 1968, 1973, and 1990; and *Wings of the Homeland* in March 1963, 1966, 1967, 1968, 1969, and 1973.

26. For example, Vera Semenova Murmantseva, "Sovetskie zhenshchiny v Velikoi Otechestvennoi voine 1941–1945," *Voenno-istoricheskii zhurnal* [*VIZh*; Military Historical Journal] 2 (1968): 47–54; A. G. Pervov and V. N. Gus'kov, "Nochnye deistviia frontovoi aviatsii," *VIZh* 6 (1988): 28–33; N. Stasiuk, "Geroicheskie dela letchits komsomol'skogo aviatsionnogo polka," *VIZh* 8 (1968): 15; M. L. Popovich, "Nebesnaia Diana," *VIZh* 3 (1995): 86–88. John Erickson's introduction to Parrish's bibliography discusses Soviet journals and notes that *VIZh* "not infrequently . . . supplies crucial information or throws sharp light on a particular Soviet controversy, as well as giving some indication of the actual competence of the author and the professional esteem in which he is held" (xix).

27. Vera Semenova Murmantseva, *Sovetskie zhenshchiny v Velikoi Otechestvennoi voine 1941–1945* (Moscow: Mysl', 1974), and *Zhenshchiny v soldatskikh shineliakh* (Moscow: Voenizdat, 1971).

28. M. A. Kazarinova and A. A. Poliantseva, eds., *V nebe frontovom: sbornik vospominanii sovetskikh letchits-uchastnits Velikoi Otechestvennoi voiny,* 1st ed. (Moscow: Molodaia Gvardiia, 1962); M. A. Kazarinova, N. F. Kravtsova, and A. A. Poliantseva, eds., 2nd ed. (Moscow: Molodaia Gvardiia, 1971); Murmantseva, *Sovetskiie zhenshchiny.*

29. Evgenia Zhigulenko, "Those Magnificent Women in Their Flying Machines," *Soviet Life* (May 1990): 12–15. The movie is called *Night Witches in the*

Sky and was directed by Zhigulenko in 1981. Wartime film footage of the 588th is included in the Soviet documentary *The Unknown War,* directed by Zoia Fomina with the participation of Harrison Salisbury, produced by Sovinfilm.

30. On the whole, the memoirs written by the women pilots seem to contain less glorification and aggrandizement of their comrades' achievements than do the memoirs of many male pilots. Overall, memoir sources provide a more balanced and detailed picture of life at the front than is given in media publications or official Soviet sources.

31. Kazarinova et al., *V nebe frontovom,* 1st and 2nd eds.

32. Madelin Blitzstein, "How Women Flyers Fight Russia's Air War," *Aviation Magazine* (July 1944): 116ff; Lael Laird, "The R.A.F. on the Red A.F.," *Life* (4 May 1942): 12ff; J. Stroud, *The Red Air Force* (London: Pilot Press, 1943).

33. Kazarinova et al., *V nebe frontovom* (1st ed.), 118.

34. Hardesty, *Red Phoenix,* 192.

35. Edgar S. Meos, "Russian Women Fighter Pilots," *Flight International* (27 December 1962): 1019–20; Grigorii Svirsky, *Proshchanie s Rossii* (Tenafly, N.J.: Hermitage, 1986).

36. Bruce Myles, *Night Witches: The Untold Story of Soviet Women in Combat* (London: Mainstream Publishing, 1981). Among the many odd spellings in the book are "Yemshokova" for Yamshchikova, "Ria" for Raia, and "Sooranchevskaya" for Surnachevskaia.

37. An example that combines both errors is Myles's portrayal of the arrival of Liliia Litviak at Stalingrad (*Night Witches,* 91–94). Myles shows Litviak arriving alone at an all-male regiment, where they are surprised when she removes her heavy winter flying gear and reveals herself to be a woman. In Myles's depiction, Budanova flies in the next day, after which the women report to regimental commander Nikolai Baranov. In fact, Litviak and Budanova were among eight women pilots who transferred to Stalingrad on 10 September 1942—too early in the year for "heavy sheepskin flying boots" and a "crackling stove." Furthermore, all the women flew in together. Litviak and Budanova were among a flight of four women assigned to the 437th regiment; they were transferred to Colonel Baranov's regiment, the 73rd, in January 1943.

38. Raisa E. Aronova, *Nochnye ved'my,* 2nd ed. (Moscow: Sovetskaia Rossiia, 1980). Gelman wrote, "Aronova was a journalist and interpreter, and very talented. About our flights, you should look in those books that I named [the list included Aronova]. Everything is written there." Polina Gelman, letter to author, 11 August 1992.

39. Gelman, letter to author, 11 August 1992.

40. Anne Noggle, *A Dance with Death* (College Station: Texas A&M University Press, 1994).

41. Ibid., 23; "[no title; designation of the 588th NLBP, 218 AD, 4 VA, Zakavakasky Front as a Guards Aviation Regiment]," TsAMO, Podolsk, Russia (11 February 1943), f. 46 GvBAP, op. 143370c, d. 1, l. 2.

42. K. Jean Cottam, *Soviet Airwomen in Combat in World War II* (Manhattan, Kans.: Sunflower University Press, 1983).

43. K. Jean Cottam, ed., *The Golden-Tressed Soldier* (Manhattan, Kans.: Sunflower University Press, 1984).

44. K. Jean Cottam, *In the Sky Above the Front: A Collection of Memoirs of Soviet Air Women Participants in the Great Patriotic War* (Manhattan, Kans.: Sunflower University Press, 1984), and *Women in Air War: The Eastern Front of World War II*, rev. ed. (Nepean, Ontario: New Military Publishing, 1997).

45. K. Jean Cottam, *Women in War and Resistance: Selected Biographies of Soviet Women Soldiers* (Nepean, Ontario: New Military Publishing, 1998).

46. I have deposited copies of my interview tapes (more than thirty hours), Gridnev's manuscript, and the photographs I received with the National Air and Space Museum.

Bibliography

PRIMARY SOURCES

Archival References

The *fonds* (collections) of the three women's aviation regiments covered in this book, like those of many other units, had not been assigned numbers at the Central Archive of the United Armed Forces of the Commonwealth of Independent States in Podolsk (TsAMO) as of the late 1990s and were simply designated as "the fond of the 46th GvBAP" or the appropriate regimental number. (Many of the documents pertaining to fighter pilot Liliia Litviak are in fond 33.) The fonds of the 46th, 125th, and 586th are extensive and contain handwritten logs of wartime combat activity; typed dispatches summarizing the more detailed combat logs; lists of personnel at various points in the war, indicating awards received, number of flights made, and positions held; and monthly summaries of combat work by regiment. What follows is not a complete list of archival materials that were consulted, but a selective list of the most useful documents. The following abbreviations are used:

f.	fond (collection)
op.	opis' (catalogue)
d.	delo (file, dossier)
kor.	korpus (file, dossier)
l.	list (page, sheet)

"Dolzhnost', zvanie, familiia, imiia i otchestvo letchika i kratkoe opisanie vozdushnogo boia." N.d. TsAMO, f. 586 IAP, op. 196818, d. 11, l. 2–7 c. ob.

Eremin, B. N. "Nagradnoi list (Lidiia Vladimirovna Litviak)." 25 May 1989. TsAMO. Komitet veteranov Velikoi Otechestvennoi voiny, f. 33, op. 686044, d. 4, l. 279.

Gridnev, Komandir 586 IAP, and Nachalnik Shtaba Moskovenkov. "Combat Order No. 7, 586 IAP Staff, Kastornoe 15 Aug 43." 15 August 1943. TsAMO, f. 586 IAP, op. 196605, d. 28, l. 4.

Gridnev, Komandir 586 IAP, and Nachalnik Shtaba Podruzhko. "Opisanie vozdushnogo boia." N.d. TsAMO, f. 586 IAP, op. 196604s, d. 2, l. 2a.

Gridnev, Komandir 586 IAP, and Nachalnik Shtaba Podruzhko. "Otchet o boevoy deiatel'nosti 586 IAP za 1944 g." 5 November 1944. TsAMO, f. 586 IAP, op. 197102, d. 8, l. 14–18 ob.

Gridnev, Komandir 586 IAP, and Nachalnik Shtaba Podruzhko. "Svedeniia a boevoi deiatel'nosti 586 IAP za ves' period Otechestvennoi voiny." N.d. TsAMO, f. 586 IAP, op. 197102, d. 8, l. 36 ob.

"Istoricheskii formuliar [46 GvNBAP]." N.d. TsAMO, f. 46 GvNBAP, op. 518931s, d. 1, l. 1–37.

"Istoricheskii formuliar [586 IAP]." N.d. TsAMO, f. 586 IAP, op. 196818, d. 15, l. not recorded.

"Istoricheskii formuliar, I: Istoriia stroitel'stva chasti [125 GvBAP]." 13 January 1947. TsAMO, f. 125 GvBAP, op. 518876, d. 1, l. 2–4, 59–60.

"Istoricheskii formuliar, II: Uchastie v pokhodax i boiakh [125 GvBAP]." 13 January 1947. TsAMO, f. 125 GvBAP, op. 518876, d. 1, l. 5–7.

"Istoricheskii formuliar, II: Uchastie v pokhodax i boiakh v 1945 g. [125 GvBAP]." 13 January 1947. TsAMO, f. 125 GvBAP, op. 518876, d. 1, l. 36–37.

"Istoricheskii formuliar, III: Boevaia podgotovka chasti [125 GvBAP]." 13 January 1947. TsAMO, f. 125 GvBAP, op. 518876, d. 1, l. 8–9.

"Istoricheskii formuliar, III: Boevaia podgotovka chasti v 1945 [125 GvBAP]." 13 January 1947. TsAMO, f. 125 GvBAP, op. 518876, d. 1, l. 37–38.

"Istoricheskii formuliar, IV: Partiinaia i politicheskaia rabota [125 GvBAP]." 13 January 1947. TsAMO, f. 125 GvBAP, op. 518876, d. 1, l. 10–12.

"Istoricheskii formuliar, VI: Nagrady i otlichiia chasti [125 GvBAP]." 1947. TsAMO, f. 125 GvBAP, op. 518876, d. 1 (Istoricheskii formuliar), l. 13.

"Istoricheskii formuliar, VII: Nagrady lichnogo sostava chasti [586 IAP]." N.d. TsAMO, f. 586 IAP, op. 196818, d. 15, l. 4–6.

"Istoricheskii formuliar, VII: Nagrady lichnogo sostava chasti [125 GvBAP]." 1947. TsAMO, f. 125 GvBAP, op. 518876, d. 1 (Istoricheskii formuliar), l. 14–19, 65.

"Istoricheskii formuliar, VIII: Znamena, godovye prazdniki, shefy i pochetnye krasnoarmeytsy [125 GvBAP]." 1947. TsAMO, f. 125 GvBAP, op. 518876, d. 1 (Istoricheskii formuliar), l. 20.

"Istoricheskii formuliar, IX: Izmeneniia v dislokatsii chasti [586 IAP]." N.d. TsAMO, f. 586 IAP, op., d. 1, l. not recorded.

"Istoricheskii formuliar, IX: Izmeneniia v dislokatsii chasti [125 GvBAP]." 13 January 1947. TsAMO, f. 125 GvBAP, op. 518876, d. 1, l. 20–27.

Kanevskii, A. "Khronika boevykh pobed Gv. Mladshchego Leitenanta Litviak Lidii Vladimirovny, komandira zvena 3 ae 73 Gvardeiskogo IAP." 25 May 1989. TsAMO. Komitet veteranov Velikoi Otechestvennoi voiny, f. 33, op. 686044, d. 420, l. 279; op. 273351, d. 3, l. 3, 65, 109; d. 2, l. 114; op. 273351c, d. 4, l. 39, 49; op. 519104c, d. 1, l. 23.

"Nagradnoi list (Evdokiia Ivanovna Nosal')." 24 April 1943. TsAMO, f. 33, op. 793756, d. 34, l. 168, 168 ob. 169.

[No title; designation of the 588th NLBP, 218 AD, 4 VA, Zakavakasky Front as a Guards Aviation Regiment]. 11 February 1943. TsAMO, f. 46 GvBAP, op. 143370c, d. 1, l. 1–3.

Podruzhko, Nachalnik Shtaba, and Nach. Oper. Otdela Makuninna. "Opisanie vozdushnogo boia (9 Feb 44)." N.d. TsAMO, f. 586 IAP, op. 196604s, d. 2, l. 10.

Raskova, Marina. "Order No. 8, Aviation Group 122, Engels, 5 Nov 41." 5 November 1941. TsAMO, f. Engel'skoi aviashkoly pilotov, No. F. 60396, op. 35912, d. 58, kor. 4014, s. 2.

"Rol' 586 Istrebitel'nogo aviastionnogo zhenskogo polka v Otechestvennoi voine." N.d. TsAMO, f. 586 IAP, op., d., l. not recorded.

"Shtatno-dolzhnosti spisok 588 Nochnogo legko-bombardirovochnogo aviatsionogo polka na 6 noiabria 1942." 6 November 1942. TsAMO, f. 46 GvBAP, op. 15726, d. 8, l. 5–9.

"Spisok lichnogo sostava 586 IAP imeiushchikh Pravitel'stvennie nagrady." N.d. TsAMO, f. 586 IAP, op., d., l. not recorded.

Stalin, Joseph. "Vypuska iz prikaza narodnogo komissara oborony soiuza SSR No. 0099." 8 October 1941. TsAMO, f. Engel'skoi aviashkoly pilotov, No. F. 60396, op. 35912, d. 58, kor. 4014, s. 103.

Timofeeva, Vrid. komandira 587 BBAP, and Nachalnik shtaba 587 BBAP Kazarinova. "Otchet o rabote 587 BBAP za period dekabr'-ianvar' 43 g." 1943. TsAMO, f. 125 GvBAP, op. 224259c, d. 4, l. 1–5.

"Vypuska iz istoricheskogo formuliara 586 IAP." N.d. TsAMO, f. 586 IAP, op., d., l. not recorded.

Interviews

Danilova-Emel'ianova, Irina Ivanovna. Interview by author, tape recording, 3 May 1993, Moscow, Russia.

Eremin, Boris Nikolaevich. Interview by author, tape recording, 10 May 1993, Moscow, Russia (Committee of War Veterans).

Favorskaia-Luneva, Irina. Interview by author, tape recording, 10 May 1993, Moscow, Russia (Favorskaia's apartment).

Gelman, Polina Vladimirovna. Interview by author, tape recording, 3 May 1993, Moscow, Russia (Gelman's home).

Gridnev, Aleksandr Vasilevich. Interviews by author, tape recordings, 12, 13, and 14 May 1993, Volgograd, Russia (Gridnev's apartment).

Karakorskaia, Elena Nikolaevna, Nina Arkad'evna Slovokhotova, and Ekaterina Kuzminichna Polunina. Interview by author, tape recording, 4 May 1993, Moscow, Russia (Karakorskaia's apartment).

Kravchenko-Savitskaia, Valentina Flegontovna. Interview by author, tape recording, 7 May 1993, Moscow, Russia (Kravchenko's apartment).

Makunina, Aleksandra Aleksandrovna. Interview by author, tape recording, 10 May 1993, Moscow, Russia (Favorskaia's apartment).

Oriefieva, Liubov Ilinichna. Interview by author, tape recording, 20 August 1992, Moscow, Russia.

Pasportnikova, Inna Vladimirovna. Interview by author, tape recordings, 8 May 1993, Zhukovsky, Russia (Pasportnikova's apartment), and 15 May 1993, Sredniaia Akhtuba airfield, Russia (near Volgograd).

Petrochenkova-Neminushchaia, Valentina Abramovna. Interview by author, tape recording, 9 May 1993, Chkalovsk, Russia (Petrochenkova's apartment).

Polunina, Ekaterina Kuzminichna, and Valentina Vasilevna Kovaleva. Interview by author, tape recording, 1 May 1993, Moscow, Russia (Polunina's apartment).

Rakobolskaia, Irina. Interview by author, tape recording, 10 May 1993, Moscow, Russia (Rakobolskaia's apartment).

Slovokhotova, Nina Arkadeevna. Interview by author, tape recording, 10 May 1993, Moscow, Russia (Slovokhotova's apartment)

Manuscripts and Letters

Gelman, Polina. Letters to author, 15 and 28 July 1992, 11 August 1992.

Gridnev, Alexander Vasilevich. "Memuary." Typescript, n.d.

———. Letters to author, 18 and 19 August 1992, May 1993.

———. Letter to Klavdia Ivanovna Terekhova-Kasatkina, n.d.

Litviak, Lidiia Vladimirovna. Letter to Anna Vasil'evna Litviak, "end of May" 1943.

Pasportnikova, Inna Vladimirovna. Letters to author, 27 August 1992 and 3 September 1992.

———. "Moi komandir." Typescript, 1989.

Polunina, Ekaterina Kuzminichna. "Evgeniia Filippovna Prokhorova." Typescript, n.d.

———. "Raisa Vasil'evna Beliaeva." Typescript, n.d.

Rakobolskaia, Irina. Letter to author, 10 August 1992.

Newspapers and Periodicals

"Iz soobshcheniia ot Sovetskogo informbiuro za 26 iiunia 1943." *Pravda*, 27 June 1943, 1.

Laird, Lael. "The R.A.F. on the Red A.F." *Life* (4 May 1942): 12ff.

"Liubimaia doch' sovetskogo naroda" [Beloved daughter of the Soviet people]. *Ogonek* 4, no. 817 (1943): 7.

Lodgauz, L. "Boevoi pochin Valerii Khomiakovoi" [The combat initiative of Valeriia Khomiakova]. *Ogonek* 46, no. 807 (1942): 5.

Mishakova, Olga. *Sovetskaia zhenshchina v Velikoi Otechestnnoi voine* [Soviet woman in the Great Patriotic War]. Moscow: Voenizdat, 1943.

———. *Sovetskie devushki v Otechestnnoi voine* [Soviet girls in the Great Patriotic War]. Moscow: Voenizdat, 1944.

———. "Sovetskaia zhenshchina velikaia sila." *Pravda*, 8 March 1945, 3.

"Nagradi za myzhestvo." *Pravda*, 6 May 1990, 1.

Nikitin, General Major of Aviation A. "M. M. Raskova." *Krasnaia zvezda*, 12 January 1943, 4.

"Pamiati Geroia Sovetskogo Soiuza Mariny Raskovoi." *Krasnaia zvezda*, 9 January 1943, 3.

"Podvig ostaetsia podvigom." *Komsomolskaia pravda*, 6 May 1990, 1.

"Prikaz verkhovnogo Glavnokomanduiushchego General-pokovniku Petrovu." *Krasnaia zvezda*, 10 October 1943, 1.

"Traurnyi miting na Krasnoi ploshchadi, posviashchennyi pamiati M. M. Raskovoi." *Krasnaia zvezda*, 13 January 1943, 3.

Tseilin, B. "Orliata" [Eaglets]. *Ogonek* 27, no. 840 (1943): 4.

"Ukaz prezidiuma verkhovnogo soveta SSSR a prosvoenii zvaniia Geroia Sovetskogo Soiuza nachal'stvuiushchemu, sostavu VVS KA." *Krasnaia zvezda*, 24 May 1943, 1.

"Vozdushnykh pobed" [Air Victories]. *Ogonek* 15–16, nos. 828–829 (1943): cover, 1.

Official Publications and Unit Histories

Anishchenkov, P. S., and V. Ye. Shurinov. *Tret'ia vozdushnaia: Voenno-istoricheskii ocherk o boevom puti VVS Kalininskogo fronta i 3-i vozdushnoi armii v gody Velikoi Otechestvennoi voiny* [The Third Air Army: a military-historical essay of the campaign record of the Air Forces of the Kalinin Front and the Third Air Army during the Great Patriotic War]. Moscow: Voenizdat, 1984.

Baranov, Lt. Col. Nikolai. *Kharakteristika (Lidiia Vladimirovna Litviak)*. VVS, 1943.

Bershanskaia, Evdokiia, et al., eds. *46 Gvardeiskii Tamanskii zhenskii aviatsionyi polk* [The 46th Guards Taman Women's Aviation Regiment]. N.p.: Tsentral'nyi Dom Sovetskoi Armii imeni M. v. Frunze, n.d.

Grylev, A. N. *Boevoi sostav Sovetskoi armii* [Order of battle of the Soviet army]. 5 vols. Moskva: Voenno-nauchnoe upravlenie General'nogo shtaba Voenno-istoricheskii otdel, 1963–1990.

Inozemtsev, I. G. *Pod Krylom—Leningrad: Boevoi put's VVS Leningradskogo Voennogo Okruga, Leningradskogo fronta i 13-i vozdushnoi armii v gody velikoi otechestvennoi voiny* [Under the wings—Leningrad: the combat record of the air forces of the Leningrad Military District, the Leningrad Front and the 13th Air Army during the years of the Great Patriotic War]. Moscow: Voenizdat, 1978.

Kozhevnikov, M. N. *Komandovanie i shtab VVS Sovetskoi Armii v Velikoi Otechestvennoi voine 1941–1945 gg.* [Command and staff of the air forces of the Soviet army in the Great Patriotic War 1941–1945]. Moscow: Nauka, 1977.

Kravchenko, V. F., ed. *125 Gvardeiskii Bombardirovochnyi Aviatsionnyi Borisovskii ordenov Suvoroba i Kutuzova polk imeni Geroia Sovetskogo Soiuza Mariny Raskovoi*. Moscow: privately published, 1976.

Martyniuk, N. M., ed. *125 Gvardeiskii Bombardirovochnyi Aviatsionnyi Borisovskii ordenov Suvoroba i Kutuzova polk imeni Geroia Sovetskogo Soiuza Mariny Raskovoi*. Moscow: privately published, 1989.

Prussakov, G. K., et al. *16'aia vozdushnaia: voenno-istoricheskii ocherk o boevom puti 16-i vozdushnoi armii* [The 16th Air Army: a military historical essay on the campaign record of the 16th Air Army (1942–1945)]. Moscow: Voenizdat, 1973.

Vershinin, Konstantin Andreevich. *Chetvertaia Vozdushnaia* [Fourth Air (Army)]. Moscow: Voenizdat, 1975.

Published Memoirs, Diaries, and Personal Impressions

Alexiyevich, Svetlana. *War's Unwomanly Face* [U voiny—ne zhenskoe litso]. Trans. Keith Hammond and Lyudmila Lezhneva. Moscow: Progress Publishers, 1988.

Aronova, Raisa E. *Nochnye ved'my* [Night witches]. 1st ed., Moscow: Sovetskaia Rossiia, 1969. Revised and expanded 2nd ed., Moscow: Sovetskaia Rossiia, 1980.

Beliakov, A. Foreword to *Zapiski shturmana/Prodolzheniie podviga*. 2nd ed. Ed. Marina Raskova and Ekaterina Migunova. Moscow: DOSAAF, 1976.

Bereznitskaia, A. M. "Pervye Dni." In *V nebe frontovom*. 1st ed. Ed. M. A. Kazarinova and A. A. Poliantseva. Moscow: Molodaia Gvardiia, 1962.

Bialer, Seweryn, ed. *Stalin and His Generals: Soviet Military Memoirs of World War II*. New York: Pegasus, 1969.

Bourke-White, Margaret. *Shooting the Russian War*. New York: Simon and Schuster, 1942.

Caldwell, Erskine. *All-Out on the Road to Smolensk*. New York: Duell, Sloan and Pearce, 1942.

Chaika, N. "Na nochnom bombardirovshchike." In *Geroini: ocherki o zhenshchinakh—Geroiakh Sovetskogo Soiuza*. 2 vols. Ed. L. F. Toropov. Moscow: Politizdat, 1969.

Chechneva, Marina. "Annushka." *Kryl'ia Rodiny* (March 1967): 4–5.

———. "Imeni Mariny Raskovoi" [Named for Marina Raskova]. *Kryl'ia Rodiny* 10 (1975): 8–11.

———. "Katiusha." *Aviatsiia i kosmonavtika* 3 (1966): 87–89.

———. "*Lastochki*" *nad frontom* [Swallows over the front]. Moscow: DOSAAF, 1984.

———. *Nebo ostaetsia nashim* [The sky remains ours]. Moscow: Voenizdat, 1976.

———. *Samolety ukhodiat v noch'* [Aircraft go out into the night]. Moscow: Voenizdat, 1961.

Cherniaeva, I., ed. *Docheri Rossii*. Moscow: Sovetskaia Rossiia, 1975.

Chuikov, V. I. *Battle for Stalingrad.* New York: Holt, 1964.

———. *Vystoiav, my pobedili: zapiski komandarma 62-y* [By enduring, we won: notes of the 62nd Army commander]. Moscow: Sovetskaia Rossiia, 1960.

Dospanova, K. *Pod Komandovaniem Raskovoi: Vospominaniia Voennoi Letchitsy* [Under Raskova's command: memoirs of a woman military pilot]. Alma-Ata: Kazgolitizdat, 1960.

Ehrenburg, Ilya. *Eve of War: 1933–1941.* 6 vols. Trans. Tatiana Shebunina, in collaboration with Yvonne Kapp. London: MacGibbon and Kee, 1963.

———. *Russia at War.* London: Hamilton, 1943.

———. *The Tempering of Russia.* Trans. Alexander Kaun. New York: Knopf, 1944.

———. *The War: 1941–45.* 6 vols. Trans. Tatiana Shebunina, in collaboration with Yvonne Kapp. London: MacGibbon and Kee, 1964.

Ehrenburg, Ilya, and Konstantin Simonov. *V odnoi gazete.* Novosti, 1979.

Eremenko, Aleksandra. "Zhizn' za tovarishcha." In *V nebe frontovom.* 2nd ed. Ed. M. A. Kazarinova, N. F. Kravtsova, and A. A. Poliantseva. Moscow: Molodaia Gvardiia, 1971.

Eremin, Boris Nikolaevich. *Vozdushnye boitsy* [Air warriors]. Moscow: Voenizdat, 1987.

Fedotova, Ekaterina. "Batia." In *V nebe frontovom.* 2nd ed. Ed. M. A. Kazarinova, N. F. Kravtsova, and A. A. Poliantseva. Moscow: Molodaia Gvardiia, 1971.

Golovachev, P. "My ikh lyubili." In *Geroi i Podvigi.* 4 vols. Ed. M. F. Loshchits. Moscow: Voenizdat, 1963.

Golubeva-Teres, O. T. *Zvezdy na kryliakh* [Stars on the wings]. Saratov: Privolzhskoe kn. izd-vo, 1974.

Griffith, Hubert. *R.A.F. in Russia.* London: Hammond, 1942.

Grizodubova, V. "Doch' naroda." In *Geroini: ocherki o zhenshchinakh—Geroiakh Sovetskogo Soiuza.* 2 vols. Ed. L. F. Toropov. Moscow: Politizdat, 1969.

Iamshchikova, Ol'ga. "Druzhba." In *V nebe frontovom.* 2nd ed. Ed. M. A. Kazarinova, N. F. Kravtsova, and A. A. Poliantseva. Moscow: Molodaia Gvardiia, 1971.

Kazarinova, M. "Liubimyi komandir." In *Geroini: ocherki o zhenshchinakh—Geroiakh Sovetskogo Soiuza.* 2 vols. Ed. L. F. Toropov. Moscow: Politizdat, 1969.

———. "Rodina zovet!" In *V nebe frontovom.* 2nd ed. Ed. M. A. Kazarinova, N. F. Kravtsova, and A. A. Poliantseva. Moscow: Molodaia Gvardiia, 1971.

Kazarinova, M., N. F. Kravtsova, and A. A. Poliantseva, eds. *V nebe frontovom: sbornik vospominanii sovetskikh letchits-uchastnits Velikoi Otechestvennoi voiny* [In the sky above the front: a collection of memoirs of Soviet women pilots who participated in the Great Patriotic War]. 2nd ed. Moscow: Molodaia Gvardiia, 1971.

Kazarinova, M., and A. A. Poliantseva, eds. *V nebe frontovom: sbornik vospominanii sovetskikh letchits-uchastnits Velikoi Otechestvennoi voiny* [In the sky above the front: a collection of memoirs of Soviet women pilots who participated in the Great Patriotic War]. 1st ed. Moscow: Molodaia Gvardiia, 1962.

Kravtsova, Natal'ia. "Shturman polka." In *Geroini: ocherki o zhenshchinakh—Geroiakh Sovetskogo Soiuza.* 2 vols. Ed. L. F. Toropov. Moscow: Politizdat, 1969.

——. "Tysiacha vosem' boevykh vyletov." In *Geroini: ocherki o zhenshchinakh—Geroiakh Sovetskogo Soiuza.* 2 vols. Ed. L. F. Toropov. Moscow: Politizdat, 1969.

——. *Ot zakata do rassveta* [From sunset to dawn]. Moscow: Voenizdat, 1968.

Krol, Tamara. "Zvezdy ishchut liudei." In *Geroini: ocherki o zhenshchinakh—Geroiakh Sovetskogo Soiuza.* 2 vols. Ed. L. F. Toropov. Moscow: Politizdat, 1969.

Lavrinenkov, Vladimir Dmitrievich. *Vozvrashchenie v nebo* [Return to the sky]. 2nd ed. Moscow: Voenizdat, 1983.

Levin, I. S. *Groznye gody* [Terrible years]. Saratov: Privolzhskoe, 1984.

Litvinova, Larisa Nikolaevna. *Letiat Skovz' Gody* [They fly through the years]. Moscow: Voenizdat, 1983.

Lomanova, Galina. "Boevye epizody." In *V nebe frontovom.* 1st ed. Ed. M. A. Kazarinova and A. A. Poliantseva. Moscow: Molodaia Gvardiia, 1962.

Makunina, Aleksandra Aleksandrovna. "Pervyi komandir polka." *V nebe frontovom.* Ed. M. A. Kazarinova, N. F. Kravtsova, and A. A. Poliantseva. 2nd ed. Moscow: Molodaia Gvardiia, 1971. 277–81.

Markov, V. V. "Gorzhus' boevymi druz'iami." *V nebe frontovom.* Ed. M. A. Kazarinova, N. F. Kravtsova, and A. A. Poliantseva. 2nd ed. Moscow: Molodaia Gvardiia, 1971. 29–32.

Markova, Galina I. *Rasskazhi, Bereza . . .* [Tell us, birch tree . . .]. Moscow: Voenizdat, 1983.

——. "Youth Under Fire: The Story of Klavdiya Fomicheva, a Woman Dive Bomber Pilot." In *Soviet Airwomen in Combat in World War II.* Ed. Jean Cottam. Manhattan, Kans.: Sunflower University Press, 1983.

——. *Vzlet: o Geroe Sovetskogo Soiuza M. M. Raskovoi* [Takeoff: about Hero of the Soviet Union M. M. Raskova]. Moscow: Politizdat, 1986.

Migunova, E. A. "Prodolzheniie podviga." In *Zapiski shturmana/Prodolzheniie Podviga.* Moscow: DOSAAF, 1976.

Morozov, A. "Vospitannitsa komsomola." In *Geroini: ocherki o zhenshchinakh—Geroiakh Sovetskogo Soiuza.* 2 vols. Ed. L. F. Toropov. Moscow: Politizdat, 1969.

Novikov, A. A. *V nebe Leningrada: zapiski komanduiushchego aviatsiei* [In the sky of Leningrad: notes of an air commander]. Moscow: Nauka, 1970.

Ol'khovskaia, Galina. "Otvazhnaia eskadril'ia." In *V nebe frontovom.* 2nd ed. Ed. M. A. Kazarinova, N. F. Kravtsova, and A. A. Poliantseva. Moscow: Molodaia Gvardiia, 1971.

Poliantseva, A. "Dvoe protiv soroka dvukh." In *V nebe frontovom.* 2nd ed. Ed. M. A. Kazarinova, N. F. Kravtsova, and A. A. Poliantseva. Moscow: Molodaia Gvardiia, 1971.

Poliantseva, A., and Ekaterina Migunova. *Zapiski shturmana/Prodolzheniie podviga* [Notes of a navigator/continuation of a brave deed]. Moscow: DOSAAF, 1976.

Raskova, Marina. *Zapiski shturmana* [Notes of a navigator]. Moscow: Molodaia Gvardiia, 1939.

Schwabedissen, Generalleutnant D. W. *The Russian Air Force in the Eyes of German Commanders*. Prepared by the USAF Historical Division as GAF 175 ed. New York: Arno Press, 1968.

Seid-Mamedova, Zuleika B. *Zapiski Letchitsy* [Notes of a woman pilot]. Baku: Giadzhlik, 1969.

Simonov, Konstantin. *Always a Journalist*. Moscow: Progress, 1989.

———. *Days and Nights*. Trans. Joseph Barnes. New York: Simon and Schuster, 1945.

———. *Ot Chernogo do Barentseva Moria: Zapiski Voennogo Korrespondenta* [From the Black Sea to the Barents]. 4 vols. Moscow: Sovetskii Pisatel', 1944.

———. *Ot Nashego Voennogo Korrespondenta* [From our military correpondent]. Moscow: Voenizdat, 1948.

Stalin, Joseph. *Sochineniia* [Works]. 3 vols. Stanford, Calif.: Stanford University Press, 1967.

Timofeeva, Evgeniia. "Pervyi boi." In *V nebe frontovom*. 2nd ed. Ed. M. A. Kazarinova, N. F. Kravtsova, and A. A. Poliantseva. Moscow: Molodaia Gvardiia, 1971.

Timofeeva-Egorova, Anna Aleksandrovna. *Derzhis', Sestrenka!* [Hold on, sisters!]. Moscow: Voenizdat, 1983.

Tokaev, Grigori A. *Comrade X*. London: Harvill Press, 1956.

Toropov, L. F., ed. *Geroini: Ocherki o zhenshchinakh—geroiakh Sovetskogo soiuza* [Heroines: biographical sketches of women Heroes of the Soviet Union]. 2 vols. Moscow: Politizdat, 1969.

Turabelidze, G. P. "Vstrecha boevikh druzei." In *V nebe frontovom*. 1st ed. Ed. M. A. Kazarinova and A. A. Poliantseva. Moscow: Molodaia Gvardiia, 1962.

Verkhozin, A. "Komandir polka." In *Geroini: ocherki o zhenshchinakh—Geroiakh Sovetskogo Soiuza*. 2 vols. Ed. L. F. Toropov. Moscow: Politizdat, 1969.

———. "Polkom komanduet zhenshchina." *Kryl'ia Rodiny* (1966): 7–9.

Werth, Alexander. *Russia at War: 1941–45*. 3rd ed. New York: Carroll and Graf, 1988.

———. *The Year of Stalingrad*. London: Hamish Hamilton, 1946.

Zhigulenko, Evgeniia. "Those Magnificent Women in Their Flying Machines." *Soviet Life* (May 1990): 12–15.

Zhoffr, Fransua de. *Normandiia-Neman: Vospominaniia Letchika* [Normandie-Niemen: souvenirs d'un pilote]. 2nd ed. Trans. G. N. Zagrevskii. Moscow: Voenizdat, 1982.

Zhuravlev, D. A. *Ognevoi Shchit Moskvy* [The fiery defense of Moscow]. Moscow: Voenizdat, 1972.

Speeches

Kalinin, M. I. *On Communist Education: Selected Speeches and Articles*. Moscow: Foreign Languages Publishing House, 1953.

Stalin, Joseph. *The Great Patriotic War of the Soviet Union*. New York: International Publishers, 1945.

SECONDARY SOURCES

Articles and Book Sections in Russian

Bashkirov, B., and N. Semenkevich. "Geroini Sovetskogo neba." *Kryl'ia rodiny* (March 1969).

Bocharnikova, Mariia. "Boi v zimnem dvortse." *Novyi zhurnal* 68 (1962): 215–27.

"Geroini sovetskogo neba." *Kryl'ia rodiny* (March 1969).

Gribanov, S. "Frontovaia 'Chaika' " [Front-line Seagull]. *Aviatsiia i kosmonavtika* 3 (1973): 46–47.

———. "Liliia." In *V nebe frontovom.* 2nd ed. Ed. M. A. Kazarinova, N. F. Kravtsova, and A. A. Poliantseva. Moscow: Molodaia Gvardiia, 1971.

———. "Ognennaia Liliia." In *Geroi i podvigi.* 1st ed. 4 vols. Ed. M. F. Loshchits. Moscow: Voenizdat, 1966.

———. "Vyletala Liliia v boi" [Lilia flew into combat]. *Aviatsiia i kosmonavtika* 3 (1968): 15–19.

Gubarev, S. "Sestry." *Krasnaia zvezda,* 8 March 1960, 4.

Kanevskii, A. "Ia samaia schastlivaia. . . ." *Aviatsiia i kosmonavtika* (March 1990): 36–38.

Lariokhin, B. B., and I. A. Tretiak. "Improved Radio Communications for Radar Support Air Operations in the Great Patriotic War." *Voenno-istoricheskii zhurnal* 9 (1986): 68–73.

Man'ko, A. "S komsomol'skim biletom u serdtsa." *Aviatsiia i kosmonavtika* (March 1983): 18–19.

Murmantseva, Vera Semenova. "Sovetskie zhenshchiny v Velikoi Otechestvennoi voine 1941–1945" [Soviet women in the Great Patriotic War 1941–1945]. *Voenno-istoricheskii zhurnal* 2 (1968): 47–54.

Pervov, A. G., and V. N. Gus'kov. "Nochnye deistviia frontovoi aviatsii" [Night operations of frontal aviation]. *Voenno-istoricheskii zhurnal* 6 (1988): 28–33.

Romanov, Col. Gen. S. "Protivovozdushnye oborony strany" [National air defense forces]. *Voenno-istoricheskii zhurnal* 11 (1982): 29–35.

Roshchin, I. "Sled na zemle." *Aviatsiia i kosmonavtika* (March 1983): 18–19.

Selivanov, F. "Tri stranitsy iz zhizni" [Three pages from a life]. *Kryl'ia rodiny* 10 (1965): 14–15.

Senin, A. S. "Zhenskie batal'ony i voennye komandy v 1917 godu." *Voprosy Istorii* 10 (1987): 176–82.

Skopintseva, A. "Knigi o ratnykh podvigakh sovetskikh zhenshchin" [Books on the feats of arms of Soviet women]. *Vestnik protivovozdushnoi oborony* (1978): 89–92.

Stasiuk, N. "Geroicheskie dela letchits komsomol'skogo aviatsionnogo polka" [Heroic deeds of the women pilots of the Komsomol Aviation Regiment]. *Voenno-istoricheskii zhurnal* 8 (1968): 15.

Vlasov, D. "Krylataia sem'ia." In *Pamiat' ognennykh let*. Ed. M. F. Loshchits et al. Moscow: Voenizdat, 1975.

Zaitsev, A. D. "Geroinia vozdushnogo tarana." *Voenno-istoricheskii zhurnal* (March 1966): 50–51.

Books in Russian

Geroi i Podvigi: Sovetskie listovki Velikoi Otechestvennoi voiny 1941–1945 gg. [Heroes and victories: Soviet leaflets of the Great Patriotic War 1941–1945]. Moscow: Politizdat, 1958.

Gribanov, Stanislav Vikent'evich. *Na Ognennykh Vysotakh* [At the fiery heights]. Moscow: DOSAAF, 1977.

Gubin, B. A., and V. A. Kiselev. *Vos'maia Vozdushnaia: boevoi put' 8-i vozdushnoi armii* [The Eighth Air (Army): combat history]. Moscow: Voenizdat, 1986.

Il'ina, Zinaida Petrovna. *Komissar Vera*. Moscow: DOSAAF, 1981.

Ionov, P. P., ed. *Voiska PVO strany v Velikoi Otechestvennoi voine 1941–1945: kratkaia khronika* Moscow: Voenizdat, 1981.

Magid, Alexander Samoilovich. *Gvardeiskii Tamanskii aviatsionnyi polk* [Guards Taman Aviation Regiment]. 3rd ed. Moscow: DOSAAF, 1960.

Murmantseva, Vera Semenova. *Sovetskiie zhenshchiny v Velikoi Otechestvennoi voine 1941–1945* [Soviet women in the Great Patriotic War 1941–1945]. Moscow: Mysl', 1974.

———. *Zhenshchiny v soldatskikh shineliakh* [Women in soldiers' overcoats]. Moscow: Voenizdat, 1971.

Ovchinnikova, L. P. *Zhenshchiny v soldatskikh shineliakh.* Volgograd: Nizhne-Volzhskoe, 1987.

Polevoi, Boris. *Povest' o nastoiashchem cheloveke* [Story of a real man]. Moscow: Detskaia Literatura, 1984.

Sovetskie Voenno-vozdushnye sily v Velikoi Otechestvennoi voine 1941–1945. Moscow: Voenizdat, 1968.

Svirsky, Grigori. *Proshchanie s Rossii* [Farewell to Russia]. Tenafly, N.J.: Hermitage, 1986.

Tarasov, V. I., A. Ya. Zotov, et al. *Akademiia imeni M. V. Frunze* [The M. V. Frunze Academy]. Moscow: Voenizdat, 1973.

Vershigora, Petro P. *Liudi s chistoi sovets'iu* [Men with a clear conscience]. Moscow: Sovetskii pisatel', 1952.

Articles and Book Sections in English

Abraham, Richard. "Mariia L. Bochkareva and the Russian Amazons of 1917." In *Women and Society in Russia and the Soviet Union*. Ed. Linda Edmondson. Cambridge: Cambridge University Press, 1992.

Atkinson, Dorothy. "Society and Sexes in the Russian Past." In *Women in Russia*. Ed. Dorothy Atkinson, Alexander Dallin, and Gail Warshofsky Lapidus. Stanford, Calif.: Stanford University Press, 1977.

Bailes, Kenneth E. "Technology and Legitimacy: Soviet Aviation and Stalinism in the 1930s." *Technology and Culture* 17, no. 1 (1976): 55–81.

Blitzstein, Madelin. "How Women Flyers Fight Russia's Air War." *Aviation Magazine* (July 1944): 116.

Campbell, D'Ann. "Combatting the Gender Gulf." *Minerva* 10, no. 3/4 (1992): 13–40.

———. "Women in Combat: The World War II Experience in the United States, Great Britain, Germany, and the Soviet Union." *Journal of Military History* 57, no. 2 (1993): 301–23.

Chodoff, Elliot P. "Ideology and Primary Groups." *Armed Forces and Society* 9 (1983): 569–93.

Clark, Katerina. "The Aviation Hero as the Paradigmatic New Man." In *The Soviet Novel: History as Ritual*. Chicago: University of Chicago Press, 1981.

Cohn, Carol. "Wars, Wimps and Women: Talking Gender and Thinking War." In *Gendering War Talk*. Ed. Miriam Cooke and Angela Woollacott. Princeton, N.J.: Princeton University Press, 1993.

Cooke, Miriam. "Wo-man, Retelling the War Myth." In *Gendering War Talk*. Ed. Miriam Cooke and Angela Woollacott. Princeton, N.J.: Princeton University Press, 1993.

Cottam, K. Jean. "Soviet Women in Combat in World War II: The Ground Forces and the Navy." *International Journal of Women's Studies* 3, no. 4 (1980): 345–57.

———. "Soviet Women in Combat in World War II: The Ground/Air Defense Forces." In *Women in Eastern Europe and the Soviet Union*. Ed. Tova Yedlin. New York: Praeger, 1980.

———. "Soviet Women in Combat in World War II: The Rear Services, Resistance Behind Enemy Lines, and Military Political Workers." *International Journal of Women's Studies* 5, no. 4 (1982): 363–78.

———. "Soviet Women Soldiers in World War II: Three Biographical Sketches." *Minerva: Quarterly Report on Women and the Military* 18, no. 3–4 (2001).

Devilbiss, M. C. "Gender Integration and Unit Deployment: A Study of GI Jo." *Armed Forces and Society* 11, no. 4 (1985): 523–52.

DiIorio, Judith A. "Feminism and War: Theoretical Issues and Debates." *Reference Services Review* 20, no. 2 (1992): 51–68.

Dobson, Richard B. "Educational Policies and Attainment." In *Women in Rus-*

sia. Ed. Dorothy Atkinson, Alexander Dallin, and Gail Warshofsky Lapidus. Stanford, Calif.: Stanford University Press, 1977.

Erickson, John. "Night Witches, Snipers and Laundresses." *History Today* 40 (1990): 29–35.

Flerovsky, Alexei. "Women Flyers of Fighter Planes." *Soviet Life* (May 1975): 28–29.

Gray, Francine du Plessix. "The Russian Heroine: Gender, Sexuality and Freedom." *Michigan Quarterly Review* 28, no. 4 (1989): 699–718.

Greenwood, James R. "Russia's Female Fighter Pilots." *Popular Aviation* (November–December 1967): 9–13.

Greenwood, John T. "The Great Patriotic War, 1941–1945." In *Soviet Aviation and Air Power: A Historical View*. Ed. Robin Higham and Jacob W. Kipp. Boulder, Colo.: Westview, 1977.

Greenwood, John T., and Von Hardesty. "Soviet Air Forces in World War II." In *The Soviet Air Forces*. Ed. Paul Murphy. Jefferson, N.C., and London: McFarland, 1984.

Griesse, Anne Eliot, and Richard Stites. "Russia: Revolution and War." In *Female Soldiers—Combatants or Noncombatants? Historical and Contemporary Perspectives*. Ed. Nancy Loring Goldman. Westport, Conn.: Greenwood, 1982.

Hardesty, Von. "Roles and Missions: Soviet Tactical Air Power in the Second Period of the Great Patriotic War." In *Transformation in Russian and Soviet Military History*. Washington, D.C.: U.S. Government Printing Office, 1986.

Holt, Alix. "Marxism and Women's Oppression: Bolshevik Theory and Practice in the 1920's." In *Women in Eastern Europe and the Soviet Union*. Ed. Tova Yedlin. New York: Praeger, 1980.

Lapidus, Gail Warshofsky. "Sexual Equality in Soviet Policy: A Developmental Perspective." In *Women in Russia*. Ed. Dorothy Atkinson, Alexander Dallin, and Gail Warshofsky Lapidus. Stanford, Calif.: Stanford University Press, 1977.

Macdonald, Sharon. "Drawing the Lines—Gender, Peace and War: An Introduction." In *Images of Women in Peace and War*. Ed. Sharon Macdonald, Pat Holden, and Shirley Ardener. London: Macmillan, 1987.

Meos, Edgar S. "Russian Women Fighter Pilots." *Flight International* (27 December 1962): 1019–20.

Meyer, Alfred G. "The Impact of World War I on Russian Women's Lives." In *Russia's Women: Accommodation, Resistance, Transformation*. Ed. Barbara Evans Clements, Barbara Alpern Engel, and Christine D. Worobec. Berkeley: University of California Press, 1991.

———. "Marxism and the Women's Movement." In *Women in Russia*. Ed. Dorothy Atkinson, Alexander Dallin, and Gail Warshofsky Lapidus. Stanford, Calif.: Stanford University Press, 1977.

Mitroshenkov, V. "They Were First." *Soviet Military Review* (March 1969): 20–22.

Pennington, Reina J. " 'Do Not Speak of the Services You Rendered': Women

Veterans of Aviation in the Soviet Union." *Journal of Slavic Military Studies* 9, no. 1 (1996): 120–51.

———. "From Chaos to the Eve of the Great Patriotic War." In *Russian Aviation and Air Power in the 20th Century.* Ed. Robin Higham. N.p.: Frank Cass, 1998.

———. "Pilot Initiative in the Soviet Air Forces." In *The Soviet Air Forces.* Ed. Paul Murphy. Jefferson, N.C., and London: McFarland, 1984.

———. "The Propaganda Factor and Soviet Women Pilots in World War II." *Minerva: Quarterly Report on Women and the Military* (summer 1997): 13–41.

———. "Stalin's Falcons: The 586th Fighter Aviation Regiment." *Minerva: Quarterly Report on Women and the Military* (fall/winter 2000): 76–108.

———. "Wings, Women and War." *Smithsonian's Air and Space* (December–January 1993): 74–85.

Quester, George H. "Women in Combat." *International Security* (spring 1977): 80–91.

Rosaldo, Michelle Zimbalist. "Women, Culture and Society: A Theoretical Overview." In *Women, Culture and Society.* Ed. Michelle Zimbalist Rosaldo and Louise Lamphere. Stanford, Calif.: Stanford University Press, 1974.

Rosenberg, Stanley D. "The Threshold of Thrill: Life Stories in the Skies over Southeast Asia." In *Gendering War Talk.* Ed. Miriam Cooke and Angela Woollacott. Princeton, N.J.: Princeton University Press, 1993.

Rosenhan, Mollie Schwartz. "Images of Male and Female in Children's Readers." In *Women in Russia.* Ed. Dorothy Atkinson, Alexander Dallin, and Gail Warshofsky Lapidus. Stanford, Calif.: Stanford University Press, 1977.

Scott, Joan W. "Rewriting History." In *Behind the Lines: Gender and the Two World Wars.* Ed. Margaret Higonnet et al. New Haven, Conn., and London: Yale University Press, 1987.

Stiehm, Judith Hicks. "The Protected, the Protector, the Defender." *Women's Studies International Forum* 5, no. 3/4 (1982): 367–76.

Stites, Richard. "Women and the Russian Intelligentsia: Three Perspectives." In *Women in Russia.* Ed. Dorothy Atkinson, Alexander Dallin, and Gail Warshofsky Lapidus. Stanford, Calif.: Stanford University Press, 1977.

Tuten, Jeff M. "The Argument Against Female Combatants." In *Female Soldiers—Combatants or Noncombatants? Historical and Contemporary Perspectives.* Ed. Nancy Loring Goldman. Westport, Conn.: Greenwood, 1982.

Whiting, Kenneth R. "Soviet Aviation and Air Power Under Stalin, 1928–1941." In *Soviet Aviation and Air Power: A Historical View.* Ed. Robin Higham and Jacob W. Kipp. Boulder, Colo.: Westview, 1977.

Zabavskaia, Liudmila. "Not a Job for the Women." *Soviet Military Review* (March 1989): 20–21.

———. "Women Fighter Pilots." *Soviet Military Review* (March 1977): 61–62.

Zaloga, Steven J. "Soviet Air Defense Radar in the Second World War." *Journal of Soviet Military Studies* 2, no. 3 (1988): 104–16.

Books in English

Abraham, Richard. *Alexander Kerensky: The First Love of the Revolution*. New York: Columbia University Press, 1987.

Alexander, Jean. *Russian Aircraft Since 1940*. London: Putnam, 1975.

Atkinson, Dorothy, Alexander Dallin, and Gail Warshofsky Lapidus, eds. *Women in Russia*. Stanford, Calif.: Stanford University Press, 1977.

Berkin, Carol R., and Clara M. Lovett, eds. *Women, War and Revolution*. New York: Holmes and Meier, 1980.

Botchkareva, Maria. *Yashka: My Life as Peasant, Officer and Exile*. New York: Frederick A. Stokes, 1919.

Boyd, Alexander. *The Soviet Air Force Since 1918*. New York: Stein and Day, 1977.

Brontman, Lazar Konstantinovich, and L. Khvat. *The Heroic Flight of the* Rodina. Moscow: Foreign Languages Publishing House, 1938.

Clements, Barbara Evans, Barbara Alpern Engel, and Christine D. Worobec, eds. *Russia's Women: Accommodation, Resistance, Transformation*. Berkeley: University of California Press, 1991.

Cooke, Miriam, and Angela Woollacott, eds. *Gendering War Talk*. Princeton, N.J.: Princeton University Press, 1993.

Cottam, K. Jean, ed. *The Golden-Tressed Soldier*. Manhattan, Kans.: Sunflower University Press, 1984.

————. *In the Sky Above the Front: A Collection of Memoirs of Soviet Air Women Participants in the Great Patriotic War*. Manhattan, Kans.: Sunflower University Press, 1984.

————. *Soviet Airwomen in Combat in World War II*. Manhattan, Kans.: Sunflower University Press, 1983.

————. *Women in Air War: The Eastern Front of World War II*. Rev. ed. Nepean, Ontario: New Military Publishing, 1997.

————. *Women in War and Resistance: Selected Biographies of Soviet Women Soldiers*. Nepean, Ontario: New Military Publishing, 1998.

Devilbiss, M. C. *Women and Military Service: A History, Analysis, and Overview of Key Issues*. Maxwell AFB, Ala., 1990.

Douglas, Deborah G. *United States Women in Aviation 1940–1985*. Washington, D.C.: Smithsonian, 1990.

Drum, Karl D. *Airpower and Russian Partisan Warfare*. New York: Arno, 1962.

Dunham, Vera. *In Stalin's Time: Middleclass Values in Soviet Fiction*. Cambridge: Cambridge University Press, 1976.

Durova, Nadezhda. *The Cavalry Maiden: Journal of a Russian Officer in the Napoleonic Wars*. Trans. Mary Fleming Zirin. Bloomington: Indiana University Press, 1988.

Erickson, John. *The Road to Berlin: Continuing the History of Stalin's War with Germany*. Boulder, Colo.: Westview, 1983.

―――. *The Road to Stalingrad: Stalin's War with Germany*. Boulder, Colo.: West-view, 1984.

Fussell, Paul. *Wartime: Understanding and Behavior in the Second World War*. New York: Oxford University Press, 1989.

Gallagher, Matthew P. *The Soviet History of World War II: Myths, Memories, and Realities*. New York: Praeger, 1963.

Gasiorowska, Xenia. *Women in Soviet Fiction 1917–1964*. Madison: University of Wisconsin Press, 1968.

Glantz, David M. *Stumbling Colossus: The Red Army on the Eve of World War*. Lawrence: University Press of Kansas, 1998.

Glantz, David M., and Jonathan M. House. *When Titans Clashed: How the Red Army Stopped Hitler*. Lawrence: University Press of Kansas, 1995.

Goldman, Nancy Loring, ed. *Female Soldiers—Combatants or Noncombatants? Historical and Contemporary Perspectives*. Westport, Conn.: Greenwood, 1982.

Gray, J. Glenn. *The Warriors: Reflections on Men in Battle*. New York: Harper, 1970.

Grossman, Vasily. *Life and Fate*. Trans. Robert Chandler. London: Collins Har-vill, 1985.

Hardesty, Von. *Red Phoenix: The Rise of Soviet Air Power, 1941–1945*. Washing-ton, D.C.: Smithsonian, 1982.

Helly, Dorothy O., and Susan M. Reverby, eds. *Gendered Domains: Rethinking Public and Private in Women's History*. Ithaca, N.Y.: Cornell University Press, 1991.

Higham, Robin, and Jacob Kipp. *Soviet Aviation and Air Power: A Historical View*. Boulder, Colo.: Westview, 1977.

Howes, Ruth H., and Michael R. Stevenson, eds. *Women and the Use of Military Force*. Boulder, Colo., and London: Lynne Rienner, 1993.

Isaksson, Eva. *Women and the Military System*. New York: St. Martin's, 1988.

Jones, Ellen. *Red Army and Society*. Boston: Allen and Unwin, 1985.

Keegan, John. *The Face of Battle*. New York: Penguin, 1978.

―――. *A History of Warfare*. New York: Knopf, 1993.

Kenez, Peter. *The Birth of the Propaganda State: Soviet Methods of Mass Mobiliza-tion, 1917–1929*. Cambridge: Cambridge University Press, 1985.

Keyssar, Helene, and Vladimir Pozner. *Remembering War: A U.S.-Soviet Dia-logue*. New York: Oxford University Press, 1990.

Krivosheev, G. F. *Soviet Casualties and Combat Losses in the Twentieth Century*. Trans. Christine Barnard. London and Mechanicsburg, Pa.: Greenhill Books, Stackpole Books, 1997.

Lauterbach, Richard E. *These Are the Russians*. 3rd ed. New York: Harper, 1945.

Macdonald, Sharon, Pat Holden, and Shirley Ardener. *Images of Women in Peace and War*. London: Macmillan, 1987.

Mamonova, Tatyana. *Russian Women's Studies: Essays on Sexism in Soviet Cul-ture*. New York: Pergamon, 1989.

Moolman, Valerie. *Women Aloft*. Alexandria, Va.: Time-Life Books, 1981.

Moskos, Charles C. *The American Enlisted Man: The Rank and File in Today's Military*. New York: Russel Sage, 1970.

Myles, Bruce. *Night Witches: The Untold Story of Soviet Women in Combat*. London: Mainstream Publishing, 1981.

Noggle, Anne. *A Dance with Death: Soviet Airwomen in World War II*. College Station: Texas A&M University Press, 1994.

Odom, William E. *The Soviet Volunteers: Modernization and Bureaucracy in a Public Mass Organization*. Princeton, N.J.: Princeton University Press, 1973.

Offen, Karen, Ruth Roach Pierson, and Jane Rendall, eds. *Writing Women's History: International Perspectives*. Bloomington: Indiana University Press, 1991.

Pantel, Pauline Schmitt, ed. *A History of Women in the West*. Cambridge, Mass.: Belknap, 1992.

Plocher, Hermann. *The German Air Force Versus Russia, 1942*. New York: Arno, 1966.

———. *The German Air Force Versus Russia, 1943*. New York: Arno, 1967.

Polak, Tomas, and Christopher Shores. *Stalin's Falcons: The Aces of the Red Star, a Tribute to the Notable Fighter Pilots of the Soviet Air Forces, 1918–1953*. London: Grub Street, 1999.

Reddel, Carl W., ed. *Transformation in Russian and Soviet Military History* [Proceedings of the Twelfth Military History Symposium, U.S. Air Force Academy, 1986]. Washington, D.C.: U.S. Air Force, 1990.

Rupp, L. *Mobilizing Women for War: German and American Propaganda, 1939–1945*. Princeton, N.J.: Princeton University Press, 1978.

Sarkesian, Sam C., ed. *Combat Effectiveness: Cohesion, Stress, and the Volunteer Military*. Beverly Hills, Calif.: Sage, 1980.

Saywell, Shelley. *Women in War*. Markham, Ontario: Viking, 1985.

Schulz, Heinrich E., Paul K. Urban, and Andrew I. Lebed, eds. *Who Was Who in the USSR*. Metuchen, N.J.: Scarecrow Press, 1972.

Scott, Joan. *Gender and the Politics of History*. New York: Columbia University Press, 1988.

Seidl, Hans D. *Stalin's Eagles: An Illustrated Study of the Soviet Aces of World War II and Korea*. Atglen, Pa.: Schiffer Military History, 1998.

Sinaiko, H. Wallace, Mady Wechsler Segal, and Robert L. Goldich. *Cohesion in Military Forces*. Washington, D.C.: Smithsonian Institution, 1984.

Stafper, Hans-Heiri. *Yak Fighters in Action*. New York: Squadron/Signal, 1986.

Stites, Richard. *The Women's Liberation Movement in Russia: Feminism, Nihilism and Bolshevism, 1860–1930*. Princeton, N.J.: Princeton University Press, 1978.

Suchenwirth, Richard. *Historical Turning Points in the German Air Force War Effort*. New York: Arno, 1968.

Sulimirski, Tadeusz. *The Sarmatians*. New York: Praeger, 1970.

Tucker, Robert C. *Stalin in Power: The Revolution from Above 1928–1941*. New York: Norton, 1990.

Uebe, Generalleutnant a. D. K. *Russian Reactions to German Airpower in World War II*. Prepared by the U.S. Air Force Historical Division as GAF 176 ed. New York: Arno, 1964.

Wagner, Ray, ed. *The Soviet Air Force in World War II: The Official History*. Garden City, N.Y.: Doubleday, 1973.

Theses and Dissertations

Griesse, Anne Eliot. "Soviet Women and World War II: Mobilization and Combat Policies." Master's thesis, Georgetown University, 1980.
Smith, Gregory Malloy. "The Impact of World War II on Women, Family Life, and Mores in Moscow, 1941–1945." Ph.D. diss., Stanford University, 1989.

Bibliographies and Reference Aids

Erickson, John, and Ljubica Erickson, eds. *The Soviet Armed Forces, 1918–1992: A Research Guide to Soviet Sources*. Westport, Conn.: Greenwood, 1996.
Fitzpatrick, Sheila, and Lynne Viola, eds. *A Researcher's Guide to Sources on Soviet Social History in the 1930s*. Armonk, N.Y.: M. E. Sharpe, 1990.
Grierson, P., ed. *Books on Soviet Russia, 1917–1942*. London: Methuen, 1943.
Grimsted, Patricia Kennedy. *Archives and Manuscript Repositories in the USSR, Moscow and Leningrad*. Princeton, N.J.: Princeton University Press, 1976.
———. *A Handbook for Archival Research in the USSR*. Princeton, N.J.: IREX, 1989.
Guide to Russian Reprints and Microforms. New York: Pilvax, 1973.
Hardesty, Von. *A Bibliography of the Soviet Air Force in World War II*. Washington, D.C.: Smithsonian Press, 1979.
Higham, Robin, ed. *Official Histories: Essays and Bibliographies from Around the World*. Manhattan: Kansas State University Library, 1970.
Horak, Stephan M. *Russia, the USSR, and Eastern Europe: A Bibliographic Guide to English Language Publications, 1964–1974*. Littleton, Colo.: Libraries Unlimited, 1978.
———. *Russia, the USSR, and Eastern Europe: A Bibliographic Guide to English Language Publications, 1975–1980*. Littleton, Colo.: Libraries Unlimited, 1982.
Horecky, Paul L., ed. *Russia and the Soviet Union: A Bibliographic Guide to Western-Language Publications*. Chicago: University of Chicago Press, 1965.
———. *Russian, Ukrainian and Belorussian Newspapers 1917–1953, a Union List*. Washington, D.C.: Slavic and Central European Division, and Serial Division, Reference Department, Library of Congress, 1953.
Jones, David, ed. *Books in English on the Soviet Union, 1917–1973*. New York: Garland, 1975.
Maichel, Karol, ed. *Soviet and Russian Newspapers at the Hoover Institution*. Hoover Institution Bibliographical Series 24. Stanford, Calif.: Stanford University Press, 1966.
Parrish, Michael. *The Soviet Armed Forces: Books in English, 1950–1967*. Stanford, Calif.: Hoover Institution Press, 1970.

————. *The USSR in World War II, an Annotated Bibliography of Books Published in the Soviet Union, 1945–1975; with an Addenda for the Years 1975–1980.* New York: Garland, 1981.

Raleigh, Donald, ed. *Soviet Historians and Perestroika.* Armonck, N.Y.: M. E. Sharpe, 1990.

Schulz, Heinrich E., Paul K. Urban, and Andrew I. Lebed, eds. *Who Was Who in the USSR.* Metuchen, N.J.: Scarecrow Press, 1972.

Scott, Harriet Fast, and William F. Scott. "Soviet Bibliographies and Their Use as Research Aids." In *Transformation in Russian and Soviet Military History.* Ed. Carl W. Reddel. Washington, D.C.: Office of Air Force History, U.S. Air Force, 1990.

————. *Bibliographic Index of Soviet Military Books 1960–69.* Defense Nuclear Agency, 1985. DNA-TR-85-325.

————. *Bibliographic Index of Soviet Military Books 1970–74.* Defense Nuclear Agency, 1984. DNA-TR-84-112.

————. *Bibliographic Index of Soviet Military Books 1975–79.* Defense Nuclear Agency, 1984. DNA-TR-84-113.

————. *Bibliographic Index of Soviet Military Books 1980–84.* Defense Nuclear Agency, 1986. DNA-TR-86-71.

Shenfield, Stephen D. "Soviet Historiography and the Operational Art: Historical Coverage of the Great Patriotic War by Period as an Indicator of the Orientation of Soviet Military Art 1959–88." *Journal of Soviet Military Studies* 2, no. 3 (1989): 346–60.

Smith, Myron J. Jr. *Air War Bibliography, 1939–1945: English-Language Sources.* Vol. 5. Manhattan, Kans.: Aerospace Historian, 1977.

SSSR v Gody Velikoi Otechestvennoi Voiny (Iiun' 1941–Sentiabr' 1945 g.): Ukazatel' Sovetskoi Literatury za 1941–1967. 4th ed. Moscow: Nauka, 1981.

Wieczynski, Joseph L., ed. *The Modern Encyclopedia of Russian and Soviet History.* Gulf Breeze, Fla.: Academic International Press, 1976–1990.

About the Author

Reina Pennington is a former air force intelligence officer with nine years' experience as a Soviet analyst. During her air force career, she worked in tactical fighter squadrons, including the Aggressor Squadrons at Nellis Air Force Base; she also served in the Defense Intelligence Agency and the Alaskan Air Command. She wrote two classified manuals on Soviet fighter tactics and a number of unclassified articles for defense publications such as *Air Force* magazine and the *Fighter Weapons Review.*

Pennington holds a Ph.D. in modern European history, with fields in Russian and military history, from the University of South Carolina, where she also completed a graduate certificate in women's studies. She has written articles for *Airpower Journal,* the *Journal of Slavic Military Studies,* and *Air & Space/Smithsonian.* Pennington is editor of *Military Women Worldwide: A Biographical Dictionary,* a survey of military women throughout history, forthcoming from Greenwood Press. She is Director of Peace, War, and Diplomacy Studies in the Department of History at Norwich University, Northfield, Vermont.

Index